THE
CRIMINALS
OF LIMA
AND THEIR
WORLDS

THE
CRIMINALS
OF LIMA
AND THEIR
WORLDS

The Prison Experience, 1850–1935

CARLOS AGUIRRE

DUKE UNIVERSITY PRESS

Durham and London

2005

© 2005 Duke University Press
All rights reserved
Printed in the United States of
America on acid-free paper ∞
Designed by Rebecca Giménez
Typeset in Adobe Minion
by Keystone Typesetting, Inc.
Library of Congress Cataloging-
in-Publication Data appear
on the last printed page
of this book.

In memory of my father,

MARIO AGUIRRE MORALES

CONTENTS

ACKNOWLEDGMENTS

Several institutions supported the research and writing associated with this project. The MacArthur Interdisciplinary Program, the History Department, and the Graduate School at the University of Minnesota; the Harry Frank Guggenheim Foundation; the American Philosophical Society; the John Simon Guggenheim Foundation; and the College of Arts and Sciences and the History Department at the University of Oregon. I express again my gratitude to all of them.

My research was facilitated by the expertise and diligence of the staffs at the following libraries and archives in Lima: Archivo General de la Nación, Biblioteca Nacional, Instituto Riva Agüero, Biblioteca Benvenuto Murrieta, Archivo Histórico, Hemeroteca, and Biblioteca Central of the University of San Marcos, Biblioteca del Congreso, and the Biblioteca Félix Denegri Luna. I would like to thank, in particular, Ada Arrieta, Yolanda Auqui, Ruth Borja, the late Felix Denegri Luna, Carlos Gálvez, and Carmen Vivanco for facilitating my access to archival and library materials. A special word of gratitude goes to Luis Jochamowitz, who, in a conversation that he has probably long forgotten, informed me that the archive of the Dirección General de Prisiones, which I had tried unsuccessfully to locate for several weeks, was indeed in the basement of the National Archive.

Numerous friends and colleagues have helped me with this book over the years. At the University of Minnesota, Stuart Schwartz, Allen Isaacman, and Robert McCaa, outstanding mentors and friends, made me and my family feel at home in the Twin Cities. A special note of gratitude is due to Stuart Schwartz, whose superb talent as a historian is matched only by his enormous warmth and kindness. He and Mari offered much needed friendship and critical assistance as well as the best Thanksgiving dinners we have ever had. I was fortunate to share workshops, readings, discussions, and picnics with a notable cohort of international Mac-Arthur fellows, especially José Artiles, Arlindo Chilundo, Ana Margarita Gómez, and Maanda Mulaudzi. Bob and Wanda McCaa, Luis González and Arlene Díaz, Kris and Pamela Lane, José and Teresa Cerna, Fernando and Ana María Méndez, Jessy and Sandra Lillygreen, Ed Letterman, David and Consuelo Romo, and Rafael Arias and Annie Achio also deserve my gratitude for their generosity and kindness.

In Lima, many friends and colleagues helped me over the years to carry on this project. I would like to thank especially Cristóbal Aljovín, Gerardo Alvarez, Tito Bracamonte, Gustavo Buntinx, Carlos Contreras, Jesús Cosamalón, Marcos Cueto, Marisol de la Cadena, Javier Flores, Pedro Guibovich, Iván Hinojosa, Walter Huamaní, Nils Jacobsen, Natalia Majluf, the late Maruja Martínez, Carmen McEvoy, Zoila Mendoza, Fanni Muñoz, Aldo Panfichi, Scarlett O'Phelan, David Parker, the late Franklin Pease, Víctor Peralta, Felipe Portocarrero, Gabriel Ramón, Carlos Ramos, Tito Rodríguez Pastor, Augusto Ruiz Zevallos, Robert Sanchez, Carlos Villanueva, Charles Walker, and many others for their support, criticism, conversations, bibliographical references, archival sources, invitations to present my work, and camaraderie. At the University of Oregon, encouragement and support came from all of my colleagues in the History Department, especially Bob Haskett, Stephanie Wood, Jim Mohr, Jeff Hanes, and Daniel Pope. A number of friends and colleagues commented on earlier versions of this book at various conferences. I would like to thank especially Ricardo Salvatore, Gil Joseph, Pablo Piccato, and Robert Buffington, from whom I have learned much more than what this modest contribution will reflect. I thank in particular Ricardo Salvatore for the many years of collaboration and friendship. At Duke University Press, Valerie Millholland was a superb editor and offered expert guidance throughout the production of this book. Charles Walker and two referees for Duke University Press read the manuscript more than once and provided valuable criticism and feedback. A trio of extraordinary friends deserves special mention: Ricardo Ramos Tremolada, Chuck Walker, and Carlos Bustamante have been a constant source of moral and intellectual support as well as faithful partners in book-hunting expeditions, discussions about Peruvian history and politics, and endless ruminations about music, soccer, Peruvian food, and almost everything else.

My greatest debt is to my family. My wife, Mirtha, and our children, Carlos and Susana, are a daily source of joy, love, and strength. I owe to their patience and understanding everything I have accomplished in my professional life. The Avalos family deserves special gratitude for everything they have done for me. My sisters and their families have made my life immensely happier and fuller. My parents, Mario and Regina, nurtured me with infinite love, sacrifice, and faith. My father passed away just before this book went to print, and I am still coping with such an enormous loss. I dedicate this book to his memory, his love of history, and his unwavering aspiration for social justice.

INTRODUCTION

This book studies the evolution of institutions of confinement for male criminals in Lima, Peru, between 1850 and 1935. It reconstructs the social, cultural, and doctrinal influences that shaped the ways in which law-breakers were treated, the fate of programs of prison reform, and the ways in which inmates confronted the experience of prison. It argues that the operation of Lima prisons during this period reveals the contradictory and exclusionary nature of modernization in Peru. The implementation of modern rules of discipline and rehabilitative treatment inside the prisons was, at best, ambiguous, and it shows the lack of commitment on the part of state officials and prison authorities to the tenets of prison reform. As a result, a combination of brutality and indifference tended to characterize the way criminals were treated by the criminal justice system, and the operation of prisons came to depend on a double-edged and fragile customary order in which arbitrariness and abuse were much more prevalent than respect for the prisoners' rights and their well-being. Prisons thus became not sites for the regeneration of criminals but bastions of authoritarianism and exclusion.

The reform of prisons—their transformation into regimented institutions for the rehabilitation of prisoners through a strict therapy consisting of mandatory silence and segregation, obligatory work, religious counseling, and constant, total surveillance—was a political and ideological drive initiated in Europe and the United States in the second half of the eighteenth century. By 1820, the movement had consolidated a new institutional structure, the penitentiary, which combined in a single setting all the elements prison reformers deemed necessary to transform unruly criminals into honest, industrious, law-abiding citizens. In Peru, the initial plan for building penitentiaries was formulated in 1853, and in

1862 the first and only penitentiary ever built was inaugurated in Lima. The ambitious plan for reforming the entire prison system by building more penitentiaries was never effected, and none of the other prisons went through a process of renovation or reform. At the Lima penitentiary, in addition, the actual implementation of the new science of punishment was rather problematic, and it definitely departed from the original plan. While it certainly was a more secure prison and exerted greater control over the daily lives of the prisoners, the alleged purposes of disciplining and rehabilitating criminals through humane treatment were never achieved. A variety of circumstances, including financial shortages, lack of adequate personnel, private interests, the inmates' own forms of coping and resistance, and the broader social and cultural matrix of Peruvian society, explain both the deficient operation of the penitentiary and the overall lack of concern with the situation at other prisons. Despite efforts by a group of criminologists in the 1920s, when scientific penology inspired a new wave of enthusiasm with prison reform, little was achieved. The Spanish penologist Luis Jiménez de Asúa offered a highly negative assessment of prisons in 1928, seventy-five years after the original plan for prison reform was made: "In Peru," he wrote to Director General of Prisons Bernardino León y León, "*we have to begin from scratch*, as you say, even with feeding prisoners and suppressing torture. Later, we can allow room for sophisticated buildings and bylaws but, for the time being, *the first thing we ought to do is to make sure that the prisoner lives like a human being and not like a beast.*"[1]

In the case of Peru, I argue in this book, the project for the reform or modernization of prisons was complicated by at least three interrelated elements. First, although the impulse toward prison reform was mostly a state-centered initiative, the actual implementation of this project reveals the limitations of the state in carrying out its own initiatives. The lack of financial resources is just one side of the problem, although certainly an important one. Much more critical, however, were the deficient mechanisms of personnel recruitment, the lack of adequate institutional forms of control over the personnel of prisons, the patrimonial character of the state, and the presence of widespread corruption. The actual operation of prisons was left to the discretion and mutual bargaining power of two sets of actors: prison staff and inmates. Prison employees and authorities were generally detached from the main issues and goals of prison reform.

They had to operate their institutions on the basis not only of common-sensical forms of "treatment," which included, prominently, the continuous display of violence, but also of the creation and preservation of a customary order that contradicted the alleged purposes of the reform.

Second, prisoners themselves were a major factor in the lack of correspondence between the ideals of prison reform and the actual operation of the prisons. Especially at the penitentiary, whose design called for the enforcement of rules of silence, discipline, and work, inmates subverted that endeavor by engaging in individual and collective forms of bargaining, coping, and resistance. They were not necessarily docile victims of an oppressive structure but instead, as we will see in part 3 of this book, resolute and creative actors who helped shape the world they lived in.

Third, the limitations and ambiguities of prison reform in Peru can be attributed, to a large extent, to the prevailing cultural values, sensibilities, and political cultures of the larger society. The implementation of a program of prison reform required a change in attitudes toward criminals—indeed, toward the lower classes generally—and the allocation of citizenship rights that, in the context of Peruvian society, were largely absent. As many studies have demonstrated, Peruvian society underwent a process of modernization without altering the structures of power and exclusion that had been in place since the birth of the republic. Instead of a republic of citizens enjoying equality before the law, Peruvian society was dramatically shaped by exclusionary practices along social, cultural, gender, and racial lines. Any call to transform prisons into institutions displaying humanitarian attitudes and respect for the rights of prisoners was a cry in the desert in view of the oppressive force of widespread and pervasive authoritarian and discriminatory social practices. The impulse behind the adoption of the penitentiary, that is, the imitation of Western models, was part of a broader set of attitudes and practices in which racism and exclusionary practices occupied a central space.

Nevertheless, evaluated on the basis of the actual operation of institutions of confinement, the state did accomplish a number of goals: more centralized, intrusive, and powerful mechanisms of surveillance, policing, and repression were implemented, especially, but not exclusively, at the Lima penitentiary. Prisons became more secure institutions of confinement, and new and more effective methods of identification and classification were adopted. They were primarily used, however, not to combat crime or to "regenerate" allegedly deviant individuals, but to help reproduce and maintain an essentially unjust and exclusionary social order.

| | | | |

For most historians, the birth of modern Peru occurred in the aftermath of the disastrous War of the Pacific (1879–83) and especially after 1895, when the civil *caudillo* Nicolás de Piérola gained the presidency and initiated a period of steady economic growth and political stability. This process is generally associated with the growing presence of foreign capital, the slow but steady expansion of capitalist relations of production, the acceleration of migration and urbanization, the importation of numerous modern technological innovations (railroads, streetcars, telegraph, and so forth), the adoption of modern ideologies like positivism, anarchism, and socialism, and the emergence of the organized working class and mass political parties.[2] The birth of modern Peru coincided with the inauguration of what the Peruvian historian Jorge Basadre called, in deliberately contradictory terms, the "Aristocratic Republic" (1895–1919). This was a period of economic growth and political stability during which Peruvian society and politics were controlled by a small number of families whose interests were mostly associated with coastal export agriculture (cotton and sugar) and who were the beneficiaries of a system of restricted political participation based upon the exclusion of the majority of the Peruvian population.[3] The institutional expression of this system of domination was what historians and sociologists call the oligarchic state, a structure that, with minor changes and occasional challenges, would last until the late 1960s. This oligarchic state was built upon a variety of components: a conflictual but nonetheless effective alliance between foreign capital, coastal landowners, and Andean *gamonalismo*,[4] or bossism, the political exclusion of large portions of the population, especially the indigenous and rural segments, the preeminence of seignorial and patrimonial relations between state and society, an incipient development of civil society, the partial privatization of power and violence, and an accentuated political and economic centralism.[5]

Peru entered its "modern" period, thus, by consolidating a model of state–society relations whose most persistent feature was the systematic exclusion of the lower, rural, and colored classes from political participation and the effective exercise of their civil rights. In electoral terms, for example, voting was restricted to a minority composed of male, propertied, and literate individuals.[6] Recent scholarship has shown the multiple ways in which different groups of subordinate peoples—in particular, indigenous peasants—actively and vigorously participated in the negotiation of political and social boundaries and the contestation of hegemonic projects. The overwhelming outcome was, however, the defeat of popular political projects and the continual exclusion and repression of the lower classes. The Peruvian state and nation were built on the basis of exclusionary practices, racially informed policies, and discriminatory cultural and institutional models.[7] As Florencia Mallon has written, "The Peruvian state, consolidated through the repression and fragmentation of popular political cultures, had no capacity for inclusion or hegemony . . . official political discourse conceptualized a limited national polity defined by quality rather than quantity. Thus structured around neocolonial principles of ethnic and spatial fragmentation, the first 'modern' Peruvian state of the Aristocratic Republic would throw its long shadow of authoritarianism and exclusion across the entire twentieth century."[8]

In 1919, Augusto B. Leguía came to power through a coup d'état. A political maverick and successful businessman closely linked to foreign, especially North American, interests, he challenged the political basis of the Aristocratic Republic. Leguía came to represent a new and dynamic sector within the ruling block, one much more committed to the goal of modernizing Peruvian society along capitalist lines. Promising the construction of a *Patria Nueva* ("New Fatherland"), demagogically flirting with populist and *Indigenista* rhetoric, opening the Peruvian economy to unprecedented levels of foreign investment, especially from the United States, and launching an ambitious plan for the modernization of state and society on the basis of supposedly rational and scientific governmental policies, Leguía was able to break the political (but only to a limited extent the economic) hegemony of the traditional oligarchy.[9] The Leguiísta project tried, with some success, to incorporate new actors into the political scenario, especially the urban middle classes, some sectors of the provincial elites, and portions of the working classes; but it did so within a framework dominated by a personalistic, centralist, and authoritarian style of leadership. When cooptation failed, Leguía resorted to brutal repression, exile, and imprisonment of political rivals and unruly subaltern groups. The army and the police were both modernized, and Leguía was able to partially dismantle the power of provincial lords.[10] The

Leguiísta state was also an instrument of capitalist penetration, especially in the form of foreign investment, a fact which was to have dramatic implications for the regions thus affected.[11] Finally, the Leguiísta administration effectively used traditional patron/client relationships to procure the allegiance of various segments of the Peruvian population. The *oncenio*, as the eleven-year Leguía administration is called, brought to new heights the traditionally personalistic nature of Peruvian politics, and adulation became a prerequisite for inclusion in the networks of political and economic power. Leguía was called Wiracocha, the Jupiter President, the New Messiah, and the Giant of the Pacific; he was compared to Simón Bolívar and Napoleon; the twentieth century was proclaimed "Leguía's century."[12]

This state was not, however, an omnipotent machine that functioned smoothly and flawlessly. Not even during the Leguía administration, when attempts were made to rationalize and modernize it, did the state experience significant improvement in its mechanisms of operation and control. It expanded its reach, but it could not get rid of the pervasive presence, within the public administration, of traditional, even colonial, bureaucratic practices. The patrimonial character of the Peruvian state, its clientelistic mechanisms of recruitment and operation (the well-known *tarjetazo*), its centralism, and the widespread corruption it nurtured all affected the implementation of state initiatives and presented serious obstacles to the consolidation of modern structures of state–society relations.[13]

Despite its traditional components, however, the modernization of Peruvian society did occur during the long period between 1850 and 1935, and it was in Lima where it was mostly felt. The population of Lima increased from ninety-five thousand inhabitants in 1858 to more than two hundred thousand in the late 1920s, while the percentage of *provincianos*, people from the interior, rose from 37 percent in 1858 to 58.5 percent in 1908 to 63.5 percent in 1920.[14] The movement of people paralleled the physical growth and urban development of the city. The first major impulse toward urban change took place in the late 1860s and 1870s, when the colonial walls were demolished to allow for the city's expansion, and new avenues, boulevards, parks, and public buildings were erected. A second moment of notable urban development came about after 1895. Spacious avenues were opened, and public services such as running water and sewage were installed. The third and most ambitious plan of urban reform took place during the oncenio. Lima was transformed in multiple ways, the most significant being probably the gradual emergence of distinct class-based neighborhoods. Lima began to have working-class districts, middle-class neighborhoods, and upper-class *balnearios* (beach resorts) and residential areas. The proliferation of foreign boutiques and department stores (Bon Marché, Oeschle), cafes, theaters, an active cultural life, and other cosmopolitan amenities gave Lima a belle-epoque flavor that seemed to fulfill the dreams of modernizing elites eager to enjoy a European lifestyle.[15] The urban and human landscape of Lima was also being altered by the growing numbers of industrial factories, which went from 69 in 1890 to 244 in 1920, some of which, like the textile factories at Vitarte, employed more than 400 workers.[16] The overall number of industrial workers in Lima was still small compared, for instance, to the number of artisans or commercial employees,[17] but a young and combative working class emerged, nonetheless, under the organizational and ideological auspices of anarchism and socialism. This emergence had an impact that went well beyond the small size of the working class. The 1910s and 1920s was a period of intense organization and political mobilization of the working class. An effort was made to create a distinctive working-class culture, with great emphasis on self-education. As a result, the working classes of Lima made their presence felt in the city and decisively shaped the contours of its political and social life.[18]

Away from the flamboyant parts of Lima and close to, but to a certain extent separate from, the nascent working classes there was a sector of the population that did not seem to be participating in either the modernization process or the efforts at political mobilization mentioned above. Alternatively known as urban plebeians, marginal sectors, parasites, or simply criminals, this population of unemployed, wandering, and frequently lawless individuals was also an important, if usually neglected, actor in Lima's urban life. They were the target of police action and made up a significant portion of the prison population. They were either left behind by the modernization drive or refused to be a part of it. They lived lives that, in the eyes of authorities and commentators, deserved punishment and containment, if not extermination. Blamed for many of the shortcomings of Peruvian society, including the alleged lack of civilization and progress, they developed distinctive forms of socialization and culture which were generally at odds with the values of those who harassed and punished them. They coexisted with other sectors of the

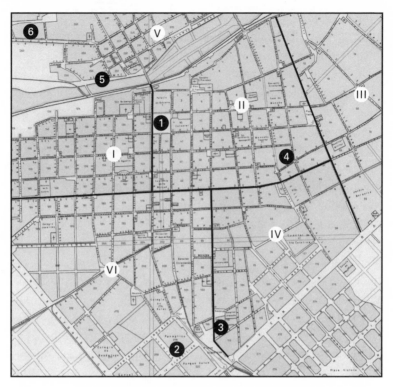

Figure 1. Map of Lima in 1908, showing the division of the city into quarters (roman numerals) and some key locations: (1) Plaza de Armas; (2) Lima penitentiary; (3) Guadalupe jail; (4) Chinatown; (5) Tajamar; (6) Malambo. Adapted by Ariel Vaughn of the Wired Humanities Project, University of Oregon, from the original "Plano de Lima" by Ricardo Tizón y Bueno (Librería e Imprenta Gil, 1908).

laboring poor, sharing with them housing arrangements (in *callejones* [tenement houses] and *casas de vecindad* [working-class housing units]), public spaces (taverns, marketplaces), and socialization practices (*jaranas*, cult of bravery), but they were looked upon by important sectors of the working classes as undesirable and undeserving. Neither suppressed nor integrated, this sector of the population represented the other Lima, not the one of cafés, boutiques, and intellectual *tertulias* (salons) or that of the factory, the union, and the political party, but the Lima of the *faite* (bully), the *ratero* (petty thief), and the vagrant.[19]

The numerous visible changes affecting Lima's society during this period should not overshadow stubborn continuities that also must be accounted for in explaining attitudes toward criminals and prisoners. I argue that attitudes toward criminals reflected the continuities affecting Peruvian society during the long period of modernization. The social and cultural scenario of Lima was continuously shaped by a central ingredient that survived the modernization process: the authoritarian and hierarchical nature of social relations. What has been called the "authoritarian tradition" of Peruvian society can be traced back to the colonial period.[20] A system of values underscoring the existence of so-called natural racial, social, generational, and gendered hierarchies, appropriate ways of interaction between superiors and subordinates, and legitimate forms of achieving conformity and obedience, including corporal punishment and other forms of mistreatment, was maintained and even reinforced throughout the nineteenth century and the early twentieth. As the historian Steve Stein, among others, has documented, Lima was a highly hierarchical, stratified society. The relationships between patrons and servants, parents and children, teachers and students, husbands and wives, and employers and employees all included diverse degrees of despotism and coercion. An appropriate symbol of this set of social arrangements would be, according to this perception, the tradition of *come y calla* (eat and shut up), which essentially underscores submission and obedience as necessary, appropriate, and even virtuous attitudes: subordinates were not supposed to reply or comment on any superior's order. The extensive use of corporal punishment was a central aspect of this culture: students were whipped at school, and domestic servants were physically punished by their patrons; in army barracks and police jails, the lash was widely used; in the domestic sphere, abuse of children and women was common.[21]

Two aspects of this situation need to be highlighted. First, the authoritarian tradition permeated all spheres of society, not just the relationship between elites and lower classes. It was reproduced, as the historian Alberto Flores Galindo emphasized, by the victims themselves in a seemingly endless chain of abusive and despotic behavior. Second, and contrary to what Stein suggests, the pervasiveness of this authoritarian tradition does not mean it went unchallenged. Stein takes at face value what contemporary prescriptive manuals and commentators said. "Obedience," he says, "was the main norm of society." But the fact that it was the norm does not mean it was always complied with. Stein goes even further when he argues that "a servile behavior was the preferred tactic in the confrontation with persons deemed as powerful," since the urban masses "assimilated a system of values that rewarded passive adaptation and personal dependence." "Deference and submission," according to Stein, would have been the most visible characteristics of lower-class social and political behavior.[22]

I would argue, on the contrary, that precisely because the norms of hierarchies and obedience were broken and challenged, an authoritarian response on the part of the superior was needed. In other words, for a parent or teacher to punish a child, the child usually had to commit a violation of the codes of appropriate behavior, and the same holds for servants, wives, workers, and other subalterns. If one accepts Stein's argument, then the numerous daily expressions of resistance and unruliness, from workers' strikes to servants' acts of defiance, are unexplainable. A seemingly appropriate example is that of criminals: they violated the codes, so they were punished. How they were punished reflects the prevalence of certain notions of appropriate punishment. Where Stein sees conformity, I see contention and struggle. What defines an authoritarian culture is not the fact that it is not contested but rather that defiance of power is met with despotism and violence.

| | | | |

Modern prisons have been the focus of intense study over the last few decades. Interpretations about their place in the development and operation of their respective societies have varied widely. Prisons have been seen, by various authors, as key instruments in the development of capitalism and the formation of an industrial proletariat,[23] as institutions revealing of the intrinsic and insolvable contradictions of liberalism,[24] as manifestations of radical changes in cultural sensibilities,[25] as sites for the production of colonial knowledge and power,[26] as loci of racial oppression and marginalization,[27] and probably most famously, as both symbols and bastions of surveillance and normalization, which are deemed central features of modern societies. According to Michel Foucault, the most prominent advocate of this view, "the carceral network, in its compact or disseminated forms, with its systems of insertion, distribution, surveillance, observation, has been the greatest support, in modern society, of the normalizing power."[28]

But prisons have also been seen as sites of resistance where alternative social and political projects are imagined and fostered.[29] The profoundly pessimistic Foucauldian rendering of total panoptical control—which left little or no room for subaltern agency and resistance—is challenged in studies that emphasize both prisoners' agency and the limits of state despotism. While, understandably, scholars tend to focus on political prisoners as carriers of resistance against oppression, studies that deal with so-called common criminals also demonstrate that even the most despotic prison regimes cannot completely subdue prisoners' resilience and determination.

The development of a network of institutions of confinement in modern societies represents, among other things, an expression of the growing intervention of the state in the regulation of the lives of ordinary citizens and its increasingly restrictive privilege in the use of legitimate coercion and violence. The emergence and operation of such institutions as the police, prisons, penitentiaries, and reformatories are intimately linked to the development of what the British historian V. A. C. Gatrell called "the policeman state."[30] The role of prisons within the overall structure of the modern state, however, is contingent upon both the nature of that state (liberal, autocratic, oligarchic, military) and the concrete manner in which specific mechanisms and actors operate. The correspondence between the ideal models of state institutions and their actual operation is complicated by the very process through which they come into being. As a result, these institutions are less dependent on the grand designs of state ideologists than on the actions and omissions of those state officials in whose hands the task of implementing them is laid. The operation of Lima's prisons demonstrates that a gulf sometimes separates the declared goals of state institutions from their practical implementation.

State institutions such as prisons cannot be dissociated from the broader scenario in which they function. Historians must be attentive to the influences exerted by prevailing cultural and mental settings. As David Garland has argued, prisons are also "cultural artifacts" that both reflect and contribute to the shaping of wider patterns of mentalities, values, and social practices.[31] Thinking of prisons as mirrors of society is not just a rhetorical trick, for they reflect deeply ingrained social values, beliefs, and practices, including, prominently, the ways in which authority and power is exercised in a given society. In the words of the historian Dario Melossi "punishment is deeply embedded in the national/cultural specificity of the environment which produces it."[32] Regardless of the specific needs that punishment may fulfill—deterrence, regeneration, control over the labor market, and so forth—or the legal and doctrinal basis upon which ideologists elaborate their designs—natural law, humanitarianism, science—the ultimate form punishment takes will always depend, at its core, on the influence of socially constructed sensibilities.[33] In other words, what is considered appropriate, just, horrendous, or well deserved is defined not just by the law or by the needs of the state but, more critically, by the dominant (though still contested) cultural values of the broader society.

The impact of these cultural values upon the operation of prisons is critically mediated by the construction of images and representations of the criminal population. These "distorting mirrors" include, but are not limited to, legal, popular, and scientific representations of the criminal population that also shaped the ways in which prisoners are treated inside the prison.[34] Perceptions about crime as a social issue, for example— whether viewed as a major threat or a minor problem, a social malaise or the result of specific deficiencies among certain groups—and the criminal as an individual—whether seen as a victim or a monster, a degenerate being or a sick person—also inform the specific forms that punishment adopts at any given time.[35]

The operation of institutions of confinement, finally, is crucially mediated by the responses they generate among the very recipients of the variety of interventions that prison regimes entailed, namely, their inmates. Prisons, like other socio-institutional settings such as the plantation and the factory, constitute arenas in which power and domination are wielded but in which contestation and struggle also take place. Despite the formally extreme differential of power existing between a prison authority and a convict, there is always room for the convict to manipulate, circumvent, and redefine the rules of engagement. The success of these strategies is always limited and very frequently fragile and ephemeral, but nonetheless they offer ample demonstration that prisoners do not totally succumb to the oppressive logic behind their imprisonment. A study of the prison that ignores prisoners' agency and the realities of daily life inside the prison is incomplete. In the words of the historian Michelle Perrot, "It is precisely the real, the daily life of this group—the prisoners— that we must try to capture at its most hidden level, the level that lies behind and beyond the serene statements and the conventions of the discourse of the penitentiary."[36]

The case of Lima's prisons reveals the profound schism existing between the promises of the Peruvian republic—democracy, rule of law, and citizenship rights for all Peruvians—and the realities of despotic and exclusionary political and social systems. Despite recent and quite valuable analyses of the development of civil society and political participation that tend to highlight the spread of democratic impulses and practices among the Peruvian population, authoritarian traditions and exclusionary practices tend to emerge in the literature as decisive features of Peruvian society.[37] In numerous ways prisons have both reflected and reproduced the inequalities of the Peruvian social and political structures: in the visibly discriminatory patterns of policing and incarceration, in the excessive punishment inflicted against vulnerable populations, in the absolute disdain for human life and dignity, and in the denial of access to fair trials and adequate legal counsel. Even though prisoners, as this book emphasizes, were not always passive or acquiescent victims, the overall picture is one in which they suffered from the state's and society's indifference and malice, if not open brutality. That these conditions continue to inform the operation of Peruvian penal institutions to date is revealing of the pervasiveness of the exclusionary and anti-democratic traditions born with the Peruvian republic almost two hundred years ago.

|||||

This book is largely, although not solely, based on a rich and for the most part unused collection of documents from various institutions of confinement and other administrative units connected to the Peruvian prison network. They were gathered by the Dirección General de Prisiones (DGP) and housed at the Ministry of Justice. When this ministry was closed in the 1970s, the papers from the DGP were sent to the National Archives, where they remain. Despite the richness of this documentation, lacunas and gaps are numerous. Certain aspects of the experience of incarceration are less represented than others in the documents. For example, I found little documentation for political prisoners before 1920, and the documents are very silent on prison employees, about which I would have liked to say much more. More important, documents on female prisoners and their institutions of confinement are quite scarce, which prevents me from including, as I wanted, an account of female imprisonment in Lima.[38]

Part 1, "Apprehending the Criminal," reviews the ways in which crime and criminals were represented by a variety of social commentators as well as the role of the police in the construction of a criminal class. Chapter 1 looks at the invention of the "criminal question" and the intersection between views about crime and discourses about race, urban life, and lower-class morals. Chapter 2 traces the early development of scientific theories of crime, stressing the continuities it had with previous, prescientific discourses. Chapter 3 analyzes the ways in which the most visible and intrusive arm of the state, the police, contributed to the construction of the "criminal classes" by displaying a highly arbitrary and class-biased pattern of abuse against certain segments of the lower classes. Part 2, "Prisons and Prison Communities," describes penal institutions and their inhabitants. Chapter 4 reviews the evolution of institutions of confinement such as the Lima penitentiary, the Guadalupe jail, and El Frontón Penal Island, while chapter 5 looks in detail at the male inmate population, highlighting their diversity as well as the ways in which they bridged the prison and the outside world. Part 3, the last section, entitled "The World They Made Together," examines in greater detail the ways in which daily interactions, negotiations, and forms of contestation shaped the world of the prison. Chapter 6 reconstructs what I call the customary order of the prison, pointing at the complexities of the prison experience and the multiple forms of interaction—ranging from partnership and complicity to abuse and neglect—between prison officials and inmates and among inmates themselves. Chapter 7 considers the formation of prison subcultures and their impact on daily life inside the prison, and chapter 8 the various ways in which inmates defied both the customary order and the overall prison regime imposed upon them. The conclusion puts the findings of these chapters in the social, political, and cultural context of Lima society and offers an interpretation of the connections between punishment, modernization, and authoritarian traditions in Peruvian society.

PART ONE

APPREHENDING THE CRIMINAL

1

On August 24, 1861, the recently founded law newspaper *La Gaceta Judicial* published an article under the title "The Moral Situation." The author, a lawyer named Gabriel Gutiérrez, outlined what he thought were the major causes of the "alarming" rise in crime in Lima.[1] "How could we explain the moral situation in which we are immersed, due to the gradual increase in the number of crimes that are committed?" Gutiérrez asked at the beginning of his article. His response came in the form of a long list of factors that, according to him, contributed to the growing levels of criminality in Lima. Intermittent political instability and civil wars, for instance, had "corrupted the [people's] customs, drained fiscal resources, destroyed agriculture, condoned militarism, eradicated the prestige of all principles, divided the population into antagonistic parties, [and] engendered profound enmities," as a result of which increasing numbers of people were taking to the streets and roads in order to commit crimes. The growing number of idle hands resulting from the decline of local production, in turn caused by an "excessive and disorganized free-trade policy," was seen as another source of crime. Because work represented an "essentially moralizing element," its opposite, idleness, necessarily led to criminal behavior among the lower classes. Alcohol consumption and gambling were also cited as major factors in criminality. Gutiérrez rejected the legal and customary practice of treating inebriation as a mitigating circumstance for criminals; in his opinion, the correct attitude was just the opposite: "The individual that has put himself voluntarily in the aptitude of committing a crime should be punished more severely."[2]

A psychological, somehow compulsory propensity to seek richness and luxury was also blamed for the growth of criminal activity. The author considered this "a sort of furor or disease," a "gangrene of all classes of society" that in the case of the poor and middle classes would require the commission of crimes to keep up with the cost of living this kind of artificial life. The situation had even added negative effects on Peruvian society because most, if not all, luxury goods were imported, thus further hurting local production. Additional fuel for rising crime rates was supplied, in Gutiérrez's judgment, by public diversions. The abundance of festivities, he posited, underscored the dimensions of unproductive idleness among the Lima population and their corruptive effects on the population's attitude toward labor and social discipline. Moreover, lack of education produced a ferociousness of character which, he stated, made people even more prone to crime and violence. Gutiérrez estimated that three-quarters of the population of Lima were illiterate.

The recent abolition of slavery (1854) also had an impact on the levels of crime in the city, according to the author. Former slaves, "abject beings with an obtuse intellect, subjugated by the lash of the overseer," were unable to differentiate the "materiality of the flesh" from "the spirituality that animates it." They bore not a single idea about the organization of society, their rights, or the respect they deserved. They were a sort of "undomesticated and enchained tigers" that, suddenly incorporated into society, given rights, and elevated to the same position of other citizens, abandoned their masters' homes and, lacking an industry, "rushed into roads and cities to make their living out of theft and the knife." Furthermore, the abolition of the death penalty in 1858 had been interpreted by criminals as a guarantee of impunity. Such a "noble reform" was "inopportune" because it came at a time when "our manners have reached a level of alarming relaxation, civil wars have corrupted our habits and character, the penitentiary system has not yet been implanted, [and] our penal legislation is extremely vicious." By protecting the criminal's life, Gutiérrez said, legislators had automatically condemned society to death. Finally, deficiencies in the administration of justice—especially leniency motivated by compassion toward the criminal and tardiness in the application of justice—as well as an inefficient and irregular police service encouraged crime, for they made things easier for criminals. Incarcerating criminals was not a solution since, instead of transforming or deterring them, jails and prisons further corrupted inmates.

Gutiérrez was not alone in depicting crime as an acute social problem, even a potentially dangerous one for the country's stability. His article belongs to a growing genre of writing that during the second half of the nineteenth century offered a critique of the material and moral defects of the city of Lima and its inhabitants, one of whose most conspicuous manifestations was criminality. Statements about crime and similar topics came from a variety of commentators, including state authorities, physicians, lawyers, hygienists, policy makers, journalists, and travelers. Although not always in agreement, these social critics shared a concern with social disorder and plebeian morals. Crime in the city of Lima was depicted as a phenomenon that went beyond the accumulation of isolated incidents of violation of the law to become a sort of social pathology resulting from multiple, complex causes, a threat to the stability of Peruvian society, a sign of social decomposition, and consequently an issue demanding prompt and energetic responses from the state.

Gutiérrez's list of factors contributing to criminality included various types of phenomena, ranging from inappropriate or inopportune state policies (free trade, abolition of slavery, abolition of the death penalty) to chronic deficiencies in the social system (inadequate judicial and police institutions, lack of education) and the endurance of popular forms of socialization (alcohol consumption, gambling, public diversions). Gutiérrez blended a critique of the morality of the urban poor and its alleged predisposition to disorderly behavior with a conservative critique of liberal social and economic policies. This conservative/authoritarian view of social problems such as crime seemed to express the anxieties of certain sectors of the Lima population vis-à-vis social and political changes, and it reiterated the demand for more severe state responses to what they viewed as the threatening increase of disorder by the lower classes. Crime, prostitution, alcoholism, poverty, gambling, and other such "vices" were discursively condensed and transformed into a single "social problem" that, at times, was deemed to be reaching alarming proportions. This semantic operation would have important consequences, for it was used to justify exclusionary policies, offered simplistic answers to very complex problems, and shaped state repressive policies. By connecting crime with certain plebeian forms of socialization and culture or, as frequently happened, by explaining crime as the inevitable result of those cultural forms, it was constructed, in addition, as a problem associated only with the lower classes of society. Crimes committed by members of the self-proclaimed decent sectors of society were rarely mentioned in those statements. The formulation of what I'm calling the criminal question thus also expressed and at the same time reinforced the class biases that shaped these efforts to "interpret" certain social phenomena.

Concern with crime in Lima was certainly not a novelty of the 1850s. There had been periods of notorious social instability, the wars of independence and the violent conjuncture of 1835, for instance, that provoked alarmist commentaries about the criminal activities of various subaltern groups, including slaves, plebeians, bandits, and the like. In fact, antecedents of the forms in which crime was perceived during the period considered here could be traced back at least to the sweeping reforms of the late colonial period. But the type of intellectual framework that sustained the emergence of the criminal question, as well as the political and cultural context in which it appeared, was quite distinct and novel. I argue that the criminal question was an intellectual and political construction that crystallized during a very concrete period (roughly, between 1855 and 1860) and not only constituted an intellectual exercise to explain the nature of crime and to promote possible solutions, but in fact was part of a much more ambitious effort to interpret society, social relations, and the nature of state intervention in the establishment of boundaries of acceptable behavior. In other words, when speaking about crime, its causes, and its remedies, these authors were also proposing a new discursive framework in which to understand Peruvian society and its problems. The new attitude toward crime emerging in the 1850s and 1860s reflected a growing concern with urban morals, labor discipline, and political control as well as a demand for more intrusive and effective state policies.

CONSTRUCTING THE CRIMINAL QUESTION

Gutiérrez's portrait of Lima's morals was in fact a mix of various sets of old-fashioned prejudices, stereotypes, fears, reactions to and interpretations of quite recent social and political transformations. The years 1854–60 witnessed a series of dramatic episodes that generated a greater sense of insecurity among various sectors of the city's population. The abolition of slavery in 1854 and of capital punishment in 1856 in conjunction with the artisans' riots of December 1858 (to name only the most notorious such episodes) were all perceived by influential sectors of the public opinion as major threats to Lima's social order. The time-honored notion that the most effective way to achieve order and obedience was through the use of harsh punishment translated into paranoia once severe forms of social control like slavery and the death penalty were removed (even if in the latter case it was only temporary).

The abolition of slavery in December 1854 was both preceded and followed by an outcry of warnings about the dangers associated with the manumission of slaves.[3] After abolition, commentators attributed the allegedly increasing levels of crime to the release of thousands of slaves who had no purpose in life other than to become involved in vice and crime. The abolition of slavery had opened up a new social and political scenario by altering, at least in the strictly legal sense, the already blurred lines between color and citizenship status and the relations of dependence between slave owners and their subjects. Landowners and other members of the upper classes expressed their fears that slaves would abandon haciendas and houses en masse to avoid work and take up a life of crime. Without slavery, they implied, blacks would not feel compelled to work. This attitude reflected racial stereotypes nurtured by centuries of slavery, but it was also related to the former owners' political battle to secure access to the labor force of free blacks. Whether or not ex-slaves turned into criminals is virtually impossible to assess. Santiago Távara, a supporter of abolition, concluded that they did not.[4] Manuel Atanasio Fuentes, on the other hand, provided statistical evidence to back allegations that abolition was indeed an important factor in the rising level of crime: in 1857, according to Fuentes, blacks represented 23.1 percent of prisoners in the Carceletas jail, a proportion more than double the black share of the Lima population, 11.34 percent at that time.[5]

The image of slaves-turned-criminals reflected the overall mental framework among important sectors of Peruvian society following the abolition of slavery. For many, former slaves did not deserve full citizenship.[6] Given their moral and intellectual handicaps, they argued, only harsh labor and social and political control would prevent them from destroying society. President Ramón Castilla, who had signed the abolition decree in the midst of the civil war he was fighting against then-president General José Rufino Echenique, responded to landowners' pressures by enacting a decree shortly after his triumph in January 1855 that forced agricultural ex-slaves to work on their former plantations for at least the next three months; at the same time, it allowed former slave owners to discharge old, sick, and troublesome ex-slaves. Former slaves who did not go back to work would be treated as vagrants and sent to the guano islands.[7] In order to check the supposedly rising incidence of crime, Castilla also reinstated in June of that year the *Tribunal de la Acordada*, a colonial institution that was viewed as a harsh and effective instrument to punish and deter crime.[8] Although the association between the abolition of slavery and the rise in criminality is far from proven, it appeared as a clear and transparent case of cause and effect in the minds of conservative commentators and in the measures adopted by the Castilla government. That image would persist in the years ahead, and authors like Gabriel Gutiérrez would embrace it as an established truth and incorporate it into a more ambitious interpretive scheme.

Other antecedents to the emergence of the criminal question can be found in debates over the death penalty. Capital punishment had existed in Peru throughout the colonial period. As elsewhere, public executions were designed as punitive rituals to chastise the aggressor and dissuade the rest of society from committing unlawful acts.[9] During the early independent period Peruvian constitutions retained the death penalty, but tended to restrict it to cases of so-called atrocious crimes.[10] Illegal executions of highway robbers and other criminals were also common during these decades.[11] Influenced by both liberalism and Catholicism, some opposition to capital punishment began to appear in the 1830s.[12] The author José Manuel Loza launched a philosophical/religious attack on the death penalty, drawing from Christian and other Western philosophers. Apart from being contrary to God's law, the death penalty was deemed "ineffective as a repressive means, useless for teaching a lesson [*escarmiento*], unjust in its application, and destructive of industry and of the most laborious and miserable race." Loza favored the penitentiary as a more suitable form of punishment.[13]

The death penalty was abolished by the liberal Constitution of 1856 following a campaign led by such liberals as José Gálvez.[14] Article 16 of the constitution was unambiguous: "Human life is inviolable; the death penalty cannot be imposed by law." This measure generated a series of alarmed complaints that the lack of "appropriate" responses to crime would cause it to proliferate. For Fuentes, for example, "the abolition of the death penalty has also been the abolition of the little public security that we enjoyed . . . never before have so many crimes been committed than in the last year."[15] The message was unequivocal: crime was on the rise because society was not severely punishing criminals. The minister of justice opined in 1858 that "a misunderstood philanthropy has declared inviolable the lives of the evil murderer, the arsonist, and other such criminals," while the law-abiding citizen had been left "abandoned to the cruel knife of the bandit."[16] The death penalty was deemed the only deterrent against potential law-breakers, especially at a time when, it was argued, former slaves were increasing their criminal activities and the Lima penitentiary (envisioned by many as the only hope to control crime) was still under construction. According to this apocalyptic vision, Lima society was at risk of being enveloped in uncontrollable crime and violence.

There were, indeed, occasions when these fears seemed to materialize. In December 1858 the cities of Lima and Callao witnessed three days of violent protests by discontented artisans against the increasing importation of manufactured goods. The protest was accompanied by unusual levels of violence and destruction. "The peaceful populations of Lima and Callao have been the scenario of dreary scenes intermixed with blood and destruction," wrote José Silva Santisteban.[17] According to several reports, the occasion had been seized by vagrants and criminals to engage in destruction and plunder that had nothing to do with the just protest of honest artisans. Both liberal and conservative observers highlighted the role played by the urban plebe in those riots and called the attention of the government to the problem of vagrancy. For some, the promotion of local industries would help alleviate the needs of the underprivileged groups, thus eliminating their inclination to violence; for others, harsher repression and stiffer police control were the only ways to avoid the repetition of such threatening scenes.[18]

In 1858 the legislature again discussed the death penalty and ultimately ratified its abolition. One of the most conspicuous supporters of the death penalty was the conservative cleric Bartolomé Herrera, for whom the efficacy of capital punishment stemmed from the fact that it was "irreparable." The execution of criminals, he posited, was "a sublime act" that restored "social order."[19] In 1860, the Peruvian congress drafted a new constitution, and the death penalty was again the subject of intense debate. Silva Santisteban, among others, passionately advocated its abolition. He was persuaded that the aim of any penalty must be the moral reform of the criminal, not his destruction, and since most crimes had social causes like poverty and unemployment or were the product of passion, the real solution was the creation of jobs, not the execution of the criminal.[20] Congressman Antonio Arenas, conversely, called for the restoration of the death penalty, citing the "alarming" increase in crime produced as a result of its abolition in 1856.[21] The assembly finally opted to reinstate the death penalty in the Constitution of 1860, albeit only for cases of aggravated murder.[22]

Debates about the death penalty continued in the following years. The most conspicuous abolitionist was the liberal writer and cleric Francisco de Paula González Vigil. He argued, in a pamphlet written in 1858 and published in 1862, that the reform of the criminal, not his extermination, must be the ultimate aim of punishment.[23] He was convinced that the penitentiary was the best means of punishing criminals. A lawyer, Nicanor Tejerina, argued that capital punishment had no deterrent effect on criminals and that the "deep" causes of crime ought to be looked for in the "vices of the social organization." Along with Vigil, he proposed increased use of prisons as the best punitive method. Tejerina shared the view that crime was a serious problem (demonstrated by "daily police chronicles"), but he used it to question the efficacy of the death penalty as a deterrent. Those who defended the death penalty used the argument of rising crime to demonstrate the opposite. In 1861, Luis E. Albertini considered abolition "a noble and generous utopia" that could not be effected without putting at risk the enire social order. He stressed that capital punishment was necessary in Peru "as a repressive and intimidating means" and as "the only brake capable of restraining evil passions." Echoing Fuentes and Gutiérrez, Albertini presented crime as reaching an alarming rate: "The horrendous events of our daily life, *the irrefutable facts of the statistics of crime*, and the growing overflow of evil passions have convinced us that the realization of this principle [the abolition of the death penalty] is at present an impossible utopia." In societies in which the ignorance of the masses was deep, Albertini further argued, and where "brutal passions" ruled over reason, punishment was most effective "when it uses terror as a means of intimidation." Confronting allegations that the death penalty did not reform the criminal, he replied that the goal was not to reform the delinquent but society as a whole, and that goal could be accomplished only through intimidation and terror.[24]

It is within this context that Gabriel Gutiérrez's article must be seen. Fear and paranoia associated with the abolition of slavery and attempts to abolish the death penalty were instrumental in the emergence of widespread concern over social disorder and crime. More important than the real or imagined statistical growth of crime in the city was the way law-abiding sectors of Lima society reacted to a changing social and political climate that produced, in their perception, a less severe and less effective system of justice and, at least in formal terms, a more fluid and potentially egalitarian social and racial structure. Another ingredient in the growing sense of insecurity felt by certain sectors of the Lima population was the active participation of the lower classes in political debates and electoral battles. As the historian Martín Monsalve has chronicled, both the presidential election of 1850 and the congressional election of 1855 generated a sense of disgust and paranoia because the lower classes "seized the streets" while elites retreated from openly public political participation. Monsalve quotes Fuentes who, in typical style, denigrated lower-class participation, especially that of blacks: "Black citizens are the saddest citizens, capable of discrediting every democratic institution [and] degrading it to the point that Whites renounce to their rights as citizens. Why are there no White water carriers or chocolate makers? Today, there are no White electors either, because that is a Black occupation."[25] The electoral act, Monsalve argues, was transformed into a "plebeian festivity."[26] Needless to say, for many members of Lima's respectable society that participation was a crime in itself.

All these events framed the emergence of crime as a social problem around 1860. Insecurity associated with political and social changes, together with a series of circumstances that seem to have affected crime rates (inflation, epidemics, and unemployment being the most important) created a climate, both psychological and political, conducive to heightened concern with the city's morals.[27] Although liberal observers like Mariátegui and Tejerina also contributed to the construction of the criminal question, it was authoritarian and conservative commentators such as Fuentes and Gutiérrez who more clearly shaped its outcome. While liberals saw crime as a serious problem closely associated with the imperfections of the social system, conservatives tended to blame it on the lack of severe punishment.[28] Concerns with crime need to be viewed within a larger conservative backlash in the Peruvian political scene during the second half of the 1850s. President Castilla, for instance, who had led the liberal revolution of 1854, shifted to openly conservative positions during those years. In his message to the Peruvian Congress on July 28, 1860, Castilla gave official sanction to the idea of a rising criminal problem: "The picture offered by recent criminal statistics, and especially the high number of terrifying crimes, is truly disheartening. A plague of malefactors that has augmented its numbers and audacity with foreign bandits is infesting our country, so it is imperative to adopt effective and severe measures for deterring the evil man from pursuing a criminal career, instead of encouraging him with impunity."

Castilla then commanded the Congress to examine whether the origin of that situation rested on the imperfections of the law or "on the morality of a corrupted and degraded part of the people."[29] President Castilla's statement highlights two of the most significant aspects of the discursive construction of the criminal question. First, he supported his claims, as did many other commentators, by referring to "recent criminal statistics." Second, he suggested the crime wave may be related not to social handicaps, but to the "morality" of the lower tiers of society.

The construction of crime as a social problem, as evidenced in Castilla's statement and in those of commentators like Gutiérrez, Albertini, Fuentes, and many others, was always related to allegations about rising levels of criminality, as demonstrated by statistical data. By citing crime statistics they tried to ascribe an aura of credibility to their assertions, although they did not generally bother to present those statistics to their audiences. This strategy was facilitated by the fact that, around the second half of the 1850s in Peru as in many other countries, statistics was consolidating its prestige as a fundamental tool both in the production of knowledge and in governmental practices. "Without statistics a state could not be well administered," wrote Juan Espinosa in his *Diccionario para el pueblo*.[30] Since the late 1840s, in fact, the Peruvian state had taken important steps in the direction of incorporating statistics into the machinery of government, and important statistical compilations were produced in the 1830s and 1840s.[31] But the beginning of what may be considered modern statistics in Peru was the result of the largely individual efforts of the most conspicuous chronicler of nineteenth-century Lima, Manuel Atanasio Fuentes.[32]

In 1858, Fuentes published his masterful *Estadística General de Lima*, a 774-page volume that included information on Lima's population, employment, bureaucracy, and production.[33] Despite its title, it was not restricted to figures and statistical tables, since Fuentes offered extensive commentaries on the many issues that attracted his attention. Although crime was not his main focus, he devoted several passages to it, presenting it as a social malady that was becoming more serious as a result of defective policing, an inefficient judicial system, the inopportune abolition of the death penalty, and the overall destruction of social life in postindependence Peru.[34] "Nobody will deny," he wrote, "no matter how great his/her patriotism is, that Lima is one of the cities that hosts the largest number of vagrants and corrupted men."[35] The growth of crime appeared to be connected, in Fuentes's view, with certain forms of popular sociability and culture. In lengthy narratives he presented gambling, drinking ("inebriation dominates the low class of the population"), and begging ("one of the malaises with the most deplorable consequences") as serious problems that threatened social order, and he demanded the creation of a "correctional police" to repress those who, lacking an "honest job," preferred to live by "corrupting public morality."[36] He further suggested the creation of houses of correction "for abolishing habits of idleness and combating vices that degrade humanity."[37]

The image that emerges from certain passages of Fuentes's book is that of a society at risk of being destroyed by crime and the lack of morality of the lower classes. His descriptions of popular dances and festivities are quite revealing: "hateful and repugnant spectacles" (the *Moros y cristianos* [Moors and Christians] dance); "obscene movements accompanied by savage gesticulations . . . horrendous procession" (the dance of *Diablos y gigantes* [Devils and giants]); "hateful, immoral, savage, a pastime in which no social consideration is respected" (carnival). He called for their repression in the name of civilization: "The people cannot be civilized or moralized if we foment their low instincts and if we respect customs born in barbarous times." To combat the volatile drives of the plebeian groups—"the lower the degree of civilization of the society to which they belong, the more pernicious they are"—he demanded "energetic and vigorous measures." Only then would they be contained "within the limits of order and moderation."[38]

Many of the statements Fuentes made, however, in particular those related to growing crime in the city, do not appear to be sustained by statistical evidence. Fuentes himself admitted that "the statistics of vice" were not easy to compile, since they involved acts that people had an interest in hiding or that in most cases were overlooked.[39] He did present figures on individuals arrested and held in Lima's jails, including their nationalities, race, occupation, and so forth, along with estimates of the numbers of beggars, gamblers, and prostitutes. It is very difficult to infer from those figures, however, the conclusions he presented in his narrative. In a revealing passage, after stating that "never before have so many crimes been committed than in the last year," he added that he could not organize a statistical compilation of the population in *Carceletas*, the local jail, because the records prior to 1856 had been stolen, and thus he had had access only to the 1857 records: "but from the records we will present, the large number of indicted men could be seen. Thefts and homicides: here is, in summary, the catalog of crimes committed in Lima; precisely the most serious; precisely those that governments attempt to repress the most."[40] This rather confusing and arbitrary reasoning was used by Fuentes to try to convince his readers that the number of thefts and homicides was really high, in fact, higher than ever before, when the figures he actually presented did not justify such an opinion.

Thanks to the prestige he acquired from his tireless efforts at chronicling the history and current events of Lima and the quite impressive amount of information he collected in his book, Fuentes became an obligatory reference for authorities and commentators and thus contributed decisively to shape the way crime, social disorder, and public morals were perceived.[41] Statistics, in Peru as elsewhere, had become not only an administrative auxiliary, but also a powerful tool to construct reality itself.[42] According to such historians as Simon Cole there was a close relationship between the development of statistics and the emergence of a view of crime as "less a series of isolated acts of individual will than an organized social phenomenon, an epidemic," a description that is applicable to the invention of the criminal question in mid-nineteenth-century Peru.[43] And even if in Peru there was much to be desired in terms of the scientific manipulation of statistics, by the late 1850s it had already become a source of authorized opinions: to rely on statistics offered a patina of veracity that was hard to contest.

The inflections and particular style of Fuentes's portrait of the city's morals had a tremendous impact on subsequent depictions of Lima and its lower classes. The emphasis on the moral aspects of popular culture, his denigrating view of popular forms of socialization, the distance he established between lettered and plebeian cultures, and his open condemnation of urban popular culture, with the concomitant call for its repression and control, all were received approvingly by the respectable sectors of the Lima population, especially those who ascribed to conservative political positions. Fuentes offered the means but also the language and the images that would inform the way in which successive generations of observers would interpret Lima society and its inhabitants. In light of this, it is not an overstatement to say that President Castilla's rhetorical question, formulated in 1860 (do public morals explain crime?), had already been answered by Fuentes: for him, the morality or, better, lack of morality of the lower classes was largely responsible for the statistically proven rise in crime levels. This formulation, not entirely original but now offered as being supported by the painstaking statistical work of Fuentes, would persist for a long time. In this, as in other aspects, Fuentes truly was, as the historian Paul Gootenberg has asserted, the "social constructor of Limeño reality."[44]

A new motif, what I call the criminal question, thus entered the intellectual, political, and legal debates in Lima around 1860. Although commentators did not always agree on the specifics, for example, causes and remedies, most of them, liberals and conservatives alike, shared a concern about the threats illegal behavior posed to public order, the state of civilization, and the prospects for the modernization of Peruvian society. In the years and decades ahead, as Peruvian society experienced a series of social and political calamities, this sense of anxiety only deepened. Explanations for criminal behavior grounded in moral and cultural traits thus became further consolidated, for they were built, not surprisingly, upon a series of pervasive discourses about the lower and colored classes that usually coalesced into a singular narrative: their supposed moral degeneration. Lack of morals became a condition associated with multiple manifestations of lower-class culture and explained by a combination of factors, one of the most influential being the lack of severe punishment. Moral degeneration was a phenomenon frequently associated with particular racial groups (blacks, Indians, Chinese), certain trades and social groups (domestic servants, peons, street vendors, the urban underclasses), and specific urban environs (certain neighborhoods of Lima). What connections were there between discourses on crime and those on race, labor, and urban hygiene?

"LA PODRE DE LIMA" (THE PUS OF LIMA)

That representations of crime were usually colored by racialized views of society will surprise no one. Although still far removed from theories of crime and criminal behavior based on racial and biological traits, the ways in which authorities, journalists, policy makers, and other commentators reflected upon crime were patently shaped by racial assumptions, prejudices, and stereotypes whose origins could be traced to the colonial period. The hegemonic view of Indians as naturally inferior, reluctant to work, intellectually impaired, superstitious, brutalized by alcohol and coca, and enemies of progress and civilization was not an invention of mid-nineteenth-century modernizing elites. Building upon theories of racial difference that emphasized purity of blood (*limpieza de sangre*), place of birth, and cultural heritage, Spanish colonists had long defined nonwhites, in particular, Indians, as racially inferior. Whether Indians were viewed as biologically condemned to inferiority or as human beings needing protection, evangelization, and education, colonial discourses laid the foundation for a view of Indians as an inferior race. And even though there were dissenting voices that attributed racial handicaps not to biology but to exploitation and abuse, there was a wide consensus about the inherent baseness of the colored races.[45] Massive, violent episodes like the Tupac Amaru rebellion in 1780 only deepened sentiments of fear and abhorrence against Indians, which would loom large during the Wars of Independence and beyond. As historians have long established, Peruvian independence did not offer full citizenship rights to large segments of its population, in particular to indigenous groups. The tortuous process of nation-state formation was plagued by violent political confrontations, economic distress, profound ethnic and social divisions, and ever-growing cultural schisms between groups. Race played a critical role in these confrontations.[46] The basic quandary for the new creole ruling class was how to realize the promises of rights and equality before the law associated with liberalism in a society in which the majority of the population was composed of people they regarded as inferior. In Peru, Indians represented about 60 percent of the more than 1.5 million inhabitants of the country in the immediate postindependent period.[47]

The first decades after Independence, although not devoid of struggle and contention, ultimately consolidated the exclusion of Indians and blacks from the creole hegemonic national project. In the case of Indians, a combination of old and new mechanisms of social, political, and labor control was implanted in order to keep them in their place. The old notions of Indians as degenerate subjects, reluctant to progress, and incapable of political wisdom were reinforced. In debates about who should be granted citizenship in the new republic, Indians were excluded almost by default.[48] As the historian Cecilia Méndez has said in reference to Simón Bolívar's views about the Indians, "Culturally speaking, in his idea of nation there was no place for Indians. The concept of Indian was incompatible with that of a citizen."[49]

Racist discourses became strengthened in the decades after independence. Anti-Indian sentiments shaped both conservative and liberal political agendas and discourses, but, as in the case of attitudes toward crime and punishment, they tended to differ in their explanations and proposed remedies, some emphasizing biological determinism, others stressing the impact of the social and historical milieu. Most creole ideologists, commentators, and state officials agreed that Indians were indeed a degenerate race. This rhetoric was used in political debates, literary constructions, official reports, demands for European immigration, explanations of the country's failures, and doctrinal justifications for the Indians' exclusion from political participation. As such, racist discourse was a powerful instrument of marginalization. Nobody expressed it with more clarity than Herrera, the ardent supporter of the death penalty, who, in a landmark speech given on July 28, 1846, used racial justifications to dismiss the doctrine of popular sovereignty as unfit for the Peruvian republic. Indians, he argued, must be prohibited from voting because their "natural incapacity" for intelligent reasoning made them unsuitable for full citizenship.[50]

Around the middle of the nineteenth century, a new generation of modernizing intellectuals also addressed issues of nation and race. Most of them reiterated the standard depictions of Indians and blacks that they borrowed from earlier authors, but they also began to depart from theories of inevitable inferiority and exclusion. One such intellectual was Fuentes. As we have seen, he repeatedly scorned Indians, blacks, and Chinese as barbarous and uncivilized; but he stopped short of embracing a biological theory of degeneration, emphasizing instead culture and morals and postulating that education could turn savage Indians into modern citizens, a posture that echoed for decades to come.[51] He seems even to celebrate racial diversity: "If the theory of a garden can be applied to human populations, that of Lima will have to be pleasant, since it is not just comprised of whites, and thus it is not homogeneous, monotonous, or boring to our senses."[52]

Other commentators of this period took a step forward. Building upon "proto-Indigenista" writers of the colonial period, they advanced an argument that would be offered more forcefully in the early twentieth century: the prostration of the Indian race was a result of colonialism and the abuses of landowners, judges, and priests. This group includes writers like Narciso Aréstegui, the author of the pro-Indian novel "Father Horán" (1848), modernizing businessmen such as Juan Bustamante, who founded in 1867 the Sociedad Amigos del Indio,[53] and social critics such as Juan Espinosa, the author of the *Diccionario para el pueblo*. While they all shared with more conservative observers the view of the Indian race as weak and degenerate, they differed in that they posited social causes to explain such prostration. They generally espoused republican ideals and, as the historian Carmen McEvoy has argued, were convinced that the realization of the Republican project in Peru "must encompass the incorporation of Indians as citizens."[54] Bustamante considered "a shame to the Republic, to civilization, and to Christianity" the fact that Indians were still treated as feudal serfs. "The Indian has no family, no property; he does not even have a right to his own person. He is forced to die like a beast in a bullfight; his woman is raped, his children sold, his land devastated, as if it had no owner."[55] Espinosa stated that the "present-day Indian is no longer the same as before; when he is taught, he is humble, helpful [*servicial*], loving, intelligent; but he is distrustful (and rightly so), stingy, and degraded when in contact with those supposed civilizers that have usurped his natural rights." He explicitly blamed priests and local authorities (prefectos and subprefectos) for having turned the Indian into a slave.[56] Francisco Laso argued that "the Indigenous race . . . is a good race . . . Had Indians been treated like men and not like beasts [they] would have displayed their good qualities, and would have leveled with the most civilized man."[57] In quite ironic ways, nonetheless, these "friends of the Indians" helped perpetuate stereotypes and negative images about them, since their common point of departure was an ideal of civilization that the Indians could not match, even if they underwent a profound, painful, and ultimately futile process of becoming civilized. But precisely because they emphasized cultural and social traits in their explanation for the Indians' alleged state of prostration, their ideas about race fit well with the way the criminal question had been constructed, that is, as an essentially moral and cultural issue.

Racialized views of subaltern groups were not limited to Indians and blacks. From the late 1840s, thousands of Chinese indentured servants (*coolies*) were brought to Peru to work on plantations, railroad projects, and guano islands. Their living conditions were similar to, maybe even worse than, those endured by black slaves. The Chinese became a source of increased anxiety over the moral, racial, and cultural future of the Peruvian population. Although initially praised by landowners for their alleged discipline, obedience, and lack of vices,[58] they later became the target of epithets and racial slurs, especially when, after their contracts expired, they moved from rural plantation areas to Lima and other coastal cities. Promoters of white European immigration scorned the Chinese for allegedly thwarting Peru's march to progress.[59] References to the Chinese usually combined physical and moral traits, as if their alleged ugliness reflected their equally evident moral impairment. In the words of the physician César Borja, the Chinese were imperfect and weak and formed a "vicious, degenerate, and decrepit race" that accelerated the "degeneration" of the Peruvian racial makeup.[60] As in the case of Indians, even those who felt some degree of commiseration toward the Chinese used racialized arguments in their defense. In 1861, a Chinese peon named Achin murdered his abusive *caporal* (overseer) and was sentenced to fifteen years in the penitentiary. Opponents of the death penalty like Ignacio Noboa applauded the judge's consideration of mitigating circumstances, such as the abuses of the overseer, and added, "An abject being like the Chinese, heartless, without ideas, lacking any knowledge of our ways, and accustomed to look with disdain not only on the lives of others but also on his own life, cannot be held responsible for such a criminal action in the same way that an enlightened man who, after pondering all the circumstances, still yields to his uncontrollable passion."[61]

As in the case quoted above, discourses about race intersected with and shaped views of crime and criminals. Since racially inferior groups were almost always portrayed as vicious, lazy, and incapable of moral judgment, accusing them of being prone to crime (when not natural-born criminals) was a foregone conclusion. Sebastián Lorente, a reputable liberal educator, portrayed the Indian as a compulsive *ratero*: "He could not get close to you without stealing something, a trifle [*bagatela*], a rag [*harapo*], a utensil that we no longer value."[62] Blacks, as we have seen, were also depicted as being prone to banditry and crime: since they had been accustomed to being restrained by slave owners and overseers, once slavery ended their fate was to become a criminal. As to the Chinese, their state of abjection and their propensity to vice made them criminals almost by definition. Again, Fuentes expressed these ideas in a blatantly clear way: the "moral conditions" of the Chinese included, according to him, "the depravation of manners, idleness, and the inclination to suicide and theft."[63]

Whether nonwhites' inclinations to crime and vice were depicted as resulting from organic defects or social environment, the relationship between discourses of race and crime was crucially mediated by a heightened concern with labor discipline. Crime as a public issue was, in fact, in the long run, much more closely associated with vagrancy and idleness than with outbursts of property or violent crimes. The lack of work discipline among Lima's urban poor and their alleged preference for idleness and vice was a recurrent theme in public discourse.[64] In 1860, the minister of government depicted vagrancy as the "leprosy" of the social body and the origin of all vices and crimes.[65] Once again, statistics were invoked to support these views: according to Fuentes, more than 50 percent of all men tried for criminal conduct were vagrants.[66] Newspapers such as *El hijo del pueblo* (The Son of the People) and *El Trabajo* (Work) were founded specifically to educate the masses to set themselves to useful, profitable work and remove them from a life of vice and crime. *El Trabajo* was very explicit about the need to transform vagrants/criminals into workers and how to achieve that transformation: "We must send to military or industrial schools all that crowd of adolescents that hang around hotel counters or pool saloons, and who seem to have no occupation other than going through elementary education in vagrancy, secondary instruction in vice, and, later, graduating in political and social crime."[67] The jurist Isaac Alzamora considered that vagrants were budding criminals who, rather than be forcefully enrolled in the army (which did not need to be contaminated with the "scum" of society) or fined (which could not modify a lifestyle that had become "second nature"), should be sentenced to forced labor.[68] The problem, according to many of these authors, began at an early age, so the solution needed to address the issue of child vagrancy. Even adolescents who offered their services as porters at different locations in the city were considered vagrants and, if not "corrected," would later turn into criminals.[69] Demands were also made to deter religious institutions from providing relief to the homeless and to beggars for, it was said, charity fomented vices and "contributed to the perversion of that part of the population."[70]

Policies geared toward curtailing vagrancy had been implemented by state authorities since colonial times.[71] During the early independent period different measures were taken to eradicate vagrancy, including forced enlistment in the army and the incarceration of all those plebeians not carrying a *boleto* (certificate of employment).[72] The Reglamento de Policía of 1839 considered as vagrants not only beggars, gamblers, and the unemployed, but also alcohol drinkers and artisans showing poor work discipline. In 1855, the boleto was made obligatory for *jornaleros* (day laborers), artisans, and domestic servants,[73] but it proved not to be a solution: *El Comercio* reported that phony passes were being sold in the streets of Lima.[74] The Penal Code of 1862 did not consider vagrancy a crime, but it punished the owners of gambling houses and other businesses that allowed "notoriously vagrant individuals."[75] The Reglamento de Policía of 1877, which included an entire section on vagrants and beggars, stretched the definition to include artisans who were absent from their work for one week. Vagrants were to be punished by consigning them to military service in the army or the navy or by committing them to perform forced labor in "any other useful job for which they may have aptitude."[76]

These anxieties about labor discipline, when merged with depictions of the lower classes' cultural impairments and racial inferiority, coalesced into a pessimistic view of urban life in general and of certain areas of the city in particular. This attitude, however, did not become pervasive until after the hopes and dreams of urban civilization had faded away. Beginning in the 1850s, the city fitfully began to abandon its colonial blueprint. A new railroad station, a marketplace, a slaughterhouse, and a mental asylum were built; in 1856, the construction of the penitentiary started; in the 1860s, the central post office building, a gas factory, and a hospice were added; and in the 1870s, even more impressive buildings and monuments contributed to the modernization of the city: the Palace of Exhibition, the Dos de Mayo hospital, and the Plaza Dos de Mayo, among others.[77] An important symbolic step in this process was the demolition of the colonial city walls, which was enjoined in 1866 but not executed until the early 1870s.[78] Arguments in favor of and against the demolition focused, not surprisingly, on issues of urban décor, but also, quite importantly, on matters of public safety. As late as 1860, public officials considered the wall an important instrument in crime control.[79] Méndez noted the almost simultaneous demolition of the walls and the erection of the penitentiary of Lima.[80] Although a certain sense of liberation may have been felt by the Lima population once the wall was demolished, it is revealing that many felt unprotected against bandits and highway robbers.[81] Simultaneously, promenades and boulevards were built, and monuments and public sculptures began to proliferate, reflecting a conscious effort, as the art historian Natalia Majluf has suggested, to instill a new, civilizing order. The new streets and plazas were imagined as symbols of stability, order, and progress.[82] As in other cities of Latin America, this modernizing drive responded to a desire to transform Lima on the model of European urban and cultural paradigms. Nobody expressed this more clearly than the anonymous writer who commented upon the fact that the new, presumably patriotic, monument to the heroes of the naval combat of May 2, 1866, had been made in a foreign country: "Bronze and marble we profusely had in our Andean mines and in our quarries [canteras]; but, what about art, the vital breadth, the soul? It did not exist then, it does not yet exist among us; it is a privilege of other peoples, a grace that will be given to us after a long time. It was necessary to search for it far away, where the warmth of enthusiasm, education, and traditions exists and is transformed by inspiration."[83]

The high hopes that modernizing elites had in such urban civilizing projects were complicated by various obstacles. First, public and private initiatives faced enormous financial obstacles, as Peru entered the postguano era and the "fictitious prosperity" gave way to the gloomy reality of an empty treasury and an economy in shambles.[84] Second, the allegedly civilizing message was generally lost on the purported recipients. Plebeian groups proved resilient when it came to their own cultural traditions, erecting quite serious obstacles to the elites' plans to turn Lima into an orderly and peaceful heaven. And third, the material modernization of Lima did not include efforts to improve the living conditions of the urban poor. Large sectors of the population continued to live under quite precarious conditions, occupying the worst housing environments of the city.

Gradually, as Peruvian society was ravaged by a series of social and political calamities, the city of Lima became the subject of reports, descriptions, and other types of representation that emphasized its maladies. Lima was depicted as a sick organism, its social problems as diseases, and the unfit population as a sort of cancerous cell that needed to be extirpated. The assassination of President José Balta and the ensuing urban riots of 1872, the assassination of former president Manuel Pardo in 1876, the severe economic crisis that followed the guano age, and especially the disastrous effects of the War of the Pacific (1879–83) all increased a sense of frustration and impending downfall among important sectors of the Lima population, especially its social and economic elites. The Chilean occupation of the capital between 1881 and 1883, immediately preceded by violent riots, further dislocated Lima's society.[85] The sense of ruin, decay, and impotence ran deep before, during, and after the war. Racial stereotypes, in particular against Indians and Chinese, fed the notion that those two groups were to blame for Peru's catastrophic defeat against Chile. As the historian Heraclio Bonilla emphasized, the war destroyed not just the physical architecture of the city but also, and more important, the institutional and political means of control that the *civilista* oligarchy had built, thus forcing an "institutional reordering of society."

Frustration with the growing awareness that Lima's society was not civilized enough to match their idealized European models was an important ingredient of this series of highly negative images of the city. While in 1867 Fuentes could still offer an optimistic, if biased and racist, picture of the city ("Lima's society has nothing to envy the most advanced capital"), a few years later that sense of optimism would disappear.[86] The country's "moral abatement" was explained by, among other things, the criminal tendencies and the racial makeup of the lower classes. The jurist Paulino Fuentes Castro demanded energetic measures against vagrancy as one means of overcoming moral prostration.[87] An article entitled "Causes of Peruvian Ruin" blamed the country's downfall not on foreign war or the amputation of the territory, but on "ethnic bastardy."[88] Although greater concern with urban hygiene would be displayed in early twentieth-century writings (see chapter 2), depictions of the city prior to 1900 already showed the combination of voyeurism, repugnance, and commiseration typical of later *higienista* (hygienist) writings. Specific areas of the city were depicted as being inhabited by dangerous criminal groups, and an image of "cities inside the city" gained preeminence.

Typical examples of the elites' contempt for specific areas and groups of the city were two articles that one "Dr. Vidrieras" wrote under the common title "La podre de Lima" (The pus of Lima). In one of them, the author described his visit to Lima's Chinatown, a conglomerate of housing units, restaurants, brothels, and opium dens that became one of the favorite targets of upper-class denigration of the lower classes of Lima.

"Does anybody know the city of the Chinese?" asked the author. "Hygiene has been proscribed, morality has been annulled, and all the vices keep the beast with its drives unbridled." He had gone to Chinatown with both "wonder and repugnance," only to find "abnormal physiognomies, which could enrich Lombroso's files." He then described both the physical environment ("each house is a pigsty") and the population that inhabited it: "disheveled women, indolently strewn in obscene positions," "men with shifty or extremely lively, asymmetric eyes, with strange ears, lifted and open nose, and disproportionate arms."[89] The morality of the Chinese, the author seems to imply, was concurrent with their physical imperfections. Demands for their forceful relocation were a common corollary of such negative depictions. Years later, in 1909, the Callejón de Otaiza, one of the most vilified housing units in Chinatown, was demolished on orders of the Lima municipality.[90]

Lower-class neighborhoods inhabited by blacks and mestizos were also described, over and over again, as indicative of a lifestyle that would shock any foreign (that is, civilized) visitor. An article in *El Comercio* offered a sordid account of Lima's miseries:

> The entrance to Lima, which until 1840 was made through the beautiful gate of Callao, and that later, until 1878, was made by railroad through the industrial area of San Jacinto, is made today through the rear of the city; through the garbage dumps, the tanneries, the ugly backside of the slaughterhouse, and then through the oldest and most horrendous façades of the urban constructions next to the railroad track. This, from the south; from the north, you have the mounds of garbage, the filthy and unpleasant Tajamar neighborhood, a bridge filled in its supports by tons of human fecal matter, the remains of some toilets, the façade of the dirtiest and most neglected stone bridge that exists in the world, and, lastly, the banks of a river without canal, with infected, stagnant waters, which is used as a toilet by the poor.

Visitors asked themselves with disdain, the reporter added: "Is this Lima?"[91]

What is at work here is the consolidation of a discourse that identified specific areas of the city and, concomitantly, specific social and racial groups as needing surveillance, hygiene, and even repression to achieve the civilized urban order that many dreamed of.[92] This, in turn, impacted the ways criminologists constructed their visions of delinquency and the punitive methods that state officers would propose and implement.

In his report on the "city of the Chinese," "Dr. Vidrieras" referred to Chinese men as subjects belonging to "Lombroso's files." By that he meant to suggest they were degenerate, deviant, repulsive, and criminal in nature. His description of their physical traits, in fact, closely resembles the increasingly common depictions of criminals offered in contemporary European treatises. Very few people in Lima, however, would have understood the metaphor, since not many had heard about the famous Italian physician Cesare Lombroso. But in just a few years he would become one of the most often quoted experts in writings and representations of crime and the lower classes. By the beginning of the 1890s, the new science of the criminal imported from Europe began to attract the attention of physicians, lawyers, hygienists, and state authorities. With it came the promise of new, scientific ways of looking at and explaining crime as well as novel and more effective crime-control policies.

2

THE SCIENCE OF THE CRIMINAL

(1890–1930)

By the late 1880s the language of experts writing about crime in Lima began to change. The transformation started in university classrooms and professional groups, especially lawyers' and physicians' associations, but soon afterward it began to influence the way policy makers, authorities, journalists, and even common folk talked about crime and criminals. Terms such as *born criminal, criminal anthropology, dangerousness,* and others became common currency. Physicians and psychiatrists influenced by positivist criminology began to play a much more prominent role in the analysis of crime and the formulation of penal policies. Prisons were visited by researchers interested not only in evaluating prison discipline but also, increasingly, in describing and analyzing the physical and clinical characteristics of the convict population. Scientific analyses of crime promised to change the way crime was perceived and explained. As happened in Europe, Peruvian authors engaged in discussions about the causes of criminal behavior. The relative importance of biological and social factors in explaining tendencies toward crime was a subject of intense debate. In their contributions to this specific issue and in the formulation of broader interpretations of criminal behavior, criminologists also offered arguments that dealt with the political, cultural, and racial construction of the Peruvian national community. These discourses about crime open a window not just on competing arguments about crime and deviance, but also, and more important, on their articulation with theories and doctrines of racial difference and national identity.

The adoption and early developments of positivist criminology in Peru are the focus here. Most radical versions of biological determinism were rejected by Peruvian criminologists in favor of a "social" interpretation of crime, but one that emphasized those social elements that were most closely related to the "moral" features of the lower and colored groups, thus reinforcing the traditional view of crime as a moral phenomenon associated with certain racial, social, and occupational groups (see chapter 1). The body of knowledge thus produced generated specific images of crime and criminals that, in turn, would influence both crime-control policies and the approaches to penal regimes, which will be explored in successive chapters. Like their counterparts in other societies, Peruvian criminologists strove to construct the notion of a clearly identifiable criminal class, separate from and at odds with the community of law-abiding citizens. This separation included a clear demarcation between the world of crime and the world of labor, which resulted in the common perception that the criminal question was not as threatening in Peru as in other countries of Europe and Latin America, where it merged with other social problems (giving birth to the so-called social question) and generated enormous anxiety about potential social distress. This discursive construction of a relatively mild criminal problem was nonetheless shaped by and reinforced authoritarian views about the lower classes that served to sustain the exclusionary policies being implemented by the modernizing state.

THE ADOPTION AND EARLY DEVELOPMENT OF CRIMINOLOGY IN PERU

Criminology, the science of the criminal, emerged in Europe during the last quarter of the nineteenth century. According to some authors, its origins are located in late eighteenth-century attempts to isolate the causes of crime, from which it gradually evolved until crystallizing, by the late 1870s, into what was known as criminal anthropology, as formulated by the Italian physician Cesare Lombroso.[1] Other scholars, while not denying the importance of those antecedents, emphasize the radical difference in nature and purpose between criminology as a scientific discourse and previous, less articulated approaches to the study of crime. David Garland, for instance, argues that late eighteenth- and early nineteenth-century efforts to explain crime are part of "criminology's genealogy" but "did not constitute a criminology." He identifies criminology with a specific genre of inquiry about criminals whose foundations lay in the idea that science can provide rational explanations of criminal behavior and that it was possible to separate, for cognitive and political purposes, criminals from noncriminals; both of these assumptions were absent in earlier approaches.[2] Positivist criminology—whether considered the first science of the criminal or only a modern version of it—built upon a series of nineteenth-century intellectual and scientific traditions such as phrenology, physiognomy, statistics, the evolutionary theories of Charles Darwin and Herbert Spencer, the positivist persuasion that laws could explain social phenomena, and the development of state records on criminals and prisons. Its influence rapidly expanded throughout the world, becoming, in less than a decade, one of the most attractive intellectual constructions of the nineteenth century.[3] Criminology reached an audience well beyond the small circle of specialists, for it offered not only new interpretations of crime and criminals but also scientific explanations to a variety of social concerns.

The birth of positivist criminology is generally associated with the publication, in 1876, of Lombroso's *The Criminal Man*.[4] Lombroso became famous for making two straightforward arguments: first, that there were human beings whose inclination to crime was innate or inherited (the idea of the born criminal),[5] and second, that it was possible to identify actual or potential criminals by observing some of their physical characteristics (what Lombroso called stigmata). Lombroso viewed criminals as "atavistic" individuals who represented a regression to more imperfect, even primitive stages in human evolution, and the idea led him to associate criminals, "primitive" peoples, and nonwhite racial groups.[6] Lombroso, in fact, made an explicit connection between the biological features of criminals and those of "inferior races" in Bolivia and Peru and even certain animals, such as apes, rodents, and birds.[7] Although Lombroso's ideas were more complex than this, and while he later somehow balanced his claims—admitting, for instance, that born criminals made up only a fraction of lawbreakers—his theory of the born criminal became the center of one of the most passionate debates in the history of the human sciences. His books and articles along with those of his disciples, especially Enrico Ferri and Raffaele Garofalo, circulated all over the world and were widely used to generate knowledge about criminals in quite different societies. Lombrosian criminology was subjected to harsh criticism by a group of French scholars, in particular Gabriel Tarde and Alexandre Lacassagne, who rejected the idea of the born criminal and emphasized the social nature of crime. "Societies," Lacassagne said, "have the criminals they deserve."[8] The two schools confronted each other at a series of international conferences, and these debates reached and were reproduced in the rest of the world.[9] In Latin America, legal, social, and medical debates about crime and criminals began to incorporate, from the late 1880s, the premises of positivist criminology. Lawyers and physicians, especially, avidly read foreign-language criminological treatises, disseminated the new ideas in newspaper and magazine articles, wrote university theses, and vehemently debated the ideas of Lombroso and his followers. Reactions to Lombrosian criminology varied widely, ranging from uncritical endorsement to furious rejection. Although actual criminological research was slow to come, some authors, among them Carlos Roumagnac and Julio Guerrero in Mexico, Nina Rodrigues in Brazil, José Ingenieros in Argentina, and Fernando Ortiz in Cuba, produced studies whose value and interest went beyond the issue of crime and criminal behavior and touched on problems of national identity, politics, and race. Although the impact of positivist criminology on penal legislation and prison reform would not be felt until later, public and official discourses on crime, race, sexuality, and related issues were greatly influenced by criminological theories from at least the early 1890s.[10]

In Peru, jurists and physicians reproduced these debates.[11] Authors such as the jurist Javier Prado suggested that the focus of criminal science should shift from the crime to the criminal, his physical and moral constitution, and the influence of nature and the social milieu on the criminal's character. Prado also considered heredity a major factor in the shaping of not only the physical and moral constitution of the subject, but also the contours of national character.[12] Paulino Fuentes Castro, a lawyer and director of the law newspaper *El diario judicial*, was probably the most enthusiastic publicist of the new doctrines. He blatantly stated that "criminality is a state of war launched by a certain type of men who have remained behind in the evolution of sentiments of humanity and probity. . . . Crime is not an isolated human act, but the revelation of an existence incapable of adapting to the social milieu."[13] The physician Abraham Rodríguez conducted a typically Lombrosian research project: he went to the penitentiary to measure the convicts' physical attributes in order to identify the features of the Peruvian born criminal. He reported that his research corroborated Lombroso's claim about the "cephalic index" of the criminal man, established a connection between types of crimes and the size of the cranial hole, and determined that born criminals in the penitentiary of Lima comprised about 10 percent of its population.[14]

More important, these early Peruvian criminologists made a clear association between the Lombrosian notion of a born criminal and the Peruvian indigenous population. Rodríguez concluded that all Peruvian born criminals presented a "plagiocephalic deformation" that he identified as the sign of innate criminality among Indians. Fuentes Castro, in a series of portraits of famous criminals, included those of indigenous murderers such as Manuel Peña Chacaliaza, who was depicted as "one of the most perfect criminal types," a "moral phenomenon, contrary to the laws of the [human] species," a person whose physiognomy revealed, among other anomalies, "a clear facial asymmetry."[15] Pedro Laredo, an Indian criminal from the central Andes, was described by the same author in the following terms: "His facial deformations, resulting from the daily use of alcohol, turn his physiognomy into that of the true imbecile, very close to the idiotism of the irresponsible . . . his features reveal a mental illness that makes him akin to the innately depraved, that is, to the organic criminals. His intelligence is harmonious with his physical condition." His trade as a muleteer in the Andean highlands, Fuentes Castro continued, where Laredo had as companions only the sky, the mountains, the frigid elevations, and a few wild animals, explained his lack of intelligence and his "atrocious cruelty." Indians, being in such close contact with nature, thus represented a regression to less civilized lifestyles. As such, they were a perfect illustration of what Lombroso had presented as typical criminal types.[16]

But enthusiasm for the theories of the Italian doctor cooled rather quickly. Even Prado distanced himself from the extreme biological bias of Lombrosian criminology and, citing Tarde, demanded more attention be paid to the social factors of crime.[17] Numerous voices of skepticism rejected the idea of inborn criminals and argued for a truly social approach to criminality, albeit this was usually done in a rather abstract, theoretical way. In some cases, they simply repeated what Tarde and others had written in discrediting the biological extremes of Lombrosian criminology.[18] In a few instances, authors did produce relatively valuable analyses, offering elements for a reinterpretation of crime in the context of Peruvian society.

Plácido Jiménez, for instance, a graduate of the University of San

Figure 2. Manuel Peña Chacaliaza. From Ismael
Portal, *Del pasado limeño* (Lima: Librería
e Imprenta Gil, 1932).

Marcos, adamantly rejected Lombroso's theories, although he admitted there were human beings of "congenital perversity" who could not be reformed by penal treatment.[19] Still, following Tarde and Lacassagne, he considered social factors the most prominent breeders of crime, a conclusion he found "consoling" because legislators "could improve the conditions of society" and thus help reduce crime.[20] The social causes of crime he referred to included "vagrancy, prostitution, gambling, pauperism, and the impunity of crimes committed by members of the upper classes."[21] He emphasized, as earlier writers like Fuentes and Gutiérrez did, that moral decay among the lower classes led to a life of crime: "Among the lowest tiers of society, moral sentiments are enervated, the notion of justice is still embryonic, and they never pause to prepare for the future."[22] Accordingly, he proposed firmer state intervention to contain social disorder and demoralization: "social prevention" would be the only means to eliminate crime. In fact, using a metaphor that was becoming increasingly common, he thought that social prevention was a matter of "social hygiene," for criminality could be compared to a contagious disease. Prevention, he added, should focus especially on children and must include education, the creation of charities and welfare agencies, the promotion of religious sentiments, the elimination of impunity, the search for political stability, the improvement of laws, and the repression of drinking and gambling.[23]

In the 1910s and 1920s, other authors would produce empirically based portraits of crime that departed from the simplistic theories of biological criminology. Although biological and hereditary factors were not totally expunged, these authors paid more serious attention to factors ranging from demoralization to exploitation, from ignorance to imitation, and from prostitution to alcohol consumption. José Antonio Encinas, for example, strongly posited that the Peruvian Indian was not a degenerate, and that an enormous proportion of crimes committed by Indians were a response to social causes, namely, exploitation.[24] The physician and psychiatrist Hermilio Valdizán, who argued that crime must be treated as a biological phenomenon, admitted that "exogenous" factors were particularly important in the case of indigenous criminality.[25] The criminologist Víctor Modesto Villavicencio, in his *Sociología criminal peruana*, argued that all the defects attributed to the Indian—cruelty, laziness, ignorance, and the absence of sentiments of honor, nationality, and class—were the result of an exploitative feudal system: "All their energies have been used not for becoming a select biological type, but in defending themselves from economic, political, and social oppression."[26] Although these and other authors challenged simplistic biological/racial explanations of social behavior, and some of them explicitly rejected the idea of the Indian as a born criminal, none disputed the established images of degenerated Indians prone to commit violent, even savage crimes.[27] As we will see below, though, these images were framed by notions of race that deemphasized its biological dimensions.

The lack of enthusiasm for biological explanations of crime responded to multiple causes. To begin with, the timing of the arrival of criminology in Peru helps explain those reactions. By the late 1880s criticism of the Lombrosian school already had a strong presence in international circles, so when it arrived in Latin America it had to compete with theories of crime that emphasized the "social milieu." The rejection of biological criminology was also connected to the evolution of racial ideas among

Peruvian intellectual elites. As seen in chapter 1, although racist views pervaded commentaries on crime, morals, and social disorder during most of the nineteenth century, biological forms of racism were not prominent. Portraits of Indians, blacks, and Chinese as *biologically* inferior were not very common. Clemente Palma's *El porvenir de las razas en el Perú* (The Future of Races in Peru), a blatantly racist pamphlet, appears to be an extreme but isolated version of racist ideas in Peru.[28] Inspired by the doctrines of Gustave Le Bon and other European authors, Palma endorsed the idea that humankind was divided into superior and inferior races. He argued that all races that had come to constitute the Peruvian population were defective: Indians, blacks, and Chinese were inferior, while Spaniards, who were "apparently healthy," carried with them the "racial vices resulting from their mixture with the African race."[29] *Mestizos*, he added, lacked "the strength of unity necessary to constitute the soul of a nationality."[30] Convinced that "useless [racial] elements must disappear, and they do,"[31] Palma predicted that Indians and blacks would wane as a result of miscegenation ("the slow advance of civilization will exterminate, little by little, that damned and inept race, incapable of developing the mentality and will proper of true nations"), while the Chinese race was to disappear as a result of its own biological weakness. But even Palma offered a way out of racial deficiency. For him, the "creole race," a term he used somewhat confusedly to refer to Peruvian *mestizos*, was the only racial group that had a future, but on the condition that it merge with a race that could offer what it was missing: character.[32] Miscegenation with the "German race" (a "virile race") was his proposed solution.

Most Peruvian commentators on racial issues espoused different views, though. For them, Indians and blacks were redeemable not necessarily through biological miscegenation (certainly a desirable possibility), but especially through social and cultural redemption. Education became the alleged basis for the regeneration of the Indian.[33] By the 1880s and 1890s, Peruvian intellectuals had begun to rethink some of the typically Darwinist racial theories and clearly expressed their preference for "benefiting and uplifting rather than suppressing and eliminating the Indians."[34] Arguments dismissing biological racism gained preeminence. Early twentieth-century political and ideological debates on the fate of the Peruvian nation and the role different social and ethnic groups would play in its construction also began to reflect this influence. Most interventions emphasized the potential contribution of Indians and *mestizos*—blacks and Chinese were not of particular interest to these authors—to the creation of the national community. Manuel González Prada, José Carlos Mariátegui, and Víctor Raúl Haya de la Torre, to mention only the most prominent, went further and presented the Indian problem as *the* central social question of contemporary Peru and the indigenous population as representing the true Peruvian nationality. The so-called Indian question, they argued, was not a racial but a social issue, one whose solution demanded radical social and political reforms.[35] As was also the case with other Latin American countries such as Mexico, Brazil, and Cuba, biological racism had to be rejected if there was to be any hope for the future of the Peruvian nation, no matter how inclusive or exclusionary that entity was to be defined. Beyond hopes of massive European immigration and the concomitant "whitening" of the population, which were never realized, Peruvian ideologists had to contend with the obvious fact that the country's future would have to be built with those racial groups that constituted the majority of the population.[36] The low reputation of radical biological racism thus helped to discredit biological explanations of crime. As Villavicencio put it, "To accept as absolute and irremediable the Indian's deficiencies would be to renounce to the great mission of incorporating them into civilization. Science has effected so many prodigies, even with abnormal beings, that we should not lose our hope for perfecting him. Otherwise, we would have to exterminate them. And to wipe out the Indigenous race would mean the disappearance of Peru as a biological organism."[37]

As part of the same intellectual awareness but responding also to a previous literary tradition, *Indigenismo* helped shape the stands criminologists took toward biological explanations of crime, particularly regarding Indian criminality. *Indigenistas* stressed the harmful legacy of colonialism, the exploitation of Indians by *gamonales* (Andean feudal landlords) and local authorities, and misery, alcoholism, and coca abuse as some of the most important causes for the degeneration or prostration of the Indian race.[38] Echoes of these claims are found in the writings of criminologists who emphasized both the Indians' wretched conditions and the exploitation they endured as factors to be considered when explaining indigenous crime.[39] More important, the Indigenistas' emphasis on the possibilities of redemption for the Indian race helped to discredit claims of an essential and immutable biological proclivity for Indian violence and crime. While Indigenistas generally espoused paternalistic, essentialist, and even racist views of indigenous peoples and cultures, and even though their approach tended to homogenize Indians as if they belonged to a single, uniform culture, they nonetheless helped to counter ideologies based on extreme biological racism.[40] For Indigenistas, as for neopositivists of an earlier generation, the uplifting of the degenerated races, instead of depending on biological miscegenation with superior races, was made contingent on education and moral reform.[41]

The relative obliteration of biological racism and the rejection of biological explanations of crime were thus mutually reinforcing intellectual trends, but equally important is the fact that both left room for the continuation of more subtle or less extreme, though not less effective, racist discourses. In fact, more often than not, Peruvian criminologists incorporated race or racial features in their list of factors contributing to criminality.[42] The portraits of Indians, blacks, and Chinese that criminologists influenced by Indigenismo presented were always negative and distant. The Indigenista Villavicencio, for instance, offered this portrait of the contemporary Indian: "Today's Indian is the Indian of colonial times. The process of his life has not gone through noticeable changes. He lives like an animal, following a routine, without any type of aspirations. His ideal is to accumulate a few cents—the result of a brutalizing effort— in order to spend them in a Sunday's drinking. If he rises over his peers, it is only to become a tyrant."[43]

Most of these authors entertained a notion of race that was an amalgam of biological, hereditary, and cultural features such as attitudes, norms, values, customs, language, and morals. As the anthropologist Marisol de la Cadena has noticed, "Since the early part of the twentieth century, Peruvians (intellectuals and nonintellectuals) have tended to define race with allusions to culture, the soul, and the spirit, which were thought to be more important than skin color or any other bodily attribute in determining the behavior of groups of people, that is, their race."[44] Although this shift did not entail the elimination of racism, it did mean, among other things, that Peruvian racial groups were considered capable of improvement, chiefly through compulsory education and the elimination of some of the factors that were causing their degeneration. Since Peruvian elites could not present themselves as belonging to a superior white race (in the European racist canon, after all, they would not qualify as such),[45] they adjusted their rationale for constructing distance between themselves and people for whom, after all, they felt little empathy. It was culture, morals, manners, and taste that would establish the difference.

By depicting the lower classes as lacking morals, habits of industriousness, and education, Peruvian elites justified energetic social control and exclusionary policies, thereby transforming the war on crime into a campaign for authoritarian moral reform and prolonging an old, prepositivist discourse. In other words, the so-called social causes of crime were constructed in such a way that criminals once again were blamed for the crimes they committed. In fact, the line between the social conditions of existence and the inner morality of the lower classes remained blurred. An illustration of such fuzziness is the way in which experts addressed hygiene and alcohol consumption and connected them with the world of crime.

HYGIENE, CRIME, AND THE URBAN POOR

The issue of social hygiene was certainly not new. The preoccupation of elites with the living conditions and health of the population, and especially with the effects of these on social order, had a long history. In the last decades of the nineteenth century, and especially after 1895, as the historian David Parker has chronicled, *higienistas* took on themselves the task of diagnosing and proposing solutions to the problems associated with housing, public health, and the living conditions of the urban population, especially its poorest sectors. A combination of good intentions and authoritarian, racist views characterized the whole enterprise.[46] Lack of hygiene was discursively connected with the degeneration of certain races, the spread of epidemic diseases, the demoralization of specific social groups, and, not surprisingly, the spread of criminal tendencies among sectors of the urban poor.[47] Lower-class housing patterns, for example, were viewed as shaping the morality of the population and fostering their criminal impulses. Most criminologists accepted the notion that certain lower-class neighborhoods, especially *callejones*, were nests of criminal behavior. Oscar Miró Quesada argued that poor housing was a proven cause of mortality, which, in turn, "must have an effect on the bio-psychical degeneration of the race, and, thus, on their criminality." In houses without proper light and ventilation, he added, "rachitic and abnormal individuals are formed."[48] For the medical student

Juan Antonio Portella, callejones were "true pigsties" (*verdaderas pocilgas*) in which "scenes of immorality and crime" were a daily occurrence.[49] Villavicencio detected a much more direct connection between crime and living conditions in Lima's callejones: "The callejón, in Lima, is the best school of vice and crime. Close to honest people live vicious individuals, exploiters of women, all sorts of rogues. Immoral or bloody scenes are frequent. . . . Callejón and crime are two interrelated words. Let us examine any recidivist criminal, any habitual delinquent, and we will conclude that his vices and criminal ideas originated in the callejón."[50] *El Comercio*, reporting on *casas de vecindad*, combined social, racial, and legal qualifications in its attempt to convey the sense that they were a "great danger" for the city: "It looks like there [in one of those casas de vecindad] live numerous unemployed and suspicious individuals. A lot of *serranos* [migrants from Andean highlands] are lodged there. It's a sort of *tambo*" (wayside stall).[51]

The connection between poor housing conditions and the world of crime was also mediated by images of uncontrollable alcohol consumption and epidemic diseases among the lower classes of Lima, which, in the view of the hygienists, were inextricably linked. Epidemics were opportunities for the display of "criminalized" views of the urban poor. As Marcos Cueto has convincingly argued, state representatives approached this issue with a mixture of medical fanaticism and a racist/authoritarian attitude.[52] Victims were blamed for their misfortune. Their living habits were seen as resulting from their degeneration, not from social or economic handicaps. In his study of tuberculosis in Lima, Rómulo Eyzaguirre described the *barrio chino* (Chinatown), the outskirts of the city, army barracks, prisons, and hospitals as loci of contagion. Echoing criminological depictions of the causes of crime, Eyzaguirre listed as "accomplices" of tuberculosis "social misery, excessive taxes, lack of employment, lack of industrial habits, vagrancy, alcoholism, poor hygiene among the population, [and] the unhealthiness of poor people's housing."[53]

Although alcohol consumption was certainly not a new issue in public debates about criminal behavior, it received a great deal of attention from criminologists, physicians, hygienists, and policy makers in the late nineteenth century and early twentieth.[54] Most authors cited alcohol consumption as a major source of criminality. Few vices, wrote Jiménez, were more easily acquired than alcoholism. It was particularly pernicious among those "who conceal their criminal instinct," for alcohol "triggers it off, revealing that fatal predisposition [to crime] that, without its assistance, would have remained latent."[55] With obvious hyperbole, Jiménez blamed alcoholism for the *embrutecimiento* (stupidization) of two million Andean Indians, for allowing demoralization to "devour us," and for weakening the "national character."[56] A heated debate took place in the Peruvian parliament in 1887 over a projected increase in taxes on alcohol sales. Although most congressmen agreed that the effects of alcoholism on the population, especially Indians, were pernicious, they debated whether a tax on alcohol would help decrease its consumption. According to Congressman Francisco García Calderón, inebriation was the only means the Indian race had to "dissipate the memories" of an endless "chain of misfortunes" that included "three hundred years of misery and *envilecimiento*" (degradation). Similarly, Senator Manuel Candamo, a future president of Peru, argued that Indians turned to alcohol because, "almost completely alien to the advantages of civilization, subject to very few necessities, and animated by so few aspirations," they found enjoyment only in drinking.[57] An article in *El Comercio* summarized the dominant views of alcoholism in Lima around the turn of the twentieth century. "Alcoholism, Social Plague" was the title of a lengthy report in which the working classes of Lima were depicted as being the victims of a disease that was "more lethal than cholera, yellow fever, or the bubonic plague" and generated "the visible and immediate degeneration of the race." Furthermore, it stated that "from the point of view of criminal law alcoholism dangerously increases crime."[58]

Antialcoholic leagues were founded in Lima and Callao between 1895 and 1899, followed by the Antialcoholic Propaganda League (1903) and the National Temperance Society (1912).[59] In January 1903 an antialcoholic conference was organized by the government. Proposals for combating alcohol consumption included an increase in taxes on alcohol production and sales, the collection and distribution of habitual drinkers' names so that shop owners would refuse to sell alcohol to them, and the incarceration of all drunkards found in the streets.[60] Debates identified the conventional link between alcoholism and crime, an argument that was allegedly supported by criminal statistics. For Francisco Graña, "alcoholism means crime, misery, dishonor, and death."[61] This common wisdom was underlined by the minister of economy in his inaugural speech: Society, he said, "has the right to repudiate the alcoholic in the same way it repudiates the criminal." More than an individual problem, alcoholism was, he argued, a social question, for its most negative effects were to be suffered by the alcoholic's offspring: alcoholism produced "degenerated, imbecile, feebleminded, epileptic, impulsive, weak, amoral, and perverted children": in other words, "Lombroso's malefactors, arsonists, suicides, and born criminals."[62] In 1916, antialcoholic education was made obligatory in all elementary and secondary schools.[63]

Discursive connections between housing patterns, epidemic diseases, alcohol consumption, demoralization, and crime were clearly overwhelming. As usually happens with these types of construction, they were repeated over and over again, thus turning them into truths sanctioned by experts and requiring no further discussion. The increasing prestige of physicians, hygienists, and criminologists as well as their scientific aura allowed these ideas to become well-established, widely accepted "facts." In more concrete terms, they fostered an interpretation of crime that not only featured culture and morals (or the lack of them) but also, more important, contributed to the fabrication of an identifiable criminal class, one whose housing patterns and hygienic habits set them apart from the rest of society.

SCIENTIFIC CRIMINOLOGY AND ITS IMPACT

Gradually, positivist criminology became the dominant paradigm in specialized discourses about crime in Peru during the period 1890–1930. Its impact was felt, first, in academic circles, then in public debates about social problems, and finally in penal legislation. The Penal Code of 1924 reflected that influence. It incorporated many of the penal principles advocated by positivist criminologists in other countries: the indeterminate sentence, the idea of criminal irresponsibility for "dangerous nonimputable criminals," the tailoring of the penalty to the degree of dangerousness of each individual and conditional freedom.[64] Following the dominant view among Peruvian criminologists and jurists at that time, the Penal Code of 1924 also abolished the death penalty.[65] The doctrine of "social defense" served as the overall ideological framework of the penal code.[66] Developed in Europe in the early twentieth century, it owed its formulation to a previous, quite successful construct, that of the dangerous individual, which appeared first in the field of psychiatry.[67] The doctrine of social defense posited that each society had the right to protect itself from those dangerous individuals, including those who were potentially dangerous.[68] Dangerousness, in turn, was understood as the state or condition of an individual who in the judgment of such experts as physicians, criminologists, psychiatrists, and others, represented a threat to others or to society as a whole. For Garofalo, one of the main proponents of the concept, dangerousness was "the constant and active perversity of the criminal and the amount of expected evil that we should fear from him."[69] Since the sources of such a dangerous state were varied, ranging from racial features and heredity to social influences and medical conditions, determining the degree of dangerousness would have to include an inquiry into the person's ancestors, education, clinical records, anthropological features, penal antecedents, and so forth. The most important implication of the notion of dangerousness was that the penalty to be applied to any criminal should take into consideration the degree of danger that such an individual posed to the community. In other words, it was not just the crime itself but also the dangerousness of the individual who committed it which must be evaluated; thus, the punishment was going to be decided not by the judge or the jury alone, but also, decisively, by the experts who evaluated the dangerousness of the individual.

The 1924 penal code ordered judges to evaluate both "the culpability and the dangerousness of the agent" in order to determine the penalty. The evaluation ought to take into account a series of factors, including the nature of the crime, the criminal's age, his or her personal and family life, and the particular emotions that may have affected behavior.[70] Criteria about what exactly accounted for a state of dangerousness varied. While Leonidas Avendaño saw recidivism as the ultimate sign of dangerousness,[71] the criminologist Susana Solano, writing in the 1930s, emphasized the need to evaluate so-called noncriminal forms of dangerousness, including prostitution, gambling, homosexuality, and alcohol addiction.[72] According to her, certain social conditions made individuals dangerous, even if they had not yet committed a crime: thus, Indians who lived in conditions of isolation and poverty or who were victims of alcohol and coca abuse or subject to the exploitation of gamonales were regarded as dangerous and in need of surveillance and treatment.[73] For others, medical conditions created signs of dangerousness that may not even show in the commission of crimes but that needed to be carefully evaluated.[74] In his analysis of the assassination of the journalist Edwin Elmore by the celebrated poet José Santos Chocano, the Spanish criminologist Luis Jiménez de Asúa portrayed the offender as an individual in an "estado peligroso," or dangerous state, demonstrated by "all his previous life, adventurous and avid of pleasures, his scarcely neat behavior, his incurable megalomania, and even his hepatic affection, which has been used to claim moral irresponsibility for his crime."[75] The difficulty of offering a precise definition of this concept was sarcastically underlined by the Spanish criminologist Manuel López-Rey, who thought dangerousness was used as a sort of "penal sulfanilamide," for it was applied to almost every situation.[76]

One of the innovations of the penal code was the treatment it accorded to the indigenous population. It demanded that tribunals take into consideration every mitigating circumstance in the commission of crimes that may result from the fact that the perpetrators were "savages"—the native tribes of the Amazon region—or "semicivilized" or "alcoholic" Indians—the inhabitants of the Andean region.[77] According to the penal code, those two groups, each of which was treated as constituting a homogenous collectivity, lacked the knowledge, sensibility, and morals of the civilized portion of Peruvian population, that is, urban, educated, non-Indian sectors, and consequently must be considered relatively nonimputable.[78] This approach was, according to Víctor Maúrtua, the author of the project that resulted in the penal code, concomitant with the supposedly benign character of Peruvian Indians: "Most [criminals] are Indigenous. Their character is sweet, their moral constitution does not require severe and prolonged repression. Among [Peruvian] criminals, depravation and permanent dangerousness do not prevail."[79] The ultimate purpose of such benign legislation was to make possible for the indigenous criminal "full readaptation into an honest and free life," and this was to be accomplished at agricultural penal colonies in which "savages" and "uncivilized Indians" were to receive a treatment that would readapt them to the "juridical framework of the country." In the words of the anthropologist Deborah Poole, the purpose was to transform the Indian into a "correct juridical subject," one who would be incorporated into the national community through compulsory education, rehabilitative punishment, and the polishing of his cultural mores.[80] Beneath the protection that the state would grant the indigenous population through tutelary legislation lay, in fact, a neocolonial attitude.[81]

The doctrinal orientation of the penal code both reflected and reinforced the growing prominence that medical views of crime were gaining in Peru, which paralleled the prominent place physicians had acquired in both the professional and political spheres.[82] Starting in the mid-1850s, physicians had been contributing to the formulation and study of social problems in general and of crime in particular. Specialized journals such as the *Gaceta Médica de Lima* paid attention to a variety of issues, including epidemic diseases, crime, and alcoholism, and also hosted debates about juridical matters, such as the legal status of crimes committed by alcoholics or insane persons. Physicians were consulted when their opinion was considered crucial for elucidating matters related to the crime, the perpetrator, or the victim, and according to José Casimiro Ulloa, "the physician's competence for elucidating certain criminal acts" was a universally recognized fact.[83] Medical language permeated discussions about crime, especially in the period after 1880.[84] For most jurists, this was quite acceptable, but the notion advanced by positivist criminologists that crimes were caused by organic dysfunction and that it was the physician's duty to evaluate the criminal and suggest a sentence was rejected by legal experts. One of the most outspoken opponents of these views was José Viterbo Arias, the author of a treatise about the Penal Code of 1862. "We don't see in crime mere disgraces," he wrote in 1900, "we don't request hospitals instead of prisons, or physicians instead of wardens, nor anthropologists and psychologists to substitute for magistrates and judges."[85]

Legal and medical views of crime and punishment repeatedly clashed, both in doctrinal debates and in court litigation. One of the most prominent of such cases was that of Lorenzo Machiavello, an Italian-Argentine immigrant who killed three coworkers, two Chinese and one Italian, in a hacienda outside Lima in July 1885. His trial prompted a passionate exchange of opinions between experts. The key question was whether Machiavello committed the murders as a result of his "mental feebleness," and, if so, whether that condition must be seen as a mitigating circumstance. When the defense requested medical exams, the prosecutor objected, denying the physicians' right to "qualify the crime and suggest the penalty." José Casimiro Ulloa, one of the physicians consulted, replied that science had produced new ideas about criminal responsibility that would eventually close the doors of prisons and open those of the asylums. After lengthy legal maneuvers, a team of three physicians, including Ulloa, concluded that Machiavello was not mentally insane but that it was plausible he was under the influence of "impulsive insanity," which they thought should be considered a mitigating circumstance. Prosecutor Manuel Atanasio Fuentes posited that impulsive insanity was just an excuse used by criminals to get away with their crimes and requested the death penalty for Machiavello.[86] In another famous case, Javier Prado defended Enrique Rojas y Cañas, who was accused of murdering his lover in 1893, by arguing that his client was a "degenerate, in whom we can find the signs of the feeble: he is lymphatic, weak, skinny . . . a great anemia is evident in him . . . he has suffered from all kinds of diseases that have further annihilated a temperament weakened by sensuality and alcoholism."[87] He did not, however, convince either the judge, the superior court, or the supreme court, for all three instances confirmed the death sentence for Rojas y Cañas. According to the prosecutor, this was a simple case of homicide, "a repugnant and vulgar murder committed by a vicious young man against an unfortunate woman." Rojas y Cañas died in prison before his sentence could be carried out.[88]

As these and other cases demonstrate, it was not easy for physicians and criminologists to convince jurists and lawyers that medical conditions may explain at least certain types of crimes and that, accordingly, criminals did not bear responsibility for their acts.[89] But within the criminological community medical explanations of crime began to gain some popularity. Hermilio Valdizán and Carlos Bambarén, among others, pressed for the medicalization of crime and in both theory and practice tried to connect criminal behavior with such maladies as insanity, epilepsy, and alcoholism. In a criminological and medical study of the perpetrator of an atrocious crime in the northern town of Pativilca, Valdizán concluded his subject was a "biopathic phrenastenic" with "high mental insufficiency (imbecile)" and could not be held responsible for his crimes.[90] During the late 1920s, Bambarén conducted a series of studies of individual criminals whom he found to be victims of pathologies beyond their control.[91] At the University of San Marcos medical school he taught numerous physicians who would later offer their own contributions to the medical study of crime.[92]

The trend toward the medicalization of crime included the adoption, by some criminologists, of the tenets of the science of race improvement, or eugenics, which became fashionable in Peru in the second decade of the twentieth century. Like positivist criminology, it was first embraced in academic circles, especially the University of San Marcos Medical School, where Carlos Enrique Paz Soldán is credited with the introduction of eugenic ideas. Bambarén also promoted the teaching of eugenic ideas among teenagers. At least twice, in 1916 and 1923, the Peruvian Congress debated proposals to enact laws requiring a prenuptial certificate to guarantee that no "unfit" individual would procreate children, an initiative clearly influenced by eugenicist ideas.[93] As in other parts of Latin America, however, eugenics in Peru is more properly called "social eugenics," to use Nancy Stepan's apt term.[94] Peruvian authors did embrace the notion that scientific engineering of marriage and reproduction patterns would allow any racial or national community to improve its stock by eliminating unfit individuals. But Peruvian eugenicists did not see these interventions as purely biological, and quite often eugenics simply meant improving the living and working conditions of the population. Augusto Peñaloza, for example, the author of a thesis on eugenics and the prevention of crime, considered himself a follower of what he called adaptive eugenics, which he pitched against the Galtonian (for Francis Galton, the English scientist) selective eugenics, understood as a strictly biological process. Peñaloza proposed a number of measures to solve the "scabrous" problem of crime, which included improving the living conditions of the working classes, educating their spirits, and opening theaters, libraries, and lecture halls.[95] Other authors did embrace sterilization as the only solution to the reproduction of "undesirable and dangerous individuals." Vasectomy would rescue thousands of useful individuals for the nation, wrote Rafael Fosalba, author of a 577-page thesis on heredity. It was, he suggested, the only way to prevent crime and other pathologies.[96] But the dominant approach was to equate eugenics with what Paz Soldán and others called social medicine.[97] At the first Pan-American Eugenics Conference, held in Havana in 1928, Paz Soldán was one of the most severe critics of the proposal to adopt a Code of Eugenics that incorporated racist notions such as the superiority of the white race and the need to discourage racial miscegenation.[98]

Thus by the late 1920s, divergent trends of criminological thought contributed to the debates about crime and crime control policies in Peru. They ranged from medical/biological views such as Bambarén's to more clearly sociological ones like those of Villavicencio and Encinas. Still other participants in these debates favored a psychological approach to the explanation of criminal behavior.[99] In most cases, however, criminological thinking reflected two characteristics: a relatively eclectic view in which various factors, including race, culture, morals, biology, and social conditions, were invoked as explanations for criminal behavior and a lack of commitment to rigorous and original research.

The absence of a serious program of criminological research among Peruvian criminologists reveals how much positivism in Peru "valued science as a source of progress and practical knowledge [but] preached a rhetoric favoring research that was just discourse and that only rarely materialized into a persistent [investigative] effort."[100] Unlike work done in Mexico, Argentina, and Brazil, positivist criminology in Peru did not produce a substantial body of empirical research that exhibited original interpretations about the local realities of crime. It was a highly rhetorical appropriation of a set of principles, hypotheses, and metaphors for explaining crime and criminals. Research guided by positivist criminology generally meant nothing more than reading foreign treatises, summarizing them, and peppering them with a few references to local realities. Peruvian criminology was hardly a scientific discipline. The psychiatrist Honorio Delgado offered a harsh analysis of these efforts: "A sesquipedalian dilettantism replaces science, and fanatical propaganda occupies the place of reason. . . . It is hard to find in any other body of writings a greater abuse of 'scientific' terminology and of a dramatic emphasis than in the study of the criminal."[101]

Despite differing opinions and opposing views on a number of issues among its practitioners, by the late 1920s positivist criminology had established itself as the hegemonic discourse on crime in Peru. The growing prestige of criminologists and their close relationship with the Leguiísta regime were reinforced with the creation and strengthening of the DGP (see chapter 4) and was reflected in the publication, in 1927, of the *Boletín de Criminología*, the official organ of the DGP.[102] The *Boletín* contributed to the legitimization of the criminological profession and to the establishment of a strong connection between this discipline and the formulation and implementation of social policies. It published doctrinal treatises on criminological theories, translations of foreign materials, studies on aspects of Peruvian criminality, and various types of legal norms on penal policies and prison management. The *Boletín* is the most telling evidence of the maturity that criminology in Peru had acquired by the late 1920s: it not only produced knowledge about a problem (namely, criminal behavior) but also participated in formulating and implementing practical solutions to it. Although the field demonstrated a rather weak commitment to scientific inquiry, it maintained a strong inclination toward interventionism. In the 1920s, as never before in Peru, prison reformers attempted to effect changes guided by the principles of positivist criminology. In fact, prison reformers were usually recruited from within the ranks of criminologists. But the translation of supposedly scientific criminological principles into practical policies regarding the treatment of prisoners was, as we will see later, rather problematic, partly because of the critical mediation of other agents of state intervention such as the police (see chapter 3) and partly as a result of the ways in which crime, its causes, and its agents were constructed. Of particular importance was the way in which experts and policy makers constructed the connections between workers and criminals in early twentieth-century Lima.

THE WORLD OF CRIME AND THE WORLD OF LABOR

In their efforts to advance interpretations of Peru's criminal and lower classes, criminologists usually adopted a view that projected a separation between the so-called criminal classes and the working classes. Very rarely, if ever, were these two constructs presented as merging and becoming a single social problem. The dangers of a confluence of discontented workers and volatile criminal groups were largely absent in the perception of social commentators. For many, the problem of pauperism, for instance, which in Europe and Latin American countries like Argentina was thought to be at the root of the social question, did not exist in Peru or was at most a minor problem. This belief was only occasionally called into question by protests and crowd violence.[103] For authors like Felipe Barreda, pauperism, defined as the combination of unemployment, low salaries, and high population density, was not present in Peru. Strikes were the result of the "prosperity" enjoyed by the working class, he suggested, and he insisted that vagrancy and begging should be prosecuted as crimes.[104] Alejandro Revoredo, writing in the aftermath of the massive food riots of May 1919, baldly stated that the social question did not exist in Peru, chiefly because capitalism did not exist there yet.[105] José B. Gandolfo thought that pauperism was a potential threat to young nations such as Peru but argued that in this case, unlike that of Europe, it was owing not to the lack of opportunities but to the absence of good work habits: it was not pauperism (unemployment, low salaries) which produced vagrancy; it was vagrancy which generated pauperism. Thus the state must assist the poor but not the vagrants, who deserved prosecution and punishment. To further illustrate his implicit distinction between the criminal/vagrant class and the laboring poor, he quoted Lima's police chief, Gonzalo Tirado, who reported that vagrants committed 85 percent of property crimes in Lima.[106] The resulting argument was that crime in Lima was the product not of social injustice or exploitation of the laboring poor, but of vicious habits among a specific sector of the population, mostly vagrants and rateros. The so-called social question—the explosive combination of poverty, unemployment, low salaries, crime, strikes, and working-class agitation—was generally seen as not having the same dimensions in Peru that it had in Europe or other Latin American countries.

As Victor Bailey has argued for Victorian England, the encompassing category of *dangerous classes*—"a threatening amalgamation of poverty, vagrancy and crime"—was gradually shrunk "to the slimmer notion of the 'criminal classes,' no longer associated with political subversion and social breakdown."[107] Bailey links this discursive and political distinction to the project of establishing moral boundaries within different segments of the lower classes. Crime was considered "a problem less of collective social breakdown than of deficient moral restraint." This allowed authorities to disassociate crime from the overall system of economic exploitation and to incriminate, instead, "urban dislocation and moral indiscipline" for the commission of crimes.[108] This construction of separate worlds in Victorian England has some similarities with the case of early twentieth-century Lima. While in the nineteenth century the association between workers, criminals, vagrants, and vicious people in general figured prominently in the rhetoric of social commentators, that connection was later somehow lost. The world of labor and the world of crime became, in the eyes of experts, discrete territories, each with its own problems and its peculiar relationship with the social order. I contend, however, that this was not only a strategic political/discursive construction from above, as Bailey argues was the case in England, but also a product of the evolution in workers' own forms of social identity and consciousness. Workers began to distance themselves from criminals and, to a certain extent, internalized the discourse on honesty and working habits disseminated by the state, the school, the church, and even the union.

Around the mid–nineteenth century, the urban working poor of Lima were still a highly undifferentiated mass, closely resembling the colonial urban plebe. Artisans, street vendors, vagrants, domestic servants, and many other social and occupational categories shared a plebeian culture distinct from that of respectable society, though, some might argue, also borrowing elements from it. As both industrial work and labor union-ization gradually expanded toward the end of the nineteenth century, important segments of the urban poor, especially artisans and factory workers, began to transform themselves into the working class, with its distinct forms of organization, cultural traditions, and forms of social behavior.[109] Because of a variety of material, ideological, and cultural influences, they began to detach themselves from those values and atti-tudes that were deemed more characteristic of criminals.[110] It partly responded to the dissemination—by the state, the church, and, more critically, anarchist and socialist unions and leaders—of notions of hon-esty, industriousness, and self-esteem. Anarchist ideology, for instance, was always very insistent on encouraging workers to behave in ethical ways, demonstrating not only their combativeness but also their indus-triousness, restraint, and integrity.[111] As Parker has suggested, "In em-bracing self-improvement and temperance as the means to a better life, organized workers could not help but accept the gulf that separated them from the thousands of other poor Peruvians who drank, who gambled, and who did not share their ideals."[112]

As several historians have emphasized, in an estamental society like Lima, certain forms of cultural identification and self-representation, for example, decency, were largely associated with the upper classes. As a conscious strategy to remove themselves (at least in appearance) from the indignities associated with lower-class status and manual labor, sectors of the working classes, including employees, artisans, and workers, devel-oped their own sense of decency, imitating but at the same time subvert-ing the cultural codes of the Europeanized elite. To be poor but decent became very much a part of the mentality of certain segments of the working poor. For this decent status to be plausible, workers needed to establish a clear separation from those habits identified with the criminal classes. To begin with, decent workers had to dress appropriately. Striking workers, for instance, as Parker notices, used to wear suits and hats even when protesting in the streets, to convey the idea that they were "men of respect."[113] The sociologist Aldo Panfichi has emphasized that a major component of the *criollo* culture of the urban poor was to behave like a gentleman (*caballero*), with honor and decency.[114] The aversion to the criminal underworld also included a political angle: the identification, real and imagined, between criminals and *soplones* (police informants) further reinforced, in a context of increased confrontation between the organized working class and the state, the disdain workers demonstrated toward criminals.[115] To be decent did not preclude workers from participating in demonstrations, strikes, and riots, but it did oblige them to fulfill their duties as workers, parents, and citizens. This idea was clearly expressed by the presidential candidate Guillermo Billinghurst when he addressed the multitude of workers that had just completed two days of rioting in support of his candidacy: "You, chauffeurs and motorists, go and reestablish the traffic; you bakers and butchers, go to work so that bread and meat will not be missing in those homes that have given you their solidarity in these moments of self-sacrificing privation; you peons and workers, students and professionals, go to your homes and bring joy to your families, bring them back the calm that you have taken from them in favor of democracy and the fatherland."[116]

Of course this does not mean that workers did not commit crimes, or that workers and criminals lived in absolutely separate worlds. These individuals, in fact, generally lived in the same callejones and barrios, sharing, to a certain extent, the urban popular culture of which *jaranas* and drinking were central components. The population of the barrio of Malambo, for example, included both workers very much engaged in working-class cultural self-education and union activism and criminal individuals identified as faites and rateros.[117] Despite their physical proximity, however, workers tended to perceive themselves as honest, decent individuals, qualitatively different from criminals, a label generally applied to the population of vagrants, drunkards, and rateros that filled the jails and prisons of Lima. For a worker or artisan to be accused of being a ratero was a terrible insult.

Instead of a Manichean division between decent and popular classes, more subtle divisions, real and imaginary, existed within those two large conglomerates. Of paramount importance is the schism between what might be called the honorable poor and the parasites or criminal underworld. The boundaries between these categories were blurry, but in people's eyes there were moral, cultural, and social divides between them: elites saw themselves as different from the working-class population; workers saw themselves as different from criminals.

The divergence between the world of labor and the world of crime had important effects on the definition and implementation of state policies of social and political control. If crime as a social problem was not linked to working-class agitation or other forms of political threat, then there was no real need for instituting costly systems of penal control in order to maintain social order. If little or no solidarity existed between "parasites" and workers, then there was little chance that the way the state treated criminals in police stations and jails would generate outrage among the organized working classes. The conditions of prisons that we will examine later are partly the result of this perception of Peruvian social problems. Prisons were no longer imagined as sites for the fabrication or redemption of workers, but for the punishment of those morally degenerated and irredeemable—the parasites, the undeserving poor, the scum of society. Unlike cases such as Argentina, for instance, where the social question resulting from mass European immigration and working-class agitation prompted prison reform, in Peru there was no link between fears of social upheaval and state-sponsored campaigns for the reform of prisons.[118]

POLICING AND THE MAKING OF

A CRIMINAL CLASS

Before entering an institution of confinement, those accused of per-petrating crimes had to deal with another branch of the state's institu-tional apparatus of surveillance and social control: the police. The arrest and incarceration of people whom the police selectively and usually ar-bitrarily targeted as enemies of law and order represent another, much more tangible, form of "apprehending the criminal." A study of police behavior—its motivations, practices, and effects—sheds light on the clash between the state and the lower classes (or between the law and those that seemed to be at its margins) in one of its crudest forms. Having reviewed the ways in which the criminal was apprehended in intellectual, legal, and academic discourses (see chapters 1 and 2) and before turning to the life of criminals inside the prison (see chapters 6 and 7), it seems appropriate to look in some detail at the ways in which the encounter between the police and the lower and criminal classes took place.

Policing, monitoring, and arresting practices were not just efforts at crime control, but critical instances in the cultural, legal, and political construction of the criminal classes. They constituted effective, albeit ambiguous, forms of social marginalization, for they targeted specific social, racial, and occupational segments of the population. The social stigmas associated with certain forms of identity, culture, and socializa-tion were reinforced by the daily behavior of police forces. More than just a response to crime, then, policing was a social mechanism that served several goals simultaneously, even if not all of them were consciously designed or consistently executed: the criminalization of specific groups of the population, the protection of order and property, the establishment and maintenance of social and cultural boundaries, the reproduction of specific forms of racial, class, and gender hierarchies, and the expansion of the state's intrusion into the lives of ordinary citizens.

GENDARMES AND CACHACOS:
THE EVOLUTION OF LIMA'S POLICE INSTITUTIONS

It is not an easy task to reconstruct the institutional evolution of police forces in Lima during the nineteenth century and early twentieth. Numerous reforms and reorganizations, changes in political regimes, and the usual discrepancy between norms and their actual implementation all contribute to complicate this endeavor. Still, even with these limitations, the picture is one of the police moving from a rather loose, ineffective, and quite unprofessional series of units to a centralized, semiprofessional, and certainly much more repressive and quasi-militarized force in the 1920s.

During the first decades of the nineteenth century the maintenance of public order was in the hands of police units belonging to the army, itself a conglomerate of irregular forces subject to constant changes resulting from political instability.[1] Additional policing duties were performed by *serenos*, an institution of colonial origin used at different times and consisting of officials who monitored the behavior of the population and, in case of infractions, notified the authorities.[2] According to bylaws enacted in 1834, serenos carried out such duties as announcing the time, accompanying neighbors who needed to run errands after 11 P.M., controlling the movement of animals, checking public lights, and making sure that no parties were held after 10 P.M.[3] As the city began to expand and modernize and the state began to take over most duties associated with public order, the functions of the sereno became increasingly old-fashioned and superfluous. By the middle of the nineteenth century the figure of the sereno was already a sort of colonial residue and would shortly afterward disappear from the streets of Lima.

During the first decades following independence, the fate of police forces became tied to the recurrent political instability resulting from *caudillista* struggles.[4] They were continuously formed, reformed, and disbanded. Successive attempts at organizing an effective Guardia Nacional (by presidents Luis José de Orbegoso in 1834, Agustín Gamarra in 1840, and Ramón Castilla in 1845 and 1855, for example) produced meager results. Although enlistment was made obligatory and universal (with the usual exceptions granted to professionals, priests, and public employees), all testimonies point to the continuous use of coercion over lower-class individuals to man police units. Quite frequently, bandits and discharged members of the army (*licenciados*) filled the ranks of the Guardia Nacional. According to a police historian, "a true and efficient police force" did not exist in Peru before 1852.[5] The minister of government in 1867 was more emphatic: "There has never existed a police in the Republic."[6]

Between the early 1850s and early 1890s, a number of institutional changes affected the nature and operation of police forces. The creation of different bodies and jurisdictions as well as the enactment of various *Reglamentos* (bylaws) aimed at the organization of an effective, national police force. Most remarkable were the changes effected by Manuel Pardo, the first civilian president of the Peruvian republic. In November 1872 Pardo organized the Guardia Nacional again, making a new attempt to establish a nationwide civil police force. As the historian Carmen McEvoy suggests, this move sought to "neutralize the power that militarism had developed over the course of several decades."[7] A year later, in December 1873, the Pardo administration issued written bylaws aimed at building effective policing by actively incorporating the civilian population.[8] The *Policía de Seguridad*, for instance, was divided into three branches. First, neighborhood organizations "to resist the attacks of malefactors," which would eventually become the *Guardia Urbana* under the command of an *alcalde de barrio*, selected from among the propertied citizens. Second, special police units organized by the municipality would offer their services at specific locations such as theaters, promenades, slaughterhouses, and rural areas. Third, "a permanent public force" for the conservation of order, prevention of crimes, and arrest of criminals would be comprised by the *Guardia Civil* and the *Gendarmería*. One of the main duties of the civil guard was to guarantee "the peaceful exercise of the rights of the citizens." The *guardias civiles*, the bylaws stated, "are guardians of public order, in charge of the citizens' safety, as the most immediate custodians of their [civil] guarantees" (art. 48). They were to be between eighteen and fifty years old and free of "organic vices" and previous "corporal penalties." The Gendarmería, charged with maintaining order and security, was to have "the same organization as the army units" and was to recruit, preferably, former members of the army.

In 1877, during the administration of President Mariano I. Prado, important pieces of police legislation were enacted, including a comprehensive "Reglamento de Moralidad Pública y Policía Correccional" for the department of Lima and a "Reglamento de Policía Rural," the latter written in consultation with Lima's landowners.[9] The first statute imposed a variety of penalties, including fines, arrests, and closure of private businesses, for infractions such as indecent behavior, obscenities, drunkenness, and gambling. It authorized not only police officers but in fact any individual to apprehend and keep in custody criminals and malefactors, thus giving legal status to a variety of private policing schemes and vigilantism that were already common, especially in the rural areas.[10] Forced recruitment (*leva*) seems to have stepped up during the Prado dictatorship. The newspaper *La Patria* reported a story about a fourteen-year-old who was levied, tortured, and eventually released.[11] The War of the Pacific and the Chilean occupation of Lima dislocated police forces in most of the territory. The German traveler Ernst Middendorf reported that "the most dangerous period in Lima" was the first year of the Chilean occupation, when "the thieves were the policemen."[12] In 1883, after the Chilean occupation ended, President Miguel Iglesias reorganized the police forces once again. In 1884, the government created rural police stations in Lima's hinterland valleys, and in 1887 a *Policía Rural* was established.[13] They were under the command of unpaid rural commissaries selected by the government from the ranks of the rural propertied class. The personnel for rural policing comprised gendarmes, but frequent complaints reveal they were insufficient in number, undisciplined, and unmotivated, in part because they very rarely received their salaries.[14] Landowners had agreed to pay for the maintenance of these rural police stations, but they did not always comply with their obligation. Several stations were closed from time to time for lack of funds.[15]

In July 1886, President Andrés Cáceres issued a decree reorganizing the police forces yet again, and the legislature approved a new law for the Guardia Nacional in October 1887.[16] The law made the Guardia Nacional a reserve force for the army. Article 10 stated that "the Guardia Nacional is the force that must immediately assist the army, and the executive will organize it so that in every circumstance it could attend to the demands of the defense of the nation and public order." Cáceres was clearly trying to strengthen the armed forces, worried as he was about the eruption of military challenges to his still fragile authority. In August 1889, a new Reglamento for the Guardia Civil de Lima divided its forces and jurisdiction into five districts, each of them under the command of an urban commissary who reported directly to the *subprefecto* of Lima.[17]

Shortly afterward, the police force of Lima entered a period of change, driven by a very ambitious and energetic official, Pedro E. Muñiz, who was appointed Lima's subprefecto and *intendente de policía* in 1890 and prefecto in 1893. Muñiz displayed unusual energy in attempting to make the police force more efficient. The number of arrests increased dramatically after he took command of the force (table 3.1). Between 1890 and 1893, the monthly average of arrests almost tripled, from 412 to 1,223. Muñiz's goals, however, were larger than just increasing police arrest rates. He had spent some time in Europe, had read and embraced the new criminological, penal, and police doctrines in vogue by the late nineteenth century, and was particularly interested in data-gathering techniques, such as statistics, "because its interest for the statesman, the moralist, the historian, the criminologist, etc. is undeniable and of decisive importance." He endeavored to gather "the most detailed data on crime in this province."[18] In 1891, he organized a census of the Lima population, using police stations to collect the information.[19] In 1892, he created the Sección de Identificación y Estadística (Section of identification and statistics, sie) at the Intendencia de Lima, under the direction of the physician Leonidas Avendaño.[20] Muñiz believed that effective identification techniques were crucial elements of an efficient police force, and he considered them to be even more necessary in Lima because of the frequent changes of authorities and personnel. If the sie had reliable anthropometrical databases, he thought, those changes would not affect the efficacy of the authorities' disciplinary efforts. As a result, the sie adopted the Bertillon system of criminal identification—then the most trendy such system in police circles worldwide and consisting of a combination of photographic and anthropometric data—installed anthropometrical equipment, and claimed to have measured, photographed, and registered a total of 1,680 individuals in its first three years of operation.[21] Being "measured" at the Intendencia, in fact, became a sort of stigma, for it was clearly identified, in the minds of the police as well as the public, as evidence of a criminal background. At some point the police began to issue certificates of proof that the bearer had *not* been measured or photographed; these were used by men wanting to enter the police forces.[22] Also in 1892, a "Police Manual" was issued and academies were created where the police personnel could gather and study the manual.[23]

Statistics of police arrests began to be collected much more consistently than before, and other mechanisms of identification and surveillance were created. In July 1892, for instance, new rules concerning domestic service in Lima mandated the formation of a register of domestic servants at the Intendencia.[24]

Muñiz's tenure as police intendente left a remarkable imprint, reflective of the larger trend toward modernization and of increasing state efforts at improving surveillance and monitoring of the population. For victims of the increased monitoring capabilities of Muñiz's police force, such modernization efforts would represent greater degrees of abuse and intrusion: despite all the changes (actually, because of them), police arbitrariness and harassment of certain segments of the population increased, as we will see below. On the other hand, police forces continued to face an endemic problem in the breakdown of discipline among police personnel. Indeed, deteriorating self-control affected not just the rank and file, but also the higher echelons. Alcohol consumption by police officers was a constant source of scandals, abuses, and other embarrassing episodes.[25] Desertion was common, especially among policemen assigned to rural areas.[26] Numerous reports by rural commissaries requested that their personnel be replaced, for they had become too familiar with the local population, had committed unprofessional acts, and thus had lost the respect necessary to exercise their authority.[27] In July 1894, the commissary of the valley of Surco Bajo reported that of the four men assigned to his unit, only one was available; of the other three, one lay injured in the hospital, the second had fled after injuring the first one, and the third was imprisoned in Guadalupe.[28] A commissary reported that police troops were so uncontrollable that "we need to keep an eye on them instead of the roads."[29] Undisciplined police members who were expelled from their units, however, could easily enroll in a different one, since effective mechanisms for checking their background were missing.[30]

Corrupt and disorderly acts tended to increase during periods of political instability, such as the 1894–95 civil war between Nicolás de Piérola and Cáceres. The archives of the Prefectura contain abundant complaints about police desertion, scandals, abuses, and overall lack of self-control during this period. In May 1895, for example, policemen and soldiers were accused by tavern owners of "scandals and abuses," for they repeatedly ate and drank without paying.[31] In July 1894, *La Opinión Nacio-*

nal denounced police officers who were requesting residents of several *callejones* to pay quotas (*cupos*) of 20 cents each.[32] The comandante de guardias of the third quarter was accused of using policemen as domestics in his house, charging arrested individuals monetary quotas to release them, and imposing illegal fees on brothels.[33] Not surprisingly, police members were frequent targets of the population's rage. In February 1895, a riot erupted at Torrecilla Street when a policeman was trying to arrest Pedro Medina—the mob managed to thwart the arrest. Another individual, Aniceto Gregorio, who was being arrested for drunkenness, incited the crowd to throw stones at the guards who were taking him to the police station, as a result of which he was let go (although he was recaptured nine days later).[34] On various occasions policemen and soldiers found themselves confronting each other. In June 1895, for example, a soldier of the Húsares de Junín regiment was accused of attempting to rape a minor, and when a police officer tried to take him into custody other soldiers came to his defense. A scandal erupted. Numerical advantage favored the soldiers, and the policemen had to abandon the arrest. In fact, according to the report, several similar incidents had taken place at that time. The intendente accused army personnel of "undermining the principle of authority among the population" with their humiliating acts against the police forces. Soldiers, he said, were "despots that have no other law than their caprices, ignorant people that disregard the barriers that society recognizes and upholds."[35]

After his accession to the presidency in 1895, Piérola attempted a new reorganization of police institutions. He increased the number of troops and raised their salaries. Most important, he established rules for the promotion of police personnel on the basis of merit, the first time there was such a system.[36] According to the police historian Víctor Zapata Cesti, this was the beginning of a truly professional police force. Following up on this, the intendente suggested in 1900 that a police academy be created at each police station, so that policemen could acquire professional skills.[37] The minister of government echoed this in 1907: due to low salaries, he said, instead of "good elements" the ranks of the police were filled with those who "seek a way of living without having to endure the efforts that industrial labor demands."[38] The situation was deemed even more critical among gendarmes who served in rural areas, where there was no "disciplined" environment. In 1905, the minister of government cited the need to build headquarters in each valley to isolate the police forces from both *hacendados* and their peons, whose proximity he thought only generated corruption. He also demanded that army *licenciados* be forced to serve as gendarmes for at least two years after completing their service, for they could be "an example and a stimulus for those who have not been soldiers."[39] To address the issue of persistent undiscipline, police institutions introduced in 1907 a form that prospective policemen had to fill out so that their names could be checked against criminal records held at police stations and the Intendencia, including the anthropometric office.[40] Record-keeping techniques conceived to help the police combat crime became useful tools for scrutinizing prospective police officers.

Because of frequent desertions, discharges for poor discipline, lack of adequate salaries, and the growth of the city and its population, urban and rural police commissaries always deemed their forces insufficient to deal with allegedly growing crime. Particularly critical were areas that police authorities reckoned were infested with criminals: Tajamar, for instance, in the Liza and Bocanegra district, "where innumerable vagrants and *rateros* have their hideouts," and Cercado and La Victoria, which included numerous factories and businesses.[41] Lizardo Revollé, commissary of the second quarter in 1908, requested that the number of inspectors be increased from 134 to at least 180, although, he added, the ideal would be 210. After the usual complaints about police indiscipline and meager salaries, Revollé came up with an innovative proposal: a police academy under the direction of a European mission, which he thought might be the only means to guarantee a professional police force.[42] It would take some time for this idea to germinate, but it was eventually embraced by state authorities, as we will see below.

Despite its institutional flaws, the police gradually became a sort of surveillance machine. All the imperfections of a bureaucratic apparatus in which clientelism, corruption, and frequent disrespect for the written norm were recurrent did not prevent the police institutions from collecting, organizing, and using all kinds of information, not just about criminals but about the population in general. This period marks the beginning of policing as a more intrusive form of social control, one that used methods of generating and manipulating data that, at least in principle, promised to monitor and check a wide range of activities among the lower classes of society. In July 1895, the intendente stated that, in order to guarantee effective policing, "daily and constant observations of the movements and habits of the population" needed to be conducted and recorded in police registers, which ought to be kept with "painstaking exactitude."[43] Following his suggestion, the police opened a series of registers in which many kinds of data were kept: not only a residential listing but also directories of street vendors, domestic servants, fugitive prisoners, hotel guests, former inmates, and many others, including a list of "criminal suspects" that the police tried to keep an eye on.[44]

In addition, the police began to use fingerprinting techniques for criminal identification in the early 1910s. An Oficina de Identificación using the Vucetich system of identification was opened in the Callao police station in June 1912.[45] In the late nineteenth century, Juan Vucetich, a Croatian immigrant living in Argentina, had invented a new system of identification based on a series of fingerprint patterns. He is thought to be the first investigator in the world to have used dactyloscopy to solve a crime, which he did in 1892. Further improvements in his techniques gave him an international reputation, although many still considered the Bertillon system superior.[46] In 1915, the government created an Oficina de Investigación Dactiloscópica (OID) at the Lima Intendencia, under the direction of Luis Vargas Prada. According to Zapata Cesti, 4,235 individuals were fingerprinted by the OID in only six weeks, resulting in the formation of a "magnificent" database.[47] As in other countries, techniques of criminal investigation were extended to monitor the population as a whole. In 1916, the OID began issuing identification cards that included a photo and dactyloscopic data to everyone who requested them.[48] By September 1920, according to Elías Lozada Benavente, 10,527 identifications had been recorded, of which 4,226 were of criminals.[49] In October 1915, a new office was created for keeping statistics on recidivism.[50] In January 1913, a Sección Obrera (Workers Bureau) had been created inside the subprefecturas of Lima and Callao: "the latest workers' [wave of] agitation" made it necessary to collect all the information available "about the moral and material condition of the salaried classes."[51] Shortly afterward, an advertisement in a Lima newspaper invited workers to register at the newly created division.[52] The form that the police created to record workers' data was similar to a criminal identification card. It included descriptions of anthropometrical features: nose, mouth, lips, hair, and so forth. Identification and surveillance were also extended to the police personnel itself. In 1916, new rules for admission into police forces were issued. All applicants were required to submit the names of two respectable neighbors of the locality as guarantors of the equipment that the potential deserter might take with him.[53] In 1920, OID director Vargas Prada, for whom the fingerprint was the "anthropological name" of each individual, proposed an ambitious plan to make identification even more functional. Besides recommending its use for electoral purposes (a proposal that was in fact embraced later), he suggested that the Intendencia gather dactyloscopic data from all criminals in the country. He was concerned that ex-convicts from the interior who came to Lima looking for jobs might end up being enrolled in the police forces. In addition, he thought that because most domestic servants were from the interior, this register would allow patrons to know the antecedents of those they were going to hire. The lack of methods of identity checking resulted, he said, in numerous crimes being perpetrated by domestic servants in Lima. Furthermore, the identification system would allow the exchange of criminal records among different countries.[54]

In 1920, the Leguía administration, under the leadership of Minister of Government Germán Leguía y Martínez, began a complete overhaul of police institutions as part of its goal of modernizing the Peruvian state. Of special interest was the creation of the Guardia Republicana, a branch of the police forces that, among other duties, was in in charge of the external and internal security of the prisons.[55] The most ambitious undertaking by the Leguía administration was the appointment of a Spanish mission to assist the Peruvian government in the formation of a professional police force.[56] In November 1921, amidst great expectation, four Spanish police officers arrived. Their duties included the evaluating and restructuring of the existing police forces. In the next couple of years, a series of new police units were created, effectively transforming the police into a much more regimented, centralized, and professional institution. In October 1922, for example, the Brigada de Investigación y Vigilancia, a special unit for combating both crime and political opposition, was created.[57] A new Escuela de Policía (police academy) was inaugurated with great pomp on November 1, 1922.[58] Located in the renovated mental asylum, which had been transformed into the headquarters of the Guardia Civil, it began to offer police training to former gendarmes and army licenciados.[59] On April 12, 1923, the entire police structure was reorganized once again. Now it was composed of three units: the Guardia Civil, the Cuerpo de Seguridad (Security Unit), and the Cuerpo de Investigaciones (Investigations Unit), the latter in charge of investigating crimes and identifying criminals.[60] Rural policing, on the other hand, somehow continued to escape the state's efforts at centralization and modernization well into the 1920s. Police stations in the rural valleys of Lima still functioned in private facilities (haciendas, for example), and commissaries were named from within the class of landowners. Some of their personnel were paid by hacienda owners, and police horses were fed at private estates. Although the minister of government had warned in 1916 that "they offer the danger that those who perform [policing] duties are dominated by a partial spirit in favor of private individuals, from whom they receive remuneration,"[61] by 1923 there were still thirteen rural police stations in Lima that depended on private resources.[62]

Of special importance was the strengthening of political policing during the Leguía administration. It went through a series of incarnations, but its presence was felt throughout the eleven-year regime, and it became increasingly sophisticated and harsh. Political police units had existed before, but during the *oncenio* they became an effective and widely used instrument of intimidation and harassment. A new secret political police force had been organized, in fact, shortly before the Leguía coup, on June 7, 1919. It was called the Sección de Vigilancia, and its first head was Damián Mústiga, who would become notorious in the 1930s as a brutal agent of state repression.[63] Another famous torturer, Rufino Martínez, was in charge of organizing the political police for Leguía, for which he used mostly criminals and former prisoners.[64] Under General Pedro Pablo Martínez's directorship, political and investigative units were further strengthened. Comisarías de Investigaciones were created with the aim of "investigating and discovering every criminal act and every political event that could go against the government."[65] Following the police reforms of 1923, the secret police became part of the Cuerpo de Investigaciones. Later, in 1928, a special brigade of social affairs (Brigada de Asuntos Sociales) was added as a special unit in charge of the surveillance of workers and labor leaders.[66] A harsh critic of the oncenio, Abelardo Solís, described the police as the main instrument of Leguiísta repression and the city of Lima as a sort of oppressive cage. The agents of *la secreta* raided cafes, taverns, clubs, churches, military barracks, and schools, instilling terror in the population. Squealers abounded: ladies at the aristocratic salons, female vendors in the marketplace, domestic servants inside households, and even pimps at brothels, all allegedly worked for the political police. The reform of the police, Solís concluded, had been in fact used as an instrument to enhance the dictatorial nature of the Leguía regime.[67]

The effects of the Leguiísta police reform were quite noticeable. Sympathetic commentators see this period as a sort of foundational era for modern, professional police forces in Peru. It is not difficult to see why: the police became a much more intrusive and repressive institution, and indeed much more powerful. The tired old gendarme and the lowly cachaco were replaced by trained policemen, perhaps not scrupulous observers of the law but certainly much better equipped and more invasive and visible than in the past. In Lima, the presence of the police was increasingly felt in many ways: they controlled traffic, rounded up vagrants, monitored the activities of political opponents, and made dozens of arrests for disorderly conduct every day. Policing had become, indeed, an effective instrument in the state's efforts at monitoring and controlling specific sectors of the population.

FROM ARREST TO INCARCERATION

Most individuals who were arrested were first taken either to a comisaría (district jail) or to the *Intendencia de policía* (the city's police headquarters). They had committed a crime, had been accused of committing one, behaved, in the eyes of the police officer, as if they lived a life of crime, or simply (as occurred quite frequently) happened to be in the wrong place at the wrong time. Shortly after their arrest (though in some cases it took days and even months), the intendente would evaluate the arrestee's legal situation (a procedure called *calificación de presos*) and then determine if he or she should be released, detained at the comisaría for a period of time while further investigation was conducted, or transferred to a prison to await trial. The evaluation process was, for many decades, a public event. *El Comercio* sarcastically invited the public to go to the Intendencia every morning to witness the evaluation of prisoners and have some fun: "It is an event to be seen, not to be told. There are faces that resemble masks, and dresses that look like tatters. The most hilarious stories are heard there, and a best-selling volume can be written with the expressions that are used."[68] Relatives and passersby gathered in the Intendencia to witness, and possibly try to influence, the evaluation of those arrested by the police. In January 1908, the subprefecto criticized the calificación as a counterproductive procedure because it allowed detainees to communicate with each other and even with the public attending the event. The public nature of the event, he thought, was inconvenient in that it violated the "absolute secrecy" that should characterize every police procedure. He thus suspended the public evaluation, and the calificación became a private event.[69]

But before their fate was decided by the calificación, the suspects had already been subjected to the usually arbitrary behavior of police officers. Mistreatment, if not brutal torture, was routine. In fact, police arbitrariness could begin with the arrest itself, for individuals were sometimes detained for no apparent reason. In 1875, *La Gaceta Judicial* denounced the fact that people were sometimes arrested for actions that were not violations of the law.[70] The arrest of an individual was sometimes violent, even tragic. An unnamed Chinese man, for instance, was killed by a police officer who was trying to arrest him. The victim, according to the police officers, was in such a "great state of excitement" and "transformed into a wild beast" that they had no choice but to beat him badly. During the trial it was revealed that one of the police officers was drunk and that, in fact, he had arrested the Chinese man only because somebody had pointed him out as being a thief. Arguing self-defense, one officer was acquitted, while the other was sentenced to one year in prison.[71] The arrest of drunken suspects was particularly difficult, but the authorities came up with a practical solution: police agents began to use *carretillas* (carts), in which they would tie up the subject and rush him to the closest police station.[72] Once inside the police premises, arrestees usually had to endure poor conditions. Jails were generally dirty and overcrowded, cells were humid and filthy, and detainees had to sleep on the floor or even in horse corrals.[73] More cruel forms of treatment such as torture and beating were also common. The case of Isidoro Torres, for example, was certainly not exceptional: accused of theft, he was taken to the comisaría and placed in the *barra*, the most common instrument of torture used in Lima's prisons and jails. It consisted of a device that held the prisoner tied to a bar by his feet, upside down and at variable heights, for periods of several hours, days, and even weeks.[74] Later, during the trial, Isidoro's guilt could not be proved, and he was eventually released free of charges, but his innocence had not prevented him from being tortured.[75] Things went even worse for the typographer Marcos Cobián. He was accused of theft, brought to the Intendencia, and then transferred to a military station, where he was put in the *cepo volador* for two hours and then in the barra for the night. The cepo volador consisted of handcuffing the prisoner with his hands behind his back, hitting, pushing, and throwing him to the floor, and rolling him over while the torturers kicked him repeatedly.[76] The next day Cobián was forced to mop the place and was tortured again. *El Comercio* called him a professional thief, which he earnestly denied: in fact, he had been detained in the past but was acquitted. Cobián ultimately died during the trial of undisclosed causes.[77] Cases like these were fairly common. In 1912, a man by the name of Carlos Duarte escaped from Guadalupe prison and was recaptured about a month later. Back in the Intendencia, he was put in the barra. Later, according to the official version of the case, in a moment of desperation he stole a rifle from a distracted guard and killed himself.[78] At La Legua district jail, one day in 1916, Juan Osorio was arrested and tortured in the barra, while his wife, Angelina Espinoza, was raped.[79] Things did not improve in the 1920s despite all the efforts to professionalize the police forces. According to a collective letter signed by prisoners at the Lima penitentiary in 1930, the Intendencia was a "cemetery for the living" where authorities used to "massacre" innocent people.[80]

Police brutality was not an issue that excited extended discussion among Lima's populace, but from time to time it did scandalize a few observers. An article in *El Diario Judicial* in May 1890 denounced the fact that police torture was commonly used to force the detainee to "declare what he has not seen or totally ignores," and compared the police's use of the lash with such degrading torments of the colonial era as mutilation and branding. It also stressed that torture was used everywhere (in jails, military barracks, the Intendencia) because of the widespread belief that "authority is more respected when it is more feared and, because of that, it is convenient to use the stick and the whip to intimidate the evil men and ease the work of the police."[81] *El Comercio* editorialized in 1890 about police abuses, reacting to denunciations that political and military prisoners had been tortured at police headquarters: "The police show among us quite bad manners, and do not have a precise idea of the respect the human being deserves. This behavior greatly discredits our society, undermining and turning abhorrent the principle of authority in its more practical manifestation." Everybody credited the allegations of police abuse, continued the paper, because almost everybody "knows of similar acts, conducted in very similar situations."[82] In April 1896, the director of *La Opinión Nacional* was arrested after the newspaper denounced abuses, tortures, and even executions.[83] The most emphatic and incensed critic of Lima's police behavior was the anarchist writer Manuel González Prada, who wrote, "There isn't anything that they don't try with the miserable [detainees] to force them to confess a crime or to attribute to themselves an imaginary one. They are jammed in rooms with no air nor light, humid and filthy; at midnight, they are woken up to get showered with cold water . . . they are put in stocks or in the cepo volador . . . and they are hung by their thumbs or their testicles."[84] Complaints like these eventually reached the National Congress, where in 1915 a congressman condemned police excesses against lower-class women, who were repeatedly treated as if they "deviated from the path of morality and good behavior."[85]

While the discretionary power enjoyed by the police was widely used to harm particular individuals, it could also be used to benefit others, generally *personas decentes*, who in the officers' eyes did not deserve such treatment or who had enough influence to avoid incarceration or indictment. That this discretionary power was used openly and consistently is revealed in the following case, based on the authority's own report. In January 1895, a commissary reported that more than twenty people had been arrested for disorderly behavior, including a few who "seem to be decent." Once inside the Intendencia, those individuals "of better aspect" were placed in a special compartment, "quite different from a filthy dungeon." The morning after, once the authority confirmed that among the arrested were "three well-known gentlemen," he ordered the release of the whole group because, in his view, "the cause of their arrest being identical, I could not have preferences in administering justice." He then cautioned police officers to carefully "differentiate among the people, in order to avoid annoying complaints."[86] *El Comercio* reported in March 1902 that drunkards were apprehended and sent to jail in police carts when they appeared to belong to the lower classes but were taken to their domiciles "with all due honors" when they were "*decent gentlemen*, as they are called in the technical vocabulary of the comisaría."[87] González Prada accused the cachaco of being "humble before the great lady and the great gentleman, but fully arrogant against the timid *chola*, the poor black man, and the miserable Chinese man."[88] In January 1916, three drunken men created a scandal when they protested the arrest of the coachman who was transporting them. The commissary ordered their arrest but later realized the men were none other than Leonidas Yerovi, a well-known writer, and two journalists from *La Prensa* and *La Crónica*. "*Given the social condition of the arrested*, and after I called their attention to the seriousness of their infraction . . . I had no problem with letting them free."[89]

Not surprisingly, the immense majority of arrests in Lima were of individuals belonging to the lower classes. Between 56.6 percent and 77.4 percent of the arrestees were members of the working classes, while another 16.99 percent to 38.9 percent were registered as unemployed, vagrants, or marginal people (table 3.2). Altogether, more than 90 percent of all arrestees were members of the lower classes. Police action thus was overwhelmingly focused on persecuting the underprivileged sectors of the Lima population. Within that population, men were clearly the majority, comprising about 85 percent of all those detained by the police.

Transgressions of public order constituted roughly half of all offenses committed (table 3.3). These included vagrancy, drunkenness, and other minor offenses that, since they did not call for incarceration, allowed the perpetrators to go free after spending a short time in the comisaría. Between one-fifth and one-quarter of the offenses were crimes against property, including *raterías*, or petty theft, while crimes against persons, such as injuries, assaults, kidnapping, and the like, ranked third. Clearly most police energies were directed either at punishing individuals for minor offenses against public order or at trying to prevent the commission of such offenses. Criminality in Lima, as shown by the available statistics, did not entail a wave of violent or property crimes but was constituted primarily of the lower classes' engagement in certain forms of social behavior that clashed with the rules of propriety, temperance, and respect for authority that the state and the decent sectors of society were trying to enforce. This pattern of arrests shows remarkable consistency over the period between the 1890s and the 1920s, as does the ratio of arrests per number of inhabitants. After 1892, that ratio remained quite stable at around 1 percent (see table 3.1).

An arrest could have further consequences for a person if, regardless of his or her culpability, the police wrote an adverse *parte policial*. This report about the facts and circumstances that led to the arrest, written by a police officer, was usually a crucial piece of evidence at the ensuing criminal trial. Poor, unemployed persons, habitual drunkards, and other such characters were very likely to receive unfavorable partes, which would be used against them by judicial authorities. A typical case was that of José Fernández, nicknamed "Chuzaso." He was accused of stealing a few items from the house and restaurant of José Calderón. The police apprehended Chuzaso and sent him before the judge with a parte policial that described him as a well-known thief (*ratero conocido*) caught while trying to remove a sewing machine from a corral. During the trial, the judge asked officials at Guadalupe jail to report on Fernández's jail record, which showed he had been detained four times, all for theft, but had never been found guilty. At his sentencing, however, the judge argued that Fernández's culpability had been *proven* by both the parte policial and his record of previous terms at Guadalupe. He sentenced him to four years in prison. In his appeal the defense attorney correctly argued that the parte policial could not be considered proof of culpability: it was simply "the narrative of an event, subject to confirmation by the judicial authority . . . it does not have value in itself." Still, Chuzaso's sentence was confirmed by both the superior and the supreme court. In this case, as in many other similar ones, the combination of an adverse parte policial and a previous (even if not quite conclusive) record of incarceration weighed heavily in the decision about the guilt of the arrestee.[90] Not even dead people escaped a negative parte policial: when the police identified a dead body found in the Rímac river as being that of Manuel Rojas, they quickly added to the report that he was "a vagrant, ratero, and habitual drunkard," well known by the police, so that "his tragic end should not surprise us, given his licentious and immoral lifestyle."[91]

Despite the arbitrariness of the parte policial, however, the number of people who actually went to prison after the initial evaluation by the police authority was a very small fraction of the total number of arrests. Only between 4 percent and 8 percent of those detained were eventually sent to prison, while more than 90 percent were released without charge (table 3.4). A small percentage of arrestees were consigned to the mental asylum, the army, or, when they died during detention in the police station, even the cemetery. Most of those who avoided criminal accusations went free immediately, but others, especially those who had committed minor infractions like drinking or fighting, for which there was no penalty of prison, might spend a few hours or even days at the Intendencia, where they were often assigned some menial work like mopping and cleaning. A subject of constant criticism and exasperation among authorities and journalists was precisely the fact that vagrants, rateros, and other undesirable individuals were taken to the police station or the Intendencia, kept for short periods (days or even hours), and then released for lack of evidence, space, legal mandate, or interest in pursuing charges against them. *El Comercio* complained in 1901 that "all too frequently, the five comisarías of Lima . . . pick up a legion of vagrants, who are then returned, in the same conditions, to that social milieu that cannot get rid of them."[92] Such exasperation seems to have been the source of many a campaign to eradicate crime in Lima that used the argument of unprecedented growth.

For the small percentage of arrested individuals who were suspected of some felony, the next stop was prison—Guadalupe, El Frontón, or the CCV—where they would wait to go on trial. If convicted, they would either remain there or be transferred to another institution such as the penitentiary, depending on the penalty they received. The inmates who spent time in prison as either *enjuiciados* (felons awaiting or undergoing trial) or *sentenciados* (convicts) were the distillation of police work and the criminal justice system; in more than a legalistic sense, they constituted the criminal population of Lima.

PART TWO

PRISONS AND PRISON COMMUNITIES

4

By the middle of the nineteenth century incarceration had become the most common form of judicial punishment in Peru. Most crimes were penalized with prison terms, while fewer and fewer were castigated with the death penalty and other forms of punishment. More infamous forms of punishment such as branding were already legally abolished. At that time, however, Peruvian prisons lacked adequate infrastructure, and a mixture of inefficiency and despotism characterized the way in which they were managed. This situation began to be viewed by some observers both as an obstacle to the state's goal of achieving an effective, centralized system of justice and as a shameful reminder of colonial times. Around 1850, new concerns regarding the treatment of criminals and the nature of imprisonment as punishment emerged among certain sectors of the Peruvian political and intellectual elite. Perceptions about the "alarming" increase in crime rates and, to a certain extent, humanitarian compassion toward the condition of prisoners fueled the demand for prison reform. Penal doctrines developed in Europe and the United States began to influence the language of state authorities, policy makers, and other experts. Prisons, it was now thought, should be used not only to punish criminals but also, and especially, to redeem and reincorporate them into society. The consolidation of the Peruvian state under liberal direction provided both the political motivation and the administrative capability to attempt a serious transformation of the penal system. The Lima penitentiary, inaugurated in 1862, was the centerpiece of the new and allegedly modern punitive strategy. It promised to replace traditional attitudes of abhorrence and hatred of criminals with a new posture that emphasized humane treatment. Such humanitarianism, it was thought, would become the best instrument for correcting and readapting offenders into the social body.

The tortuous process of prison reform in Lima between the early 1850s and the early 1930s reveals the ongoing tension between two conspicuous doctrinal and cultural constructions of punishment: for some, it was an instrument of retribution and deterrence, for others, a means to reform and redeem the criminal. At no point during this period can one identify a single consensual paradigm, for there was always contention, whether open or veiled, between the two approaches. I contend, however, that a despotic approach to punishment, one that emphasized revenge and deterrence over rehabilitation and reform, generally prevailed, if not always in the official discourse, certainly in the perception and behavior of prison experts and state authorities.

The ambitious goals of building a modern prison system in Peru clashed with political inertia, logistical obstacles, and, even more centrally, the persistence of exclusionary state policies and dehumanizing attitudes toward subordinate citizens, including prisoners. An important element in this story is the pervasiveness of an authoritarian political culture and the absence of sentiments favorable to the cause of prisoners among the public at large. Intermittent and isolated efforts to ignite interest in this issue were met with apathy and indifference on the part of the public. In a society in which racism and authoritarianism were much more prevalent than egalitarianism and democratic rights, the way prisoners were treated was not bound to become a source of widespread, sympathetic concern. The lack of dissenting voices made it easier for successive governments to perpetuate the status quo. Although important changes took place in the way prisons were administered, and allegedly scientific methods were later employed in the provision of punishment, those changes were superseded by strong continuities in the implementation of punishment and the treatment of prisoners.

PRISONS IN LIMA, c. 1850

In 1853, the young lawyer and future historian and statesman Marino Felipe Paz Soldán wrote a devastating report on the conditions in prisons and jails throughout the country.[1] Paz Soldán, a former justice of the peace in the northern city of Cajamarca, had taken an interest in this issue after witnessing the atrocious conditions in the Cajamarca local jail, whose demolition he later ordered. A disturbing indictment of the nation's criminal justice system, the report highlighted the pressing need that existed to address a problem that had not hitherto attracted serious public attention.

Lima's jails and prisons shared many of the deficiencies Paz Soldán found in centers of detention around the country. The local jail, commonly known as Carceletas, was located in the same building that had held the Inquisition jail during colonial times. It was supposed to house only offenders awaiting trial (*detenidos*), but its inmates included people who were being tried (*enjuiciados*) as well as criminals already sentenced to prison (*rematados*).[2] According to observers, Carceletas hosted an "abominable confusion" of petty offenders, occasional criminals, stubborn recidivists, and innocent people. The building was highly unsuitable for use as a jail, and surveillance and security were dismal. Paz Soldán dubbed it a "tomb of the living." Prisoners were treated like "savage beasts," occupied small, filthy, and overcrowded rooms, wore tatters instead of clothes, and used mats for beds. The lack of any principle of organization inside the jail was underlined by commentators. It was almost impossible to know, for instance, how many inmates were there at any point, what kind of crimes they were being held for, what their sentence was, if any, or even whether or not they deserved to be incarcerated. Prison records simply did not exist.

Another local jail was located in the police headquarters building (Intendencia de Policía). Known as the *cárcel de policía* (police jail), it was used to hold petty offenders who had to spend time in custody as well as those awaiting a judge's decision on whether or not they should be tried. Those who merited a trial were transferred to Carceletas. Abuse was rampant in the cárcel de policía. Whipping and various other forms of physical torment were common currency once an arrested person crossed the Intendencia's gate, as we saw in the previous chapter.[3] Equally infamous was Casasmatas, a jail inside the Real Felipe fortress in Callao that held offenders sentenced to prison terms. Casasmatas accommodated as many as two hundred prisoners in two small rooms of less than 250 square meters each. Lack of ventilation, poor illumination and hygiene, the mixing of different types of inmates, and the absence of principles of discipline and work also characterized this facility. Women occupied a separate, smaller room, not far from the guards' quarters. Alcohol consumption and gambling were widespread, and communication between inmates and people outside the prison was common. Escapes were reportedly facilitated by corrupt guards. Prisoners were employed in various types of public works, including cutting stone on San Lorenzo Island, five miles west of Callao, where an equally sordid jail was located.[4]

These facilities, hardly prisons in the modern sense of the term, coexisted with an extended network of private, informal, and illegal forms of punishment. Bakeries, for instance, used as centers of seclusion during the colonial period, continued until 1854 to house insubordinate slaves sent by their masters and, after slavery was abolished, black and Chinese workers sent by their patrons as a means of punishment.[5] Haciendas in Lima's rural hinterland often had their own jails for punishing unruly peons. Other illegal forms of punishment were used by state authorities, including the extrajudicial execution of bandits and robbers.[6] In this context, incarceration was viewed as just another part of a socially sanctioned web of authoritarian, arbitrary, and usually illegal forms of punishment.

Paz Soldán strove to change this situation. Mixing humanitarian sentiments with the search for efficacy in crime control and following fashionable European and North American developments in penal doctrine, he began to advocate the reform of prisons and the adoption of the penitentiary in Peru. A new type of prison with an internal disciplinary regime aimed at enforcing silence, repentance, and working habits, the idea of the penitentiary was conceived in England during the late eighteenth century. The original penitentiary act was enacted in 1779, and a small number of prisons were built in England following the new model. In 1787, the utilitarian philosopher Jeremy Bentham had designed an architectural model, the *panopticon*, to serve the needs of surveillance and control in hospitals, factories, schools, and prisons. Although Bentham's scheme would eventually come to influence the construction of penitentiaries, it was not readily accepted by English reformers.[7] The idea of the penitentiary crossed the Atlantic and was embraced in the United States, where several states built new prisons in the 1790s and 1800s. It was in the United States, in fact, where the penitentiary model would acquire its definite institutional consolidation in the 1820s.[8] Two penitentiary models competed for the favor of penal reformers worldwide, those corresponding to the penitentiaries of Auburn (New York) and Philadelphia. As is well known, the Auburn, or congregate, model placed a strong emphasis on productive work, aiming to transform prisons into factories. Prisoners worked together during the day but were separated in individual cells at night. The Philadelphia, or cellular regime, on the contrary, was based on the complete, permanent isolation of inmates. They had to work, eat, and sleep inside the cell, segregated not only from the external world but also from every other person inside the prison. Prisoners had to wear a mask to minimize contact with other persons every time they left their cell. Both systems, however, mandated strict rules of silence and aimed at the segregation of prisoners, so ultimately the differences between them were, in spite of all the polemics involved, more of form than of substance.[9]

President Echenique commissioned Paz Soldán to visit the United States with the explicit aim of examining the two models and recommending which would be the more appropriate for Peru. Paz Soldán chose the Auburn regime for the Lima penitentiary. The Philadelphia system, he thought, was very expensive, did not bring benefits, and could not achieve absolute isolation. He distrusted the reformative power of isolation, for rehabilitation of the criminal would be easier "in the company of his peers [and] motivated by the good examples." Racial criteria also influenced Paz Soldán's choice, for he thought that Indians—who were expected to comprise the majority of the inmate population—would actually enjoy solitude since "they consider themselves happy being in a desert taking care of their cattle." Paz Soldán's inference was that the Philadelphia cellular regime would have no punitive effect on Indians who, in addition, because of their "natural laziness," would benefit more from working in congregation than in solitude.

Paz Soldán's project encompassed the basic principles of reform. The building had to be in a good location and offer security and ventilation, while the façade had to be severe and somber. Strong emphasis was placed on discipline, obligatory work, and religious instruction as means to transform criminals into industrious, reliable workers. Prisoners were to be prohibited from talking among themselves, silence was to govern all prison activities, total obedience was expected from inmates, and a rigid system of surveillance was designed to exert total control over the prisoners.[10] Replicating the setup of U.S. penitentiaries, various workshops were to be placed inside the penitentiary with the explicit purpose of teaching labor skills and discipline to the inmates. Work inside the prison was to complement the "domestication" of the inmate, who was to be not only convinced through religious preaching that work was necessary and

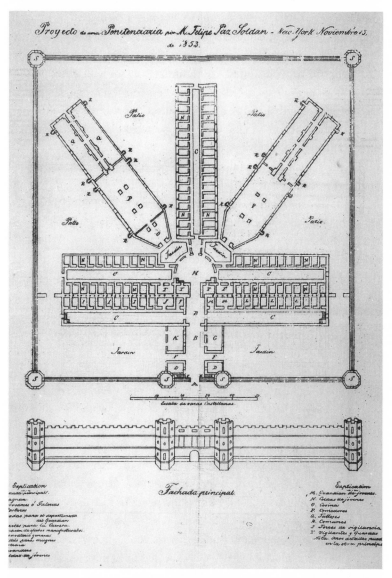

Figure 3. Proposed plan of the Lima penitentiary drawn by Mariano Felipe Paz Soldán in 1853. From Mariano Felipe Paz Soldán, *Examen de las penitenciarías de los Estados Unidos* (New York: Imprenta de S. W. Benedict, 1853).

virtuous, but also trained in its practice through the daily regime in the prison workshops. Criminals, it was thought, came from a population that had always had aversion to work, and thus the only way to transform them into useful subjects and to remove them from the world of vice and crime was by teaching them a trade and training them in constant and productive work.[11] This approach to punishment, in addition, connected with the centuries-long perception of Indians, blacks, and other non-white people as being naturally resistant to work and closely associated with the world of crime. Prison labor was thus conceived as a necessary step in the moral regeneration of the Peruvian lower classes and in the march toward material progress.

THE PENITENTIARY AT WORK

Under Paz Soldán's direction, the Lima penitentiary took almost six years to build and was inaugurated on July 23, 1862.[12] Located on the outskirts of the city, its impressive walls framed a total expanse of more than forty thousand square yards. Its massive stone structure became both a symbol of modernity for Peruvian elites and a source of admiration (or fear) for visitors and passersby. For several decades the penitentiary was the most visible and monumental edifice in Lima.[13] It was indeed, as the historian Alberto Flores Galindo observed, the very first modern building of Lima.[14] Although it did not quite follow the architectural model of the panopticon, the Lima penitentiary came to be known in popular parlance as *el panóptico*. At the center of the façade was a sober two-story edifice that housed the administrative offices. This was connected with a rotunda at the center of the construction, from which the five branches of the penitentiary building extended "like radii from a common center." Three of the five pavilions contained departments intended to accommodate male, female, and juvenile inmates, while the other two held the director's apartment, administrative offices, and other facilities such as the infirmary and the chapel. Inmates' cells occupied the first and second floor of each department; punishment of unruly prisoners took place in gloomy dungeons in the basement. The penitentiary, which accepted prisoners from the entire country, could house up to 315 inmates, each occupying an individual cell of about 9.75 cubic meters that was ventilated through a skylight in the back wall and was furnished with a retractable bed, a nail on the wall for hanging clothes, a small shelf for personal

Figure 4. Façade of the Lima penitentiary. From *Album de Lima y sus alredededores* (Lima: Librería e Imprenta Gil, n/d).

effects, and a crucifix. Inmates were to follow a rigid daily schedule of work, pray, and sleep but, more important, were expected to learn and practice the rules of obedience, silence, and industriousness.

The penitentiary introduced what other Peruvian prisons lacked, a daily, preestablished schedule of activities for both employees and inmates. That alone had important effects on the prisoners' lives and allowed the administration greater control over the inmates. By multiplying the rules convicts had to follow—punctual dressing, bathing, and eating, constant work and silence, and so forth—prison authorities were able to limit prisoners' movements and improve mechanisms of surveillance. The "rehabituation" of inmates, to use Adam Hirsch's term, began by familiarizing them with routines and obedience to commands.[15] Other, more visible elements such as the use of striped uniforms and numbers instead of proper names added to the regimented nature of the prison and reveal the intention of depriving inmates of any sense of individuality.[16]

Incarceration in the penitentiary was, according to the Penal Code of 1862, the most severe penalty after capital punishment. A long list of crimes, including most types of homicide, assault, rape, dueling, arson, piracy, and counterfeiting, brought sentences of four to fifteen years in the penitentiary.[17] *Penitenciaría* identified not only the edifice but also the penalty (as in *pena de penitenciaría*, penitentiary penalty), which underscores the uniqueness of this type of correction in the view of the authors of the penal code: the rules-enforcing discipline, obligatory work, and all the other elements were seen as intrinsic to the punishment the convict must endure. Although the *Reglamento* mandated the separation of prisoners in different departments according to the length of their sentences, that directive was not implemented.[18] Instead, prisoners were segregated by degree of dangerousness as estimated by prison employees: the first floor was for those considered to be "truly menacing" and the second for those deemed less dangerous.[19] Penal experts and authorities always recommended further separation according to the character of the prisoner or the nature of the crime, but it was not possible to enforce such a classification in the Lima penitentiary.[20] Regardless of length of sentence, type of crime, or criminal background, prisoners lived and worked beside one another inside the penitentiary's departments, workshops, and prison yards.[21]

In charge of keeping internal discipline, regulating the prisoners' work, and attending to penitentiary services was a group of guards, officers, and employees whose numbers varied constantly. Staffing the new penitentiary proved to be an endemic problem for authorities. Most employees had no experience with prison administration (not to mention a commitment to the ideals of prison reform) and owed their employment to personal and political patronage networks. It was not uncommon, in fact, for individuals with criminal backgrounds to be hired as workers or guards. A number of penitentiary employees were *meritorios*, people who worked as unsalaried apprentices in the expectation of being offered a future appointment. They commonly received some kind of unofficial compensation in the form of meals or other benefits for them and their families. The idea that military officers were suitable to run the penitentiary and that army veterans would be excellent prison guards was paramount, resulting in the frequent appointment of military men to fill positions at the penitentiary. Director Demetrio Saco would find in 1906 that army veterans were "very appropriate" as prison warders, for they were "accustomed to the military discipline, which is very rigorous and which, to a certain extent, is adopted for the internal regime of the establishment."[22] Between 1862 and 1920, the directors of the Lima penitentiary included at least eight military officials, who served for a total of more than seventeen years. Colonel Manuel Panizo y Zárate, for example, had the longest tenure as director of the penitentiary, from April 1897 to August 1905.

One of the main hurdles to the operation of the penitentiary was its chronic financial shortages. The critical economic situation Peru faced during most of the second half of the nineteenth century meant that the state could not adequately fund the penitentiary. The penitentiary was projected and constructed during the guano age, when fiscal resources seemed inexhaustible, but its operation was complicated by funding shortfalls, as the state's finances were never again as lavish as they had been in the 1850s.[23] Many prison authorities blamed the lack of financial resources for the shortcomings of the penitentiary. Yet many of the inconsistencies of the prison regime had their origin in decisions and omissions not necessarily connected to the institution's financial situation. As a result of the continuous financial shortcomings there was greater pressure, first, to transform the penitentiary into a productive institution, one that could sustain itself on the basis of the prisoners' work, and second, to encourage prisoners to take advantage of the opportunities offered by private contractors to earn money with which to procure the goods and services that the meager budget of the prison administration could not offer them. Prison work, a central component of penal rehabilitation, became the subject of a series of negotiations between administrators, authorities, private contractors, and inmates, as we will see in chapter 6.

Between 1870 and 1890, the penitentiary underwent a number of changes and reforms. In response to a critical report written by a *Junta Inspectora* (Inspection Committee) in 1873,[24] President Pardo enacted a series of ordinances to improve the performance of the penitentiary. He ordered that the Reglamento be strictly enforced, established monthly inspections, appointed new personnel, increased the prison budget, and requested stringent accountability from prison administrators.[25] Pardo's initiatives did not last long: only a few years later Peru was devastated by the War of the Pacific and the concomitant financial crisis of the state. Prison resources became even more scarce. By 1881, the penitentiary was found to be "in the most regrettable state of disorganization." According to the director, prisoners enjoyed "undue considerations" and exhibited "arrogance, insubordination, and immorality," which resulted in "daily mutinies."[26] Another director, Rosendo Samanez, resigned in 1887 when his repeated requests for funds were met with the "ridiculous" sum of 20 soles. Prisoners, he reported, did not have clothes, beds, soap, or kitchen utensils, a situation that, he protested, greatly hurt "the first monument of the Republic."[27] After his resignation, the Junta Inspectora was reinstated once again and in 1890 produced another, equally devastating report. "It would be preferable," it concluded, "to shut this house of correction and reform and go back to the old and repulsive penal regimen, than to tolerate disorder in this institution that used to be unique in South America."[28] This sense of failure was shared by many experts, policy makers, and criminologists, and somehow matched the frustration they felt with urban life in general in Lima after the 1870s, as discussed in chapter 1. From the point of view of the inmates the situation was far less clear: while it is true they usually lacked basic services and material goods, they also took advantage of, and contributed to, the state of generalized undiscipline that authorities repeatedly denounced, as we will see in chapter 6.

THE LIMA PENITENTIARY IN THE ERA OF SCIENTIFIC PENOLOGY

By the late nineteenth century, there were repeated demands to tighten the penitentiary regime. The failure of the penitentiary was associated with lack of resources and adequate personnel but, more centrally, with prisoners' indiscipline and demoralization and the corruption of the strict regime of regulation the penitentiary was supposed to enforce. This perception gave way to the widespread inference that what was needed to achieve prison discipline was not just enforcement of rules, but implementation of a harsher regime. Paul Pradier-Foderé, an influential French jurist who spent several years in Peru, found the prison regime too comfortable (*muy dulce*, literally, very sweet), partly because intimidation of prisoners was almost nonexistent.[29] The jurists Manuel Atanasio Fuentes and Miguel A. de la Lama expressed their preference for the Philadelphia regime because "it easily achieves order and discipline and prepares the inmate for moral redemption."[30] Numerous theses written at the University of San Marcos advanced the idea that the cellular system was the only "effective, intimidating, and repressive" prison regime.[31] A more radical stand was taken by some commentators for whom the reform of the criminal, now clearly a secondary goal of the punitive scheme, would be achieved not through humane treatment or contemplative attitudes but through severity, even cruelty, for "suffering is indispensable for the regeneration of the criminal."[32] On the basis of my survey of the literature, it is fair to conclude that most penologists regarded a harsher penal regime as the only solution to the endemic problem of crime and prison discipline in Peru. The tone of the debates both mirrored and reinforced the political and social climate of this period of authoritarian modernization.

A new Reglamento for the penitentiary was issued in 1901.[33] Drafted by the jurist Juan José Calle, known for his conservative approach to legal issues, it actually sanctioned the status quo, disappointing most penal experts who were demanding a stricter regime. For others, the Reglamento was a missed opportunity since it failed to adopt the newest ideas and practices regarding the treatment of prisoners. Thanks to the increasing diffusion of international innovations in criminology and penology (part of what Felix Driver has called "the international trade in models of social policy"),[34] Peruvian experts began to entertain other alternatives. The progressive or mark system was now offered by some as the best alternative to the inappropriate regime of Peruvian prisons. It was originally developed by Alexander Maconochie in New South Wales and later put into practice by Sir Walter Crofton in Ireland (thus the name it was also given, the Crofton or Irish system).[35] Unlike the traditional system of penalties, in which a convict received a fixed sentence based on the crime he or she had committed, the progressive system involved a disciplinary regime tailored to each prisoner and subject to change according to the individual's behavior in prison. Through hard work, good habits, and school attendance prisoners could earn marks or points that would allow them to move up through increasingly rewarded stages.[36] For Enoch Wines, a prominent North American prison reformer, the Crofton system was "a magnificent triumph of reason and humanity over coercion and brutal force."[37] The model gained an international reputation, and its universal adoption was recommended at the National Prison Association meeting in Cincinnati in 1870, whose final Declaration of Principles stated, as a major principle of reform, that "the prisoner's destiny should be placed, measurably, in his own hands."[38] The Elmira Reformatory, created by the New York legislature in 1869, became under the direction of Zebulon Brockway the institutional embodiment of the progressive system.

Peruvian penologists of the turn of the century debated the progressive system.[39] Although some presented it as a system that encouraged deception and hypocrisy among inmates, others like Oscar Miró Quesada expressed their admiration for the Elmira Reformatory, emphasizing the fact that reformatory goals could not be achieved without the cooperation of the prisoner. Elías Lozada Benavente, whose area of special interest was the treatment of juvenile criminals, also concluded that Elmira was "the best penal institution in the world."[40] The intellectual elites' fascination with foreign social and institutional models was again playing a major role in the formulation of proposals for penal reform, although they would have a hard time convincing policy makers to adopt them.

The rise to power of Augusto B. Leguía in 1919, whose administration was intent on improving the state's efficiency through institutional modernization and the strengthening of mechanisms of social control, gave impulse to a renewed interest in issues of prison management and discipline. The daily press reported with growing frequency the conditions of prisons and the threats they allegedly posed to the stability of the country. The publication in 1920 of another damning report on the Lima penitentiary written in 1916 by a commission led by Calle also seems to have affected the decision to seek changes in the penitentiary and other prison institutions.[41] The judicial system in general and the deficiencies in criminal legislation and prisons in particular received more attention from the Leguía regime than from any previous government since the mid–nineteenth century. Several prominent jurists, including Plácido Jiménez, Oscar C. Barrós, Abraham Rodríguez Dulanto, and Germán Leguía y Martínez, influenced in one way or another by positivist penal doctrines, became part of the Leguía administration and contributed to the formulation of state policies. One of the main guidelines of the Leguía government was the idea that society's problems could be corrected by the application of scientific and rational administrative methods.[42] The question of what to do with prisons and how to improve their administration thus was inserted within this larger project to modernize Peruvian society. The mutually beneficial cooperation between an aggressive and authoritarian administration and a set of experts eager to apply scientific solutions and gain individual and collective legitimacy resulted in the formulation of an ambitious, though no less ambiguous and inconsistent, program of prison reform.

The first step was actually a bold one. In 1921, Leguía created the Inspección General de Prisiones, later the DGP, a centralized bureau for administering the entire national prison system. The DGP was expected to supervise all penal facilities nationwide, keep statistical records of their operation, oversee the functioning of workshops and schools inside prisons, and organize a central register of anthropometric data for the identification of criminals.[43] It would take a few years for this entity to effectively control the national network of prisons and similar institutions, which were hitherto dispersed under various administrative schemes, but the importance of its formation can hardly be exaggerated.

The next step was the creation of a new legal framework, which came into effect with the enactment of the Penal Code of 1924, which replaced that of 1862. The adoption of the principles of social defense and dangerousness, which I analyzed in chapter 2, brought some changes in the types of penalties and in the administration of penal institutions. The code included, for instance, the new penalty of *internamiento*, which would send convicts to a penitentiary for a minimum of twenty-five years, after which prison time to be served under that classification would be indeterminate. During the first year of confinement, prisoners would be subject to continuous solitary confinement and obligatory work. The penalty of penitenciaría entailed between one and twenty years at a penitentiary, an agricultural penitentiary (*penitenciaría agrícola*, which did not yet exist), or a penal colony. The penalty of *prisión* (prison term) could last from two days to twenty years and was to be served at local jails. Finally, the penal code also contemplated prison terms for "political and social delinquents," for whom separate facilities would have to be built.[44] Of much more immediate impact was the adoption of parole, that is, conditional freedom given to inmates who demonstrated good behavior and had served two-thirds of their sentences, and conditional sentence, or probation, the temporary suspension of the enforcement of the penalty. What some penologists missed in the new penal code was a more explicit progressive regime, with a system of marks or points that would allow prisoners to track their performance inside the prison. Being paroled was thus entirely dependent on the evaluation of the inmates' behavior by prison administrators and physicians; the inmates could exert very little leverage over the decision. Still, it introduced a new terrain of contention for prison officials and inmates, one that would have important effects in the negotiation of the terms of imprisonment, as we will see below.

Perhaps the most ambitious endeavor of criminologists everywhere was the transformation of penal institutions into laboratories for the production of knowledge about the criminal and, indeed, about the lower classes of society. Strong traditions of criminological inquiry in such countries as Italy, France, and Argentina developed largely as a result of the launching of research projects that used inmate populations to propose and test theories about criminals. Between 1890 and 1920, investigators at the Lima penitentiary had used inmates as subjects of research on such topics as sexual behavior, diseases, and tattooing. The transformation of the Lima penitentiary into a research facility was an endeavor the Penal Code of 1924 tried to effect by mandating the formation of an Instituto de Criminología modeled after a similar institution created at the Buenos Aires penitentiary in 1907 by the prominent criminologist José Ingenieros. In Ingenieros's hands, the instituto became a major research facility, collecting enormous amounts of data, conducting numerous research projects, and advancing bold hypotheses about crime and its connections with biology, psychology, hygiene, and politics.[45] It was not until 1929 that the penal code's mandate became a reality, and an Instituto de Criminología was created at the Lima penitentiary under the academic umbrella of the University of San Marcos Law School.[46] The physician Carlos Bambarén, its first director, had long subscribed to the idea that establishing "laboratories of penitentiary anthropology" to study the criminal population would reveal "the intimate personality of the criminal" and would facilitate the implementation of appropriate and individualized punitive strategies.[47]

Among the initial tasks of the new institute was the introduction of a system of criminological cards for gathering as much information on each prisoner as possible.[48] The *Cartilla Criminológica* was composed of fifteen categories, including the prisoner's genealogy, anthropometric data, fingerprints, medical records, and sexual life. In October 1930, both the cartilla and a questionnaire for evaluating the inmate's *estado peligroso* were made obligatory in all Peruvian penal institutions.[49] The determination of the inmates' estado peligroso, following a model developed by the Spanish penologist Luis Jiménez de Asúa, included five main classes of data: the inmate's personality (anthropological, psychological, behavioral, and moral); his or her personal background; the crime and its motives; the inmate's behavior while in prison; and a criminological-medical appreciation of his or her degree of dangerousness.[50] Although the institute intended to conduct criminological studies of the prisoners in order to effect the individualization of the penalty, that endeavor was never realized.[51] By 1933, the institute was unfunded and was thus condemned to languish until it reached total inactivity.[52] In the mid-1940s, Bambarén was still trying to resurrect it.

Less ambitious goals were easier to reach. A Tribunal de Conducta was formed in 1929 to evaluate the inmates' behavior and make decisions regarding requests for either parole or pardon.[53] At its first meeting the tribunal evaluated 119 files of inmates slated for pardon. In the session of June 1930, the tribunal discussed a number of disciplinary cases, pondering what sanctions, if any, should be taken. In the months ahead, the tribunal met regularly to evaluate large groups of inmates. In its December 1931 session, for instance, 187 inmates were evaluated, of whom 98 were found to have displayed good and very good behavior, 4 excellent, and 84 bad.[54] The 98 inmates with good behavior were rewarded: they were allowed to listen to the radio, have electric light in their cells, visit the library, and even wear their own clothes instead of the prison uniform. The tribunal's assessments were also used later to classify inmates on the basis of their behavior. The 1924 code had stipulated that at each internment center inmates be classified according to "their physical and psychical conditions and their previous life and aptitudes for work."[55] In 1931, it was ordered that prisoners with bad or mediocre behavior would have to be separated from those showing good conduct.[56]

As might be expected, some of the tribunal's evaluations were challenged by the inmates, and in some cases they were indeed revised, but obviously it was always the tribunal that had the final word. The way the Tribunal de Conducta carried out its evaluations was far from rigorous. Each member gave the inmate a monthly grade (*nota*) for his behavior during leisure time and, for those who worked, another grade for performance at the workshop. Both grades were recorded along with a qualification pretentiously called *Apreciación criminológica*, which involved no systematic inquiry and was nothing but an arbitrary label imposed on each inmate. The categories included normal, dangerous, semidangerous, minimally dangerous, and nondangerous, with no indication as to what exactly those terms meant. On July 10, 1935, for instance, 437 inmates were evaluated. Forty-seven were found to be normal, 5 dangerous, 4 semidangerous, 3 minimally dangerous, and the remaining 378 nondangerous.[57]

The duties of the Instituto de Criminología and the Tribunal de Conducta overlapped in that the institute did little other than evaluate the criminal population. As far as I have been able to establish, no systematic research-oriented programs were carried out at the instituto, whose duties were mostly restricted to the gathering of data on the inmate population. A division of penitentiary statistics was organized within the DGP in June 1927 for recording prison populations, sentences, escapes, recidivism, mortality, output of prison work, attendance at prison schools, and prisons' infrastructure and budgets.[58] It was meant to help identify criminals, monitor recidivism, and individualize prisoners' treatment.[59] About the same time, an office of dactyloscopic identification was established at the penitentiary.[60] During the next two years, about 1,500 inmates were identified by means of biographical cards (*cartillas biográficas*) that included dactyloscopic and morphologic data as well as a picture of each inmate bearing his number. At the very least, the card system helped administrators keep records of occurrences such as diseases, escape attempts, disciplinary violations, and the like. A *Libro de Conducta* was also created to record inmates' behavior inside the prison, and this was used in weighing the decision about parole.

While the implementation of evaluative bodies, research facilities, and huge databases was more difficult than penologists expected, the few steps that were effectively taken proved to be quite important indeed. By far the most consequential such reform was the adoption of a parole provision and, along with it, the use of the Tribunal de Conducta for assessing those inmates who requested it. To be sure, this was not what advocates of a progressive system wanted, but, still, it had its effects. The possibility of getting parole was a powerful incentive for prisoners to be on their good behavior, but it also became an important element in the daily negotiations occurring within the penitentiary between inmates and authorities. Although prisoners resorted to a variety of strategies to take advantage of the possibility of getting parole—writing letters, simulating good behavior, engaging in negotiations with prison guards and authorities (which I will analyze in part 3 of this book)—the ultimate decision continued to lie in the hands of the experts. Their authority and thus that of the increasingly ubiquitous Leguiísta state were reinforced.

FROM GUADALUPE TO THE CÁRCEL CENTRAL DE VARONES

A few blocks away from the penitentiary, occupying the building of a former convent, was the infamous Cárcel de Guadalupe, where the majority of Lima's criminals served their prison terms. At its peak, it held more than seven hundred prisoners, although its real capacity was probably around two hundred. The physical layout of Guadalupe comprised two yards surrounded by various compartments. The first yard, the smaller of the two, was surrounded by administrative offices and quarters for prisoners "of some consideration." The second was surrounded by prisoners' rooms. The prisoners spent most of the day in this yard, playing cards, buying and selling goods, or just hanging around; in fact, it resembled a sort of street market or fair, for a series of booths had been installed by inmates to sell groceries, clothes, personal items, and even coca.[61] The prison also included several workshops or, more appropriately, rooms where inmates worked voluntarily, generally without the intervention of the authorities and often for outside private entrepreneurs.

Guadalupe opened for the first time in 1821, immediately after Peruvian independence. It functioned irregularly during the next few decades, and in the late 1850s it was reopened and remained in operation until 1928.[62] Despite the fact that it was the main institution of confinement in Lima prior to the inauguration of the penitentiary, its first bylaws were not issued until 1879. Written by a five-member team that included the prominent jurists José Silva Santisteban and Manuel Atanasio Fuentes, the Reglamento mandated the separation of inmates by sex and legal status, the creation of workshops for the prisoners, the censorship of the inmates' communications, and a regime of rewards and penalties "to foment their dedication to work and morality." It prohibited the use of the whip and the stick (*palo*) but did allow the *cepo de pies* (stocks). It also forbade canteens inside the prison. The authority resided in the *alcaide* (prison warden), who was supposed to live inside the prison and could not leave "except temporarily to attend serious matters related to his service." The Reglamento also contemplated the use of "as many *caporales* [aides] as needed," which were to be selected by the director from among the prisoners with better behavior. The caporales secured all internal locks, cell bars, and doors, oversaw order in each department, monitored the isolation cells to prevent other inmates from approaching those being punished, and controlled contraband. In fact, in the absence of prison personnel (the Reglamento specified only the alcaide, sub-alcaide, a chaplain, a doctor, an intern, and the doormen), the entire internal disciplinary and security system was placed in the hands of the caporales.[63] Outside security was provided by a contiguous military station.

From the day it opened, Guadalupe epitomized everything that prison reformers were ashamed of. Descriptions of the prison are consistently scathing throughout the period. Dr. Vidrieras described it in 1890 in the following terms:

> Down by the city outskirts I came across a house, what a house!— dirty and somber like an eighteenth-century jail! . . . the inside, it is not a yard, not even a ward, nothing like that; it is a filthy plot enclosed by four walls . . . a crowd of men were lying down, like incarnations of brutal idleness! . . . huge rooms, humid and poorly ventilated, serve as bedrooms; each bed is used by 40 or 50 prisoners; long benches serve as mattresses; warm clothing? each inmate tries to use somebody else as a blanket . . . dauntless prison! . . . Such a jail is unimaginable in this City, so proud of its luster.[64]

For some commentators, conditions at Guadalupe were so bad that it had become dangerous to the stability of Peruvian society.[65] *La Gaceta Judicial* warned about the risk posed by the six hundred inmates of Guadalupe, who could easily open its doors, "going over society like a tiger over its victim."[66] Official communications among judicial authorities constantly pointed to Guadalupe as being in disastrous condition and needing urgent reforms, but not a single meaningful action was ever taken.[67] The admixture of different kinds of inmates, the relaxation of discipline, the lack of an internal regime for inmates, and the widespread recourse to illegal practices were mentioned over and over again as signs that Guadalupe was a prison in urgent need of radical reform. This almost unanimous depiction of Guadalupe as a prison in shambles raises some questions. There is no doubt that the conditions at Guadalupe were, to say the least, lacking. Not just the testimonies quoted, but also prisoners' letters and other sources all coincide in depicting the place in the worst possible terms.[68] But it is equally important to take notice of the fastidious exasperation authorities and commentators expressed for what they interpreted as leniency toward prisoners. They were scandalized at the "freedom" inmates "enjoyed" inside Guadalupe and at the absence of a more rigid disciplinary regime. The images of inmates moving around freely, playing cards, engaging in leisure activities, and trading all sorts of goods and services bothered elite commentators for, in their view, inmates should be suffering the consequences of their crimes. It is true that some commentators also pointed out the needy conditions of at least some of the prisoners, but the overwhelming impression is that it was the lack of discipline that prompted the condemnations of Guadalupe.

While Lima was rapidly changing and acquiring a cosmopolitan look, Guadalupe, the largest local jail, remained virtually unchanged. Several projects were planned to replace it. In 1873, the government ordered the construction of a new prison, but both financial and political obstacles prevented the realization of the project. In 1893, a new commission studied the feasibility of the project and recommended the construction of a new prison with a capacity for five hundred inmates, but no action was taken.[69] Years later, in 1905, the project was resumed by the minister of justice, only to be abandoned shortly thereafter.[70] In 1928, the Leguía administration closed Guadalupe and transferred its population to the hastily created Cárcel Central de Varones (CCV), or central jail for men, which occupied two departments of the Lima penitentiary.[71] Conditions at the CCV, not surprisingly, were no better than those at Guadalupe or the penitentiary. According to the director in 1931, about 50 percent of the prison population was "almost stable," made up of stubborn recidivists.[72] Material deficiencies, including overcrowding and the lumping together of disparate types of prisoners, were blamed for the bad conditions.[73] Descriptions of the prison coincided in their depictions of its atrocious conditions: lack of adequate sanitary services forced inmates to use their cells as lavatories; inmates ate with their hands for lack of silverware and slept on the floor for lack of mattresses; most remained idle because of the lack of occupation; more than half stayed there for a year or more without attending a single court hearing and thus not knowing their real legal status.[74] Prison authorities manifestly admitted the inadequacies of prison conditions: in October 1931, the director asked the minister of justice to try to speed up the trials of CCV inmates because their continuous incarceration allowed them to "learn vices and bad habits they did not have when they entered here." The CCV was, in the eyes of its own director, a school of vice.[75]

EL FRONTÓN

A penal colony began operations in the late 1910s on the island of El Frontón, a few miles off the coast of Callao.[76] It was used by the Leguía administration as the terminus for a variety of lawbreakers, including

Figure 5. El Frontón inmates working at the *canteras* (quarries). From Colonia Penal "El Frontón," *Memoria presentada por el director Sr. Manuel Hermilio Higueras al Ministro de Justicia, Instrucción y Culto. 1922* (Lima: Litografía e Imprenta T. Scheuch, 1923).

political opponents, strikers, vagrants, recalcitrant inmates from other prisons, and *penitenciados* for whom there was no room at the penitentiary. The penal colony of El Frontón comprised a series of stone constructions housing administrative offices, a small regiment of gendarmes, prisoners' cells and rooms, a chapel, cafeteria, and workshops. By the early 1920s, there were at least three departments for inmates. Prisoners generally spent the day working or, when the authorities allowed them to do so, hanging around the island, while at night they were locked inside the pavilions. The main occupation for inmates—and the main source of income for the prison economy—was the cutting of stones to make paving blocks (*adoquines*) used in the rapidly developing urbanization of Lima. By 1922, for example, the prison was producing more than thirty-four thousand blocks a month.[77] Prisoners also worked as carpenters, shoemakers, bakers, and blacksmiths.[78] According to the director in 1922, the penal colony was economically profitable. He estimated even that by 1924 the central government would not need to disburse funds to maintain the prison because it could balance its budget "with its own profits."

In order to keep this economy profitable, a continual flow of prisoners to maintain the necessary minimum population of 250 was needed.[79] By 1922, a decrease in the number of inmates was seen by the director,

Hermilio Higueras, as "a threat to the progress of the prison," for fewer inmates meant also fewer workers.[80] The solution was to transfer inmates from Guadalupe, where they were "a burden for the state," to El Frontón, where, by contrast, they would become productive prisoners/workers. Another boost to prison productivity came during the heyday of the vagrancy law in 1925–28, when hundreds of vagrants were sent to the island, thereby guaranteeing enough manpower to keep its production levels steady (see chapter 5).

In spite of the authorities' efforts to present El Frontón as a location beneficial to prisoners—especially because, they said, inmates were able to work outdoors and enjoy clean air—both independent and official visitors testified to the horrors endured by most inmates.[81] On one of her visits to the island in 1927, the prison activist and journalist Angela Ramos encountered inmates who were bleeding working in the stone quarries, prisoners who resembled "vagabond cadavers," others who did not even know why they were being detained, and children living with their parents. She pointed to the irony of prisoners manufacturing shoes for the navy and private contractors while going shoeless themselves because they had not received the shoes the administration was supposed to furnish.[82] An official delegation from the Department of Public Health visiting in September 1932 found ruinous buildings, overcrowding, abundance of rodents, and so forth.[83] The Chilean citizen René Mendoza, incarcerated at El Frontón for espionage in 1921, left a horrific testimony: El Frontón was even worse, he stated, than "the filthiest Russian prisons."[84]

El Frontón was managed as a quasi–slave plantation.[85] It even had a cemetery not sanctioned by the state to bury the inmates who died.[86] During the tenure of Higueras, a former director of the penitentiary and director of El Frontón from 1921 to 1925, a true regime of terror reigned.[87] In June 1924, for instance, when the inmates threatened to strike if they were not given their wages, Higueras wrote a message to the inspector of El Frontón, "[I suppose] you have put your hands on them, and that if needed you may shoot them with my authorization. Let them know if you wish, especially the *rateros*, who must be the promoters, that if anything happens I will go immediately to terminate their temerity and to put my hand on them so they will never dare to try it [the strike] again; that I will not pay them now because I don't want to, and that they have to work themselves to death while they are at the Island." He ordered the lieutenant in charge of the military post to shoot, if necessary, at some of the prisoners, "preferably the rateros, for whom nobody gives a damn."[88] Such language does not reveal the attitude of a dutiful authority compliant to the law (not to mention a compassionate protector of the rights of prisoners), but closely resembles the despotism of slaveowners or Andean *gamonales* (bosses), who considered themselves almost omnipotent and who treated their subjects in whatever way they wanted with impunity.

Torments and torture were daily occurrences at El Frontón, to an extent difficult to find in the other prisons. One of the most infamous sites of torment was the *lobera*, a fetid, dark natural cave in which the inmate was permanently exposed to ocean water. The lobera was described by an inmate in 1936: "This lobera is a cave made by the ocean in a cliff. The dungeons are in its deepest area. When the ocean tide rises and hits the rocks, the water reaches the inmates. The ocean's noise concentrated under that cellar is deafening, and at nighttime bats and the wolves' howling make it impossible to sleep."[89] Many left the lobera with diseases such as tuberculosis, and some would later die as a result of it. *La parada*, another torture site, was "a sort of vertical coffin, stamped against the stone wall of the island." When placed inside la parada, prisoners were forced to stay on their feet. After some time, their feet would start swelling and bleeding. In wintertime it was cold and wet; in the summer, horribly hot. When the punishment ended and the guards opened the door, the prisoner, not able to remain standing, would fall to the floor. A political prisoner who refused to eat the filthy food he was given was sent to la parada and died there, according to the testimony of the *Aprista* writer Julio Garrido Malaver.[90] A similar site was called *la sepultura* (the grave).[91] Besides these, there were the usual solitary confinement cells. Corporal punishment was rampant. Víctor M. Villavicencio described a punishment called *carreras de vaqueta* (beating race), in which naked inmates were thrown into the water and, when retrieved, were forced to run between two rows of guards, who would beat them about the body with sticks, being careful to avoid the head, so as to prevent possible life-threatening injuries.[92]

| | | | |

Guadalupe, the Cárcel de Varones, El Frontón, and even the Lima penitentiary offer compelling evidence that, almost eighty years after Paz Soldán launched his program for prison reform, penal institutions continued to be places where inmates suffered the combined effects of despotism, neglect, corruption, and indifference. Lima's architectural and urban landscape had been radically transformed over time, especially during the *oncenio*, but Lima's prisons were largely untouched by the modernizing drives. As Ramos said in reference to Guadalupe in 1927, "What does it matter that we have avenues, boulevards, hotels, statues, monuments, and houses that are real palaces, when in the heart of the city three hundred or more disgraced subjects writhe [with pain], for whom the word *piety* has not yet been invented?"[93] Mistreatment, corporal punishment, lack of basic services, and a denial of the fundamental rights of prisoners characterized the operation of these institutions.

During the 1920s, attempts were made to ameliorate the conditions of some of the prisons, but beyond small administrative measures related to food, work, surveillance, infrastructure, and prison schools, little else was actually changed. As late as 1929 President Leguía himself admitted that most Peruvian prisons were still "centers of useless suffering" and sites for the "reproduction of crime." He envisioned a plan to build a new penitentiary, a new prison for women, a new agricultural and industrial reformatory, and many other prisons. The problem of prisons was to be solved, apparently, by the massive construction of new facilities. As had become distinctive of the Leguía regime, social and political problems were addressed through narrow technical solutions. For the case in point, however, not even the proposed alternative was realized, for none of Leguía's proposals ever came to fruition.[94]

The ambiguities of prison reform during the oncenio are further illustrated by a little-known episode. At a time when criminologists and experts were eagerly trying to develop a penal complex in which both scientific punishment and criminological research would offer clues to solving the problems of crime and disorder, Peruvian state authorities began to take steps toward procuring a European religious society to run the Boy's Reformatory of Surco and, eventually, also the Lima penitentiary and the penal island of El Frontón. It seems as if certain sectors of the administration had finally given up: the state needed to get out of the prison mess.[95] In 1928, formal requests were made to the Vatican to permit the Fathers of the Providence or any other fraternal order with experience in the administration of prisons to come to Peru. The Peruvian ambassador contacted several Italian, Belgian, and German orders, but the results were disappointing. A representative of the Brothers of

Our Lady of Mercy actually went to Lima but was negatively impressed by the situation of Peruvian prisons. The order decided not to accept the invitation, and no further attempts were made in this regard.[96]

The conditions at El Panóptico, Guadalupe, and El Frontón evoked in the imagination of most residents of Lima visions of horror, suffering, and despair. While these representations of Lima's prisons are almost unanimous, the ways in which their inhabitants were perceived were much more mixed: for some, convicts constituted the scum of society and deserved the suffering they endured; for others, they were victims of injustice and oppression and were worthy of commiseration and pity. But none of these images of prisons and prisoners could ever do justice to the complex realities of prison life and the ambiguous relations inmates established with the institution and its multiple layers of authority. The horror and suffering those names evoke were always accompanied by other types of interaction that made prison existence a little more tolerable, as we will see in chapter 7. And imagining the occupants of these places as belonging to a single class of criminals would obscure the diversity of backgrounds and the complexity of the hierarchies that shaped their lives behind bars.

5

One of the goals of locking people up behind bars is to isolate them from the communities who consider them dangerous, worthless, or simply undesirable. Having been extirpated from their milieu, they are expected to detach themselves from the daily occurrences, habits, and other contemptible features of their lives in the outside world. Prisoners, in the imagination of prison reformers, would have to abandon their cultural and social baggage the moment they set foot in the prison—or at least shortly thereafter, following rehabilitative therapy or simple exposure to a different set of rules and routines. In reality, however, that never happens. Prisoners, in fact, carry the outside world into the prison—and vice versa. They confront the challenges of the prison with the resources and the handicaps they acquired in the outside world; they also learn inside ways of coping and surviving that, once they are released, will shape their readjustment to free society.

The world in which the male prisoners of Lima lived was shaped less by the written bylaws and doctrinal manifestos of criminologists and penal experts than by the multitude of interactions that took place among and between them and prison authorities, guards, and employees. These human congregates, however, and in particular the community of inmates, did not constitute homogeneous entities, for they were permanently divided by multiple fissures (of class, race, regional origin, legal status, age, culture, and so on) that effectively made the community of peoples we call prisoners a highly heterogeneous, fragmented body.

The various segments that composed the male population of Lima's prisons exhibited diverse backgrounds, roles, and hierarchies as well as the peculiarities of their collective personas. While faites, for instance, were both feared and admired and strove to defend their conceptions of honor, respectability, and masculinity, rateros were constructed as pitiful, pathetic, and even effeminate characters of the Lima underworld. They were not the only such criminal types, though, and most likely they do not represent the whole range of characters the prison populations encompassed. Ordinary workers and parents, so-called vagrants, serial killers, and even members of the "decent" classes were also part of this assorted conglomerate of inmates. The most sui generis of these groups was that of political prisoners, who shared with common criminals the same buildings, but not the same conditions or physical space. Altogether, an account of the male prison communities offers an opportunity to highlight their diversity and the potential sources of solidarity and tension existing within them.

In exploring the communities of inmates in Lima's prisons, one will also start to decipher some of ways in which prisons were "resonance boxes" of the society in which they operated: the hierarchies, values, and tensions existing in the outside world reverberated in the interior. Lima's prisons, as we will see, were among the few truly *national* institutions in the sense that they reflected the diversity of regional, ethnic, social, and cultural backgrounds of the Peruvian population to a greater extent than such institutional settings as schools, universities, the state bureaucracy, or the clergy. It was through their very relationship with the state (in this case, the criminal justice system) that thousands of individuals, mostly of lower-class origin, came into close contact with other members of the national community of Peruvians. This chapter reconstructs the multiplicity of worlds that coalesced in the space of the prison.

PRISON COMMUNITIES: FIGURES AND PATTERNS

During the period 1850–1935, male criminals of Lima were incarcerated in three main institutions: the Lima penitentiary, Guadalupe jail, and El Frontón penal island. Given the variety of legal statuses of inmates in those prisons and the diversity of terms they were serving, each institution held a disparate assortment of inmates. *Enjuiciados*, individuals undergoing trial, were generally kept at Guadalupe; *rematados*, those sentenced to various prison terms, spent their prison time at El Frontón or Guadalupe; *penitenciados*, those sentenced to a so-called penitentiary penalty, as well as political prisoners could be sent to any of the three; most vagrants were sent to El Frontón. Each prison thus housed an assortment of inmates who differed widely in terms of their legal status.

In the period between 1862 and 1908, the Lima penitentiary accommodated a maximum of 315 prisoners, each occupying an individual cell. Because the number of criminals sentenced to the penitentiary always exceeded its capacity, authorities sent the overload to other prisons, such as Guadalupe, Casasmatas, and later the penal island of El Frontón, none of which had the infrastructure to even attempt to enforce the strict regimentation and rules-learning process embodied in the penitentiary penalty.[1] At times as many as 274 criminals sentenced to the penitentiary were serving their terms at Guadalupe. In 1908, the penitentiary's capacity was increased to 411, and in 1920 to 515.[2] When in 1928 an entire section of the penitentiary building was transformed into the Cárcel Central de Varones (men's prison), the average number of inmates at the *panóptico* decreased to around 250.

The population of Guadalupe was much more mixed and heterogeneous than that at the penitentiary. It housed suspects awaiting sentence, criminals already sentenced to various prison terms, penitenciados sentenced by different tribunals from all over the country, convicts sent from the nearby provinces of Canta and Huarochirí, and also political prisoners and felons sentenced by military tribunals—deserters, undisciplined soldiers, and military men guilty of other crimes. Guadalupe was always depicted as being terribly overcrowded. Available statistics seem to confirm that picture: as many as 728 prisoners jammed the prison at one point. According to figures collected by the physicians Francisco Graña and Hermilio Valdizán, a total of 26,431 criminals entered the Guadalupe prison during the period 1870–1915, an average of 573 entries per year (table 5.1).[3] Fluctuations in the number of criminals entering each year are attributable to multiple factors, including variations in the actual levels of criminality and in arrest and conviction rates. The relative importance of such elements is impossible to assess. Particularly noteworthy is the low number of criminals that entered Guadalupe in the period after the occupation of Lima by Chilean forces, which may be related not to a decline in crime, but to the state of disorganization of police forces after the War of the Pacific.[4] On the other hand, hundreds of inmates were also released every year upon their acquittal. During 1874, for example, 563 Guadalupe inmates were released, 472 of whom were acquitted of

Figure 6. Interior view of the Lima penitentiary. From
Album de Lima y sus alrededores (Lima: Librería
e Imprenta Gil, n/d).

all charges. Inspector of Prisons Tomás Caivano pointed to the obvious
quandary: "We are either arresting innocents or releasing criminals."[5]
The practical consequence of this situation was the constant presence of a
floating population of individuals who repeatedly spent short periods at
Guadalupe. According to the authorities, that population included a core
number of criminals who were incarcerated only to be released after a
short period. This high turnover rate allowed the prison population as a
whole to remain strongly connected to the outside world, a "privilege"
that penitentiary inmates, for example, did not have. Guadalupe, some
authorities suggested, was for some criminals more a sort of "summer
camp" than a place of suffering and penitence.[6] Those who were convicted spent periods ranging from a few months up to fifteen or twenty
years (in the case of penitenciados).[7]

The mixture of various types of inmates was also a characteristic of the population on the penal island of El Frontón, which hosted rematados, penitenciados, vagrants, and political prisoners. Statistics about the population of this colony are quite scarce. The largest figure I have encountered is 387 prisoners in December 1929, which included 156 political prisoners, 186 common criminals, and 45 military inmates.[8] A list from 1922 included 182 rematados and 121 penitenciados.[9]

The statistical profile of the inmate population in Lima's penal institutions duplicates well-known patterns in prison populations around the world. Most prisoners belonged to the poor and working segments of the population, were relatively young, and belonged to nonwhite ethnic groups (tables 5.2 through 5.8). There were more differences in the types of crimes these criminals had been accused of or were sentenced for. Most penitentiary inmates (82 percent in 1927, for instance) were serving lengthy sentences for various types of homicide (table 5.9), while those at Guadalupe had been accused of or sentenced for a variety of crimes. In 1877, for example, only a third had been accused of violent crimes, including murder, while another third had committed property crimes.[10] At El Frontón in 1922, 40 percent of rematados had been sentenced for theft and 34 percent for homicide (table 5.10). The regional origins of these inmates is also revealing of the universe from which they were drawn. The proportion of penitentiary inmates sentenced by Lima's tribunals declined over time (from 53.3 percent in 1877 to 18.3 percent in 1926), while the share of those sentenced in other jurisdictions, particularly Piura, Puno, and Cajamarca, increased (table 5.11). This is likely a reflection of the gradual expansion of policing and the criminal justice system, particularly during the Leguía administration, to areas in which its presence had not been particularly strong in the past.[11] As a result, an increasing number of felons were convicted by provincial courts and sent to the Lima penitentiary. At Guadalupe, 56.8 percent of all the inmates between 1870 and 1915 were *provincianos* (from the interior) and only 25.3 percent were natives of Lima. In 1930, of 92 inmates at El Frontón only 22 were from the Lima/Callao area and 5 were foreign. The remaining 65 came from the interior, especially the northern provinces of Cajamarca, La Libertad, and Piura.[12] These figures clearly reflect an increasing migration from the interior to Lima, but also the rather difficult adaptation of many of those immigrants to the city.

What was the background of these inmates? Were they long-term criminals? Was their incarceration the culmination of a life of vice and crime, as was usually portrayed? For penitentiary inmates, those who had allegedly committed the worst crimes of all, fragmentary evidence suggests that, contrary to common impressions, most seem to have been first-time offenders. In his study of tattooed inmates at the Lima penitentiary (1917), Marino Alegre y Pacheco offered detailed biographical sketches of 27 inmates. Seventeen of them (63 percent) were presented as having lived a "regular life" with no criminal antecedents, and although 8 were depicted as having lived an "irregular life," only 2 were explicitly associated with a criminal career.[13] The short sketches the author offers, a mixture of the inmates' self-portraits with Alegre's frequent observations about them, describe some details about their background. Inmate no. 294, for instance (he did not identify them by name), was literate, lived a regular life, and had parents who were described as being "laborious and honest."[14] Inmate no. 175, a thirty-two-year-old literate Indian, had never shown poor behavior and was well esteemed by his superiors in the army, where he had served.[15] Inmate no. 319, a twenty-two-year-old mestizo, had never been involved in criminal activities, had been a dedicated worker, and enjoyed a family environment described as good.[16] Evidence about recidivism among penitentiary inmates tends to confirm this pattern. In 1909, only 10 out of 411 inmates (2.3 percent) were listed as recidivists.[17] Occasional and first-time offenders seem to have abounded among the population of the penitentiary, and a good number of them, in addition, claimed to be victims of injustices, errors, or acts of vengeance.

Such evidence tends to cast doubt on the well-established association between the *panóptico* and a population of dreadful assassins that some commentators, prison experts, and the common folk had created. These images were triggered by the widely and sensationally reported cases of a few murderers who were interviewed by journalists, reported on in the press, and carefully studied by criminologists, which conjured up notions of truly inhuman characters. Murderers such as Manuel Peña Chacaliaza, Lorenzo Machiavello, Enrique Rojas y Cañas, Alejandrino Montes, and Emilio "Carita" (Little Face) Willman, to name only a few, are among those celebrities of the criminal underworld whose careers seemed to epitomize what was most terrifying about Lima's criminals. Chacaliaza, an Indigenous murderer, became famous and, according to various reports, widely feared after he carried out one of the most publicized escapes from the penitentiary.[18] Machiavello, a triple homicide, was the subject of lengthy and at times quite heated discussions among experts seeking to determine his legal and mental status.[19] Rojas y Cañas, who murdered his lover for no apparent reason, was also the focus of attention of criminologists and newspaper reporters.[20] Montes, an indigenous domestic servant who murdered his employers in 1916, was the subject of the most detailed criminological study ever conducted on a single criminal and also received abundant coverage in the daily press.[21] Willman, as we will see below, was one of the true criminal celebrities of his time, even acquiring literary status.

But more often than not, murderers were quite regular people who lived ordinary lives, not the sort of monsters the sensational press and a few criminologists wanted to portray. Most lodgers of the panóptico belonged to the working classes and shared many of the cultural and physical spaces that, as outlined in chapter 2, were common among the popular sectors of Lima. Many of them lived in callejones, frequented taverns, attended *jaranas*, and got into fights for apparently trivial reasons. Many murders were the result of personal disputes, usually turning on the minutiae of daily life; alcohol consumption played a large role, although its effects were probably exaggerated by the perpetrators in an attempt to diminish guilt. Some of the situations leading up to homicide reflect patterns of socialization founded upon profoundly hierarchical and *machista* ideas about how interpersonal relations should be. It was not uncommon to see murders resulting from systematic spousal abuse or despotic behavior toward subordinates (domestic servants, peons, and others). Horizontal forms of violence were also at the basis of many tragic episodes that resulted in the commission of homicides. Violence, after all, as we saw in the introduction, was a central component of social relations in nineteenth- and early twentieth-century Lima. The violent episodes that led to the commission of homicides and ended in penitentiary convictions were usually unpremeditated, but they were not senseless. They resulted from patterns of behavior and mentalities that shaped the lives of large numbers of Peruvians. A few examples drawn from the hundreds of criminal cases will illustrate these patterns.

Take, for instance, the case of Pablo Bambarén, a twenty-nine-year-old mestizo policeman who lived with his common-law wife Victoria Macedo in a callejón of the Plazuela Santo Tomás. According to his testimony, Victoria had developed such a strong devotion to alcohol that he left her and moved out of the callejón. One day in 1911, following a few hours of drinking in a tavern with a fellow police inspector, Pablo went to the police station, picked up his gun, and went on duty. He passed by the callejón where Victoria still lived and saw her drinking in the company of other people. He was invited to stay, and he did so. Shortly afterward, a discussion between Pablo and Victoria began and resulted in two shots being fired at Victoria. She died, and Pablo was sentenced to thirteen years in the penitentiary.[22] Melchor Bustamante, a *zambo* (person of black and indian background) musician born in Lima, was fifty-four years old in 1896. He lived with a woman named Faustina, also known as Cascabel (jingle bell) with whom, according to some testimonies, he administered a brothel in the southern city of Chincha. Because of Melchor's abusive behavior, Faustina decided to leave him and return to Lima. Bustamante apparently came after her, found her, and, when she refused to go back with him, killed her. He managed to escape and was on the run for about two years. Described by police as "a disorderly subject with an unruly character," he was captured in 1898 in Guayaquil, Ecuador, and extradited to Peru. He was convicted to fifteen years in the penitentiary. In fact, this was his second conviction: he had already spent twelve years there.[23] The case of Ambrosio Flores, a fifty-five-year-old farmer and doorkeeper of the Callejón de Camaroneros illustrates a different angle of interpersonal violence among the lower classes of Lima. He intervened in a heated discussion between two residents that ended, according to witnesses, with Flores stabbing one of them. Ambrosio and his defense attorney insisted that the victim was an ex-convict with "bad antecedents," that the witness was prejudiced against him because Ambrosio, as the doorkeeper, did not allow her husband to bring rum into the callejón, and finally, that the death was the result of the victim's provocation. Nevertheless, Ambrosio was sentenced to twelve years in the penitentiary, later reduced to eleven by the Supreme Court.[24] The next case took place in an ambience closer to the criminal underworld. Acam was a forty-eight-year-old Chinese employee at a gambling house in Callao. One night in October 1900, one Manuel Guerrero came to the place to gamble and seemed to be having good luck, winning fourteen *soles*. Acam asked Guerrero to lend him one sol, to which Guerrero responded by punching Acam in the face. Furious, Acam went to the kitchen, grabbed a knife, and killed Guerrero. In spite of the defense's argument that Acam could not be considered a balanced ("ecuánime") person, he was given the death penalty, although the sentence was later reduced to fifteen years at the penitentiary.[25]

A number of penitentiary inmates were agricultural workers in the *chacras* and haciendas of the rural valleys surrounding Lima. Despite their relative distance from the city, these rural inhabitants were not necessarily dissociated from the population of the urban environment. They constituted a multi-ethnic conglomerate of regular and irregular peons and employees, many of whom lived in the *rancherías* of those agricultural estates. Many also worked on their own as woodcutters, traders, and itinerant workers. In September 1869, Pedro Reyes, a fifty-eight-year-old black peon and woodcutter of the Carabayllo hacienda was accused of murdering his fellow black peon Manuel Cárdenas. Reyes asserted that he did not recall what had happened because he had been inebriated that day, but he admitted that the knife used to commit the crime belonged to him. It turned out the apparent cause of the crime was a dispute over two *reales* (ten-cent coins). Although the judge admitted the defender was drunk, he also noted that Pedro had always been "a formal man." Nevertheless, Pedro was sentenced to eleven years in the penitentiary.[26] That same year, in another hacienda of Lima, Pedro Pablo García, a young black peon, killed Cipriano Tenorio, an elderly co-worker. They had been drinking heavily one Sunday after finishing a woodcutting job. Upon returning to the hacienda, they began to engage in some horseplay during which, according to several witnesses, Cipriano threw a handful of sand into García's eyes. García took out a knife and killed him. According to his attorney, García was "in a state of quasi-insanity because of his excessive drinking." He too was sentenced to eleven years in the penitentiary.[27] Another case involved Pablo Alemán, a forty-three-year-old brick-maker who ran a tambo in the Huachipa estate, a few miles outside Lima, where he sold alcohol and food. One evening, the estate's overseer, an army captain named Ismael del Campo, and the local commissary went to drink at the tambo. As they were about to leave, a discussion began between Alemán and del Campo. Alemán took out a knife, stabbed del Campo, and ran off. He was later apprehended. According to the commissary, Alemán had an old quarrel with del Campo, who apparently had once humiliated him, a story that was later confirmed by the estate owner. In order to demonstrate the nature of the murderer, the commissary observed that Alemán had been previously sentenced to eleven years of prison for homicide. Alemán was found guilty and sentenced to fifteen years in the penitentiary.[28]

Biographical sketches of inmates from the interior present similar patterns. Ricardo Carmona lived in Huambocancha, a hacienda in the northern department of Cajamarca. One day in 1904, he claimed, he was violently attacked by a few individuals "of bad antecedents" while he was drinking alcohol after finishing his daily duties. In trying to defend himself, he committed murder, for which he was condemned to nine years at the penitentiary.[29] Aurelio Cueto was, in 1900, a soldier in the Húsares de Junín regiment in Trujillo. A fellow corporal stole money from him, but no action was taken. The corporal kept harassing him and one day even attacked him with a knife: Cueto ended up murdering the corporal, as a result of his "tremendous obfuscation." He was sentenced to twenty years in the penitentiary.[30] Saturnino Fuertes was from Canta, a province near Lima, and spent some time away from home grazing his cattle in the Huampaní estate with his wife and three children. One day in 1898 he was invited to have a few drinks and upon returning home was greeted with insults and other hostile actions by his wife. Quite "obfuscated," he killed her. He was sentenced to fifteen years in the penitentiary.[31]

These stories and the statistics given above show that the Lima penitentiary was used first and foremost to punish a segment of the population that had committed crimes that not only the law but also religion and common judgment defined as serious, if not horrendous and morally appalling. These inmates, however, were not monsters or inhuman characters; in fact, they were all too human. They were the distillation, so to speak, of certain patterns of cultural interaction that were widespread and persistent. Their behavior was not necessarily aberrant in the sense that it was exceptional. After all, abusive and violent behavior also characterized the very institutions of the state such as the police, the army, and the school, which were supposed to instill civilized values among the population. Most inmates came from the lower and working classes, but the penitentiary could not be seen as a penal institution aimed at transforming idle, lazy individuals engaged in a war against property into industrious citizens. Instead, it was meant to segregate and punish individuals expiating "atrocious" crimes and deemed "dangerous" to society.

Although murderers were the subject of the most sensational reports about Lima's criminality and although, understandably, they elicited fear and revulsion among different sectors of the Lima population, they were not the kind of characters commentators usually had in mind when they addressed the criminal question. Instead, two conspicuous criminal types stood out from the community of outlaws and inmates and came to represent the quintessential criminal population of Lima: rateros and faites. Rateros were almost unanimously condemned to occupying a low status, but faites acquired within the criminal underworld and beyond a solid, if ambiguous, reputation for alleged bravery and manliness.

The population of Lima, including police authorities, journalists, criminologists, and the public, commonly saw the ratero as a repugnant, ubiquitous, opportunistic, and recidivist male petty thief who was never punished enough and was essentially irreformable. He did not commit crimes out of necessity but because of his aversion to honest, steady work. He was, in this view, the product not of injustice, poverty, or hunger but of a lack of authority and discipline, at school, at home, and in society at large. The ratero, in addition, owed his career to widespread tolerance from negligent authorities. In October 1892, *La Gaceta Judicial* editorialized about this "plague": "There are very few cities [like Lima] in which this class of criminals abounds, and this is due not only to the ineptitude of the police but, in the first place, to the impunity they enjoy after perpetrating their iniquities." The *intendente*, the paper explained, sent rateros to the judge, who as a rule dismissed the charges because of the pettiness of the crimes, then sent the files to the local judge (*juez de paz*), who in turn released them free of charges.[32] The view of the ratero as an opportunistic, semicowardly criminal also informed the views of prison reform activists like Angela Ramos, who despite the sympathy she felt for prisoners, described the rateros as pathetic figures: "Our local rateros are only capable of telling the *cuento del tío* [the story of the uncle],[33] stealing a few hens, going out and eating without paying, or, the most daring, stealing a purse. Only rarely do we hear about a serious burglary at a department store. This is why our unfortunate thieves constitute only a horde of *harapientos* [men in rags] in our prisons, whose aspect alone generates compassion. . . . Our ratero is a vulgar thief who takes what is out of its place, and that's it."[34] José Gálvez, in his highly romanticized view of Lima's past traditions, added a gendered dimension to the scorn with which rateros were usually depicted:

> True bandits belong to ancient history; today, only rateros remain, usually ridiculous and even effeminate. Yesterday's bandit used to have charm and strength. He was bold and astute. He did not refuse to fight, committed great thefts, was able to sack a house and save a life, and frequently died, with his forehead facing death, from a bullet to his heart, convinced that he had had a splendid and fiercely masculine life. The thief has degenerated into the insignificant job of stealing hens. What appeared then was a crowd of rateros . . . the great robbers disappeared with the increase of police action and general progress.[35]

The generalized impression that rateros enjoyed impunity and were tolerated by the police and judges did, to a certain extent, reflect the low rates of conviction to which I have already referred. It was not the case, however, that police and judges had any sympathy for them; the fact was that they did not have the means for ensuring that every individual accused of *raterías* was to be convicted and sent to prison. In fact, police officers did everything possible to assure that conviction. The *parte policial*, in particular, as we saw in chapter 3, reflected police efforts to convince other authorities of the culpability of the individuals arrested. By labeling an individual as a "very well-known," "recalcitrant," or "professional" ratero the police both justified their own behavior—which usually included, as we have seen, large doses of abuse and arbitrariness—and tried to influence the outcome of any potential trial. This did not per se guarantee conviction, but in numerous cases it helped to condemn the suspect.

Rómulo Calonge, nicknamed Marcolfa, for example, was arrested in July 1897 for an attempted burglary in a house located in the callejón where he lived on Maravillas street. The parte policial stated that Rómulo was "very well known owing to the numerous times he has been sent for the same reason to the Intendencia." Although he denied the accusation, there was a witness, a laundress who lived in the same callejón, who testified she had seen him leaving the crime scene. Her testimony and the parte policial convinced the judge of Rómulo's culpability, and he was sentenced to four years in prison.[36] Aurelio Pinto, a Chilean baker, was caught inside a house in the port of Callao stealing some clothes and other items. The parte policial referred to him as a "recalcitrant ratero" who needed to be sent to a "secure place." He was sentenced to four years in prison.[37] Julián La Rosa was released from prison on January 16, 1899, after serving a five-year conviction. The very next day he went to the chacra Mirones, entered a peon's compartment, and allegedly stole a poncho and a dress. He was apprehended by the owner of the chacra. According to the parte policial, the offender was "an incorrigible delinquent whose case has been filed in the anthropometric department . . . and his card shows repeated recidivism." This was in fact his fourth time in prison. La Rosa, a black peon born in the southern province of Ica, asserted that he was actually celebrating his release from prison(!) that day and was completely drunk, so he could not recall why or how he ended up in the chacra. La Rosa could well have been part of the floating population of peons who used to go from chacra to chacra seeking temporary jobs. From the point of view of authorities and estate owners, though, there was little or no difference between them and certain groups of criminals who plagued the area. Whether the accusation was real or the result of the owner's paranoia is an irresolvable issue. La Rosa went back to prison for another fifty-two months.[38]

Andrés Farfán, a forty-eight-year-old shoemaker born in Piura entered a pawnshop one day in 1902 to reclaim a few items. After he left, he noticed that two police officers had been watching him, and, according to the report, he threw a packet into the river. That was enough for the police to apprehend Farfán, a "very well known thief," and search his house, where they found several items and pawnshop vouchers. Because of his "bad antecedents," the police officers concluded the objects were all stolen, as it was unthinkable that he might lawfully own jewelry or items of gold. The police made their case credible by noting in the parte that Farfán was already "measured and photographed" in the Intendencia and was a recidivist. He admitted to having been in prison four times, but only in two of them as a convict. He was sentenced to forty months in prison.[39] A final example is that of Pedro Aguirre Villar, who was arrested for theft in March 1915. In his parte policial, the police officer stated that "the arrested is the famous and incorrigible ratero known as Chivatito [Little Goat], with whom there is nothing we can do, for he enters this Intendencia on a daily basis for similar occurrences." Aguirre's attorney argued there was no proof against his client. However, a report was requested from Guadalupe, which showed that he had been there five times in the past but had been released all five times with no charges. This time he was also acquitted, but the Superior Court changed the sentence to one year in prison.[40] Again, it was the antecedents of the defender, not the evidence of his culpability, that ultimately decided his fate in the trial.

Rateros became the quintessential character of the Lima criminal world. When authorities or commentators talked about crime in the city, what most of them had in mind was the image of a multitude of rateros getting away with their thefts. The Penal Code of 1862 mandated only brief arrest for thefts under one hundred pesos. That penalty entailed jail time of two to thirty days (*arresto menor*) or forty days to six months (*arresto mayor*). Because rateros could not be held in prison for longer periods, authorities and commentators expressed their exasperation for what they saw as a revolving door that allowed rateros to get away with their crimes. The negative depictions of Guadalupe and the profound disdain these commentators expressed for those held there responded, in part, to the perception that the system did not work, since rateros had a free hand to commit crimes that went almost totally unpunished. According to a reporter, there were inmates who had been incarcerated at Guadalupe as many as eighteen times, so when they were released they simply said, "See you later" and left their possessions and even their place with another inmate, so that when they came back they could recover them. "It could be said that it is the only right these people acquire: the undisputable right to [prison] property." Most inmates, he said, had been in Guadalupe six or more times.[41]

The presence of rateros in Guadalupe, with their high turnover rate and their familiarity with the prison and its written and unwritten rules, served, in addition, as a transmission belt between the outside and the inside worlds. As a result of this constant transit of rateros through the prison yards and departments of Guadalupe, key components of the culture and forms of socialization of certain sectors of the Lima urban poor (jaranas, drinking, gambling, criminal jargon) were reproduced inside the prison, while the subculture of the prison also reverberated in the outside world. It is to be expected that a great deal of the traffic (commercially and culturally speaking) in and out of the prison was carried by these short-term guests of Guadalupe. Hence the image of Guadalupe—with its own callejones, shops, taverns, and gambling spots—as an extension of certain environs of Lima does not appear to be too farfetched.

Guadalupe was also renowned for being home to another particular variety of Lima's criminal underworld: the faite, sometimes also referred to as *matón*. Usually also a thief, the faite was, most distinctively, a fearless, violent, well-trained fighter (from which the term *faite* derived) who lived a semilegal life and was very close to the underworld of prostitution, alcohol, gambling, and other sorts of illegal activities. Many of them, in addition, worked in close proximity to the police as *soplones* (snitches) or agents of the secret police and were frequently recruited to join in fomenting political melees by assaulting voting locations or rival political demonstrations. In Gálvez's version, the faite was a "degenerate and vulgar" criminal with "inferior and denigrating habits," a degeneration of the traditional *palomilla*, or middle-class, decent teenager or young adult who mischievously engaged, generally as part of a larger group, in minor offenses such as throwing stones, stealing valueless things for fun, engaging in highly ritualistic fights between rival gangs, and so forth. For Gálvez, it was difficult to distinguish the faite from the bodyguard, the torturer, or the police informer. "They live a bad life, oscillating between the gloomy corridors of the Intendencia and the sinister yards of the prison."[42] The novelist José Diez Canseco described the world of faites in his stories: "Andrades, Rubios, Espinoza, the whole coarse mob of crooks, bullies, and party-goers. Lords of the blade and the head butt. Rogues and scoundrels of the daily fighting. Buddies of the guitar and pimps. Hidden gamblers in ruined and filthy tenements. Brothels of Chivato, taverns in Tintoreros. Romances at the Descalzos. Tajamar, cockpit for the brawls. Brave men from Abajo el Puente!"[43] Carlos Miró Quesada was more specific in locating the faites in the traditionally black barrio of Malambo: "The man from Malambo was a specialist in fighting; he was into cockfighting, played the guitar, and threw into the air some songs. . . . He exercised in the use of a sharp blade known as *chaveta*, was a good fighter, and threw compliments [*piropos*] to all the girls they came across with. Malambo was and continues to be the expression of the faite who evades the police, commits a theft in the street, and drinks rum at the dirty counter of a cheap canteen. . . . The paper's criminal section is for them [the inhabitants of Malambo] the daily social chronicle of the neighborhood."[44]

Although generally despised, faites could also generate admiration for their valor and bravery.[45] In fact, for some—and not only those belonging to the criminal world—faites were synonymous with manliness and even honor, as we will see below.

The condition of faite was, during the early decades of the twentieth century, almost always associated with black people and black neighborhoods, especially Malambo, thus becoming also a racial in addition to a legal and social marker of identity.[46] Malambo, as the sociologist Luis Tejada has chronicled, was originally a sort of warehouse for newly arrived black slaves during the early colonial period and gradually evolved into a predominantly poor black neighborhood of the city. It developed a reputation for being a hotbed for criminals, *jaraneros* (party-goers and heavy drinkers), and other characters of the Lima underworld. It would eventually become also a working-class neighborhood and develop its own culture of working-class organization and protest. While Malambo's reputation as a crime-infested neighborhood was clearly an exaggeration created by commentators from Lima's decent society, at least some inhabitants of the neighborhood fit the description, and many more sought to capitalize on its reputation. Being a faite from Malambo, it seems fair to suggest, was an asset that helped certain individuals establish themselves as powerful members of the criminal community.[47] Faites and those who wrote about them, constructed their image on the basis of cultural stereotypes that attributed to blacks in general and to the inhabitants of certain neighborhoods in particular both an inclination toward criminal behavior and an innate ability to fight. From a certain perspective this construction of the faite reflects deeply held prejudices and stereotypes, yet one must also consider the extent to which it was also fed by faites themselves: within the criminal underworld, to be considered a true faite almost instantly ascribed to an individual certain qualities that made him respectable. Although this is impossible to document, it may not be too much of a stretch to imagine faites bragging about their skill with a knife or about being from a specific neighborhood (that is, Malambo), both being considered important markers of their reputation as daring criminals.

Inside the prisons, faites stood out and not surprisingly became respected, even feared inhabitants of the prison. The faite was indeed as much a product of the outside criminal underworld as he was of the prison.[48] Faites constituted potential sources of conflict and violence, but they were also important elements within the customary order of the prison, as we will see in chapter 6. Some of them, in fact, became *caporales*, thus acquiring an important degree of authority vis-à-vis inmates and prison officials alike. Precisely because of their ability to stand out in the prison population, they also became important players in the administration of the prison. For authorities, they were ideal intermediaries and, accordingly, were given privileges and positions of command within the inmate population; in return, they became allies of the administration in the maintenance of internal order.

No faite of this period enjoyed a greater reputation than "Carita" Willman and Cipriano "Tirifilo" Moreno, protagonists of one of the most publicized events of the early twentieth-century criminal underworld of Lima: the knife duel they had in May 1915 that ended with the death of Tirifilo. The fight was almost immediately dubbed Duelo de Caballeros (Gentlemen's duel) and was later given literary status in a short story of the same title written by the Peruvian novelist Ciro Alegría, who met Carita at the penitentiary in 1932 while he, Alegría, was being held as a political prisoner.[49] Both Carita and Tirifilo were black residents of Malambo. According to *El Comercio*, Tirifilo was a matón, a bad man, perpetrator of numerous misdeeds, and also a secret police agent.[50] Since at least 1911 Tirifilo had taken part in the repression of political demonstrations as a soplón working for the government's secret police, and according to some reports he was a well-known torturer in Lima's jails. During the electoral campaign of 1912 he was almost killed by a mob supporting the Guillermo Billinghurst candidacy. He was depicted as a "veteran of the [criminal] profession, a terrible man . . . without conscience, always certain he could impose his will on everybody, authorities included, with his misdeeds proper of a brave man." He had "brutal manners" and "low instincts," as a result of which he made a lot of enemies, one of whom was Willman. After being killed by Carita, he became the subject of popular verses and songs that depicted him as both a brave and a cruel man.[51] Carita, on the other hand, was much younger and less experienced than Tirifilo, although *El Comercio* editorialized that "his soul [was] well prepared for the fight and the scandal." The mere fact that he dared to challenge Tirifilo was bound to boost his status and even generate admiration.

There are different versions as to what exactly provoked the duel. According to *El Comercio*, the two men's enmity stemmed from a dispute at a brothel over a woman's favors. After a discussion that had no apparent consequences, Tirifilo used his connections with the police to send Carita to prison, something Carita would not easily forget. Some time later, Carita challenged Tirifilo to a fight in the Tajamar area. Tirifilo, confident in his abilities with the knife, replied, "Okay, but hurry up because I have to go somewhere."[52] Alegría's version, based on his recollection of Carita's rendering of the fight, was very different. Tirifilo went to Carita's house to try to convince him to collaborate with him on a "job." Carita was not at home, his mother told Tirifilo, who responded by hurling insults at both Carita and his mother. Upon hearing this story, Carita became furious, went to Tirifilo's house, and challenged him to fight that night. Tirifilo responded, "I'll be there."[53]

The fight was incredibly fierce and bloody, with both fighters receiving multiple injuries. Although Tirifilo was a much more experienced fighter, Carita had the advantage of his feline agility. The duel was witnessed by scores of other criminals from Malambo, who saw in disbelief how Tirifilo, upon receiving a precise stab in the chest, fell to the ground dead. The death of Tirifilo was sensational news throughout Lima. A crowd of about two hundred incredulous people gathered outside the morgue to "confirm with their own eyes" that Tirifilo was dead.[54] "A new popular hero had been born," wrote Alegría. Carita had not only challenged and defeated the dreadful Tirifilo: he had done so in defense of his honor and that of his mother and in the way gentlemen usually did it, in a duel. "The soul of the people vibrated," wrote Alegría, and songs and poems were reportedly written celebrating Carita's triumph.[55] Afterward, Carita was caught by the police and taken to the hospital and then to prison. Interviewed at the hospital by José Carlos Mariátegui, the future Marxist ideologist and then young journalist, Willman defined himself as a formal man who did not want to be taken as a vagrant or a "bad man." He did make clear, however, that he was not a coward and that he had been ready to die in the fight.[56] Willman was sent to Guadalupe before being transferred later to the penitentiary and then, surprisingly, pardoned in December 1918.[57]

These two "heroes of the blade," as Mariátegui called them, epitomized the faite and fulfilled the expectations of courage and bravery attached to the faite condition. They also exemplify ways of understanding honor among the lower classes of Lima, which included the observance of rules of proper behavior and unwritten laws of respectability within the criminal underworld. Honor was certainly at the center of their dispute, and it encompassed loyalty to certain principles. Carita knew he could die but went ahead with the challenge in defense of his honor. Tirifilo could have rejected the challenge, but doing so would have been an act of cowardice. Their fight resembles the logic behind elite duels, whose main foundation was always the defense of one's reputation and the willingness to die in that endeavor. According to Alegría, even the courts considered "the brawl between a Negro and a Mulatto a clear question of honor."[58] Rivalry and vengeance were also key elements in this episode: in the end, it was a dispute over power, for the place as the most feared faite.

This episode is revealing of some of the ways in which masculinity was constructed among different sectors of the urban poor. Manliness was associated with all the qualities of a good faite. While Carita told Mariátegui he was a formal man, that is, a man of principles, rectitude, and honor, Tirifilo could have said he died like a real man. Not only bravery, but also respect for certain rules was at the bottom of this understanding of manliness, one that shared certain ingredients with elite definitions of honor and masculinity. That some faites were admired by members of the literate classes further highlights these shared perceptions about how a man should behave. As in other social realms, notions of masculinity were the foundation on which to construct and hold power in the criminal underworld. Hierarchies of power and prestige were built, as we will see in chapter 7, on the basis of gendered and racialized dichotomies such as the manly, black faite versus the effeminate, sly ratero.

LIMA'S VAGRANTS: CRIMINALS OR SLAVES?

Vagrancy, as I noted in chapter 1, was always considered a serious social problem, and attempts to curtail it generally produced meager results. Vagrants were the usual residents of Lima's jails, but except for the few hours or days they spent locked up, they wandered the streets. The army and navy became at times destinations for dozens, maybe hundreds, of vagrants, a government strategy that drew criticism because it allegedly brought the "scum" of society into the institutions that were supposed to protect the highest interests of the fatherland. By far the harshest and most comprehensive vagrancy law was enacted on January 18, 1924, by the Leguía administration.[59] The law defined a vagrant as somebody who, "lacking properties and income, does not exercise a profession, trade, or occupation; does not have employment, destination, industry, or licit occupation, nor another legitimate or known means of subsistence; or who pretending to have them, lacks a domicile; or who, having as his or

her own that of a different person, lives out of the tolerance, compla-
cency, suggestion, subjection, abuse, or exploitation of the latter." Other
categories included were parolees who failed to report to the authorities,
habitual gamblers and drunkards, and unregistered prostitutes. Vagrants
were to be punished with prison terms and forced labor for periods
between thirty days and five years, depending on the circumstances and
their degree of recidivism. Former prisoners who failed to secure an
occupation during the six months following their release were also subject to a penalty of one year of forced labor. Although the law was not
explicit about where those vagrants were going to be incarcerated, El
Frontón became the preferred destination for them. Hundreds of so-
called vagrants were sent there every year.

Suspects were first evaluated by a *Junta Calificadora* functioning at the
Intendencia de Policía, which, if it found the subjects merited conviction,
sent the cases to the political authority, the *prefecto*. The prefecto would
then order the incarceration of the vagrant at El Frontón or some local
jail. As a result of Angela Ramos's campaign against the highly abusive
methods used by police authorities, the procedures for evaluating vagrant
suspects were later changed. On March 6, 1928, the government made the
calificación a public event and placed jurisdiction in the hands of a jury,
not the prefect. In addition, suspects were given the right to a defense
attorney, although Ramos observed that the public defenders assigned to
these cases tended to act instead as "another prosecutor."[60] In a clear
violation of their constitutional rights, vagrants were not allowed to use
the writ of habeas corpus to appeal their arrest or the penalty imposed
upon them. The de facto judicial prerogatives accorded to the police,
although criticized by activists like Ramos and Mariátegui, were deemed
necessary by police authorities, for "they [policemen] live closer to the
suspects of vagrancy, they are the ones that are well informed about their
maneuvers, can follow them, and can form, thanks to this continual
observation, a precise idea about the dangerousness of the supposed
vagrant."[61]

The outcome of this campaign against vagrancy was a large-scale, quite
exploitative experiment with forced labor. Leguía's vigorous program of
public works—street paving, public buildings, housing for working-class
families, and so forth—required abundant cheap labor. One way of procuring such labor was to sentence vagrants to perform public works or, in
the case of those sent to El Frontón, to work in the *canteras* (quarries)

manufacturing stone blocks. In Lima, vagrants were put to work on projects like road building and marketplace construction as well as in street and ditch cleaning. Ramos wrote, "As the need for ornateness and hygiene in Lima grows, so does the number of vagrants."[62] Hundreds of so-called vagrants were also sent to the Amazon region to a sort of penal colony near the Perené River, where they built roads under horrendous conditions.[63]

The vagrancy law has been correctly considered a "slavery law" by another name.[64] It invites comparison with the infamous Road Conscription law, also enacted by Leguía, which forced all male citizens between the ages of eighteen and sixty to work from six to twelve days per year, depending on the age of the individual, in road construction or repair. This law became a source of exploitation and abuse mostly of the indigenous population and reinforced existing social and racial hierarchies: it exempted, for instance, men who were willing to pay a monetary "redemption" or who were able to send somebody to replace them, usually a peon or some other social subordinate.[65] Both the vagrancy and the road conscription laws underline the exclusionary, highly exploitative nature of the modernization process on which the Leguía administration embarked. The so-called vagrants and the indigenous peoples being forcefully recruited to work in road construction had virtually no legal rights. Arbitrariness and abuse reached dimensions comparable to those of black slavery, Chinese servitude, and the exploitation of Indian labor under *gamonalismo*.

During the first six months after the law was passed, 286 individuals were investigated, of whom 218 were condemned as vagrants.[66] Information on the vagrant population sent to El Frontón during the period between April 14, 1926, and July 31, 1927,[67] reveals that a total of 119 convicted vagrants were consigned to the island for periods of 18 months to 2 years.[68] More than half (68) were sentenced to 1 year, about 25 percent (38) to 6 months, and the rest to various terms. Of the 119 convicts, 30 were sent by the Prefectura of Lima and 89 by that of El Callao. They were accused of diverse crimes in addition to their condition of vagrants—however, as is evident, they had not faced trial, and the accusations were generally vague (15 were "malefactors," 15 had "bad habits," 3 were "pernicious foreigners"). Though convicted of vagrancy, they were still able to profess to having an occupation: 23 were *jornaleros*, 20 artisans, 18 seamen, 16 dockworkers, 12 fishermen; 26 did not declare an occupation.[69]

Most occupations they cited had a seasonal or temporary character, which may indicate that instead of being vagrants these individuals, or at least some of them, were workers forced into temporary idleness by fluctuations in the job market. Ramos, among others, denounced the high numbers of vagrants in Lima, declaring they were the result of official interest in fabricating them: police agents were paid "by the piece," so they took to the streets, arrested as many people as they could, and even destroyed their work certificates in order to charge them with not having proof of employment.[70] Individuals with supposedly criminal antecedents were the main targets of this campaign.

One such victim was Enrique Ortiz, a former Guadalupe inmate who, after serving a thirty-month prison sentence began work as a shoemaker in Callao. He ran his own shop and hired three workers, including Félix Zamudio, a former penitentiary inmate. On February 15, 1928, all four were arrested by the police at their workplace and sent to jail, charged with vagrancy. They were put to work in the construction of new residences in Malambo.[71] Another case was that of Juan Zapata, a thirty-four-year-old shoemaker from Camaná who admitted he could not always earn enough to make a living. He contended that when he ran out of money he survived by pawning a few items of his personal property. He was detained during a popular riot against the police and, because of his antecedents, was considered a vagrant. According to the authority in charge, he ought to be put "in a place where he can work in public works, as a means to achieve his moral regeneration and [his acquiring of] industrious habits." He was sentenced to twelve months at El Frontón.[72]

The records of the DGP contain numerous arrest orders for vagrants sent to El Frontón. Regrettably, the information they contain is very sketchy, being limited to names and aliases. The inclusion of the alias reveals a conscious effort by police to convey the notion that they were in fact criminals or at least persons of dubious antecedents, as they used to say.

Although vagrants were only temporary residents of Lima's institutions of confinement, their case is important, for it reveals the explicitly utilitarian uses of punishment and the totally arbitrary implementation of legal mandates by a government that, in theory, was striving to modernize Peruvian society. So-called vagrants belonged to the most vulnerable sectors of the Lima population, precisely those segments that had been criminalized not only in legal and political discourse but also by daily police action. They were deprived of their fundamental rights and forced to perform harsh labor to realize the dreams of modernizing elites. Despite the efforts of advocates like Ramos and Mariátegui, abuses against vagrants continued for the rest of the Leguía administration and beyond.

DISGRACED GENTLEMEN: POLITICAL PRISONERS

A final category of inmates, indeed the most sui generis, is political prisoners. Political prisoners did not belong to the criminal world, but they did belong to the world of the prison. The category political prisoner was in itself very imprecise. During the period under discussion in this book, it encompassed a variety of inmates, including participants in military insurrections, members of opposition parties, workers involved in strikes, and members of recently overthrown regimes. Some were imprisoned for brief periods while others got lengthy sentences or endured long-term illegal incarceration. The Penal Codes of both 1862 and 1924 established a variety of political crimes, including rebellion, plotting, mutiny, riot, disobedience of the authority, crimes against the constitution, and crimes against the right to vote. Punishment for those crimes included prison terms of various lengths, expatriation, and, in the case of state employees, disqualification from public office. Most political prisoners were not put on trial. Depending on a variety of circumstances—their political influence or position, their social status, their personal connections with government officials, and the actual number of political prisoners—they were sent to the penitentiary, the penal island of El Frontón, San Lorenzo island, the Casasmatas jail, the Intendencia de Lima, or, later, the ccv and the El Sexto prison. Other police and military stations were also occasionally used to hold political prisoners. It is impossible to offer even approximate figures of the extent of political imprisonment because records are very sketchy, largely because of the extrajudicial character of most of those incarcerations. While some were convicted at trial, most were illegally detained and incarcerated.

As recent studies have shown, although political power was controlled by coalitions of members of the upper classes, including *gamonales*, merchants, coastal planters, urban professionals, and military officers, subaltern groups were not absent from political struggles. They participated in riots, mutinies, and *montoneras* (irregular armed forces) and in the numerous informal armies competing for power in the various civil wars that erupted throughout the nineteenth century.[73] As a result, the ranks of political prisoners were filled with individuals not only whose social backgrounds, regional origins, and political affiliations differed, but whose legal status and treatment were also diverse. Although random lists of political prisoners are found in the documentation, very few details are known about their fates inside the prisons, their relationship with other inmates, or the treatment they received. In the late nineteenth century and early twentieth, when the press reported on political prisoners, they would typically include only upper-class participants of failed conspiracies or members of outgoing administrations.[74] The documentation about political prisoners is, not surprisingly, much richer for the period after 1919 because in that period not only did political repression increase, but also record keeping became more consistent. By then, political repression had begun to hit hard not simply members of opposition parties, but labor leaders and anarchist workers. The labor movement was becoming an important political actor and working-class forms of protest and confrontation were answered with repression and imprisonment.[75]

In the aftermath of the coup that brought Leguía to power, numerous members of the deposed administration were imprisoned, including President Pardo himself, who was confined in the panóptico. On various occasions between 1919 and 1921 the Leguía administration sent numerous journalists and political opponents to prison on allegations of conspiracy.[76] Repression increased after 1923. At different times, dozens, maybe hundreds, of labor activists and members of opposition parties and groups were imprisoned.[77] Some of them spent a few days in confinement, others several years.

San Lorenzo island, a few miles offshore from El Callao, became a major destination for political prisoners. According to the historian Jorge Basadre, it was Leguía's cousin, Minister of Government Germán Leguía y Martínez, who opened San Lorenzo in 1921 for the detention of political prisoners.[78] The buildings that were constructed to quarantine passengers arriving at the port of Callao began to be used to accommodate political prisoners. According to the writer Abelardo Solís, San Lorenzo became "an *hacienda*, a big business," and prisoners were "sort of cattle, whose number had to be increased with further detentions and kept imprisoned at any cost."[79] In addition to San Lorenzo, the government also used the penitentiary, Guadalupe, the ccv, El Frontón, and, after

1928, the yet-to-be-completed El Sexto prison. Workers and activists from different parts of the country were also sent to Tequile Island, in the Andean department of Puno.

As Basadre put it, Leguía sent to prison "the great *señores* of the highest economic aristocracy as well as young students and modest workers."[80] Labor leaders, university students, and anarchist and socialist activists suffered repression. Dozens were also sent into exile. Víctor Raúl Haya de la Torre, president of the students' federation and future leader of APRA (Alianza Popular Revolucionaria Americana), was jailed and sent to San Lorenzo in October 1923 in the aftermath of protests in May of that year against the consecration of Peru to the Sacred Heart.[81] Also in October 1923, Leguía y Martínez and numerous members of his clique were imprisoned at San Lorenzo.[82] Among the most noted cases of political repression was the "Communist conspiracy" that involved Mariátegui and his closest circle of friends and collaborators. Up to 40 of them were sent to San Lorenzo in June 1927, including the young Basadre. In November 1929, another wave of repression against radical intellectuals and activists put Mariátegui under house arrest and up to 180 persons in prison.[83]

After Leguía's fall in 1930, the political scenario became much more convulsed. The Aprista party lost the election of 1931 to Luis M. Sánchez Cerro and, accusing him of fraud, stepped up its sometimes violent opposition, while the government increased its repression. In March 1932, President Sánchez Cerro survived an assassination attempt by a young Aprista militant, José Melgar, as a result of which both Melgar and Juan Seoane, an Aprista lawyer and the owner of the pistol used in the attack, were thrown into prison, tried, and sentenced to death. Later, the sentence was commuted to twenty-five years in the panóptico.[84] In May of the same year Haya de la Torre was also detained in the panóptico and kept there for fifteen months. In July 1932, an Aprista insurrection in Trujillo left hundreds of Apristas dead or in prison and numerous army officers assassinated. A wave of anti-Aprista repression swept the country. In April 1933, a young Aprista militant assassinated Sánchez Cerro, making the division between APRA and the army even more bitter. Political imprisonment reached greater dimensions, its targets being mostly members of the middle, professional, and working classes, many of whom came from provincial backgrounds. Although most were Apristas, repression also hit Communist and labor activists.

Except for the Ley de Represión (Law of repression) enacted in November 1889, which stipulated that political crimes ought to be treated and punished in the same manner as any other crime—a legal approach that did not last long—political prisoners were always treated in the criminal law codes, by the courts, and inside the prisons as belonging to a community of offenders that was fundamentally different from common criminals.[85] A law of 1859 mandated that in defense of "the nation's decorum and the honor of citizens," the "degrading custom" of locking political prisoners up along with common criminals had to be terminated.[86] Accordingly, they had to be held in different buildings, a prescription that could not be satisfied since there were no special buildings to be used for that purpose.[87] The solution arrived at was to accommodate political prisoners on different floors, in different rooms, and in different pavilions inside the prisons they were sent to, so as to keep them physically separated from common criminals. At the penitentiary, for instance, the department for political prisoners was, in 1914, a forty-eight-square-meter room with little air and light located near the prison entrance.[88] Years later, other areas of the penitentiary like the administrative offices and classrooms would also be used to hold political prisoners. At El Frontón political prisoners occupied an entirely separate building. At Guadalupe they were kept in a special room. The rationale for these regulations and practices was the notion that social and cultural, not just legal, differences distinguished political from common criminals, a perception that was almost unanimously endorsed. *Variedades* summarized this view: "A revolutionary, a partisan [*faccioso*] can never be equated with a vulgar criminal, not even by the government, and this is the reason why, in one way or another, they are granted considerations: even when condemned to the stocks, political prisoners would not constitute, in the public concept, just 'numbers,' but disgraced gentlemen."[89]

Political prisoners, including those belonging to radical or leftist parties, always felt they had little in common with most common inmates. They belonged to different social worlds, even in the case of working-class political prisoners. Partly because of social and cultural prejudices and partly because of their desire to get the recognition and the treatment they thought they deserved, political prisoners almost always demanded to be kept at a physical distance from the other inmates. Although there was room for individual relationships of friendship and camaraderie, albeit not without hierarchical overtones, political prisoners always tried quite consciously to maintain strict separation. More often than not they felt alienated by the habits, language, and even physical appearance of common criminals. They looked on them with a mixture of abhorrence, aloofness, and commiseration and thus could not avoid revealing deeply ingrained racial stereotypes, which in some cases demonstrate their familiarity with notions of organic deformities and personal hygiene as revealing of a criminal or quasi-criminal complexity. The Aprista lawyer and writer Seoane, for example, offered numerous physical descriptions of common prisoners in his novel and testimony *Hombres y rejas*, including this collective portrait of penitentiary inmates that closely resembles a physiognomic depiction of Lombrosian characters:

> Hermetic Indians, impenetrable Chinese, eyes with a resigned look, loudmouthed criollos, expressions of anguish, firm looks, baleful gestures, faces plunged in pain, prognathic criminals, obscene zambos, severe men, a venerable black man. Traces of vices, syphilitic noses, bloodshot eyes, epileptic pupils, faces eaten by *uta* (leishmaniasis), yellowness from malaria, contractions of the mentally insane, haggardness from tuberculosis, asymmetries, the violent profile of the hypersexual, disheveled heads, gloomy faces. . . . Vice, pain, indifference, evilness and perversion, rancor and hatred, and bitterness, and sadness.[90]

It would be hard to exaggerate the sharp contrast prison life represented for most political prisoners when compared to their life at home, their usual habits and surroundings. Seoane described how his cultural habits, formed in decent schools and "petit bourgeois" homes, clashed with the realities of prison.[91] On the basis of the almost universal perception of their status as being that of noncriminal individuals who belong to decent society—and, as such, deserving of different treatment—and thanks to their personal connections with state authorities, political prisoners usually, although not always, received better treatment than common criminals. Some of these privileges, including relatively comfortable accommodations, visitation rights, and decent food, were in fact mandated by law for all inmates, but given the conditions of Peruvian prisons they were generally seen as resulting from special consideration. The special treatment of political prisoners was visible even in the way they were addressed. Guards, employees, common inmates, prison authorities, and also the press called them Don, Doctor, or Señor, the usual signs of respect accorded to social superiors in Lima.[92] During the Aristocratic Republic, upper-class political prisoners were allowed to receive visits and enjoyed a considerable degree of comfort.[93] On at least one occasion, a political rally was allowed inside the panóptico.[94] A reporter for *Variedades* visited a group of political inmates incarcerated after the liberal conspiracy of May 1908 against President Leguía and told his readers that "*los señores presos* [the Messrs prisoners] enjoy freedom and comfort."[95] And then, with obvious sarcasm, he mentioned all the celebrities he had seen: "Don Carlos de Piérola shows up for a minute with a meditative look. Colonel Tirado . . . appears briefly behind the gate. Don José Carlos Bernales yawns on a bench, with a closed book between his hands; he reveals a bit of indignation. Don Pedro de Osma gallantly stamps his heels while heading to the living room. The honorable Del Valle, the honorable Cornejo, with a forested beard, Colonel Lanfranco, with his hair dotted with white locks [*mechones*]. Isaías de Piérola, calm and ironic, vigorous and fattening. I've seen them all."[96] Several group pictures of political prisoners showed them to be very well dressed, clean, shaven, and assuming the same posture they would have if the picture had been taken at their homes or studios.[97]

During the *oncenio*, special considerations for political prisoners, although clearly diminished, appear from time to time in testimonies and archival documents. In the late 1920s, for example, the Intendencia paid a private supplier (the Hotel Comercio) to deliver food to political prisoners at both the penitentiary and the Intendencia.[98] While at El Frontón, Basadre, through personal connections, managed to have his family send him food and books, which made his days "shorter and more interesting." Later, again thanks to personal contacts, he was transferred to a much more comfortable "first-class" single room in a special pavilion, where he joined, among others, the *indigenista* writer Hildebrando Castro Pozo. His room was cleaned by prison personnel, and he was served breakfast, lunch, and dinner. Although being in prison was certainly quite a torment nonetheless—especially, says Basadre, at nighttime, when the lights of Callao came on as a "symbol of life [and] freedom"—his situation was clearly much more comfortable than that of most common prisoners.[99]

Political prisoners may seem to have been privileged when compared to common criminals, but they still faced a hostile environment. On countless occasions they were subjected to psychological torment and physical torture, although the degree to which they were mistreated varied widely over time and from one case to the next. Treatment of political prisoners worsened visibly during the *oncenio* and became even more harsh during the 1930s, when members of radical political parties, workers' unions, and leftist organizations filled the prisons of dictatorial regimes.

One of the most humiliating forms of punishment political prisoners endured was to be forced to share the same physical space with common criminals. According to a report written in 1934 by Carlos Alberto Izaguirre, when the authorities of El Sexto wanted to punish political prisoners, they were forced to share their cells with vagrants and were actually treated as such. Don Samuel González Montero, for instance, a worker accused of being a social agitator, was later labeled a vagrant by prison authorities. Other political prisoners, reported Izaguirre, were held in the *calabozos* (dungeons) of the Intendencia, where they shared space with rateros and vagrants and were subjected to humiliating treatment, including the frequent flooding of the space, which forced inmates to sleep over a wet floor. Bad food, frequent insults, and other degrading aspects of the detention infuriated the reporter.[100] Luis Felipe de las Casas, an Aprista leader imprisoned in 1934 after a failed conspiracy against the government, was taken to the Intendencia and locked in one of the calabozos along with a multitude of common criminals. He and the other political inmates protested and started a hunger strike, demanding they be transferred to the area for political prisoners. They found it offensive to be lumped together with "two types of rodents [rats and rateros], each more repugnant than the other," a situation Las Casas deemed degrading given their status as "decent individuals and political prisoners."[101]

Another common form of punishment was solitary confinement. Prisoners were forced to stay in their cells for lengthy periods without being allowed to see natural light or take fresh air. Seoane and Melgar, the two Apristas accused of the assassination attempt against Sánchez Cerro, were isolated for an entire year.[102] At the penitentiary, a cell called *la aislada* was used to isolate prisoners for days, weeks, and even months. Haya de la Torre spent more than eight months of solitary confinement in his cell in the panóptico, unable even to confer with his lawyers.[103] He commented later on the conditions of his imprisonment: "Even the lion at the zoo enjoys better conditions of seclusion. He has air, sun, and his female companion."[104] At El Frontón, as we saw, the *lobera* and the *parada* were widely used. Jorge García Mendizabal, a political inmate who tried to escape from the penitentiary in May 1936, was caught by guards and placed in the aislada for two weeks, then sent to solitary confinement for a month. Later he was transferred to El Frontón, where he was immediately placed in the parada, "from which he was not taken out until the swelling reached his thighs and made it impossible for him to walk." Then he was locked in the lobera for several months with no bed, light, or cigarettes.[105] Instruments of torture like the *barra* and the *cepo volador* that were used on common criminals were also used on political prisoners.

The presence of political prisoners in Lima's prisons was to have an important effect on the internal order of those institutions, on the relationship between authorities and common criminals, and on the development of certain forms of cooperation between political and common criminals. It also added to the complexity and diversity of the community of human beings who occupied the cells and compartments of Lima's prisons. Prisoner, then, as we have seen, was a category that encompassed persons from quite diverse social, racial, regional, legal, and political backgrounds, and as a result inmates had to learn not only how to cope with the prison environment and its (written and unwritten) rules but also how to forge human relationships with other inmates. Making such adjustments brought into play highly complex interactions, tensions, and mutual forms of negotiation and accommodation.

PART THREE

THE WORLD THEY MADE TOGETHER

6

DAILY LIFE IN PRISON—I:

THE CUSTOMARY ORDER

Inmates at the famous Elmira Reformatory in New York, according to the historian Alexander Pisciotta, "had a clear choice: total submission or severe corporal punishment."[1] If this depiction is correct (and I'm not sure it is), prisoners at Elmira had become victims of a despotic regime that left them no alternative other than complete obedience and submissiveness. Obeying prison rules would have been the only means prisoners had of coping with their conditions of confinement and avoiding the most extreme forms of brutality. But the radical dilemma prisoners at Elmira apparently faced does not seem to be what most prisoners in other parts of the world and in other periods of history have had to confront. In fact, there is an extensive literature that shows that even under very severe prison regimes inmates have always been able to challenge, with varying degrees of success, the imposition of a rigid prison order; they do so either by manipulating the inevitable weaknesses in the administration of prisons or by creating their own, proactive forms of resistance and accommodation.[2] The case of Lima's prisons, as we will see in this chapter, confirms this pattern. What emerges from my review of daily life inside Lima's prisons is a rich and complex scenario in which prisoners displayed a variety of strategies in their attempt to cope with the realities of incarceration. In doing so they avoided some of the most inhumane aspects of prison life and decisively helped shape the world of the prison.

Besides the rare occasions on which prisoners openly challenged the prison order, in the form of escapes and riots, for instance, most of their efforts reflect a strategy of accommodation rather than open confrontation, a strategy whereby they took as much advantage as possible of the prison administration's flaws. Prisoners engaged in types of relations that contributed to the building of a different type of order, not the one prescribed in the prison bylaws, but one resulting from the series of negotiations, transactions, and mutual accommodations between inmates and prison officials and guards. I call this alternative pattern the "customary order" of the prison. Order in Lima's prisons, understood as continual operation with the minimum disruption possible, was generally maintained less by absolute coercion or despotism on the part of prison officials than by a mixture of control and tolerance, abuse and negotiation, the infliction of suffering and the allocation of small concessions. The practice of this regime included, as a central component, the establishment of widespread illegal and informal relationships between inmates and prison staff. It is worth emphasizing that this order did not render inoperative the severe mechanisms of coercion and control that greatly constrained prisoners' lives. Any betterment prisoners gained in terms of their living conditions or bargaining power was always fragile and provisional, revealing of the intrinsic vulnerability of their condition.

If the general principle outlined above seems to have worked in all three of the prisons discussed here—the penitentiary, Guadalupe, and El Frontón—it did so to different degrees. At El Frontón, with its plantation-like regime and much more exploitative labor structure, both the threat of coercion and brutality and the need to employ them were always present, and so room for negotiation was smaller than in the other prisons. At Guadalupe, the extraction of labor from prisoners was never a pressing issue, and the authorities, facing overcrowding and the lack of adequate infrastructure to impose a more despotic regime, realized that tensions would be alleviated if they showed leniency and tolerance toward the inmates' management of their time, money, and personal relations. Permissiveness was usually accompanied by a sort of hands-off approach: the greater the degree of autonomy prisoners were allowed, the less prison authorities felt compelled to attend to prisoners' material needs. At Guadalupe, intervention into the lives of prisoners was not as oppressive as at the other two prisons. At the penitentiary, on the other hand, much greater degrees of regimentation are found; inmates there enjoyed less autonomy than those of Guadalupe but did not suffer the extent of arbitrary despotism found at El Frontón. Clearly, these variations are not always evident or meaningful: little difference may exist between being secluded in a *calabozo* or being tortured at any of the three prisons. But excessive punishment was the exception, not the rule, for more often than not inmates sought accommodation, not confrontation.

The disciplinary regime prison authorities and penologists tried to enforce in the prisons and jails of Lima, and particularly at the penitentiary, was always subverted by the various widespread forms of partnership and complicity between prison personnel, including employees, guards, and even higher authorities, and the inmates. This customary order included varying degrees of violation of the written norms. Some of them were almost never questioned, while others were more volatile and contingent upon specific individuals or circumstances. Mutual economic interest was the foundation, and it dominated the forms and extension of this partnership; but economic gain led to, and was intimately linked with, the negotiation of power boundaries inside the prison. Poorly paid, inadequately trained, and not entirely committed to the cause of the reform of the prisoner, prison employees found in these illegal arrangements some compensation for their otherwise unrewarding job. According to several testimonies, prison employees were frequently recruited from within a population of dubious antecedents, if not in fact from the criminal underworld.[3] Limited financial resources forced prison authorities to use a common practice in the recruitment of white-collar employees for governmental positions, that is, the hiring of *meritorios*.[4] Not being on the regular payroll and confronting an unstable economic situation, they tried to benefit as much as possible from their relationship with inmates. In October 1901, for example, the presence of meritorios was denounced as "a constant perturbation of the penitentiary regime," for they were usually "corrupted" by the prisoners who, through gifts (*dádivas*), were able to get from them "illegal services."[5] These relationships offered inmates the opportunity to access a variety of goods, services, and privileges that would have been inaccessible to them if the bylaws had been enforced by uncompromising employees. Meritorios and other civil employees were not the only ones involved in these practices, for very frequently soldiers and policemen in charge of the custody of prisons and even higher authorities entered into these arrangements.

The most persistent of these forms of partnership was illegal trafficking in alcohol and coca inside the prisons. Both were widely consumed by the prison populations, although coca was more commonly associated with indigenous prisoners. In August 1870, for example, the director of the penitentiary arrived at the "sad conclusion" that it was the employees themselves who supplied alcoholic beverages to the prisoners.[6] Two meritorios were caught, in January 1876, bringing in alcohol for the inmates.[7] There were also cases of soldiers trafficking in coca and alcohol in the penitentiary.[8] In January 1927, seven guards were caught supplying coca to the prisoners. After 1928, soldiers began to smuggle coca and alcohol between the penitentiary and the CCV.[9] In June 1929, the penitentiary inmate Antonio Llamo was caught with two big packages of coca which, according to the report, "could not have entered the prison without being noticed by the doorkeepers." It turned out that it was the chauffeur of the prison director who was selling coca and alcohol to the inmates.[10] Coca, in fact, was at times openly sold at the *cantina* or *oficina de auxilios* (prison canteen) of the penitentiary, a practice clearly condoned by the authorities despite the fact that the *Reglamento* prohibited it.[11] Inmates also consumed an alcoholic beverage known as *chicha* or *fresco* that could not have been prepared and consumed without the complicity of prison personnel.[12] Prison employees and guards not only introduced alcohol and coca but also consumed them, sometimes in the company of inmates with whom they had developed friendships or formed partnerships. In April 1892, for example, a guard introduced rum and coca to the penitentiary, unlocked a group of inmates, and spent the night drinking and chewing with them.[13] On November 5, 1877, *El Comercio* complained about the numerous *jaranas* that took place both outside and inside the Guadalupe prison. "The prison is not a place for diversion, but for correction," the paper thought it had to remind state authorities. One soldier in charge of policing the street in front of the prison got so drunk he lost his rifle and ended up sleeping in the street. "What a police! What a police! What a police!" lamented the paper.[14] One day in 1881 three guards of the Guadalupe prison did not show up for work because, the warden realized, they had been arrested for inebriation. The situation forced him to use two trustworthy inmates as doorkeepers.[15]

Partnerships between prisoners and prison staff involved many other activities besides the illegal trading and consuming of alcohol and coca. Prison employees served as intermediaries in various legal and illegal errands that inmates needed to undertake, such as negotiations with outside contractors and the writing and delivery of legal documents.

Inmates from the interior especially, who did not have relatives or friends in Lima and who, in many cases, did not have a good command of the Spanish language, often availed themselves of the secretarial services. On the illegal side, inmates bribed authorities for a variety of favors, including sometimes even pardon or release.[16] When prisoners needed to acquire items from outside, for example, they used so-called *canasteros*, employees who, generally in exchange for a commission or some favor, agreed to provide different sorts of goods for the inmates.[17] At Guadalupe, prisoners were sometimes allowed to walk outside the prison for short periods.[18] Cash loans between prisoners or, more frequently, from prisoners to employees were also very common. The fact that it was inmates who generally lent money to employees must be viewed as an important source of leverage prisoners had to extract concessions and favors. While they could be critical for overcoming emergency situations, these transactions frequently generated conflictive and even violent confrontations between lenders and borrowers.[19] In 1892, such financial dealing prompted an investigation into the custom of penitentiary employees borrowing money from prisoners. According to the director, "the circumstance of becoming a debtor of a prisoner obliterates all the authority an employee could have over the inmate, and makes him unworthy of the confidence the institution has placed in him."[20] The practice, however, was never halted. A list submitted to the director of the penitentiary in 1925 included four employees who owed a total of almost fourteen *libras* (pounds) to various inmates. One employee owed money to four prisoners.[21] At El Frontón, the inmate Martín Saniz filed a complaint against a number of employees who owed him a total of three hundred *soles*. Although he was accused of being mentally ill and was later transferred to the penitentiary and isolated in the underground dungeons, Saniz doggedly fought his case and was able to get his money back. The last payment came in 1935 from none other than the widow of Adán del Río, the former director of El Frontón, who had borrowed money from Martín when he was an inmate on the penal island.[22]

The existence of a cash economy inside prisons forms the backdrop of this widespread practice of borrowing and lending money. A thriving underground economy existed in these institutions, and it involved both inmates and prison employees. There was always an unstoppable trafficking in products like coca, alcohol, cigarettes, and candles, but there were also sexual and other types of services. Inmates also made money from the

jobs they performed in prison workshops or by working for private contractors, as we will see below. In addition, there were forms of entrepreneurship that allowed some inmates, usually those in positions of power
and authority, to significantly increase their earnings. One of the most
common businesses in Lima's prisons was chicken farming, an activity
that involved employees, inmates, *caporales*, and even higher authorities.
Víctor M. Villavicencio, for example, the noted criminologist and director of the penitentiary school, had an interest in such an enterprise.[23]

By participating in these partnerships inmates improved their living
conditions inside prison and satisfied some of their most pressing needs.
Having access to cash made an important difference because money
made it possible to establish relations of clientelism and friendship with
prison guards and authorities. Since guards and employees were faced
with severe working conditions and meager salaries, the opportunities
for inmates to enter into those negotiations were abundant. A sense of
relative empowerment seems to emanate from the participation of prisoners in these arrangements, although, as we will see below, not all
prisoners benefited from them, and they contributed to the establishment of hierarchies within the prison population.

Prison personnel from top authorities to meritorios were also engaged
in myriads of illegal actions that did not generally benefit the prison
population but added to the informal nature of the prison order. Corruption among prison staffers was pervasive, as it was, after all, in most
branches of the Peruvian state. Examples are abundant: fraud in the
administration of prison funds and provisions,[24] the use by prison authorities of both workshops and prisoners' labor for private advantage,[25]
authorities forcing prisoners to pay for clothes and other supplies that
were supposed to be free,[26] and authorities' use of prison facilities for
their comfort and profit.[27]

The organization of businesses and trades inside the prison was generally condoned by authorities. At Guadalupe, for instance, prisoners had
supposedly acquired the right to install booths in the main prison yard,
where they traded a variety of commodities like cigarettes, clothes, personal utensils, and coca in a sort of "European fair," as one reporter
described it. There were even stalls devoted to the provision of legal
services, performed by ubiquitous *tinterillos* (informal legal intermediaries), and others that operated as casinos, where inmates entertained
themselves by playing and betting.[28] Other, less visible illegalities such as

skipping school classes, not complying with work obligations, and circulating through reserved areas of the prison were also widely tolerated.

The most important effect of all these practices was the collapse of the disciplinary regime that was supposed to govern the prisons' internal affairs, especially that of the penitentiary. The close relationships between inmates and employees led to a variety of situations that flagrantly violated prison bylaws and undermined the principle of authority. According to the Calle Commission in 1915, "Very little respect is shown [by penitentiary inmates] to the employees."[29] One of the most important manifestations of this was the common practice of prison employees of overlooking inmates' infractions or not enforcing penalties mandated against certain prisoners. In 1887, the director described the penitentiary as a place where "prisoners obtain from employees commodities for fomenting their vices at a fabulous price, and they [inmates and employees] were united by a close friendship, which precluded the effecting of discipline." He remarked that many, if not most, prisoners' acts of indiscipline went unrecorded because employees could not denounce those who were not only their friends but in some cases their creditors.[30] After a prisoners' riot at El Frontón in 1921, the director announced that upon restoring order among the inmates it was necessary to impose discipline on the prison's employees as well, for he had noticed "the great intimacy existing between employees and *penitenciados*."[31] In 1922, a Guadalupe employee was described as being dangerous in regard to the disciplinary structure of the prison because "he has been bought by the prisoners."[32] In February 1892, authorities feared that Guadalupe prisoners were preparing a massive escape during carnival. The warden requested military forces but warned that troops who had previously served in the prison should not be used this time as "they already have friendly relations with most prisoners, which is reason enough to help them in their [escape] plans."[33] A letter signed by a group of inmates who called themselves *Presos amigos del orden* (Prisoner friends of order) denounced the loose discipline at Guadalupe. The prison, they said, had been "abandoned to its own fate," for, among other things, the warden did not comply with the rules, alcohol was sold "shamelessly," and prisoners were in possession of weapons.[34]

The presence of caporales contributed to the forging of this customary order. They were a small group of individuals drawn from within the convict population to aid the administration in the management of prisons. The use of prisoners as caporales was a common practice in Peruvian prisons, as in prisons elsewhere.[35] According to a report from the penitentiary in 1877, for example, four caporales helped the administration in running both the hospital and the laundry room and in taking care of sanitation and the general infrastructure of the prison building. Each had under his supervision a number of other prisoners who worked as de facto employees of the prison.[36] According to the 1901 Reglamento of the penitentiary, the subdirector had to choose from among prisoners observing good behavior one caporal for every section of each department, and a *caporal mayor*, who was not only to ensure that those in charge of order and cleanliness inside the prison did their jobs, but also to report any occurrence taking place in the prison.[37] The caporal mayor was, in fact, the most prominent, powerful, and rewarding position an inmate could hold inside the prison. Caporales became particularly critical elements in the operation of the prison, for they belonged to both the inmate population and the prison mechanisms of authority and control. In order to perform their duties they needed to fulfill various, sometimes contradictory roles, which required them to construct elaborate networks of loyalty and partnership. They enjoyed some privileges awarded to them by prison officials, but they were not always fully trusted by them; at the same time, they might enjoy friendships or partnerships with some inmates, but they were also looked upon with suspicion by their fellow convicts. According to Juan Seoane, the caporal of the penitentiary was perceived as being superior even by prison employees. They respected and feared him but, not surprisingly, also hated him.[38] Their crucial position gave caporales control over certain aspects of prison life, including illegal businesses. At the penitentiary, a caporal mayor was denounced for having acquired total control of the delivery and distribution of food inside the prison and its illegal commercialization outside. In addition, he owned more than one hundred hens, a very profitable business indeed.[39] In another case, a warder accused the inspector of taking a bribe of five soles per day from the caporal mayor, presumably for allowing him to run illegal businesses. He also charged that "huge amounts of coca" were being brought in by the inspector to be sold inside the prison.[40] In Guadalupe, caporales had a presumed right to receive visitors without having to pass through the routine inspection at the entrance. The spouse of the caporal mayor Francisco Espantoso took advantage of this privilege to smuggle in alcohol that Francisco later sold inside the prison.[41]

At Guadalupe, in particular, caporales enjoyed great leverage in their relationship with authorities, especially because prison officials, having to negotiate from a relatively weak standpoint, tended to give greater power to prisoners with ascendancy among the prison population, which basically meant prisoners with a great capacity for coercion (such as faites) ended up fulfilling the role of caporales.[42] The case of one of the most famous Guadalupe inmates, "el negro Arzola," illustrates this point. Arzola was convicted of murdering the wealthy Spanish moneylender Miguel de Orueta, a crime that was widely covered by the media and gave Arzola instant celebrity status.[43] Sentenced to a term in the penitentiary, Arzola was able to avoid being transferred to the panóptico and remained at Guadalupe, where he became caporal. As such, he was able to move freely throughout the prison, generally heavily armed. In a dramatic letter to the *prefecto* of Lima, the *intendente* described how during a confrontation between a police officer and a detainee, the officer noticed that Arzola was prowling about nearby holding a knife. When the prison warden was notified, he made no attempt to disarm Arzola and feebly warned him "to be very careful of his actions."[44]

In cases like this, the caporal was less a puppet in the hands of prison officials than a sort of *cacique*, or headman, of the prison population governing under a pact with the prison authorities.[45] This was especially true in Guadalupe, where the mechanisms of control over the prison population were far less strict than in the penitentiary, and the need for a particularly respected caporal was much more pressing. Authorities had to accept the fact that prisoners like Arzola enjoyed greater leverage and considerations than his status as an inmate would otherwise accord him. But even powerful inmates like Arzola could not avoid the vagaries of the prison customary order. He surfaces in the record again in 1915, this time locked up in one of the *calabozos* of Guadalupe. He was still involved in trading inside the prison and was denounced as the leader of a riot, but apparently he no longer held enough power to avoid being sent to the isolation cell.[46]

The customary order did not guarantee that every inmate would benefit equally from it—quite the opposite. It inevitably led to situations in which split loyalties and partnerships could in fact make things miserable for those on the wrong side. The customary order, indeed, involved a high degree of arbitrariness, mostly on the part of authorities, but also on the part of powerful inmates vis-à-vis those who were vulnerable. Despite all their weaknesses, authorities still held much more leverage than inmates and could impose, restore, or alter the rules of the game with relative ease. The behavior of one subdirector of the penitentiary illustrates the highly arbitrary nature of the customary order: he was accused of revoking penalties imposed on disruptive prisoners, presumably in exchange for money or favors, drinking alcohol with other employees, torturing prisoners, and authorizing others to move freely about inside the prison.[47] Why he seems to have been permissive with some inmates and brutally strict with others can be explained only by assuming his involvement in some of the informal networks of corruption and trade that existed inside the penitentiary.

All these practices were possible, ultimately, because of the willingness of prison staff members to get involved in them. Poorly paid and poorly motivated prison personnel were eager to take advantage of the opportunities presented to them. Barely aware of the ideologies of prison reform, penitentiary regimes, and rehabilitative therapies, they were mostly concerned with getting by and assuring that the prison kept operating. A penitentiary employee quoted by Seoane in *Hombres y rejas* put it blatantly: "Here, we only have to check that the people do not escape, and then close our eyes to many other things. Why should we care about men who would leave [the prison] today and will come back tomorrow?"[48]

An important component of the disciplinary regime of prisons was the system of rewards and penalties. In theory, penologists and prison authorities agreed that prisoners needed some sort of stimulus for transforming their morals, and they recognized that pure brutality would never achieve that goal. Proper behavior, respect for discipline, hard work, school attendance were to be rewarded, while resistance to the rules would be penalized. The original Reglamento of the penitentiary, for instance, included such rewards as lessened workloads, more time to read, permission to cultivate plants for sale, consumption of tobacco and coca, and the right to send letters to relatives and receive visitors. Conversely, bad behavior would lead to mandatory performance of personal services to the institution, reduced food rations, prohibition of reading time and visits, isolation in underground cells, withholding of earned wages, and the "rain shower."[49]

The implementation of the system of rewards and penalties was generally inconsistent and varied widely from administration to administration. Naturally, it became entangled with the many other interactions taking place between authorities and inmates. Prison authorities disagreed as to the proper way in which to use rewards to stimulate prisoners' allegiance. For most of them the first priority was to avoid mutinies and maintain prison production, even if that would involve the violation of internal rules. In 1873, for instance, the Junta Inspectora reported that the two cigarettes per day that had been assigned as a reward for good behavior were actually being given to all inmates, so "rewards have become customary" and thus had lost their initial purpose of encouraging allegiance.[50] At certain points, conversely, rewards were made more difficult to obtain, in an attempt to force prisoners to make even greater efforts to acquire them.[51] The most common (and attractive) rewards, as we will see below, were the monetary incentives prisoners received from private contractors. On occasion, "rewards" included services and goods that prisoners were legally entitled to. There was the case of a director who rewarded well-behaved prisoners with two glasses of wine.[52]

Similar contradictions surrounded the administration of penalties. Generally speaking, unruly prisoners were subjected to harsher penalties than those outlined in the Reglamento. Prison officials, prompted by exasperation and prejudicial sentiments against the prison population, tended to resort to violence and cruelty in dealing with insubordinate inmates. When escapes, mutinies, and revolts openly challenged prison discipline, penalties became swifter and harsher, with flogging and long-term seclusion in underground isolation cells—without air or light, and sometimes even without beds or blankets—being the most recurrent. Juan Bautista Mariscal, the director of the penitentiary in 1867, admitted he had ordered the whipping of prisoners involved in a riot. When charged with cruelty, he defended his actions through cynical reasoning: if, in spite of legal prohibition, whipping was used in the army, in the household, and at school, why couldn't he use it to punish "obstinate criminals"?[53]

While the infamous rain shower would be officially abolished in 1904, the most common corporal penalty, the *barra*, survived well into the twentieth century. In a list of penalties applied in the penitentiary during the year 1906–07, the most frequent were solitary confinement (including the case of an inmate who spent 151 days in seclusion and two who were there "permanently"),[54] the barra, and the *subterráneo*, underground isolation cells.[55] An inspector of the penitentiary is quoted as saying that "we have to treat the criminal as such," thus justifying the application of brutal penalties.[56] A survey of disciplinary measures applied to penitentiary inmates in 1918 shows the range of offenses and penalties: the most common offenses were insolence, theft, fighting, coca possession, sodomy, insult to the authority, and disobedience, while the most common penalties were the barra, underground or cell confinement for days or weeks, and *pentágono*, confinement in an isolation cell whose shape resembled a pentagon.[57] Beyond these penalties, as we saw in chapter 4, the use of illegal forms of punishment ranging from isolation and privation of food to corporal punishment was a daily occurrence. What needs to be stressed is that the inconsistency and arbitrariness in the use of penalties generally reflected the state of affairs of the customary order: it is clear, for instance, that different inmates committing the same violation of the rules would elicit quite different responses from authorities.

For prisoners, the relaxation of discipline and the actual disregarding of the Reglamento associated with the customary order represented a double-edged situation of which they nonetheless strove to take advantage, even if that meant, eventually, stepping over other inmates. Prisoners, as much as authorities, employees, and guards, learned what was permissible and what was not, realized that violating the laws was neither impossible nor always punishable, knew they could take advantage of the existing situation, and, especially, realized that by doing so the prison would be a much more tolerable place to live for some, if not for all. For authorities, on the other hand, it was evident that without these informalities the prison would have become an unbearable place to rule and live in. They recognized that by allowing inmates to get involved in a series of illegal operations they would be less inclined to revolt, escape, or otherwise challenge the paramount authority of prison officials. Obviously, too, the need for this tolerance was inversely proportional to the capacity of the prison to feed, cloth, and attend to the needs of the prisoners: the less satisfied the prisoners were, the more the prison administration would need to tolerate their entering into informal practices inside the prison. The customary order thus helped to keep the prison order—understood not as a disciplinary regime geared toward redemption, rehabilitation, and industriousness but, more pragmatically, as the absence of major eruptions of violence and unrest.

An important component of the daily routine inside the penitentiary and, to a lesser degree, in the other prisons was prisoners' work. While in doctrinal terms work was considered a key moralizing tool, in practice it became not only a source of profit for different sectors of the prison community, including officials, private contractors, and inmates but a central component of the negotiations between authorities and inmates and an arena of contention around key elements of the administration of prisons. This section, based on the much better documented case of the penitentiary, will highlight the contested nature of prison work and the ways in which it fit or clashed with the prison's customary order.

When work inside the penitentiary was initially instituted in 1862, male prisoners could choose between the shoe-making, leather-working, tinning, carpentry, and blacksmith workshops.[58] Each workshop was placed under the direction of a master hired by the penitentiary, who would earn a wage and receive a percentage of the sales. Private interests, together with the unsatisfactory performance of prison workshops, led to gradual changes in the rules governing prison work. In February 1865, a private contractor was given the administration of all workshops in exchange for a percentage of the sales,[59] but he was not able to increase the workshops' output, so by early 1867 advertisements were placed in Lima's newspapers to auction the administration of workshops. In the meantime, the penitentiary authorized Lima artisans to hire prisoners' labor as a means to counteract idleness and generate revenues for the institution, in practice establishing a system of concessions.[60] This arrangement was interrupted when, in the aftermath of the violent riot and attempted escape that took place in December 1867, prison authorities confined the inmate population to their cells permanently, which virtually paralyzed prison production.[61] By the beginning of 1868, according to a report, most prisoners were idle.

The projected solution was a mixture of private entrepreneurship and state patronization. Private contractors would assume the administration of the prison workshops. They had to supply materials and tools and pay a fee to the state for the use of prisoners' labor as well as a stipend to the prisoner/worker. The state was expected to place its orders, especially for supplies for the armed forces, with the penitentiary workshops. The Penal Code of 1862 had mandated that the inmates' earnings must be divided into three equal parts: to compensate the prison for the inmate's subsistence, to pay civil reparation to crime victims, and to form a savings account for the prisoners to be used upon their release. The new system being implemented altered the stipulations of the penal code, allowing prisoners to have the last portion split, so that one-fourth of their earnings, the so-called *vales de cuartas partes*, were given to them in cash to purchase "licit" goods.[62] Director Tomás Lama explained the rationale behind the system: "Work is, without doubt, the most efficient way of moralizing the human being, but in order to fulfill that goal, he [the prisoner] needs the incentive of the profit that [his work] must entail, thus guaranteeing his future and his leaving behind misery, almost always the source of shame and crime."[63]

The major flaw of this model was the inability of prison administrators to convince state bureaucrats to refrain from placing their orders with private entrepreneurs and use the penitentiary shops instead. Lama proposed using the highly publicized Exhibition of 1869 organized by Lima's mayor Manuel Pardo to display the prisoners' products and to demonstrate that the penitentiary workshops could produce everything the state needed. To his disappointment, not a single governmental authority visited the exhibit.[64] For decades to come, the state's reluctance to become the main (or sole, as some demanded) purchaser of articles produced by prison labor was deemed a major factor behind the failure to transform the penitentiary into a self-sufficient institution.[65] The state did place orders with the prison workshops, but never in the amounts required to guarantee their profitability.

The practice of stimulating prisoners with monetary advances, while certainly welcomed by prisoners, contractors, and some authorities, did not enjoy general approval. Here, the conflict between profitable work and prison discipline was the main issue. To put money into the hands of prisoners as a way of stimulating productivity was, some outside observers argued, to generate an almost unstoppable chain of corruption—monetary exchanges, loans, gambling, contraband, bribing—that clashed with the disciplinary goals of the prison regime. In 1873, President Pardo condoned the contract system but decided to ban the "corrupt custom" of giving the prisoners their vales de cuartas partes and ordered the strict observance of the Penal Code.[66] There is evidence, however, that in spite of the prohibition the vales were still being distributed to prisoners. During the next twenty years or so, prisoners who worked were able to get some type of cash compensation. That priority was given to prison production is evident in the common practice of moving handicapped prisoners out of the penitentiary and bringing in skilled *penitenciados* from other prisons.[67] Prisoners who were nearing completion of their sentences but were healthy and skilled were kept at the penitentiary instead of being sent to Guadalupe, for "it is convenient to use their services until the last minute," explained the director.[68] In periods of high demand, during the War of the Pacific, for example, when articles of war were being manufactured in penitentiary workshops, or whenever the private contractors deemed it necessary, prisoners were authorized to work even during holidays and at night.[69]

Cash incentives became the norm, and for inmates it was a sort of acquired right. In addition, they received other rewards from contractors eager to stimulate their productivity; after all, prison labor was cheaper and maybe even more reliable than on the outside. Contractors' eagerness to use prison labor also led to abuses. In November 1878, when a congressman visited the penitentiary and complained about the excessive workload of the prisoners, he was told that the contractor paid inmates by the piece; only those who finished their tasks quickly could make good money, and this forced prisoners to work until they reached the point of exhaustion. According to the director, however, prisoners had the supposed freedom to choose whether they wanted to work overtime or not.[70] In June 1881, when an attempt was made to eliminate cash incentives, the director rejected the idea because of the grave disturbances he thought the measure would generate.[71] Accustomed to receiving part of their earnings as cash wages, prisoners were not willing to tolerate their being eliminated. Instead, monetary rewards were fully and legally reinstated. By December 1883, a public auction was called again to assign the workshops to private contractors. Each contractor had to pay the state a fee for every prisoner they used and a reward to each prisoner. In addition, the contractor was required to supply two sets of uniforms, shoes, shirts, and underwear to the prisoners.[72] The director in 1890 suggested that this system had in fact prevented riots and mutinies, for prisoners were more content with it and their cash incentives than with the previous system of direct administration.[73]

Obviously it was the private contractor who benefited the most from this system, usually by abusing the inmates. Numerous complaints were voiced against the exploitation of prisoners, especially when accumulated wages were not paid at the time of the prisoner's release. The ex-convicts' frustration over unpaid wages is illustrated by the case of an allegedly insane ex-prisoner who, according to *El Comercio*, was living in a public park in front of the penitentiary and whose "theme" was that after fifteen years of incarceration he had not yet received his wages.[74] In 1892, Ricardo Heredia, president of the Patronage Society, criticized the contractors' abuses, stating that "private interest exploits the prisoners' disgraced condition" by not paying them their wages.[75] The Patronage Society initiated legal actions against contractors who failed to give the prisoners their remunerations, uniforms, and meals. Prisoners were exploited, Heredia said, because they were considered legally dead (*muertos civilmente*).[76] On the other hand, the vile conditions at the penitentiary forced some inmates to seek whatever means were available to them to improve their living standards. They seized the occasion for earning some cash that, in addition, would allow them to assist their families. Prison authorities would claim credit for the inmates' compliance with the rules of work: "Generally speaking," said the director in 1896, "the inmates of the panóptico are not reluctant to work, and I can assert, on the contrary, that they usually demand it, stimulated by the paternal deference [*sic*] with which the Administration rewards work and good behavior, and by the small compensation they receive every week from the contractor, apart from the small amount that is left for their savings."[77]

The prisoners' handling of cash, regardless of the amounts involved, increased their leverage to barter and to conduct negotiations with fellow inmates and prison guards. As we have seen, money was used for a variety of purposes, including the trading and purchasing of illicit goods and services such as alcohol, coca, and sex. On payday, one journalist reported, most inmates went to the prison canteen, the Indians to purchase coca, the *limeños* to buy cigarettes.[78] Money could also be used to pay for basic stuff such as food, personal items, and even legal services. For some observers and administrators, the relaxation of discipline this system entailed made it unacceptable. The "ill-fated contract system" was blamed for the loosening of discipline and the deviation from the true purposes of penitentiary reform. All efforts to reform the criminal, the director of the Junta Inspectora said in 1890, "collide against the wall that the contractor's selfishness has erected between the prisoners and the possibilities of their reform." The system, so the criticism went, generated widespread corruption, impeded application of the system of rewards and penalties, allowed contact between prisoners and outsiders, and failed to guarantee the private contractors' compliance with the terms of the contracts. The contractor, according to the director in 1892, "sees in the prisoners only instruments of work, factors that serve his utilitarian goals, without actually caring if the prisoner is reformed or not, or if he leaves the prison more or less perverse than he entered; whether or not he learns a craft, whether or not he will become a good citizen: he is indifferent to all this."[79]

As this and many other similar statements make clear, the key issue was no longer the alleged prisoners' reluctance to work—the old idea that criminals were inherently adverse to it. Instead, the issue became the corrupting effect of money. Prisoners had clearly demonstrated that under a system of incentives, which, given their living conditions, they certainly needed in order to satisfy a series of basic needs, they could positively respond to work demands; after all, as we saw in chapter 4, most penitentiary inmates were indeed workers. But prisoners, in the grand design of penal experts, were supposed to become obedient, submissive workers, not active barterers and consumers. The penitentiary's rehabilitation project was supposed to instill in the prisoners appreciation for work and money, but when prison experts realized that money gave the prisoners partial control over their living conditions inside the prison, increased their leverage to negotiate with prison employees a series of internal arrangements, and allowed them to subvert the rules of discipline, they began to censure the system. It was the prisoners' increasing bargaining power and autonomy which prompted criticism of the contract system and of the penitentiary regime as a whole and produced a consensual demand for a harsher penal regime, as we saw in chapter 4. From the point of view of prison authorities, however, those same characteristics were generally welcome: prisoners' work took care of a number of potentially explosive issues, so they sacrificed any expectation, real or not, of complying with the prison regime and chose to go with the customary arrangement of giving incentives to prisoners.

Under external pressure, however, the contract system was eliminated in 1896, when the *Junta Económica* of the penitentiary took over the administration of the workshops. Within two years, the workshops' production and demand for labor as well as the quality of and demand for their products had all decreased.[80] Prisoners seemed to be negatively affected by the new system: their savings had been eliminated, and they received only "an insignificant reward," as a result of which they lost their "enthusiasm for work."[81] The Reglamento of 1901 sanctioned the new system. Prisoners were still supposed to get a stipend besides their savings, but, being contingent upon sales, it was very unlikely prisoners were satisfied with it.[82] By 1903, forty-eight inmates did not work at all, and only forty-five were fully occupied all year long. At any one time, 20 percent of the prisoners were reported as being idle. The director tried to explain the situation by arguing that convict workers did not have the same incentives as outside workers. "Penitentiary work, because it is mandatory and because it is not an indispensable means for the satisfaction of the prisoner's immediate necessities, is considered [by convicts] a torment, a consequence of the crime." He failed to realize, however, that it was the lack of incentives which had turned prison work into a form of suffering, something that was evident to the minister of justice, who admitted that because they did not participate in the revenues, prisoners showed little interest in performance. The minister demanded that prisoners be rewarded in proportion to their work.[83] In May of that year the minister of justice ordered that prisoners should be paid by the piece, which, authorities hoped, would generate an increase in both the prisoner's productivity and earnings and the state's profits.[84]

The years 1905 and 1906 indeed yielded good profits to the prison, mainly because the state placed numerous orders for articles for schools and the police, but a decline in such orders put the economy of the workshops back in the red in 1907.[85] Direct administration, with the state as the main patron, was very erratic. By 1911, the workshops were almost paralyzed and half of the prison population was unemployed.[86] A return to the contract system seemed inevitable. Without actually changing the legal regulations, prison workshops began to be transferred to private contractors. In June 1911, the printing and binding workshop was leased to Manuel Aduvire. He was to pay a monthly rent, supply all the materials, sign contracts without the intervention of the Junta Administradora, pay a daily wage to the laborers, and collect all the profits.[87] In 1914, a five-year contract was signed with the firm Manufacturing Company for running an electrical-sewing workshop, and in July 1915, two private contractors, Luis E. Olazábal and Carlos Otero, were awarded the administration of all workshops. The profits generated by prison production were to be divided between the contractors (50 percent), the prisoners (30 percent), and the state (20 percent).[88]

In 1915, the Calle Commission conducted a thorough examination of the penitentiary, including its workshops. Some were closed down and others functioned irregularly; only the bakery was operating uninterruptedly. Verbal contracts had become customary, making it difficult to assess the economic performance of prison work. Independent of any involvement by prison authorities, the shoemaking workshop, one of the few that were still profitable, supplied shoes to private firms, many of them owned by immigrants of Italian origin such as Onetto, Canessa, and Bevestrello. The commission, confirming the usual hostility prison experts had toward the customary order, favored direct administration, but it demanded a more forthright commitment on the part of the state to using the penitentiary workshops to fill most of its needs. The opportunity for the state to jump in again and enhance the system of direct administration came in 1921, when two labor organizations initiated a campaign against the "unfair" competition of prison work, which, they thought, had caused a rise in unemployment rates.[89] The government responded by temporarily suspending the sale of prison products and by restricting prison production to the manufacture of goods needed by the central government. It also required all branches of the public administration to place their orders exclusively with the penitentiary workshops, except those whose nature made it impossible.[90] Both the complaint and the solution were very much political gestures, though. The search for culprits in the midst of a severe decline in urban employment found in prison work a potential target.[91] It seems the Leguía administration was trying to divert attention from the real causes of unemployment. In fact, despite the decrees, the system of private contracts and production for sale was maintained.

In March 1925, the penitentiary workshops were put under direct administration once again, but now prisoners were allowed to choose their own occupation and earn a fixed wage. The distribution of their wages, in compliance with the Penal Code of 1924, was to include a small amount of cash but only for prisoners with good behavior.[92] Pragmatism had triumphed, issuing in the recognition that cash incentives were, as prison administrators knew all along, the best way to get inmates to work. Prison work became indeed a "therapeutic" device, although not in the sense that nineteenth-century reformers had imagined it. Since it was clear that prisoners were interested in doing prison work, by making cash advances contingent on behavior the authorities were trying to secure, at least from some of them, a higher degree of compliance with prison rules. At the same time, the expansion of the state's services and bureaucracy taking place during those years promised to guarantee the penitentiary workshops a steady demand for their products.[93] While in 1926 the new system had not yet produced good results—only 40 percent of inmates were being employed, according to the director—prison work gradually began to improve its economic performance.[94] Pragmatism went even further: at the hat-making shop (*sombrerería*) inmates worked completely on their own. They purchased their materials and sold their products without any intervention by the authorities. Profits went directly to the workers, "as it should be."[95] Numerous orders, especially for school desks and stationery and other printed materials for state agencies, are found in the internal documentation. In 1927, for instance, there was an order for twelve hundred school desks.[96] Prison labor was in such demand that, on October 1, 1927, the director ordered that "not a single inmate should be without occupation."[97]

The penitentiary was becoming a sort of industrial complex. A total of eleven workshops were in operation. Production destined for private consumption also expanded, especially shoe making. A new mechanized shoe factory inaugurated at the penitentiary by President Leguía in 1922 dramatically increased productivity.[98] With its sixty-four machines, it was praised as the best shoe factory in the country. By 1929, the penitentiary produced roughly one hundred pairs of shoes a day, which made shoe making the greatest source of income for the prison. According to the director, if well managed, the shoemaking factory could become "the penitentiary's salvation."[99] The combination of state demand, improved machinery, and incentives to inmates/workers produced a relative bonanza in the financial situation of the penitentiary. In March 1929, thirty-five inmates from El Frontón—ten potters, ten carpenters, and fifteen shoemakers—were transferred to the penitentiary to alleviate the "shortage of men" in its workshops.[100] The international economic crash of 1929 and its political and economic effects in Peru, however, put an end to the good times. By 1930, confidential memos alerted authorities to the lack of financial means for keeping the penitentiary and other prisons in operation. Because of the dramatic decrease in the price of copper, cotton, and sugar, Peru's primary exports, and the resulting decline in state revenues, the minister of finances summoned the director general of prisons in August 1930 to observe strict austerity in prison expenses during the next few months. In October, the news was even worse: the budget would not cover anything beyond salaries and other "absolutely indispensable necessities."[101] A year later, the penitentiary workshops were almost paralyzed, inmates were generally idle, and very few orders were being received from private individuals and almost none from the state.[102]

Prison work, as this review has shown, was always a central ingredient in the operation of prisons and, as such, became entangled with the vicissitudes of daily life and the negotiations of power inside the prison. As happened with other types of transactions between inmates and prison officials, work was subject to intense negotiations in which various actors, including inmates, prison authorities, and private contractors, struggled to gain an advantage. While their bargaining power was, as usual, vulnerable and contingent on numerous other factors, prisoners demonstrated their ability to "work the system to its minimum disadvantage."[103] Earning cash wages and participating in the prison economy increased the prisoners' leverage in their negotiations with other inmates and prison staff, thus allowing them to have greater input in the making of the customary order. Prisoners' agency, however, was not limited to their ability to intervene in the prison's cash economy, benefit from working opportunities, and engage in transactions with fellow inmates and prison authorities. They also, as we will see in chapter 7, actively constructed semiautonomous prison subcultures.

7

DAILY LIFE IN PRISON—II:

PRISON SUBCULTURES AND LIVING CONDITIONS

Living inside a prison ought to be a traumatic experience for most human beings. Besides the obvious fact that inmates are deprived of their freedom and are kept confined within the walls of a building, incarceration usually imposes radical constraints upon the most intimate and ordinary aspects of life. At least potentially, these facets of inmates' lives are subjected to observation and intrusion, not only by the prison staff, but by fellow prisoners as well. Life inside a prison forces upon inmates a process of mental, behavioral, and physical adaptation to their new environment. Since prisoners are rarely willing to give up all their privacy, autonomy, and agency when they enter a prison, they must create a series of mechanisms, individual as well as collective, that enable them to cope with the prison environment. Prison communities thus develop unique patterns of communication, interaction, and coexistence which, because they develop within a (real or potential) hostile environment, necessarily adopt a clandestine and surreptitious, albeit highly adaptable, nature. The result is the emergence of what scholars call "prison subcultures."[1] Although these subcultures are quite distinctively a product of life inside the prison, they still have strong and visible links with the outside world. As the historian Patricia O'Brien among others has noticed, prisoners do not discard their arsenal of attitudes and practices but, at the same time, they have to adjust and adapt them to their new circumstances.

Male prison subcultures encompass some elements that are found consistently in penal institutions around the world. These include tattooing, the use of a peculiar criminal slang, distinctive patterns of sexual behavior, and a cult of violence and bravery usually associated with what is regarded as manliness. Don Sabo and his collaborators have described the prison as an "ultramasculine" world, one in which "intermale dominance," that is, the imposition of a power hierarchy among male prisoners, structures the inmates' daily life. Although perceptions and self-definitions of what it is to be a man are usually contested, the authors point to the existence of a "hegemonic masculinity" that typically recognizes violence, sexual aggressiveness, and bravery as truly manly forms of behavior. This pattern is confirmed by the case of Lima's prisons, with the usual qualifications and specificities of the local circumstances.[2]

The effects of these practices upon the prison community at large are always complex and ambiguous. They can help forge a collective identity based on common understandings of certain rules and forms of behavior, but they can also create or reinforce patterns of conflict and power hierarchies among inmates. Prison subcultures, as shown below, are inextricably linked to and may even depend on the existence of hierarchies and split loyalties within the inmate population. The sense of community that inmates are able to forge is always shaped by the conflictual nature of most interactions taking place within such a collectivity. This chapter reviews various expressions of male prison subcultures in Lima and their connections to the customary order analyzed in the previous chapter.

THE SEARCH FOR SELF-EXPRESSION AND IDENTITY

Among the most common markers of identity among prisoners are the use of tattoos and the development of a peculiar criminal jargon. Both have to do with the prisoners' need to create their own forms of group identification, distinctive ways of communication between them aimed at defying control and surveillance, and unique forms of individual and collective self-esteem. Tattooing has always been depicted, since the emergence of positivist criminology, as an important component of prison subcultures.[3] For a Peruvian criminologist, tattoos can be considered not only as "ideal identification signs" but also, and more important, "indications of certain tendencies, evidence of the preeminence of certain psychical functions, and [a] guide for the forensic doctor in the psychological investigation of the convict."[4] More recently, tattooing has been read as a sort of subversive social practice in that it allows inmates to openly defy attempts by authorities and the state to control their minds and bodies.

According to O'Brien, "in contrast to branding as a state-imposed mark of infamy and means of ostracism, tattooing was a self-imposed form of identification. It is likely that tattooing constituted a reaction to the institution and its power."[5] Tattooing can thus be depicted as an important element in the inmates' search for autonomous forms of expression with which to counterbalance the overwhelming intrusion of the prison system in their lives.

Documentary evidence about tattooing in Lima's prisons, however, is quite scarce. The psychiatrist Hermilio Valdizán wrote a brief, quantitative report of tattooing among prisoners.[6] He reviewed a sample of 620 individuals registered between 1892 and 1901 by the anthropometric office of the Intendencia, and found only 18 individuals with tattoos, a rather small proportion that may result from the fact that most of those registered by the Intendencia were suspects who had not spent time in prison, where most criminals got their tattoos. A second sample that included an unspecified number of individuals registered between 1903 and 1908 identified 82 who had tattoos. The themes depicted in those tattoos represented several categories: romantic (26), occupational (14), religious (4), and patriotic (4), while 14 had somebody's initials. The rest had various other types of inscriptions. Valdizán seemed to believe that the tattoos of Lima criminals lacked originality, although he found it interesting that a ratero had the inscription "Viva Piérola" on one of his arms. He also attempted an explanation of the fact that, in his sample, most criminals with tattoos were of indigenous origin: "We could explain that [fact], perhaps, by the cult our aborigines have of symbols in their most silent manifestations, those that speak to the spirit in the most intense tones." Their "devotion" to signs such as initials, stars, anchors, and eagles, Valdizán thought, may be related to "the delirious enthusiasm that the intense colors in objects and clothes provoke in them."[7] Valdizán's disciple Marino Alegre y Pacheco conducted a more thorough investigation of tattooing among the population of the Lima penitentiary. In his sample, he found a distribution of tattoo themes very similar to that of Valdizán: religious (9), romantic (14), occupational (5), patriotic (6), and initials (15). Thirteen had other types of emblems.[8] Some inmates had more than 1 and as many as 5 tattoos on their bodies. Most had been inscribed inside a prison (17 of the 23 for which he gave that information), and 5 were done at military institutions such as the army or the navy.[9] Alegre y Pacheco considered Guadalupe, along with prisons in the provincial cities of Piura, Trujillo, and Ica, true "foci of tattooing."[10] One of his conclusions was that most inmates he interviewed regretted having been tattooed. "Imitation" appears most frequently in Alegre's account of the inmates' explanation as to why they decided to get tattooed.

Tattooing does not seem to have enjoyed widespread popularity among the Lima prison population during this period, and so its importance as a marker of criminal identity was probably secondary. In addition, the shortage of sources and the lack of serious attention given to this issue by criminologists and other observers of the criminal population—which may reflect the relatively modest importance tattooing had in prisoners' lives—prevent us from offering a more thorough account of the practice. The use of a criminal argot was much more common. Criminal slang is both a means of concealing information and a vehicle for the formation of a peculiar type of group identity. Its features include not only a rich and original dialect but also the exultation of double-meaning expressions, mental agility, and endless creativity in subverting the forms and content of official and lettered culture. For positivist criminologists, the use of criminal jargon was a sign of retardation and atavism among the criminal population and was a recurrent topic of study in different parts of the world. Apart from brief mentions in reports about prison life and in a few glossaries included in descriptions of prison life, Peruvian criminologists failed to incorporate this issue into their research agenda.[11] Newspaper reports did notice the importance of slang for the criminal population in Lima's prisons. In November 1919, a reporter for *El Comercio* who visited Guadalupe and offered an account of the realities of prison life, considered criminal jargon a form of expression that was "close to the language of primitive peoples." The use of onomatopoeic expressions, for instance, and the fact that criminal language conferred "life" to inanimate objects while it "animalized" human actions were presented as evidence of "primitivism." Although the reporter did note the richness and creativity of criminal slang, counting, for instance, 72 synonyms for *drinking* and 32 for *money*, he nonetheless depicted it as "absolutely poor" and unable to express higher sentiments or concepts.[12] According to another observer, the jurist Pedro José Rada, "the detached irony, the shameless sarcasm, and the clumsy epigram constitute the form and meaning of their peculiar jargon." Rada located the origins of criminal jargon in the need to bypass police repression, in the customary practice among persons belonging to the same "profession" of having a common language and, especially, in "atavism." Through criminal jargon and its allegedly onomatopoeic nature, he argued, "malefactors reveal their savage instincts."[13]

These interpretations tended to miss an important dimension of criminal argot: for its practitioners, it was an assertive way of mastering a language of their own and, at the same time, ridiculing and subverting so-called proper behavior and culture. Jargon also allowed the criminal community inside and outside the prison to forge elements of a common culture and identity. One of the most important aspects of criminal jargon, in fact, was its role in connecting the world of the prison with the outside urban environments, in particular those of the lower classes of Lima. Terms and expressions invented inside the prison found their way into common parlance among sectors of the noncriminal world, and this, in turn, made it necessary for criminals to constantly renew their verbal arsenal to keep a certain degree of secrecy and group identity. Criminal jargon, in addition, like other shared cultural artifacts, helped strengthen ties of friendship and intimacy between inmates. Numerous expressions that were considered proper of the criminal underground, in fact, are still found today in common parlance, and some have made their way into official or quasi-official usage: *jato* (house), *causa* (pal), *carreta* (friend), *mochila* (stolen bundle, now backpack), *deschavarse* (to tell or confess), *bobo* (clock), and *choro* (thief).[14] But many other such terms have been lost—at least, to my knowledge—like *relucindo* (soldier), *estrilar* (to protest), *aurimarse* (to get scared), and *chascarro* (a lie).

The consumption of coca was another important aspect of everyday life inside the prison, especially among indigenous inmates. Coca-leaf chewing has been and still is in fact a central element in Andean culture, to the extent that it came to embody sacred meanings and for centuries has been associated with religious and propitiatory rituals.[15] The coca leaf is a natural stimulant that increases the individual's capacity for performing hard work, helps one endure long periods of fatigue and deficient food, and reduces the adverse effects of a variety of illnesses. Partly because of its close identification with indigenous culture, coca chewing was and continues to be depicted by physicians, criminologists, and hygienists as a terrible vice that produces degeneration. Negative portraits of the indigenous population generally point to coca consumption as one of the factors behind their supposed prostration.

Inside Lima's prisons, coca became a major component of everyday life for indigenous and nonindigenous inmates alike. According to Lorenzo Esparza, all indigenous inmates at the penitentiary consumed coca, but at least half of all the other racial groups, including whites, blacks, mestizos, and Chinese also did.[16] The physician César Valdez estimated that four hundred pounds of coca were consumed in the penitentiary each month, some prisoners consuming up to a pound per day. Although it was deemed a dangerous and corrupting vice by prison experts and authorities, they generally tolerated and even promoted it, which explains, said Valdez, the "alarming levels" it had reached in the penitentiary. As we have seen, an extended informal network of coca contraband existed inside prisons. Authorities always tried to make sure there was a generous supply of coca, as its scarcity could cause disruptions in the operation of prisons. On paydays, indigenous prisoners at the penitentiary, according to a reporter, rushed to the prison canteen to purchase coca, "a stimulant, a means of forgetting. At nighttime, in the solitude of their cells, they chew it with pleasure and devotion."[17] An inmate was allowed to walk through each department offering coca for sale to every prisoner.[18] There were instances in which coca was not only legally distributed but also used by prison authorities as a reward for good behavior.[19]

In the context of prison life, then, coca came to perform several roles simultaneously. For many prisoners, chewing coca was both a means of maintaining their cultural traditions and a way of finding some relief from the otherwise overwhelming regime of the prison. Valdez thought that "idleness, hunger, the pernicious example [of other inmates], or the habits acquired in the *chacra* or the mine" were the main reasons it was consumed so widely. The political prisoner Juan Seoane depicted coca consumption in the solitude of the cell as one of the very few pleasures prison life offered to many inmates. For the authorities, indulgence and tolerance toward coca consumption seem to have been a calculated strategy for diminishing the risks of violence and commotion inside the prison, while for employees, some prisoners, and even some higher authorities, coca leaves became a source of profit and an important component of the overall distribution of power inside the prison.

One of the most recurrent sources of criticism of the state of discipline and morality in Lima's prisons was the alleged prevalence of homosexuality among male prisoners. According to Julio Altmann Smythe, the author of one of the very few studies about the so-called sexual problem in Lima's prisons, "the number of homosexuals [in Lima's prisons] is considerable."[20] César Valdez found that number to be alarming indeed.[21] An inmate interviewed by Altmann asserted that the number of homosexuals was larger at El Frontón, Guadalupe, and the ccv than at the penitentiary: in those prisons, he said, they abounded "in an incredible manner."[22] For others, such as Gabriel Seminario Helguero, the problem of sexuality was at the roots of all the vices of prison life.[23] Numerous other sources tend to confirm the image of extensive homosexual behavior, but it is impossible to assess how commonplace it was and how it changed over time. Its impact on prison life, however, is undeniable, as most sources tend to corroborate. What seems clear also is that homosexuality in prisons encompassed a variety of situations and practices that were crucially shaped by the tensions, conflicts, and forms of accommodation typical of an institution of confinement, but that, once again, reflected values, assumptions, and practices existing in society at large. Reaching a solid understanding of sexual behavior inside the prison is a difficult endeavor, especially because of the nature of the sources being utilized, almost always hostile observers of the inmates' sexual practices. The historian Pablo Piccato has recently called for an effort to pay more attention to sexual practices than to fixed sexual identities, and he suggests that a better contextualization of those practices will help researchers decode their meanings.[24] The challenge for the historian is to document those practices and to read them from the perspective of the inmates themselves.

The diversity of situations that the category homosexuality encompassed was recognized by contemporary observers, although they did so by framing them within the well-known dichotomy of active versus passive homosexual roles.[25] According to Valdez, for example, there were four categories of homosexuals inside the Lima penitentiary. First, the occasional active, who was thought to be a heterosexual individual in his life outside prison and was believed to resume that status once released from prison. Second, the occasional switcher, who behaved as either active or passive depending on his relative power vis-à-vis other inmates. If confronted with a more powerful, that is, "masculine," individual, he would be forced to assume the passive role in the relationship, but he would take the active role if he were to encounter a more vulnerable fellow inmate. The third type was the feminine, who was, according to Valdez, the only truly homosexual prison character and who owed his alleged inversion to purely individual factors. Finally, Valdez mentioned the prostitutes, homosexuals who had acquired their supposed vice in the army, the navy, or the correctional school and who sold their sexual services inside the prison.[26] Gabriel Seminario Helguera, whose analysis is based on his observation of the population at the CCV, came up with a similar typology: active homosexuals who had a woman, that is, a passive homosexual, with whom they formed a stable relationship; occasional actives, those who engaged in homosexual relations only to satisfy a necessity without any long-term commitment; passives, those who had a powerful lover and behaved like a wife; prostituted passives, that is, feminine homosexuals engaged in prostitution; and finally, the *cambiaos*, those who adopted both passive and active roles.[27]

Stable homosexual relationships were seemingly common and probably even widely accepted. Some witnesses refer to the true affection existing between homosexual partners: they shared money, food, and other material possessions and exchanged letters, presents, and caresses. Although not everybody would approve of these relationships, it was quite typical to have such partners expressing their sentiments openly in public.[28] Homosexual couples behaved, witnesses said, like man and woman. Marriages between homosexual partners, an inmate testified, were respected "like the normal marriages we know in life."[29] In fact, marriages and reconciliations between homosexual partners constituted some of the "great events" inside the prison and gave way to celebrations involving heavy alcohol drinking.[30] To be sure, fighting, abuse, and even violence were also part of the daily experience of homosexual partners. Because these relationships tended to reproduce the prevailing marital codes informing heterosexual relationships, they could not avoid the specific roles assigned to both members of the couple. To give but one example, passive homosexuals were reportedly prohibited from drinking alcohol, for their male lovers wanted to avoid any circumstances leading to conflictive situations and also because drinking was considered a virile, masculine right.[31]

The existence of relatively stable, harmonious homosexual relationships should not conceal the fact that, in numerous cases, homosexual intimacy was the result of coercion and physical abuse. Even in the case of marriages, the original conquest took place, very frequently, within a context of coercion and unequal relations of power. Very commonly, brutality and violence were used to compel an inmate to engage in homosexual practices against his will. A few examples illustrate this point. A convict from Lambayeque who entered the penitentiary when he was only twenty-one years old was sexually abused by other convicts and forced to live as a homosexual inside the prison. Seven years later, he was determined to change his fate, but there was one convict who had threatened to hurt him if he did not yield to his sexual advances. He requested transfer to El Frontón.[32] Another inmate accused a fellow prisoner of forcing him to practice homosexual acts, which he firmly resisted. He had received death threats, so "for the protection of my manly dignity," he too requested that either he or his harasser be transferred to El Frontón.[33] In El Frontón, a prisoner seriously injured another one and tossed the body into an abyss after he did not comply with an alleged previous agreement to practice sexual intercourse.[34] In Guadalupe, Juan Marín repeatedly stabbed another inmate, Santos Romero, with whom he shared a room along with two other inmates, when Romero refused to have sexual intercourse.[35] There are, indeed, numerous cases like these, but despite the denunciations prison authorities did not feel compelled to act. When in December 1911 Manuel Chumpitaz injured another inmate with a knife because of his repeated propositions to have sex, Chumpitaz was sentenced to fifty days in isolation, but no inquiries were made into the existence of sexual relationships or the use of knives inside the prison. Both practices were clearly accepted, maybe resignedly, as inevitable components of the prisoners' daily life.[36]

The initiation of a new inmate into homosexuality could be a traumatic experience, as described by Seminario Helguera. Upon entering prison, new and inexperienced inmates were usually scared, even terrified, a circumstance seized upon by veteran inmates, generally *matones*, to approach a newly arrived inmate, offer him protection, and make sure that nobody else put his hands on him. He would gradually gain his trust and introduce him to alcohol and coca. Once the victim had developed an addiction to those substances, the report continued, he came to depend on his protector for money and supplies to satisfy his new vice; at some point, Seminario Helguera tells us, he would accept propositions for sexual intercourse as a means to secure alcohol or coca. He would eventually become the "wife" of the matón or end up as a prostitute in order to be able to purchase alcohol and coca.[37] Sex commerce inside the prison was quite frequent, and not only powerful inmates but also prison employees were involved in the business of controlling it. An observer compared Guadalupe with a brothel because of the extensive practice of homosexual prostitution.[38]

As some of these examples demonstrate, homosexual relations inside Lima's prisons offered inmates the possibility of building affectionate relations and satisfying their sexual needs. There was a need on the part of inmates to build relations of affection, care, and mutual trust amidst a generally brutal and inhuman environment, and homosexual relationships offered a way to attain them. As O'Brien emphasized, "Sexual expression was a crucial factor in the prison subculture and was one means whereby the prisoner adapted and adjusted to the rigors and dehumanization of prison life."[39] But homosexual relationships, like other interactions between inmates, were quite frequently built upon hierarchical and abusive practices: in numerous cases it was commerce, blackmail, or pure coercion which sustained them. As such, homosexuality was undoubtedly connected to the dynamics of conflict, contestation, and accommodation that characterized prisoners' lives inside the prison.

According to most testimonies, sexual practices such as homosexuality were not really a great source of concern for prison authorities.[40] In fact, it is fair to argue that tolerance to homosexuality in the prison was a key element of the customary order of the prison. By accepting it as an inevitable component of prison life, the authorities sought to diminish the tensions between the inmate population and the prison administration and to transfer some of those tensions to the prison population. Powerful inmates such as faites and *caporales* exerted greater control over homosexual behavior inside the prison, but they also performed key roles in the maintenance of prison order. Economic interests, in addition, were also behind the authorities' tolerance of homosexual practices. There were instances, of course, in which authorities decided to take measures such as transferring one of the partners to another prison, but most of the time homosexuality was accepted as an inevitable, routine component of prison life, maybe even a source of stability for important segments of the prison population. In this, again, the attitude of prison authorities was at odds with that of criminologists and penal experts, who considered the extensive practice of homosexual relations a scandalous breach of prison discipline.

As the examples of sexual behavior, coca consumption, and the use of tattooing and argot demonstrate, the emerging of prison subcultures was an ambiguous and contradictory process. While these behaviors certainly reflected the prisoners' struggle to create a world of their own and had the potential to forge horizontal relations among inmates, they also reinforced social and cultural values that included important doses of coercion, abuse, and violence. Solidarity and conflict, harmony and antagonism coexisted side by side within the world of the prison. Prison subcultures could not escape the fact that they developed inside an oppressive structure, one that was usually confronted by resorting to its very own (perverse) mechanisms of power and control: coercion, violence, and deception. Prison subcultures at once subverted and reproduced the status quo.

A VIOLENT WORLD

One of the most pervasive features of daily life in Lima's prisons was the overwhelming exercise of violence, certainly in the form of punishment and the cruelty shown by prison officials toward inmates, but also, and possibly more commonly, in the form of interpersonal violence between inmates. I have referred above to the continual use of torture and corporal punishment in the treatment of prisoners. But inmates' fear of aggression coming from fellow prisoners was at times greater than their fear of the authority's strong hand. What place did interpersonal violence in day-to-day interactions assume among prisoners and in the making of prison subcultures?

Some instances of interpersonal violence have already been mentioned, in particular the frightful practices associated with the sexual exploitation of vulnerable inmates. Violence within the inmate population, however, had many other components. It was at times a routine way of dealing with apparently trivial but tension-filled situations. A few examples will suffice. A penitentiary inmate was stabbed to death during a fight that erupted at a soccer game.[41] Another penitentiary inmate killed the caporal of the leather workshop with a knife. The perpetrator was sent to an isolation cell, where he reportedly committed suicide.[42] Two inmates at Guadalupe who were working in the shoemaking workshop suddenly began fighting. Several knife injuries sent one of them to the hospital.[43] In October 1924, four prisoners at the penitentiary were injured after they got involved in a knife fight.[44] One day in September 1920, during lunchtime, one inmate killed another "without any apparent provocation."[45] An inmate demanded that the penitentiary inspector intervene after he was injured by a fellow prisoner. There was a risk, he argued, either of his being attacked again or of him murdering the attacker.[46] When Rafael Sosa, a Guadalupe inmate who was serving as a doorkeeper, laughed at somebody, another inmate, Manuel Orué, reprimanded him, to which Sosa responded by stabbing him with a knife. In his deposition, Sosa said they were good friends, and the injury was inflicted playfully (*jugando*). Orué died a few days later.[47]

These examples—and there are many more—demonstrate the extent to which violence was used in dealing with all sorts of situations, including some relatively trivial ones, such as a discussion in the midst of a soccer game.[48] These trivial incidents, however, were also occasions in which deeper sentiments of rage and frustration surfaced, revealing the overwhelmingly violent climate of the prison world. Violence, thus, was not senseless. It was the concrete manifestation of an environment in which inmates confirmed what they had experienced outside, in society at large: that is, the continuous use of physical violence against other human beings in order to achieve obedience, subjection, revenge, or consent. They had plenty of reasons to be angry, frustrated, jealous, and rancorous. They confronted those situations in many ways, including, prominently, the use of physical violence. While prisons were not just an extension of free society, they were, in more than a metaphorical way, a mirror of it. Authoritarianism and violence were central components of Lima's cultural and social climate; prisons were microcosms of society at large.

Violence among inmates played many different roles, one of which was the setting of boundaries and hierarchies of power within the prison community. The tougher the inmate was, the more respected and feared he became and thus the greater the authority and power he could exercise. This is an example of what James Scott has called "domination within domination," a situation in which some inmates imposed "a tyranny as brutal and exploitive as anything the guards can devise."[49] At the Guadalupe prison, according to a witness, "the tough guy imposes his will. Anybody not willing to give or lend money is inevitably beaten and mistreated in the most cruel and barbarous way." Newly arrived inmates, the reporter said, had to make themselves respected from the very beginning or else they would end up being a victim of the matones.[50] This was, indeed, a major element in the distribution of power inside the prison: newcomers were always more vulnerable and fragile than veteran inhabitants of Lima's prisons.[51] It was the old inmates who generally set the tone in the relationships between inmates. Because of the obvious fact that they knew how the prison really operated and were already in a position to control critical aspects of the internal customary order, they could take advantage of the newly arrived, usually through the use of open or surreptitious violence. Abuse and coercion tended to go in one direction: experienced prisoners against novel inmates. The result was an extremely hierarchical world, one in which the toughest and most experienced prisoners exercised important quotas of power and consideration.

Closely related to this issue is yet another dimension of the conflictual relationships among prisoners. Regional and ethnic affiliations played an important, albeit generally obscure and difficult to document, role in the shaping of prison life. While Peruvian prisons, unlike those in other parts of the world, did not implement separate facilities and penal regimes for different ethnic and racial groups, divisions along geographical, ethnic, and racial lines did exist and, what is most significant, were usually driven by the prisoners themselves.[52] Divisions between *criollos* (residents of urban and coastal areas) and *serranos* (people of indigenous background) were prominent sources of friction within the population of Lima's prisons. Differences in language and customs as well as deeply ingrained notions of racial and regional superiority on the part of criollos kept them generally apart, although this was hardly an insurmountable division.[53] Criollos saw serranos as inferior and treated them as such, thus duplicating the tenets of racist doctrines and hierarchical social practices in the larger society. Within the culture of Lima's prisons, serranos, especially those who came to the penitentiary directly from their Andean provinces and had little knowledge of the prison underworld, were potential victims of mistreatment and abuse by authorities and criollo inmates alike. Indigenous prisoners seem to have occupied the most vulnerable position within the community of inmates in Lima's prisons. They faced numerous obstacles that *limeños* and *costeños*, people from Lima and the coast, respectively, did not. An inmate who wrote to the minister of justice to complain about the behavior of the penitentiary caporal told him that most victims of abuse were the *serranitos*, who were particularly abused because they resignedly accepted the whip applied to all inmates by the caporal.[54] Indigenous prisoners, in addition, seem to have faced more difficulties than their criollo counterparts in processing and acquiring such penal benefits as pardon and parole. "The Indian," wrote Lorenzo

Esparza, "always serves strictly the [incarceration] period mandated by the Courts, if his life is not truncated by tuberculosis."[55] But the vulnerable situation which newly arrived indigenous inmates seem to have faced was not irreversible, and (as we will see in chapter 8) many of them soon learned to manipulate the system to their advantage. I'm not suggesting there was a clear-cut hierarchy, with criollos as the dominant group and serranos as subordinate; that could imply that serranos resignedly accepted their fate. Portraits of serrano acquiescence like the ones quoted above were undoubtedly shaped by commonsensical notions about the indigenous population's attitudes toward superiors. At the very least, the prison environment echoed divisions and tensions existing in the outside world, and, within such environment, serranos were usually attributed an inferior position, although that did not mean passive or hopeless acceptance of their condition.

But differences in perceptions, behavior, and tastes patently tended to erect barriers between criollos and serranos. One notable episode reveals the extent of ethnic divisions within the prison population. Inside the Lima penitentiary there were two recreation areas known as the Pampa del Tawantinsuyo and the Pampa de los Criollos that were used mostly to play soccer.[56] The first was used by indigenous inmates, while the second was used by criollos or costeños. Presumably, this distribution of space was reached by agreement between the two groups of inmates and the authorities. In 1929, prison authorities proposed to build new classrooms for the prison school on the Pampa del Tawantinsuyo, which would have forced the two groups to share the other pampa. Once they found out about the proposal, inmates sent a letter to the minister complaining that the reduction of the area available for sports would negatively affect all inmates. It is impossible to know what the ethnic background of the inmates promoting the petition was, but it may be fair to assume it was the criollos who filed the complaint. The hidden argument was that they wanted to keep the ethnic separation of the recreation fields. In his report, the director of the prison admitted that serious rivalries existed between the two groups of prisoners, and he argued it was necessary to overcome such division by forcing the prisoners to share physical space and try to get along. "Ethnic prejudices have flourished in the penitentiary," he continued, "since long ago. There are some terrible criminals . . . who exhibit a supremacy that rests upon the color of their skin, or the accidental fact that they were born in a coastal city." He insisted that costeños and serranos, indigenous and whites should play on a single field, for "in a democratic society [*sic*] we should not incite animosities [*odiosidades*] built upon racial features." "Superiority," he further argued, "does not originate from morphologic signs, but from virtue, talent, or capacity for work." His seemingly democratic and tolerant spirit soon faded away, however, as he strongly opposed the right of the prisoners to voice their opinion about this or any other matter: "We should not tolerate that inmates express their opinion, discuss, and oppose these technical projects, conceived by superior authorities. . . . we ought not to confuse humanitarian treatment with sentimentalism, which is incompatible with prisoners, who are, ultimately, criminals." The inmates, however, did express their opinion. They sent another collective statement to the prison authorities reaffirming their opposition to the construction of classrooms and arguing that health and recreation were even more important than education. Quite tellingly, they used a racialized argument, but one that did not explicitly address ethnic rivalries among inmates: according to them, physical exercise can help create a "vigorous race," such as the ones existing in England, Germany, and the United States, which produced "strong, rational, and entrepreneurial men." The lack of any explicit mention of ethnic rivalries between criollos and serranos as a justification for keeping both pampas demonstrates the prisoners' awareness that such an argument would not have been accepted; but they knew racialized arguments would resonate among prison officials, so they tried to convince them that, ultimately, keeping the two pampas would help improve their (the criollos') race. The implicit message was that keeping serranos apart would advance such improvement by avoiding contamination. The "vigorous race" they (and their addressees) must have had in mind was definitely not the "indigenous race."[57]

Ethnic hierarchies are also evident in the usual, although not uncontested, preeminence that black faites enjoyed within the prison community. The kinds of assumptions about roles, hierarchies, and values that sustained the prestige of faites also functioned to buttress stereotypes and practices that assigned blacks certain positions of command within the criminal underworld. Racialized interpretations of social hierarchies inside the prisons tended to duplicate those prevailing in the outside world but with some inevitable adjustments: because of the centrality of bravery in the setting of power boundaries inside the prison and the reputation of blacks as excelling at that, they emerged, as noted in chapter 5, as generally superior to serranos and even mestizos. Despite the scarcity of sources that document the impact of ethnic divisions on daily life inside Lima's prisons, it is clear that racialized perceptions and stereotypes permeated the relationships between different ethnic groups and, in some cases, exacerbated tensions between different segments of the inmate population. As in the case of interpersonal violence, ethnic divisions were reproduced not necessarily through the imposition of despotism by prison authorities, but, to a large extent, through the prisoners' own daily strategies of coping and survival.

FOOD, HEALTH, AND DEATH IN THE PRISONS

Living conditions for inmates in Lima's prisons were generally poor. Cells and corridors at the penitentiary, for instance, were described as real "swamps" and "foci of infection."[58] But these conditions were probably not much worse than those of the city's lower and working classes. The physician Rómulo Eyzaguirre, in an exhaustive study of tuberculosis in Lima, for example, depicted prisons as being as dangerous as lower-class housing (*casas de vecindad*), army barracks, and hospitals as loci of contagion of that disease.[59] Numerous reports from different periods stressed the poor health and sanitary conditions of Lima's prisons. In the early twentieth century physicians and medical students began to pay attention to prisoners' health, as part of their overall concern with social hygiene. The "pathology" of prison populations was a recurrent topic for degree theses.[60]

The most common disease in penitentiary inmates at any one time was, indeed, tuberculosis. Although reportedly many inmates entered prison already infected, conditions inside the penitentiary were propitious for contagion. Not only poor sanitary conditions but imprisonment itself, that is, the lack of freedom, were listed as factors in the spread of tuberculosis.[61] In 1905–06, for example, 216 inmates visited the penitentiary hospital. Seventy-seven of them, more than 30 percent, were suffering from respiratory problems.[62] According to Seminario Helguero, 25 percent of all visits to the infirmary at the CCV were also caused by respiratory problems.[63] Between June 1910 and May 1911, 18 prisoners died at the penitentiary, 8 of them victims of tuberculosis.[64] According to another study, tuberculosis was rampant because inmates came from very unhealthy backgrounds, were exposed to exhausting work routines, were weakened in prison by their vices, were poorly fed, and, in addition, were exposed to contagion by using the same beds, clothes, and utensils that former infected inmates had used. Statistics for the years 1904–13 show that of the 109 prisoners who died inside the penitentiary, 72, or 66 percent, were victims of tuberculosis.[65] In the case of indigenous prisoners, it was thought that the cold weather of Lima and especially the humidity and cold of the penitentiary building condemned them to sickness, if not death.[66]

According to Valdez, work routines, environmental conditions, the regime of incarceration, and the prisoners' habits both before and during their incarceration, especially alcoholism, coca consumption, and masturbation, all combined to produce very unhealthy conditions among the inmates. The rudimentary state of the prison's health services made things even worse, for medical facilities inside all prisons were, to say the least, lacking. In some cases, sick inmates had to lie on the floor for lack of beds. At the ccv, Seminario Helguero reported, the dental facility shared the same space with the toilet.[67] The so-called hospital of the penitentiary, reported Valdez, was an "infected site."[68] At El Frontón, things were not any better: in fact, medical service was available only once a week, and sometimes not even that often.

Associated with poor health conditions was inadequate nutrition. Generally speaking, prisoners' food was almost always deficient, even though at the Lima penitentiary, some reports suggest, there were periods in which it was quite acceptable.[69] The supply of food at the penitentiary was initially the responsibility of the administration, but it was later assigned to either the workshops' contractors or private concessionaires, who most of the time failed to provide satisfactory meals to the prisoners.[70] In March 1872, to cite just one example, after successive complaints by the inmates, the physician of the penitentiary confirmed that food was generally meager and meat was "of the worst class."[71] In 1870, a group of prisoners complained to Paz Soldán, who was visiting the penitentiary, about the quality of the bread and the amount of food they received. After explaining to them he was no longer in charge of the administration of the prison, Paz Soldán remarked that convicts did not come to the penitentiary "to eat better than at their homes." The statement infuriated the inmates and prompted them to riot. Two prisoners were sent to solitary confinement while the rest became involved in a noisy protest that forced the guards to fire their guns and call for external military support. Two prisoners died during the incident.[72] In 1914, Valdez contrasted the ration stipulated by the *Reglamento* with the actual ration served to prisoners, concluding that meals never included the prescribed amount of meat, beans, and other components of the prisoners' diet. In January 1930, the new director of the penitentiary, Pablo Chueca, found food to be "not scarce, but of bad quality."[73]

At other prisons the situation was not too different. At Guadalupe, the feeding of the inmates was the responsibility of the Lima Municipality during most of the period 1850–1935. At various times there were complaints about the quality and quantity of the food served at Guadalupe. In August 1869, Guadalupe inmates sent a petition to the mayor of Lima asking for an additional cup of tea in their ration, for they were not being given anything to eat or drink, not even tea, until 11 A.M., when they were served lunch. In the afternoon, at 4 P.M., they had supper, and then nothing until the next day. Both lunch and supper seemed to have been relatively acceptable, but they complained about spending too many hours without ingesting any food. The inspector of prisons found the petition had merit and apparently granted the prisoners' request.[74] But things were typically less acceptable. In October 1883, for example, the accountant at Guadalupe wrote to the mayor of Lima, Rufino Torrico, declining to accept any responsibility regarding "any uprising [*invasión*] the prisoners may generate" because of the absolute lack of food.[75] The very next month the food there was found to be deplorable by the municipal inspector of prisons: two ounces of meat in a light soup in the morning, and a small plate of rice with beans in the afternoon, plus one piece of bread at each meal.[76] In 1885, a Supreme Court justice described the food at Guadalupe as "a piece of trash that should not be given even to the dogs."[77] At the ccv, in October 1931, a riot erupted when prisoners complained about the inadequate food they were being served.[78]

Living conditions inside Lima's prisons, as all this evidence suggests, were far from comfortable. Quite frequently, prisoners found themselves deprived of adequate clothing, food, and sanitary conditions, a situation that resulted from both economic shortages and the persistent indifference of authorities to living conditions in the prisons. The attitude of Paz Soldán during the prisoners' protest is highly revealing: a kind of "principle of less eligibility" operated in the minds of prison administrators. Criminals had been sent to prison to expiate their offenses, they tended to think, and hence should not expect good treatment or, at least,

Figure 7. El Frontón inmates waiting for their *rancho* (daily food ration). From Colonia Penal "El Frontón," *Memoria presentada por el director Sr. Manuel Hermilio Higueras al Ministro de Justicia, Instrucción y Culto. 1922* (Lima: Litografía e Imprenta T. Scheuch, 1923).

treatment that was better than what they experienced in the outside world. Otherwise, it would send the wrong message to would-be offenders.[79] Inadequacies in the provision of food, clothes, and medical attention made it more necessary for prisoners to use whatever resources they had to counter the negative effects of negligence and indifference.

Yet Lima's prisons, in spite of all the privations inmates had to endure, seem to have been for some prisoners a fairly acceptable place of residence. This is not ironic, and it is not an exclusively Peruvian phenomenon.[80] Lima's prisons, especially the penitentiary, offered some individuals a better standard of living than they could secure outside. At the very least, they found in prison a place to live, a way of earning some money, and food. Although this should not be mistaken as an endorsement of living conditions in Lima's prisons, one has to recognize that some prisoners preferred to live there than in the outside world. In 1890, for example, a Chinese inmate reportedly wrote a letter to a friend who worked as a peon on a hacienda outside Lima. He wanted his friend to come to the penitentiary and enjoy its comfort and suggested he kill the hacienda owner and join him at the prison. If it had been carried out, the murder would have had an inescapable retaliatory character. The horrendous living conditions Chinese coolies endured on some haciendas of coastal Peru would give credence to this story. For a Chinese peon subject to harsh exploitation and inhumane treatment at a hacienda of Lima, living in the penitentiary would have certainly represented an improvement.[81] According to the author who reported this case, it showed that for many inmates being at the panóptico was a gain (*ganancia*) because there they could enjoy comforts (*comodidades*) they did not have in free society.[82] A similar case was reported in 1893. Two inmates held at the Casasmatas jail refused to be released, alleging they were better off inside than outside. "Such a situation is not uncommon among us," commented *El Diario Judicial*, since the lack of enforcement of obligatory work inside prison was attractive to criminals, for whom "imprisonment is taken as a sort of vacation."[83] Some Guadalupe inmates, according to a reporter, were somewhat sad when they had to leave the prison.[84] There was also the remarkable case of one individual whose "job" was to live in Guadalupe serving other individuals' prison sentences. He charged one pound per day, a sum that apparently allowed him to live "an oriental life" inside the prison, with plenty of cash to satisfy all his caprices.[85] Seminario Helguero reconstructed the dialogue between a new inmate at the ccv and his fellow prisoners: " 'Don't worry, Yarlequé,' Medio Cohete tells him in a sardonic tone; 'here we have a lot of fun: we drink, we gamble, and we. . . . Guards are bastards, they want to exploit us, but . . . we are machos, and we screw them. Have you brought a drink?' "[86]

In addition, prison administrators, especially those of the early twentieth century, realized the importance of offering inmates moments of amusement, no matter how ironic or hypocritical this may have seemed from the point of view of the prisoners themselves. Religious festivities, which normally included processions, dancing, music, and sometimes even special dinners, played an important role in providing the prisoners some relief. Easter, Christmas, the day of the Virgen del Carmen, and many other religious celebrations were occasions for the prisoners to have a break from the everyday routine of the prison.[87] Preparations for those events kept the inmates busy for longer periods, and they demonstrate the willingness and capacity of inmates to carry on collective endeavors, usually in coordination with prison authorities. Soccer and, to a lesser extent, boxing also became popular distractions for prisoners by the turn of the century, especially at the penitentiary and El Frontón. Tournaments were organized, sometimes by the inmates themselves, sometimes by the prison authorities, and various soccer clubs were formed by groups of inmates, who conducted fund-raising campaigns and used these organizations to try to forge clientelistic relations with prison authorities and outside patrons. Seeking *padrinos* (godfathers) for their teams and inviting prominent individuals to attend their tournaments are examples of those initiatives. Later, in the 1920s, following recommendations from prison reformers, inmates were allowed to listen to the radio, watch movies, and attend music concerts.[88] An orchestra created inside the penitentiary in 1921 was thought to have a beneficial influence on the inmates.[89] When state finances made it possible, important holidays such as Independence Day were also celebrated inside the prison.[90] Philanthropic organizations and individuals, especially in the 1920s, contributed to give the inmates some spiritual relief. Events such as the *Navidad del preso* (Prisoners' Christmas), for instance, were generally welcomed by inmates. They were given presents like cigarettes, *panetones* (sweet bread), refreshments, and the like and participated in sports tournaments and musical soirees.[91] All these events were meant to instill allegiance among prisoners, for more often than not they were made contingent on good behavior. Some of these activities were attended by higher state officials, including the president of the republic and his ministers, and they were used by both prison administrators and inmates to display their own political strategies: the former to sell the image of a harmonious climate inside the prison, the latter to try to build clientelistic relationships with governmental and prison authorities (see chapter 8). Some even saw the activities as a way of diminishing sexual impulses and alleviating the anguish of sexual deprivation among inmates.[92]

In spite of the occasional periods of respite, most prisoners did face deprivation, suffering, insufficient food, and an overwhelmingly unhealthy environment. In 1926, a group of prisoners wrote a letter to the director general of prisons in which they denounced the highly adverse living conditions inside the prison: "We have been sentenced to prison," they stated, "but not to penalties against our life and health." The fact they had committed a crime, they argued further, did not authorize anybody, "not even the state," to increase the burden imposed upon them.[93] This letter, written and submitted collectively to denounce the prisoners' daily living conditions, reveals yet another dimension in the relationship between inmates and prison and state authorities, namely, confrontation and defiance.

8

The existence of a customary order (see chapter 6) did not preclude the emergence of more confrontational forms of interaction between inmates and prison staff. On the one hand, not everybody benefited from the customary order, or at least not all the time or to the same degree. There were always plenty of reasons for some prisoners to be dissatisfied with the state of things, including, as we saw in chapter 7, deficiencies in food and health care. On the other hand, there was always the temptation or the need for prison officials to resort to violence and corporal punishment to enforce certain rules or to make sure prisoners were not gaining too much leverage in the negotiation of internal rules. Numerous situations could be resolved only through the use of violence: corporal punishment by prison authorities, escapes, riots, and other forms of confrontation by prisoners.

Prisoners' challenges to the prison order—both the strictly legal order and the customary order created in daily life—adopted many forms, including suicide, individual insubordination, escapes, and riots. Less visible, but no less effective forms of protest developed throughout the period in the form of verbal and written denunciations. Some of these acts were reactions to extreme abuse, violence, and suffering. Others reveal a more conscious effort to resist the imposition of rules and norms perceived as unjust or abusive. And still others were the result of violations of the customary order by prison authorities and employees. While most of these actions did not transcend the prison walls, some of them broke through the shell of isolation and reverberated throughout the outside or at least reached outside targets, thus expanding the sphere of contention in the setting of prison rules. Writing a letter to a public authority or talking to a newspaper reporter could make the prisoners' voices resonate among wider audiences. By the late 1920s and early 1930s, albeit not always successfully, prisoners began to openly discuss the regulation of life inside the prison and attempted to have a more decisive input in the setting of prison rules. A decisive influence in this development was the presence of political prisoners and the always contentious links they established with the community of common prisoners.

PROTEST AND RESISTANCE

Prison escapes were the most obvious, although not the most common, form of protest against the prison order. During the eighty-five-year period covered in this book, escapes were rare and tended to decrease over time as prison security became tighter. Generally speaking, escaping was a much more difficult endeavor for inmates at the penitentiary or El Frontón than for those at Guadalupe. The Lima penitentiary, with its high walls and daunting architectural impediments, presented a serious obstacle to inmates wanting to break free. Still, escape attempts were numerous, though not always successful. Fragmentary evidence points to a visible decline in escapes from the penitentiary over the course of the years. The very first escape occurred only a few weeks after the inauguration: on September 15, 1862, the inmate Francisco Retroux broke out, apparently with the help of a French employee in charge of the prison's gas system. He was recaptured two weeks later in the town of Huaura, north of Lima.[1] In February 1863, another inmate, Francisco Risco, who had simulated insanity and was transferred to the physician's own apartment, managed to escape from the penitentiary.[2] There were two more escapes in July 1867, two in November 1868, and two in August 1870.[3] In the eight years between 1871 and 1879, a total of twenty-four inmates escaped from the penitentiary, an average of three per year.[4] In fact, these are rather high numbers, considering the type of prison the Lima penitentiary was. Each escape or attempted escape from the penitentiary had an impact on the outside world, and there were indeed occasions when panic seems to have spread throughout Lima as a result of prisoners' escapes.

One of the most publicized escapes from the penitentiary was that of Manuel Peña Chacaliaza in 1876, the same Chacaliaza who was the subject of a "criminological" inquiry by Paulino Fuentes Castro (see chapter 2).

He had been in the penitentiary for less than two years when he got away. He planned his escape with another prisoner, a man called Hidalgo, during conversations they had in the prison yard. Hidalgo worked in the shoe-making workshop, where he had spotted a ladder that could serve their purposes. Chacaliaza and Hidalgo first escaped from their cells by using a chisel they had stolen from the shoe-making workshop to chip away patiently at the wall and remove several bricks. It took Chacaliaza about four or five hours to complete the task. They then met at the workshop, carried the ladder to the prison wall, climbed to the top, and then, with the help of bedsheets, lowered themselves far enough to jump to the ground, getting "very banged up" (*muy maltratados*) in the process. Afterward, they reportedly walked to the port of Callao.[5] Although there was a rumor that Chacaliaza had cut his heels to get out of the stocks, this version was never confirmed.[6] The director of the penitentiary attributed the escape to "construction flaws that are very difficult to correct" and, in a move that reveals the seriousness of this breach of prison security, resigned from his position.[7]

I have not found reports of escapes in the three decades after 1879, though very likely this is a reflection of gaps in the documentation. The next prison escape to surface in the documentation was also truly spectacular and involved three political prisoners incarcerated at the penitentiary by the Leguía administration in 1910. Amadeo de Piérola, Enrique Llosa, and Orestes Ferro, prominent leaders of the opposition, had been imprisoned along with dozens of other members of the Liberal Party after the plot of May 1909 against Leguía. In January 1910, penitentiary employees discovered numerous metal files, knives, and other instruments in Piérola's room (he was not confined to a cell), tools obviously intended to facilitate his escape.[8] Shortly after, Piérola, along with Llosa and Ferro, managed to escape through a hole in one of the walls of their room. According to the official report issued later, the hole had been made from the outside. They passed on to one of the compartments of the director's apartment and from there jumped to the street with the aid of bedsheets. Suspicions of complicity on the part of prison authorities were immediately raised, but many in the opposition celebrated the successful breakout.[9] Other escapes occurred in March 1912 and November 1915, when five prisoners fled the panóptico.[10] Later, when sections of the panóptico were transformed into the CCV, escapes became seemingly easier. Escapes from the CCV are recorded in the early 1930s. Seven inmates escaped in just five months, from August to December 1934, and one of them, Enrique "Monito" Vinces, escaped four times.[11]

At Guadalupe, escapes were both more frequent and less shocking in the eyes of public opinion. In 1893, the anonymous group Presos amigos del orden blamed relaxed discipline and the state of abandonment of the prison for the numerous escapes and attempts that took place at Guadalupe.[12] Unlike breakouts from the penitentiary, many of the escapes from Guadalupe involved large groups of inmates. In August 27, 1884, for instance, twenty-two inmates escaped;[13] two months later, on October 14, another seven inmates escaped with the aid of a *caporal* who unfortunately could not avail himself of the escape tunnel "because of his corpulence";[14] on January 27, 1890, three inmates escaped from Guadalupe, this time by slipping through the bars of the window in the shoemaking workshop.[15] In February 1892, an inmate in charge of electric power management at Guadalupe and also a guard of the *calabozo*, positions for which he was chosen because of his good behavior, escaped only to be recaptured shortly afterward.[16] Overall, attempts to flee Guadalupe were much more numerous than at the penitentiary.[17]

Escapes from El Frontón, conversely, were much more difficult and rare, owing to the considerable distance between the island and the coast as well as to the turbulent ocean waters. Still, some fugitives succeeded. On February 23, 1925, three military prisoners escaped in a *chalana* (raft) used for the transportation of food.[18] In February 1927, Domingo Castañeda, described as an "old and hardened thief," successfully escaped. He first hid from view for two days in the island's hills, and when he was sure nobody was looking for him anymore, he swam to Callao.[19] On May 27, 1930, two inmates tried to flee the island in a chalana they built "little by little, working on Saturday afternoons." They planned the escape to coincide with Sunday visiting hours. When they were already on the water, they were spotted by other inmates who, not knowing if they were escaping or drowning, notified the guards. With the help of the motorboat that transported visitors the fugitives were captured. Olazabal, one of the frustrated fugitives, who had been sentenced to twenty-five years of *internamiento*, told the authority he was going to try again, for he considered his sentence totally unjust. He believed he had the right to execute his plan of escape. Shortly afterward, he was transferred to the penitentiary.[20] In his description of prison life at El Frontón, Aprista writer Julio Garrido Malaver suggested that while numerous prisoners tried to escape, "very few reached shore."[21]

Riots and mutinies were also exceptional events in the history of Lima's prisons. Most were spontaneous and, although some had the distinct purpose of forcing a massive escape, more frequently they lacked clear objectives. Riots and mutinies exploded at moments of extreme tension and were expressions of accumulated frustration and rage on the part of the prisoners. Alcohol consumption was also behind some of the riots. In most cases, there were individuals who acted, if not as leaders, at least as instigators or promoters. Although in a few cases some prisoners were able to escape, most times riots were violently subdued, and inmates suffered severe retaliation from prison authorities.

At the penitentiary, the sources indicate, riots were common in the early days of the prison but became quite rare as time passed. At Guadalupe, riots seem to have been even less frequent. I hesitate to assert what the situation was at El Frontón, as the information flowing from the island was less plentiful than for the other prisons. Yet a pattern can be identified: riots and mutinies were less frequent in those prisons and during those administrations that more closely sanctioned the customary order. That mutinies and riots were generally scarce could be interpreted as a sign that the customary order was prevalent throughout most of the period under study. Other factors also contribute to the relatively low incidence of prison riots: the multiple schisms dividing the prison population, the pervasive presence of *soplones* (informants), and the fear of harsh retaliation from prison authorities.

On October 31, 1864, for example, a riot erupted among prisoners working at the penitentiary's shoemaking workshop. Led by three inmates armed with knives the insurgents took several employees as hostages and demanded to be transferred to Guadalupe, arguing they had not been sentenced to the penitentiary. They were subdued with the help of soldiers from a nearby army post.[22] In 1867, two major riots erupted at the penitentiary. In March of that year, twenty-three inmates revolted, took hostages, and were finally subdued only with the aid of external armed forces.[23] In December, an even more serious uprising exploded. Eighty inmates reportedly tried to scale the wall to escape, and a battle between inmates and guards ensued, the would-be escapees using stones and utensils to attack the guards. The director ordered the troops to shoot at them. External armed forces came to help, and the inmates finally surrendered. In the end, two individuals were dead and sixteen injured, two of them seriously.[24] Two weeks later, undoubtedly still under the impression caused by the December episode, the new director reported that another escape was being planned, one which included setting fire to parts of the building. He quickly acted to avert it, ordering confinement to cells for all inmates except those who worked in the kitchen.[25] Several other riots were halted thanks to timely warnings by soplones.[26] In February 1868, the penitentiary director visited the workshops and reported he had noticed "serious discontent" and "menacing" faces among the inmates, which revealed that "their only goal is to escape by any means and at any cost."[27] On numerous occasions prison authorities discovered arms and utensils in the hands of inmates, instruments which could have been used in planned mutinies. On December 9, 1866, a riot that included massive flight was aborted. The detailed inspection that followed revealed ten cells with holes already opened and, in almost all the cells, stolen tools from the workshops were found.[28]

After this initial series of mutinies, however, I have not found information regarding similar incidents inside the penitentiary until the late 1920s and 1930s, as we will see below. The frequency of riots seems to have decreased around the late 1860s, when the system of private contractors and cash incentives to prisoners/workers was established. This may suggest that the system of cash incentives did work for prison administrators, at least in terms of obviating major disruptions of prison order.

At Guadalupe, riots were apparently less frequent. One major eruption, usually referred to as the great uprising, took place on January 18, 1881, coinciding with the disorder and confusion that accompanied the Chilean occupation of Lima.[29] Overcrowding, alcohol consumption, and the private interests of some inmates were behind another riot at Guadalupe. On July 28, 1915, a caporal went to open the door of a calabozo in which more than one hundred prisoners had spent the night together. He was suddenly assaulted by the crowd, which was reportedly led by Apolinario Arzola. The inmates then directed their rage against the prison canteen, calling for its sacking and destruction. Most of them were reportedly drunk and furious "like crazy." They calmed down when the prison physician came and apparently convinced Arzola to yield. Later versions located the origin of the mutiny in "certain food business" Arzola had with the prison store.[30] Although the information is sketchy, this case may demonstrate that riots sometimes flared when inmates and authorities clashed over some aspect of the customary order such as the control of food traffic inside the prison.

Information on riots at El Frontón is scarce. On one occasion, in March 1921, owing to the "prevailing indiscipline" among prisoners, the director decided to impose the same *Reglamento* as that of the Lima penitentiary, a move that was to produce a serious perturbation in the prisoners' daily lives. The convicts' response was quite radical and unanimous: they gathered in one of the barracks and refused to work. According to the director, he later convinced them to yield, but still the leaders of the mutiny were put in solitary confinement, which infuriated the inmates and led to a noisy protest. The disturbance was finally put down with the use of firearms and the application of "the penalties they deserve."[31]

Discontent and frustration were also reflected in various forms of individual protest. One of them was suicide, albeit it happened quite rarely. From the available records, only three suicides were registered in all of Lima's prisons during the period under study, and in all three cases the victim was a Chinese inmate.[32] Shortly after the inauguration of the penitentiary, in fact, the director asked the minister of justice not to send Chinese convicts to that prison because "owing to their religious beliefs and their education they very readily commit suicide, no matter how insignificant is the difficulty they are facing." He actually refused to admit the first Chinese convict sent to the penitentiary.[33] Suicides committed by Chinese persons were not rare in Lima. According to the historian Augusto Ruiz Zevallos, of a total of 121 suicides committed in Lima between 1904 and 1919, 79 (65 percent) were committed by Chinese.[34] More common individual acts of protest involved violence against guards and authorities, generally without too much premeditation or clear purpose other than expressing their rage and discontent. These situations would typically end with the inmate being severely punished if he was not dead already. In July 1874, a penitentiary inmate attacked some employees with a knife and took refuge in his cell, threatening to resist to the death. He incited others to follow his example, without too much success. Only after two days did he finally yield.[35] Another inmate attacked the inspector with a knife and then attacked the employees who tried to calm him down. He was shot to death by the guards.[36] Another inmate at the penitentiary, years later, insulted a guard, as a result of which he was confined in his cell; later, when a search of his belongings was being conducted, he attacked the caporal mayor and injured another inmate with a knife.[37] Abel Silva, a Chilean inmate at the penitentiary, injured the inspector with a knife and was shot dead by prison guards. During the showdown he was heard to say, "Quiero morir pero matando" (I want to die, but killing.)[38] Many similar situations probably went unrecorded, as did the ensuing punishment applied by prison employees. Some inmates chose to vent their frustration after their release from prison. An inmate named Manuel Contreras was released from the penitentiary in 1875 after twelve years of incarceration. His first night out he got drunk and walked to the house of the penitentiary director, Camilo Martínez, but did not find him. He told members of Martínez's family he would kill him and "drink his blood, along with that of four other [penitentiary] employees."[39] Years later, in February 1900, the warden of Guadalupe, Don Víctor Germán Pastor, was assassinated. The main suspect was Manuel Barrientos, who had been released from Guadalupe four months earlier, "which make us think," said the report, "that the crime's motivation was vengeance."[40] Although it is impossible for us to corroborate this version, it is a credible story to the extent that prison authorities were quite frequently seen as abusive and unfair by scores of inmates.

Particularly troublesome, recalcitrant prisoners like the ones involved in these impassioned actions were often portrayed and treated as being insane. The issue of the mental condition of prisoners was indeed a very controversial one. As one prison official admitted, "There isn't a more difficult or delicate issue than the assessment of the true mental condition" of convicts.[41] Ruiz Zevallos has demonstrated that diagnosing an individual as mentally insane during this period was very commonly an arbitrary procedure resulting from specific personal, political, or family motivations. A condition of mental illness was attributed to an individual anytime he or she behaved in ways that deviated from the established norm: feminists, spiritualists, and other such supposedly abnormal characters were sent to the mental asylum and treated as being insane.[42] Inside Lima's prisons, the sources indicate, authorities used the argument of insanity as a means of getting rid of stubborn, dangerous inmates.[43] The case of Leonardo Gómez, a black soldier imprisoned at Guadalupe, illustrates this issue. One day in February 1904, while being held in the dungeons, he asked the caporal for permission to talk to the warden. The caporal responded by beating him. Some time after this incident, in a moment of distraction, Leonardo attacked the caporal, which resulted in a medical report stating that Leonardo presented "symptoms of insanity." Later, physicians argued that his insanity was permanent, and he was transferred to the mental asylum. Leonardo managed to escape from the asylum—an action that, according to the judge, proved he was not insane—but was recaptured. He was sent back to Guadalupe but, in September 1905, authorities ordered him to be transferred once again to the asylum, where officials refused to admit him because of his dangerous character. New medical reports now depicted him as the offspring of alcoholic parents, an alcoholic himself, epileptic, and even as having an asymmetric organic development. The conclusion was he had "impulsive and involuntary convulsions which make him a dangerous individual." The judge ordered him to be held in the mental asylum, but again he was denied admission.[44]

The too-facile association between nonconformist behavior and madness in this and other cases reveals the manipulations prison authorities were prone to effect when it came to the issue of prison discipline. In 1891, there was a proposal for constructing special cells for "furious insane men," a category that simply meant stubborn and recalcitrant inmates.[45] Instead of dealing with such inmates, prison authorities preferred to label them as insane and pass the problem along to psychiatrists and the authorities of the mental asylum.[46] At the same time, labeling them as insane was a way of discrediting any claims made by these unruly prisoners. Accusations of physical or economic abuse, as in the case of Martín Saniz discussed in chapter 6, were transformed into discussions about the mental health of the inmate.

These disparate responses to prison order on the part of inmates suggest some observations. Openly confrontational strategies such as riots and escapes were, generally speaking, rare events in the history of Lima's prisons. At Guadalupe, escapes were seemingly more frequent than at the other prisons, a consequence of the rather loose security. Riots were also very unusual events at all prisons. When they did erupt, they proved to be quite unsuccessful, which may explain why prisoners preferred not to engage in such activities and concentrate instead on day-to-day forms of accommodation and coping with prison life. The absence of major eruptions of violence is attributable not to the acquiescence or submissiveness of the inmate populations, but to the relatively successful implementation of the customary order and other forms of coping with the experience of the prison.

The customary order of the prison did not represent, as we have seen, an ideal situation in which both prisoners and authorities fully complied with its rules. There was ample room for conflictive situations that were resolved through various means, including the use of violence. Neither prison authorities nor the inmate population ever considered that a certain status quo would last forever and without perturbations, and mutual suspicions pervaded the relationship among authorities, employees, and prisoners. At the same time, none of these groups was a homogeneous collective, and the potential for dissension and disagreement was always present. This reality generated the need, first, for authorities to seek the collaboration of specific individuals drawn from within the inmate population and, second, for certain inmates to engage in a relationship that could offer tangible benefits. There was always a small group who, sometimes openly, sometimes covertly, collaborated with the prison administration. These included the aforementioned caporales, soplones, and a variety of other individuals performing different duties for the authorities.

Soplones are a common presence in prisons everywhere, and so they were in Lima's prisons. They played an important role in the surveillance of the prisoners. Being part of the prisoners' community and having access to the channels of information and organization developed within the inmate population, they could offer authorities valid information about the state of mind of the inmates and the occasional preparations for escapes, riots, and other forms of collective or individual protest. The activities of soplones are detected in the communications between authorities in which they shared information about the prisoners' plans. Numerous uprisings and escape attempts were aborted thanks to timely *soplos* (tips). Because of their nature, they lived on a very precarious edge. In 1867, for example, a soplón was about to leave the penitentiary. According to the subdirector, he had made "revelations of such nature that have prevented the escape of all his fellow inmates and the shedding of blood by the employees." Because of this, his fellow inmates detested him and had made serious threats on his life, so he was allowed to spend his last days in prison in the director's office.[47]

Besides soplones there were always prisoners who were semiofficially recruited by the prison administration to perform a variety of duties for which, because of insufficient budgets, regular employees could not be hired. By filling these positions with inmates, prison authorities also sought to establish closer links with a segment of the prison population that could be co-opted by offering them rewards for performing their duties. For the inmates thus recruited, this was an opportunity to earn some money, obtain privileges, and forge a good relationship with prison personnel. Inmates worked in diverse aspects of the administration, in positions such as doorkeepers, kitchen assistants, cleaners, and even personal servants for prison authorities. Being in those positions also entailed some perils. They were under pressure from above, that is, from prison authorities, and also subject to the scorn or the retaliation of their peers. They lived life in a delicate balance. A telling example is the inmate who was hired as a doorman at Guadalupe because there was no money to hire a person from the outside. The director, however, thought the inmate did not cooperate with the authority and preferred to side with his *compañeros*, either out of fear or camaraderie. "We never get prisoners who are loyal to the Warden," insisted the director.[48] But collaborators did not need to have specific assignments within the prison administration. There were always inmates whose attitude tended to be spontaneously collaborative and who, because of fear of retaliation, the expectation of receiving certain privileges, or the disgust they felt toward their fellow inmates, helped the authorities preserve prison order. Such inmates were praised by the director of the penitentiary in April 1868 for "their precision in performing their duties, the morality and resignation with which they suffer their misfortunes, the respect and subordination to their superiors, [and] their industriousness," but especially for the help they offered in defeating the insurrection of prisoners that took place in December of that year.[49]

On the other hand, there was a segment of the prison population that was neither involved in open collaboration nor shared with the rest of the prison population the risks and agitation of both the prison customary order and the prisoners' subculture. These were the so-called *presos tranquilos* (quiet inmates). They were described as never being involved in behavior that authorities most feared, like fights and riots, or that most prisoners practiced with or without the authority's consent, like coca consumption, sexual relations, and so forth. They were inmates who most likely considered themselves too decent to be treated as or to live the life of a criminal. In order to be able to live in a separate section, they certainly needed money or contacts, for that was a privilege reserved for influential inmates. At Guadalupe, for instance, a special section was reserved for the tranquilos, who with the aid of authorities protected themselves from the threatening rateros and faites. These prisoners, according to one description, were not real criminals, even though they had committed crimes, but just "victims of their passions," rage, love, or ambition. "Their faces," a reporter concluded authoritatively, "do not provoke fear or distrust." In the tranquilos section, the director of Guadalupe added, neither violence nor vices were to be found.[50] At the penitentiary, inmate no. 41 was described in 1868 as being one of those presos tranquilos: "The resignation with which he has suffered his misfortune, and the exemplary behavior he has demonstrated, have earned him appreciation and trust from his superiors and respect from his fellow inmates."[51] According to a number of testimonies, some *penitenciados* confined at Guadalupe joined the ranks of the tranquilos in order to avoid being transferred to the penitentiary as retaliation for poor behavior.[52] This strategy was quite different from that of the bulk of the prison population. The tranquilos tried to keep themselves out of trouble, not necessarily challenging the customary order—after all, they also sought special arrangements—but keeping some distance from the "true" criminal population of the prisons. It is hard not to see in these attitudes the reverberations of the distinctions between criminals and workers discussed in chapter 2. While they were criminals in the legal sense of the term, they did not regard themselves and were not regarded by others as belonging to the criminal class.

The fact that some prisoners accepted positions as de facto employees of the prison did not necessarily mean they were satisfied with the status quo or had submissively accepted their place inside the prison. Good behavior and acquiescence were not always signs of conformity. They were, first and foremost, strategies for earning some compensation from prison authorities in the form of immediate privileges or, eventually, even pardon or parole. The inmate Reynaldo Agüero is a good example of this. He was very well known for his respectful attitude toward prison authorities and for his rather embellished speeches during official ceremonies, many of them attended by the president of the Republic. His "public transcript" was clearly stated: "If misfortune has brought us to this place, where we remain deprived of our freedom, let's seek conformity, resignation, and peace of spirit, for, if we come to obtain these virtues, we will be happy in any circumstance; without them, we will be completely unfortunate even if surrounded by the greatest luxuries of the world." He eventually solicited presidential pardon, and he certainly made sure that all his speeches were included in his file.[53]

Whether or not this strategy was successful—in the case of Reynaldo Agüero or in any other similar case—cannot be easily documented. As in so many other instances of subaltern power struggles, acquiescence was clearly a strategy to survive and, eventually, to leave the prison, not an indication of ideological compliance. This is further demonstrated by the numerous cases of collaborators who ultimately became involved in various forms of open resistance. One prisoner at the ccv, for example, was named *corneta* (bugler) of the prison because of his good behavior. As such, he enjoyed ample freedom to walk throughout the establishment at any time. One day he escaped by just leaving the prison through the main entrance. The prison guards did not stop him because they did not know (or at least alleged they did not know) he was a prisoner.[54] A caporal at the penitentiary created a scandal one day in March 1925 when, in a state of drunkenness, he abused another inmate, insulted a guard and a few prison officials, destroyed some items, and attempted to enter the observatory of the prison. He then called on the rest of inmates to revolt, though only seven of them joined the protest. They were later contained with the aid of other prisoners.[55] Seven prisoners escaped from Guadalupe in October 1884 thanks to the help of one of the caporales. After the incident, the warden reported that "far from assisting us in our goals, they [the caporales] become in cases like this natural allies or accomplices of the rest of the prisoners."[56] This ambiguity toward caporales, indeed, was an almost permanent feature of the prison order. Prison authorities needed them, but they could not fully trust them. Collaborative prisoners did everything they could to gain the authorities' trust by demonstrating acquiescent behavior, but they clearly had an agenda of their own, one which could eventually led to conflictive situations.

THE DEFENSE OF PRISONERS' RIGHTS

Prisoners' proactive forms of coping with the prison environment were not limited to negotiations and confrontations with prison officials. They also actively strove to engage external agents in their effort to ameliorate their situation. Although in principle communication between prisoners and the outside world was severely limited, inmates found ways to exploit the numerous opportunities that existed to attempt to open those channels of communication. Writing and often smuggling letters was one of the most common tactics used by inmates in Lima prisons, as in prisons elsewhere.[57] Prisoners have always tried to reach the outside world in search of help, understanding, love, and support, but also for voicing complaints, accusations, demands, and requests. In the case of Lima prisons, and especially during the 1920s, inmates wrote numerous letters to political and judicial authorities requesting or demanding attention be given to their situation. Illiterate prisoners realized, maybe for the first time, the importance of the written word and sought assistance for conveying their feelings through paper and ink. Despite certain inevitable ambiguities, a clear trend emerges from the study of this set of letters found in the archive of the Ministry of Justice: by the late 1920s, their nature and content began to reflect recently acquired political and doctrinal tenets that marked a double shift. First, there was a change from a strictly individualistic to a collective approach in the pursuit of prisoners' goals. By the late 1920s, numerous letters signed by large groups of inmates began to reach authorities and other outsiders, a fact which clearly discloses both a new awareness of the importance of collective action and the emergence of new mechanisms for putting action in motion. Second, there was a change from a subservient, deferential tone to a more assertive, denunciatory style, revealing the appropriation by inmates of some of the rhetorical tools used by criminologists and prison experts in their bid for the implementation of modern prison disciplinary regimes.[58]

In explaining this shift one must take into account at least two concurring factors. First, the proliferation of organizations and individuals, including philanthropists, professionals, criminologists, physicians, penologists, and journalists, that since the 1890s had begun to disseminate, among other ideas, the principles of prison reform not only outside but also inside the prison walls. Not intended to enlighten the inmates about their rights but rather to convince them of the worthiness of hard work and obedience, the discourse of these outsiders nonetheless seems to have alerted the prison population to the potentially subversive nature of the rhetoric of prison reform, especially when contrasted with the nasty realities of Lima's prisons.

By the 1890s, following the introduction in Peru of positivist criminology, prisons became, to a degree unknown in earlier periods, the focus of attention by several groups of outsiders. Criminologists, penologists, and physicians began to tour Lima's prisons in search of clues that would help them understand the nature of crime and the characteristics of the criminal population. Journalists began to explore and report on the living conditions inside prisons and the peculiarities of the prison population, exploiting the voyeuristic appetites of an urban population eager to uncover the mysteries of prison life. Philanthropists gave birth to patronage and humanitarian societies and began to visit Lima's prisons to offer consolation and relief to their inmates. People like Angela Ramos initiated energetic campaigns for the relief of prisoners, visiting them and organizing events such as the Navidad del Preso. The most traditional of all these interventions was the customary *visita de cárcel* (prison inspection) public authorities had to perform every week in order to check on the conditions of the prisons and make sure prisoners were treated according to legal mandates. In the 1920s, in addition, and following the dictates of scientific criminology, authorities organized lectures inside the prisons to indoctrinate inmates in such issues as hygiene, discipline, industriousness, and, more generally, the ideas behind prison reform efforts. While the experts naturally wanted the prisoners to internalize the rules of appropriate behavior like obedience, hard work, and sexual abstinence, inmates seem to have paid attention to the potentially subversive nature of some of the tenets of the ideologies of prison reform: humane treatment, a healthy environment, and the elimination of corporal punishment.[59]

Second, the shifts demonstrate that broader changes in Peruvian society resonated inside the prison walls. At a time in which growing sectors of the population began to organize in political parties, labor unions, and other civil organizations, inmates at Lima's prisons began also to organize themselves and to assert their demands in collective rather than individual ways. The presence of large numbers of political prisoners in Lima's prisons during the latter period of the Leguía administration (1919–30) must have further aided the inmates' efforts at organization and collective action. Although the relationship between common and political criminals was usually distant and difficult, as we saw in chapter 5, conversations and interactions between them did occur, and political detainees certainly helped common prisoners develop or consolidate a much more independent and assertive political consciousness. The search for forms of collaboration between the two groups was influenced by the doctrinal commitment progressive and radical political prisoners had to the popular classes and, most important, to social justice. Their condition as victims of state repression encouraged them to find, despite their abhorrence of common criminals, issues that affected both groups and thus got engaged in actions of protest aimed at ameliorating conditions inside the prisons. On the other hand, given their experience inside the prison and especially with the way things actually worked, common prisoners proved to be extremely helpful when political inmates needed to procure certain goods like food, cigarettes, and newspapers or to circulate secret information.[60] According to the Aprista veteran leader Nicanor Mujica, it was mostly indigenous inmates who helped the Apristas smuggle out letters and documents.[61] Despite the risks involved, common prisoners did cooperate out of friendship, monetary interest, the search for clientelistic relations with the *políticos* (common criminals realized that political prisoners had important connections and might even become state authorities one day), and even political allegiance.[62] Political prisoners saw in common criminals not just collaborators but also a potential source of political clientele. Thus, they tried to indoctrinate them and get them involved in political activism. In November 1932, for instance, it was reported that Aprista inmates at the ccv were "inculcating subversive doctrines among the prison population."[63] In June 1934, the director of the penitentiary reported that Aprista prisoners "persist in their criminal purpose of inciting the spirit of the common prisoners, in order to produce disorder in the prison." "They are tireless in asking the common [inmates] to follow their ideology and contribute to their fund, which goes to sustain what they call the National Executive Committee." The leader of this movement was, according to the director, Juan Seoane.[64]

Despite the radical differences of status, culture, and legal condition that separated political from common prisoners, certain forms of cooperation, some of them collective and well organized, did emerge. In August 1930, for example, a riot that erupted at the penitentiary was led by political prisoners and seconded by common prisoners armed with knives, sticks, and stones. External military aid helped the authorities put it down, but not before a guard was killed.[65] Abuses against common criminals sometimes generated expressions of solidarity from political inmates. In 1934, Pantera Negra (Black Panther), an inmate who dared to challenge the authorities at El Frontón by initiating his own coca business, was brutally tortured. Political and common prisoners initiated a noisy protest by shouting and banging on pots; the authority was forced to suspend the punishment.[66] In October 1935, the director of the penitentiary decided to suspend the common practice of allowing prisoners to send home part of their food ration, mostly bread, but also other foodstuffs. The prisoners responded with a strike that paralyzed the penitentiary workshops. They received support from political prisoners, a move that the director condemned because, he said, "they want to give a political aspect [to this issue] with the goal of destroying the prison's discipline." Four of the leaders of the common prisoners were sent to El Frontón in retaliation. The director later reported that the issue had been resolved, but did not say what his decision was.[67]

Political prisoners brought to the prison their own cultural and ideological baggage, including what was probably the most important tool they had to contest the legitimacy of their imprisonment: a principled position in defense of their *rights*. Although political prisoners also learned how to avoid extreme confrontation that almost certainly induced retaliation,[68] they usually displayed strength and resolution in the defense of their legal and constitutional rights. This language of rights, indeed, was not exclusive to radical political prisoners, for those belonging to elite social groups and to conservative political parties also used, quite vehemently, the defense of political rights and the constitution when protesting their incarceration. Not before the late 1920s, however, did this language begin to affect the forms of organization and the rhetoric used by common prisoners, as we will see below. This principled defense was put forward before, during, and after the actual incarceration, and although not all those instances were recorded, still the language of rights comes from numerous sources. Letters sent to newspapers, public communiqués, judicial allegations, and testimonies showed that political prisoners tirelessly used all means possible to denounce the arbitrariness and injustice of their incarceration. In this, their belonging to relatively solid organizations and the fact that they were part of the educated classes and had important social connections (with lawyers, for instance) definitely helped them make their voices heard, despite the government's repressive efforts. The case of José Carlos Mariátegui is revealing. During the persecution he suffered in 1927, he wrote a letter from the hospital that was published by the daily *La Prensa* in which he forcefully denied being involved in any "communist plot," while, at the same time, he took full responsibility for his ideas and writings, which were not "according to the law, subject to censorship or even less the action of the police and the courts."[69] "I have the right to be heard," he added. After a second incident with the police in 1929, in which he was held on house arrest and most of his personal archive was confiscated, Mariátegui wrote a letter to the director of the police himself, demanding the return of those valuable belongings.[70] The case of Haya de la Torre's imprisonment and trial in 1932–33 generated an energetic legal and political campaign. Besides denouncing the illegal nature of his imprisonment, the intolerable conditions in which he was being held at the panóptico, and the arbitrary nature of the interrogation to which he was subjected, his lawyers also presented him as a champion of social justice and the incarnation of Peruvian citizens' aspirations: "This trial, thus, is of interest not only to the Justice system and the State, but also to thousands of citizens that anxiously await the tribunal's resolution."[71] The cases of political prisoners such as Mariátegui and Haya de la Torre thus could bring to the confrontation with the state a whole arsenal of legal, political, and moral arguments whose echoes would resonate throughout the social body, including, not surprisingly, those other victims of state arbitrariness, common criminals.

Beyond the two cases quoted above, which involved the two most important ideologists of twentieth-century Peru, numerous other episodes divulge the ways in which political prisoners forcefully defended their rights. As one might expect, this defense included the explicit rejection of any suggestion that they were criminals. In August 1927, for example, Silvestre Sánchez sent a letter to the *prefecto* protesting his seventy-five-day arrest. "I am not a murderer or a thief," he complained, adding that he was detained "only because I have simply talked about working-class organization." He also demanded better food for his cell mate, apparently a common prisoner, who suffered from poor health. Sánchez started a hunger strike and a few days later was released.[72] In April 1930, the director of El Frontón reported that military inmates incarcerated for political reasons resisted classification, demanded special food, and refused to work. They did not even attend the ceremonies of allegiance to the national flag. In other words, they refused to be treated like common criminals.[73] In February 1932, Aprista inmates protested the lack of electric light in their cells and demanded they be transferred to a different section of the prison where, according to them, political prisoners ought to be.[74] Jorge García Mendizábal, a political prisoner who was prohibited from receiving visitors, told the director, "What I do not accept is that you mistreat me in cowardly fashion, taking away my right to receive visits. . . . You are a prison Director, and I am a social prisoner whose crime is no other than, precisely, to fight against injustice and in favor of social well-being [*bienestar social*]."[75] The relatives and supporters of political prisoners also did their part in raising their voices in defense of their rights. In December 1933, hundreds of relatives, mostly mothers, of Aprista prisoners wrote a petition to the president requesting pardon (*indulto*) for them: "They still suffer the burden of unjust sentences issued by the Court Marshall that, without the most elementary criteria of justice, only responded to political vengeance."[76] In May 1936, the mother of the Aprista prisoner Pedro Muñiz sent a letter censuring the prison authorities, and then stood in front of the penitentiary protesting loudly because, she claimed, her son was being starved.[77]

All these interventions had important effects on the prison population that, I argue, are reflected in the shifting content and nature of the letters they wrote. The circulation of criminologists, philanthropists, journalists, authorities, and political prisoners inside the prison not only made the isolation of prisoners virtually impossible, but also allowed them to be better informed about both political developments and public debates on penal doctrines and practices. Both were reflected in the letters they wrote to newspapers, authorities, and other outside individuals.

Many letters were addressed to prison and state authorities. Most of them, especially those sent by individual inmates, appealed to the compassion and humanitarianism of authorities by depicting the inmate's miserable existence, the submissive attitude with which he was dealing with his incarceration, and his promise of future regeneration and repentance. A good example is the letter written by the inmate Manuel Cáceres to Colonel César Landásuri, the director general of prisons, in 1924: "I am, my good Sir, one of those unfortunate individuals who, far from being malevolent, but rather a victim of the fatal force of destiny, committed an error for which I am sincerely repented. . . . For twelve years and eleven months I have been crying due to a mistake that I made because of my lack of experience, bearing the rigors of prison." He had been sentenced to twenty years of seclusion at the Lima penitentiary. The judge, he said, did not take into account his young age, good antecedents, and state of inebriation at the time of the crime. He asked Landásuri "with sincere tears" to solicit from his friends in the government his pardon on the occasion of the anniversary of the Battle of Ayacucho (the final military action of the Peruvian independence campaign against the Spaniards in 1824): "My gratitude for you will be eternal, and my personal services will be at your order, if I cannot correspond in a more dignified way." Manuel was told shortly after that he was indeed included in the list of pardoned inmates but, after several months and various letters, he discovered that nine other inmates had already left the penitentiary while he was still waiting. He wrote another letter, which he signed, "A man buried alive, who foresees his resurrection, salutes you, and blesses you."[78]

This tone pervaded numerous individual letters addressed to state authorities. Another inmate who requested transfer from El Frontón to the penitentiary depicted himself as a "disgraced man," "victim of misfortune," "submerged in this valley of tears." If his transfer was granted, he said, he would patiently wait at the penitentiary "without major moral sufferings that make my life even more bitter, until my long-awaited freedom is effected."[79] Another inmate wrote in 1930 to his "godfather," Minister of Justice José Angel Escalante: "I look forward to your goodness and your support for leaving this unjust incarceration. You well know, my dear and respected godfather, that I have not committed any crime, and that I am the victim of a woman of bad antecedents, with the complicity of a police sergeant." In this case, he asked the minister to intercede with the judge and a friendly lawyer to have his case revised.[80]

Indigenous inmates used their ethnic background to reinforce the same tone of deference and suffering that was thought to be effective in reaching out for help. Matías Suma, an indigenous prisoner, wrote to the director general of prisons requesting parole: "Your indisputable superiority would facilitate solid support for us, the unfortunate Indigenous inmates of this prison, many of whom, perhaps, are here due to strange or unjust causes."[81] Another Indian, Mariano Condori, who had just been released from prison but lacked enough money to return to his hometown in Azángaro, Puno, wrote a letter to the archbishop of Lima depicting himself as "a humble Indigenous vagrant" and explaining how "my Indigenous condition and the bad situation that I confront, force me to ask your high authority to take care of a poor man who is not culpable of his current situation." He had not mastered the Spanish language, he said, which made his situation even more difficult.[82] These and similar letters reveal the degree to which a common trope of *indigenista* rhetoric was used by Indians themselves to foster their requests: that of the "miserable Indian race," which, victim of abuse and exploitation by landlords, authorities, priests, and other non-Indian groups, was needy of protection and guidance. Indigenous inmates, likely following advice from intermediaries,[83] tried thus to capitalize from the "official indigenismo" of the Leguía regime.[84]

Other inmates chose to stress their honesty and industriousness in order to convey a positive image to the authorities. This strategy implied a desire on the part of some inmates to detach themselves from "the world of crime," an attitude consistent with my depiction of the working classes as increasingly separate from, even antagonistic toward, the criminal classes (see chapter 2). Many individuals who, technically speaking, had committed a crime thought their social, cultural, and employment condition made them different from the actual criminal population. Hence being treated as common criminals or being forced to associate with them was a terrible source of shame and discredit. Abel León, for instance, despite admitting he had committed a sexual crime, claimed, "I am neither a murderer nor a vulgar criminal. . . . I am an honest artisan, industrious, who used to support my tender children with my daily work." He requested a pardon, but it was denied.[85] Another inmate, Isaac Mayta y Castillo, actually mixed the honest-and-industrious self-portrait with the more pervasive discourse of resignation and submissiveness. He wrote a letter to President Leguía requesting pardon. He had been sentenced to twelve years at the penitentiary for homicide—which he claimed he did not commit—and for three years already had been suffering "with Christian resignation . . . as a national artisan, formal, honest, and vice-free worker." In addition, his letter employs yet another component of the prisoners' strategies: the appeal to political clientelism as a way of addressing state authorities. Besides stressing that he was a "national artisan, a tailor," Mayta y Castillo wanted to make sure the president knew he was a member of a Leguiísta political club. He promised to be an "exemplary artisan," but vowed also to be "intimately united to your very noble and patriotic action." He "implored" pardon and invoked Leguía's "well-known benevolence and philanthropy."[86]

There are strong resonances among these various ways of addressing public authorities. Inmates clearly preferred to appear as resigned victims rather than whiners; and instead of asserting rights, they chose to request mercy, a tactic that was seen as better suited since many of these letters were requesting pardon or parole. They also stressed loyalty, whether personal loyalty to a political leader or more impersonal allegiance to the principles of industriousness, obedience, and lawfulness, which, prisoners knew, authorities expected them to adhere to. Because these letters were written to request what inmates depicted (and authorities certainly considered) as favors or rewards, it would probably have been unwise on their part to use aggressive and seditious language. In reading these letters, one might recall they usually reveal what James Scott refers to as the "public transcript," which the subordinate uses to convey messages "in close conformity with how the dominant group would wish to have things appear."[87]

Mayta y Castillo was not exceptional in appealing to political loyalties. In the context of the Peruvian political culture of this period this is not surprising. The paternalistic and clientelistic nature of Peruvian political culture has been emphasized by numerous historians. Leguía's second regime (1919–30), with its highly personalistic methods and the overwhelming presence of adulation as an avenue for social and political climbing, reinforced these features of Peruvian political culture.[88] Paternalism and vertical political and social relationships were in fact pervasive in a multitude of social forms of interaction and organization: political parties, trade unions, labor relations in factories and haciendas, education, family structure, and many others. Prisoners also developed strategies of accommodation that obviously followed the lines of clientelism. They organized sports clubs, for instance, and called prison authorities *padrinos* (godfathers); they wrote poems, speeches, and songs, and played them during patriotic or religious ceremonies. In February 1928, for instance, Guadalupe inmates organized a reception for President Leguía on his birthday. "Recognizing the authority of the law," said the inmates' representative, "we obey its mandates, and from our cells, we applaud the representative of the Peruvian people. . . . The affairs of the state are conducted today with talent. . . . Oh Señor Leguía, [who has] uncommon perseverance and possesses a bullet-proof energy, is reaching the goal of his patriotic aspirations. He has a weapon: Character. And a shield: la patria."[89]

A few examples will illustrate the ways in which clientelism was deployed in prisoners' letters. A letter signed by 90 inmates was sent to President Leguía in June 1929 to congratulate him for the solution he had reached in the ongoing dispute with Chile regarding the territories of Tacna and Arica. Following the congratulations, prisoners expressed "our most fervent votes that the Divine Providence will prolong indefinitely your priceless existence, so that the Fatherland can benefit from your initiatives in favor of true progress and national prosperity."[90] Another collective letter, signed by 140 inmates at the Lima penitentiary and sent to the president in May 1930, offered him their solidarity after he had survived an assassination attempt: "We pledge our most fervent desire for your continual command of the state, and we also express our most loyal adherence to your person."[91] Once Leguía was removed from power in August 1930 (and was, indeed, himself sent to San Lorenzo and then to the penitentiary as a political prisoner), similar letters began to reach the new government authorities. Inmates at the CCV wrote a letter to the new minister of government in which they expressed their pleasure over "the recovery of civil liberties [*libertades ciudadanas*] after eleven years of oppression." They blamed the Leguía regime both for their convictions, which were attributed to corruption among judges, and for their plight inside the prison, where they were victims of abuses, injustices, and generalized corruption. They demanded the formation of a commission to review their cases.[92] Shortly after, a collective letter with more than 100 signatures was sent to President Sánchez Cerro, asking for a reassessment of their sentences. They protested that their confessions had been extracted under torture, but they also made sure to proclaim their remorse for their offenses.[93] Another group of prisoners wrote to the minister of justice, "Why in this hour of social emancipation, thanks to the brave crusade of the fearless military man Luis M. Sanches [*sic*] Cerro, have you not thought to send back to their desolated homes a good number of parents incarcerated for minor crimes, whom the old regime had sentenced almost in perpetuity?" The old regime, they added, had subtracted "a good number of citizens ready to collaborate, either with the plow or with the hammer—the ferrous symbol of the worker—to the betterment of the fatherland." They asked to be allowed to unite with all Peruvians in the "cry for freedom" promoted by President Sánchez Cerro.[94]

Whether state authorities were moved by these letters is unclear. Given the lack of meaningful initiative on the part of state authorities to improve the overall state of prisons and the living conditions of prisoners, one can probably infer that this stratagem was not really successful. After all, what would state authorities or political leaders receive in exchange, other than gratitude, from the prisoners? It is highly dubious, in the political and cultural ethos of Peruvian society during this period, that paternalistic attitudes toward prisoners would have represented major assets in the political capital of military or civil leaders. According to Angela Ramos, many people refrained from intervening in favor of inmates because they considered there was "nothing to gain" from such actions.[95] Thus, in spite of efforts by individuals such as Ramos herself, neither public opinion nor state officials were moved to act upon the deplorable situation of prisons and prisoners. An authoritarian society like Peru's, in which the political, social, and racial exclusion of the majority of the population was being reinforced during the period of modernization steered by Leguía, was not a propitious site for the development of widespread support for the cause of prisoners, and thus political rulers did not feel compelled to respond to prisoners' demands.

But more aggressively accusatory letters were also written, letters in which the submissive and clientelistic posture of those reviewed above was absent. In April 1929, for instance, three inmates wrote a letter to Director General of Prisons Bernardino León y León denouncing the torture of prisoners in the penitentiary.[96] Another letter to León y León was signed by a larger number of inmates at the ccv: "We obey the rules of discipline, but the employees, besides punishing us with underground seclusion, have begun to whip us, in an arbitrary and abusive manner." One inmate, they added, was tied naked by his hands and feet and whipped with a stick. "We are certain that the cries of that *compañero* must have been heard even outside the prison," they asserted. The letter demanded sanctions for the abusive employees. León y León read the letter, went to the prison, and verified the signs of torture. The extreme measures were then explained to him: the inmate had seriously offended a guard. Apparently no further action was taken.[97]

Inmates also wrote letters to newspapers, although only in seemingly desperate situations because of the inevitable retaliation public denunciations were bound to generate among prison officials. On the other hand, newspapers were not always receptive to inmates' protests. In August 1915, *El Comercio* published the letter of a Guadalupe inmate who had spent eight months in jail only because a policeman had accused him of insolence.[98] In September 1929, when a reporter and a photographer for *El Tiempo* visited El Frontón, inmates used the occasion to hand them letters addressed to both the director of the newspaper and the president of the Republic, but they were confiscated by the authorities.[99] In November 1930, an inmate whose letter was published in the newspaper *La*

Libertad was punished with six days of solitary confinement.[100] *La Prensa* published in July 1929 some news sent by inmates of the penitentiary with the help of an employee, who received a one-day suspension after his cooperation was revealed.[101] A prisoner wrote a letter to *La Prensa* in May 1931 accusing guards of trafficking in alcohol, coca, and food. In retaliation, he was transferred to El Frontón, for, according to the director, he was "an undisciplined and incorrigible subject."[102] Even the threat of publishing a letter could be hazardous: a note was sent by an inmate to a penitentiary inspector, warning him that if the punishment imposed on him was not suspended, he would send a letter to the media, "denouncing the abuses against the prisoners that are committed here, and revealing that you are just a bland stick without any authority." Shortly after, the prisoner's name appeared in a list of penitentiary inmates transferred to El Frontón.[103]

| | | | |

As we have seen, the continuous visits and activities organized inside Lima's prisons by both private individuals and state officials to discuss reform of the prison system gradually made more evident to inmates the flagrant contradictions between discourse and reality where their treatment was concerned. These contradictions were then underlined in their communications with authorities such as the director general of prisons and the minister of justice. As a result, the subservient and clientelistic inflection was no longer the only way of negotiating with higher authorities the living conditions inside the prisons. Prisoners began to appropriate some of the fundamental tenets of prison reformers in order to foster their own goals. This appropriation was, inevitably, quite selective. As in other cases of subaltern subversion of hegemonic and oppressive discourses, inmates turned the rhetoric of prison reform on its head and began to convey the notion that, if prison reformers and authorities had been more devoted to effecting what they preached, then the working and living conditions inside the prisons would have been quite different— indeed, more humanitarian.

A few examples will illustrate this process. In a collective letter to the director general of prisons signed by numerous penitentiary inmates on January 3, 1926, following the almost inevitable confession of resignation, prisoners denounced the fact that "*discipline*, in the noble sense of the word," did not exist at the penitentiary. What prevailed was malevolence:

"We live amidst confrontation between authorities, employees, and inmates. To enjoy tranquillity and certain benefits and privileges, it is necessary to be part of the criminal group of soplones." Prisoners demanded of the new authorities the eradication of all evils "by their roots," for, if not, "every *modern system* you would like to implement will be corrupted by the weeds."[104] Another collective letter from El Frontón inmates to President Leguía conveyed their gratitude for a project regarding new rules for conditional freedom: such a bill, they said, "will change the impenetrable look of the misfortune in which we are submerged, and will make us resurface in a climate of *readaptation*, bringing us closer to the *social milieu* from which our ill fortune removed us."[105] In one of the numerous collective letters written after the triumph of Sánchez Cerro, prisoners complained about the inhumane treatment they received in the prison. Such abuse, they argued, "far from helping us in our *readaptation to the social milieu*, from which we should have never departed, only brings bitterness and hatred to our hearts."[106] Terms such as *discipline, modern system, readaptation,* and *social milieu* were prominent within the ideology of prison reform, in Peru and elsewhere. The prisoners' use of such locutions in their letters shows the extent to which they were aware of those developments; more important, they brought the terms to bear in such a way as not to challenge the entire array of prison reform proposals—which, after all, was regarded as a means to subdue criminal behavior and impose effective surveillance and control over the inmate population—but rather to highlight the contradictions in the reformers' and authorities' actions.

Prisoners, therefore, made it very clear that the way they were being treated not only affected them as individuals and made them suffer, but also belied the whole enterprise on which the government had embarked, namely, the implementation of modern and scientific prison regimes that would consummate the transformation or readaptation of criminals into honest, industrious citizens. The abyss separating rhetoric from reality was obvious to prisoners' eyes, but they selectively chose those aspects of the reform program that fit their own agenda. The reformers' emphasis on readaptation through humane treatment, adequate infrastructure, and, especially, the eradication of physical abuse and torture was particularly appealing to the prisoners.

As a result, prisoners came up with their own "prison reform" program. By this I mean the formulation, not always explicit or systematic, of a comprehensive design of how prisons should operate, something that had always been the exclusive prerogative of penal experts. This was, indeed, a big leap for inmates: they (or at least some of them) overcame both the subservient inflection traditionally used in their requests and the clientelistic appeals to political loyalty as means of achieving their goals and moved on to articulate their own platform of prison reform. This program appeared in fragmentary form in numerous letters and in a much more systematic way in a collective letter signed in December 1931, which, significantly, also demanded, among other things, the removal from his position as director of the penitentiary school of one of the most prominent penal experts of his time, Víctor M. Villavicencio. It was as if Villavicencio had come to personify the incongruities of the official rhetoric of prison reform, and thus inmates wanted to get rid of him while, at the same time, they outlined their own, different agenda for prison reform.[107] The platform presented in this letter was quite extensive. They demanded fairness in the calculation of their wages, an issue that had been raised over and over again by penologists since at least the 1860s; the elimination of all restrictions on visitors; the regulation of parole procedures, especially regarding which infractions and penalties should be counted in the Tribunal de Conducta's evaluation; the provision of appropriate food, clothing, and medicines; the allowance of greater freedom to work on their own, as sort of free workers, so as to be able to feed their families; the release of all restrictions on the sale of goods manufactured by them; and the hiring of female employees to conduct the searches of female visitors.[108]

Some of these proposals affected one of the most crucial aspects of the organization of prison life—in particular, at the Lima penitentiary—namely, the organization of prison work. The demand for fairness in the allocation of their wages, together with the proposal to be allowed more freedom to work on their own and to sell unrestrictedly the products of such work—shoes, furniture, handcrafts—were meant to offer inmates a greater degree of control over their own time, work, and money, undermining the exploitation they usually suffered at the hands of private contractors and prison administrators. The other items in the agenda point to basic humanitarian reforms that would have dramatically improved their living conditions: appropriate food, clothing, and medicines, conspicuously and consistently poor in Lima's prisons.

This was the most ambitious plan for prison reform ever proposed by the prison population itself; it was almost as exhaustive as those designed by penologists and criminologists in the late 1920s. Although, not surprisingly, prisoners did not get what they asked for, such a comprehensive platform was both the culmination of a period of increased awareness and organizational and ideological maturity and the foundation for future collective action.

CONCLUSION

A unique series of colored drawings painted by an inmate at El Frontón in 1932 offers a rare opportunity to apprehend the experience of the prison as perceived by a member of the inmate community. The artist was Julio Alberto Godínez, who was sent to El Frontón under the apparently false accusation of participating in the Aprista insurrection of 1932 in Trujillo.[1] With a gaze full of irony and sarcasm, Godínez presents a series of caricatures depicting various scenes of daily life on the penal island. Unlike the portrayals of prison life in novels, poems, testimonies, and paintings, which tend to emphasize suffering, cruelty, and pain, Godínez's representations unambiguously invite the viewer to laugh, even when some of the scenes are not pleasant. One of them, for example (fig. 8), depicts a group of inmates enjoying a *jarana*, a festive celebration that would be unthinkable in a militarized, oppressive penal institution, but that may have occurred at El Frontón, as at other prisons in Lima, with relative frequency. The prison resembles, indeed, a *callejón* from any of the populous neighborhoods of Lima. Another group of images represent individual characters: a couple of faites, an "inoffensive idler," and Valdez, an inmate of allegedly decent background and a "victim of that high society" to which he belonged, who is depicted as mentally insane, sick, and abandoned. There is also a set of caricatures that offers a distinctly sarcastic angle on political prisoners. "Occasional Fraternity" (fig. 9) depicts the irony of an Aprista inmate and a Communist inmate embracing a soldier (apparently also a prisoner), while a common criminal stands alone, watching them from a distance. Godínez's caption is quite telling: "The soldier, ironically in this environment, fraternally embraces the citizens of the fatherland; but the sickle and hammer and the Aprista star do not embrace the Fatherland." He seems to imply that

Figure 8. A *jarana* inside El Frontón, by J. A. Godínez.
Reprinted by permission of the artist's widow, Lilia Rengifo
de Godínez, and his sons Alberto and Luis Godínez.

common criminals were also part of the *patria*, but that both political
prisoners and soldiers did not consider them as such, a forceful critique
indeed of the frequent lack of solidarity between the political and common prisoners. In another picture an inmate, apparently Godínez himself, appears to be totally indifferent to the militant attitude of both
Apristas and Communists (significantly, marching in separate columns),
while a common prisoner carrying a bottle of liquor as well as books
seems to have appropriated their political rhetoric and posture and appears to be presiding over the parade. Other elements appear in successive pictures: common criminals laughing at an Aprista speaker and
mimicking the Aprista symbol; a common criminal speaking the language of the political prisoners as he serves the ration; and the "comfort-
ably hard and hygienic" cell of a political prisoner, where rats also found
some comfort. Individual characters such as Cutipa, a black ratero, and
Zapata, a multiple murderer, "the only case that has repeatedly occupied

Figure 9. "Occasional Fraternity" by J. A. Godínez.
Reprinted by permission of the artist's widow, Lilia Rengifo
de Godínez, and his sons Alberto and Luis Godínez.

the attention of Peruvian criminologists," are also portrayed. Finally, Godínez offers two other very telling scenes: one depicts a guard (Saca-ronchas, literally, "Welt-maker") as a drunkard and an abusive officer who imposes his authority in brutal fashion; the other, entitled "Efficient Vigilance" (fig. 10), shows an inmate urinating behind the back of a sleeping guard, a suggestion that the principles of order and discipline have become fully eroded.

Godínez's drawings illustrate the vicissitudes of the customary order at El Frontón, an order in which a mixture of despotism and corruption, leniency and abuse, arbitrariness and suffering govern the world in which prisoners live. Partly the result of prisoners' agency, the emergence of a customary order is one of the most distinctive features of Lima's prisons. It was born of multiple factors and fulfilled different roles. It helped inmates overcome some of the most oppressive elements of penal institutions, but at the same time it perpetuated arbitrariness and corruption.

Figure 10. "Efficient Vigilance" by J. A. Godínez.
Reprinted by permission of the artist's widow, Lilia Rengifo
de Godínez, and his sons Alberto and Luis Godínez.

The result was an environment that in the final analysis helped maintain and reinforce the exclusionary and authoritarian nature of Peruvian society but also revealed the porosity and ambiguities of state-imposed mechanisms of social control.

Prisons around the world enjoy the unquestioned reputation of being dreadful places in which human suffering is perpetuated. Every scholarly study of the history and operation of prisons tends to confirm this depiction. "Next only to death," "tombs of the living," "worse than slavery": these are the ways in which prisons have been depicted in the scholarly literature.[2] Similar images emerge from the present review of the operation of prisons in Lima between 1850 and 1935. But to just confirm this is to add little to the understanding of the history of institutions of confinement. Prisons are worth studying because, among other things, they reveal a great deal about the values and obsessions of a society, the ways in which power and domination are both exercised and contested, and the connections between legal mandates and cultural values, on the one hand, and state policies and ordinary citizens on the other. My reconstruction of the history of Lima's prisons over an eighty-five-year period of political and social change has visited a series of issues connected with the role of penal institutions in the maintenance of social and political order. Viewed from the point of view of the alleged purposes of incarceration and prison reform, the dominant image would be one of failure. The Peruvian state failed to implement what, since the 1850s, had been proposed and officially embraced as the necessary, scientific, humane, and rational solution to the problem of crime and social disorder: the building of modern institutions of incarceration that would accomplish the goal of transforming criminals into honest, law-abiding, industrious citizens. A regime of rigorous and methodical work, strict rules of silence and obedience, the combination of rewards and penalties, humane treatment and moral suasion, and the tailoring of the penalty to the individuality of the lawbreaker were supposed to effect that transformation. It is not the case, however, that the regime failed. Indeed, the regime was never applied—it was perverted from the very beginning. What must be explained is not the failure of prisons to transform criminals, but the failure of the state to transform prisons by implementing what the codes, prison bylaws, and penal doctrines mandated. While there is no need to lament this failure, it is worth exploring what caused this outcome.

This book has identified at least three elements that help explain the fate of Lima's prisons during the period under study: first, the inability of the Peruvian state to meet the administrative challenges necessary to implement a thorough and comprehensive program of prison reform, inadequacies that ranged from fiscal insufficiencies to corruption and from lack of adequate personnel to defective infrastructure; second, the varied strategies used by prisoners to challenge the imposition of tighter forms of control and discipline inside the prisons and to create proactive forms of negotiation and resistance; third, and most important, the authoritarian and exclusionary nature of the modernization process and the pervasiveness of traditional forms of social domination. The period between the 1850s and the 1930s encompassed a series of dramatic changes in Peruvian society that are generally lumped together under the label of modernization. This was certainly not a smooth, even process, for it affected some geographical regions, economic sectors, social groups, and areas of state-society relations more than others. The birth of modern Peru was a process that reinforced various forms of social, ethnic, gender, and regional marginalization. These were not just super-fluous residues of times past, but central components of the modern-ization process. The persistent exclusion of a large majority of the popu-lation from the exercise of civil rights and political participation thus formed the backdrop of the oligarchic regime that brought Peru into the twentieth century and into the first stages of capitalist modernization.

It is within this context of an exclusionary political culture and the reinforcement of authoritarian social practices that the history of Lima's prisons must be located. Proposals for building a network of mod-ern institutions to replace the old, inefficient, and inhumane jails were launched as early as the 1850s, kept emerging (with seemingly decreasing enthusiasm) in the decades following the inauguration of the peniten-tiary in 1862, and, under slightly different doctrinal impulses, received new impetus in the 1920s. Regardless of the specific model advocated in the penal blueprint—the congregate model of penitentiary seclusion, the more rigid Philadelphia regime, or the so-called progressive system used at the Elmira Reformatory—these proposals implied that criminals were reformable, that they needed to be subjected to a rehabilitative treatment designed by scientific experts, and that state and society should look at them with compassion and humanitarianism, not hate and abhorrence.

All three components flagrantly contradicted the dominant social and cultural climate of Peruvian society during this period. Images of crimi-nals were dominated by the notion that they were individuals deserving neither compassion nor humane treatment (not to mention civil rights) but severe punishment or, at best, indifference. In this context, to de-mand, as penal doctrines did, the investment of economic and political capital in the rehabilitation of criminals was bound to generate eclecti-cism and apathy. After all, most subordinate groups, that is, children, workers, women, domestic servants, students, were treated with large doses of violence and despotism.

The lack of correspondence between penal theory and practice also relates to a salient feature of Peruvian intellectual history. As Carl Her-bold correctly pointed out, intellectual debates during the period dis-cussed here are characterized by a visible rhetorical and formalistic char-acter. Discussions of social policies were generally conducted with very little consideration as to the applicability or practicality of the ideas being discussed.[3] Many proposals looked grand on paper but their implementation lacked consistency. In the case of scientific criminology and penology, the distance between theory and practice was indeed quite marked. "Scientific criteria, specialization, and experience," complained Victor M. Villavicencio in 1927, did not exist among prison administrators. Empiricism and improvisation prevailed.[4] Actual research guided by the "science of the criminal" was also wanting, turning the doctrinal debate over crime and punishment into a usually vacuous exercise.[5]

Instead of science and humanitarianism, what guided the application of punishment, in particular incarceration, was a series of images and representations of crime that explained unlawful behavior in terms of the moral degeneration of criminals. This political and cultural construction of the criminal classes would shape not only the treatment they received in prison but also the very first encounter between them and the arm of the law: the arrest and jailing of (usually lower-class) criminal suspects. The police, one of the central institutions of modern societies, played a key role in the setting of moral, cultural, and political boundaries in Lima during this period. It was one of the most visible arms of the state, and probably the one that reached deepest into the lives of ordinary citizens. The widespread use of corporal punishment, the arbitrariness of arrest patterns, and the disregard for the most elementary rights of those who came within their sphere of action, all speak to the persistent role of the police as a manufacturer of injustice and inequality. Notions of appropriate treatment, that is, punishment, applied by the police were shared, not surprisingly, by other state institutions, most notably prisons, as we have seen in previous chapters.

Prisoners, nonetheless, were not passive victims of their fate. They responded in myriad ways: they escaped and rioted, showed strategic compliance with prison rules, resorted to diverse forms of individual and collective protest, used both patron/client relationships and more assertive forms of expressing their demands, built a rich, complex prison subculture, and actively engaged in the construction of what I have called a customary order inside the prison. Prisoners seized the occasion offered by the defective implementation of prison policies to build a series of informal and illegal arrangements that allowed them to escape some of the most oppressive aspects of prison life and to preserve some degree of autonomy within the overall oppressive structure of the prison. This order was fragile and double-edged, did not annul the essential vulnerability of prisoners, did not include all prisoners and all members of the prison administration, did not benefit (or harm) all of them equally, and frequently fostered internal divisions and exacerbated antagonisms between inmates. The customary order did not eliminate corruption, exploitation, corporal punishment, and deprivation. More important, it buttressed the overall institutional order of the prison, which otherwise would have been exposed to higher levels of stress. Given the subordinate position from which prisoners always had to operate, the construction of such an order reflects, nevertheless, their capacity to circumvent the rules, increase their bargaining power, and overcome the intermittent attempts at imposing more rigid penal regimes. To a certain extent, however, the prisoners' success in accommodating themselves to the customary order—which allowed them, for example, to supplement their diet, accumulate money, maintain contact with the outside world, generate partnerships and human relations inside the prison, and so forth—influenced the responses of state authorities to the realities of prisons. In the face of relatively modest levels of open defiance shown by the population of Lima's prisons, the government felt little need to invest significant amounts of financial and political capital in the amelioration of prisons.

The presence of political prisoners underlines the contradictions and ambiguities of prisoners' agency. They brought with them, especially in the 1920s and 1930s, an arsenal of political and ideological weapons that helped shape the strategies common prisoners used against prison authorities, including collective action, riots, and other forms of protest. Political prisoners used, in a much more assertive way, a language of rights that definitely impacted the relationship between authorities and inmates. But very seldom did they translate this into a commitment to the amelioration of prisons or the defense of the rights of prisoners after they left prison and, in many cases, became important state authorities. When they wrote about their prison experience, they did so to highlight their own vicissitudes and to denounce their own conditions of incarceration; and although they included common criminals in their narratives, they generally did so in an aloof, disdainful, if not racist, tone. Criminals, as we have seen throughout this book, were treated by the police and the criminal justice system as second-class citizens, were deprived of fundamental rights, and were forced to endure usually subhuman conditions in Lima's prisons. The sometimes terrible and life-changing experiences political prisoners endured left no room for them to become seriously concerned either with the prison situation as a whole or with the common criminals whom they met, befriended, helped, sought as political clients but, alas, also generally abhorred.

If the implementation of modern penal regimes was, at best, fragmentary and contradictory, existing prisons still fulfilled a variety of functions that made them indispensable to the state. Most obviously, prisons served the purpose of removing supposedly dangerous and undesirable individuals from society and subjecting them to punishment. As such, so the authorities expected, prisons served as a deterrent to potential criminals. Prisons also served as a sort of psychological relief to those who saw their lives threatened by (real or imagined) waves of crime. A more utilitarian aspect of prisons concerns the benefits private individuals and the state accrued from the exploitation of prison labor: private contractors running the penitentiary workshops, elegant stores selling shoes made by prisoners at Guadalupe, and the state's utilization of cheap labor in road construction are examples of the multiple ways in which prisons were used as sources of profit.

Prisons, in Peru as elsewhere, reflect the social and human landscape of the larger society. Lima's prisons congregated, like virtually no other social institution with the exception of the army, individuals from most corners of the country and from quite different social and racial backgrounds. They also reproduced existing social and cultural patterns: hierarchies based on gender, class, and racial status were reinforced and amplified within the world of the prison. Notions of *criollo* superiority over *serranos* and the display of peculiar understandings of manliness among faites, for example, resonated both outside and inside the prison. Prisons reflected, but also helped shape, the conflicts, tensions, and miseries afflicting Peruvian society. They reveal the exclusionary character of Peruvian society and the marginalization of subaltern groups imposed and strengthened by the state. Lima's prisons did not produce honest citizens; they did not even attempt to do so. Instead, they subjected criminals to further marginalization, leaving a legacy of disdain and exclusion that lingers still today.

APPENDIX

TABLE 3.1

POLICE ARRESTS IN LIMA, 1890–1927

(MONTHLY AVERAGE)

Period	Arrests per month	Total Population	%
Oct 1890–June 1891[a]	412	107,114[b]	0.38
July–Dec 1891[c]	519		0.48
Jan–May 1892[d]	1072		1
July 1892–Jun 1893[e]	1223		1.14
July 1894–Jun 1895[f]	855[g]		0.8
Jan 1892–Jun 1895[h]	1033		0.99
Jun 1905[i]	1506		
Jan–Jun 1915[j]	923		
Apr, Jun 1921[k]	1804	176,000[l]	1.025
July 1926–Dec 1927[m]	1629	200,000[n]	0.81

Notes: [a]Memoria, Subprefecto, 1891. [b]AGN, Prefectura de Lima, Serie 3.9, Legajo 16.6, August 8, 1891; 16.5, July 22, 1891; Capelo, *Sociología de Lima* (120), estimated the population of Lima in 1895 at 100,000. [c]Memoria, Prefecto, 1892. [d]Memoria, Prefecto, 1892. [e]Memoria, Prefecto, 1893. [f]Memoria, Subprefecto, 1895. [g]The decline in the number of arrests in 1894–95 must be due to the distraction of police forces during the Cáceres–Piérola civil war. [h]Jiménez, "La sociedad y el delito," 256. [i]*El Comercio*, July 20, 1905. [j]Boletín Municipal, no. 783, 1915. [k]AGN, Ministerio del Interior, Prefecturas, Paquete 219. [l]Alexander, *Los problemas urbanos*, 12–13. [m]Memoria, Guardia Civil, 1928. [n]Alexander, *Los problemas urbanos*, 12–13.

TABLE 3.2

ARRESTS IN LIMA, BY OCCUPATION, 1892–1921

	1892–93				1896				1921 (June)			
	Men	Women	Total	%	Men	Women	Total	%	Men	Women	Total	%
Working classes												
Industrial workers	1343	173	1516		2152	506	2658		42		42	
Artisans	4208	97	4305		3011	66	3077		207	57	264	
Peons	2883	1131	4014		3039	560	3599		423		423	
Agricultural workers	492	42	534		385	23	408		44		44	
Domestic servants	536	186	722		357	140	497		146	48	194	
Chauffers									57		57	
Subtotal			11091	75.5			10239	77.4			1024	56.6
Middle/upper classes												
Merchants	536	31	567		308	23	331		14		14	
Professionals	77		77		115		115		9		7	
Rentists	1		1		12		12					
Subtotal			645	4.39			458	3.46			21	
Military personnel												
Military	387		387		222		222		16		16	
Navy cadets	48		48		52		52		5		5	
Students					147	2	149		38		38	
Subtotal			435	2.96			423	3.2			59	3.26
Unemployed/marginal												
Employees	473	37	510		371	60	431		67		67	
Unemployed	611	393	1004		560	331	891		217		217	
W/out profession	547	369	916		382	311	693		142	56	198	
Rateros	66	66										
Rufianes y meretrices									63	93	156	
Subtotal			2430	16.55			2015	15.23			704	38.9
Unknown	52	25	77	0.52	57	33	90	0.68				
Total	12194	2484	14678		11170	2055	13225		1556	254	1810	

Sources: Memorias, Subprefectura de Lima

TABLE 3.3

ARRESTS IN LIMA, 1892–1927,
BY TYPE OF OFFENSE (PERCENTAGES)

	1892–1908	1896	1905	1921	1926–27
Against persons	19.49	13.06	15.11	11.47	16.07
Against property	24.42	9.21	21.59	21.68	21.59
Against honor	3.57	1.26	4.52	2.53	0.88
Against individual guarantees	0.93		0.49	0.31	
Against public order	51.59	49.87	45.24	50.98	49.89
Crimes by public employees		7.28		6.21	
Other		21.74	13.05	6.78	

Sources: 1892–1908: Valdizán, "La delincuencia en el Perú." 1921: AGN, MI, Pref, Paq. 219. 1896: Memoria, Subprefectura. 1905: El Comercio, July 20, 1905. 1926–27: Memoria, Guardia Civil.

TABLE 3.4

FINAL DESTINATION OF ARRESTED INDIVIDUALS, 1877–1921

Year		Total arrests	Sent to Prison	%	Released	%	Other	%
1877	Men	14804	1250	8.4	13527	91.3	30	0.2
	Women	2717	125	4.6	2587	95.2	5	0.2
	Total	17521	1375	7.8	16114	91.9	35	0.2
1892–93	Men	12194	515	4.2	11231	92.1	448	3.7
	Women	2484	62	2.5	2376	95.6	46	1.9
	Total	14678	577	3.9	13607	92.7	494	3.4
1921 (April–June)	Total	3608	217	6.0	3271	90.6	120	3.3

Sources: 1877: Fuentes, Estadística de la Penitenciaria. 1892–93: Memoria, Subprefectura, 1893. 1921: AGN, Prefecturas, Lima.

TABLE 5.1

NUMBER OF PRISONERS ENTERED IN GUADALUPE PRISON
PER YEAR, 1870–89

Year	Number	Year	Number
1870	662	1896	454
1871	849	1897	459
1872	470	1898	399
1873	827	1899	541
1874	964	1900	562
1875	810	1901	594
1876	606	1902	528
1877	604	1903	485
1878	565	1904	685
1879	488	1905	806
1880	542	1906	717
1881	258	1907	680
1882	302	1908	918
1883	309	1909	935
1884	236	1910	919
1885	229	1911	767
1886	408	1912	677
1887	366	1913	825
1888	330	1914	862
1889	360	1915	824
		Total	26,340

Source: Miró Quesada, *Breves apuntes de mesología criminal*

TABLE 5.2

INMATES AT THE LIMA PENITENTIARY, BY RACIAL GROUP,
1877–1928

Year	Total	White	%	Black	%	Indian	%	Chinese	%	Mixed	%
1877	386	55	14.2	33	8.5	187	48.4			111	28.8
1891	313	36	11.5	15	4.8	175	55.9	19	6.1	68	21.7
1900	315	24	7.6	14	4.4	168	53.3	16	5.1	93	29.5
1901	315	18	5.7	11	3.5	189	60.0	16	5.1	81	25.7
1903	315	14	4.4	13	4.1	178	56.5	14	4.4	96	30.5
1904	315	14	4.4	15	4.8	171	54.3	14	4.4	101	32.1
1905	311	24	7.7	14	4.5	155	49.8	13	4.2	105	33.8
1906	359	21	5.8	17	4.7	158	44.0	7	1.9	156	43.5
1907	411	44	10.7	17	4.1	340	82.7	10	2.4		
1908	411	32	7.8	11	2.7	359	87.3	9	2.2		
1909	411	35	8.5	15	3.6	351	85.4	10	2.4		
1910	410	39	9.5	22	5.4	337	82.2	12	2.9		
1925	354	47	13.3	7	2.0	89	25.1	3	0.8	208	58.8
1926	291	36	12.4	5	1.7	152	52.2	3	1.0	95	32.6
1928	234	17	7.3	7	3.0	114	48.7	3	1.3	93	39.7

Source: Memorias, Penitenciaria de Lima

TABLE 5.3

INMATES AT THE LIMA PENITENTIARY, BY RACIAL

DISTRIBUTION (PERCENTAGE), 1870–1927

	1870–1916	1917–27
Whites	17.4	15.8
Indians	36.1	52.2
Blacks	13.3	1.7
Chinese	6.2	1.0
Mestizos	27.0	29.2

Source: Fosalba, "La herencia como principal factor"

TABLE 5.4

INMATES AT GUADALUPE PRISON, RACIAL PROFILE, 1870–1915

	Number	%
Indian	9516	36.1
Mestizos	7102	27.0
White	4584	17.4
Black	3509	13.3
Chinese	1630	6.2
Total	26341	

Source: Miró Quesada, *Breves apuntes de mesología criminal*

TABLE 5.5

INMATES AT THE LIMA PENITENTIARY,
BY OCCUPATION, 1877–1925

	1877	%	1892	%	1906	%	1925	%
Artisans	141	38.7	109	36.1	253	71.1	110	37.5
Shoemakers	[67]		[46]		[122]		[43]	
Agriculturists	122	33.5	127	42.1	59	16.6	168	57.3
Armed forces	46	12.6	19	6.3	10	2.8		
Services	36	9.9	35	11.6	31	8.7	10	3.4
Without profession	9	2.5						
Mine Workers	5	1.4			3	0.8	4	1.4
Servants	3	0.8	9	3.0				
Teachers	1	0.3						
Engineers	1	0.3						
Veterinary							1	0.3
Cattlemen			3	0.99				
Total	364		302		356		293	

Sources: Memorias, Penitenciaría

TABLE 5.6

INMATES AT GUADALUPE PRISON, BY OCCUPATION, 1870–1915

	Number	%
Artisans	9692	36.8
Workers	4963	18.8
Agriculturalists	4200	15.9
Commerce and Industry	2677	10.2
Employees	1440	5.5
Military men	1424	5.4
Domestics	1109	4.2
Mariners	326	1.2
Professionals	217	0.8
Students	164	0.6
Artists	76	0.3
Proprietors	53	0.2

Source: Miró Quesada, *Breves apuntes de mesología criminal*

TABLE 5.7

INMATES AT THE LIMA PENITENTIARY, BY AGE GROUP, 1900–28

Year	15–19	20–29	30–39	40–49	50–59	60–69	70–79	80+	Total
1900	6	76	114	59	50	10	0	0	315
1901	7	88	111	58	44	7	0	0	315
1903	10	114	133	30	18	9	1	0	315
1904	13	120	128	28	18	7	1	0	315
1905	3	59	89	78	45	28	8	1	311
1908	9	105	148	86	42	17	4	0	411
1910	2	107	163	81	30	22	5	0	410
1911	3	102	141	84	37	34	5	0	406
1925	0	88	128	82	33	16	5	2	354
1927	0	95	109	59	16	7	4	1	291
1928	3	96	72	54		9*			234
Average	5.09	95.45	121.45	63.55	30.27	15.09	3.00	0.36	334.27
%	1.5	28.6	36.3	19.0	9.1	4.5	0.9	0.1	100.0

*60+

Sources: Memorias, Lima Penitentiary

TABLE 5.8

INMATES AT GUADALUPE PRISON, DISTRIBUTION BY AGE,

1870–1915

Age groups*	N	%
10–20	3198	12.1
20–30	11322	43.0
30–40	6893	26.2
40–50	3190	12.1
50–60	1215	4.6
60–70	409	1.6
70–80	103	0.4
80–90	11	0.0
Total	26341	

*As presented in the original table.

Source: Miró Quesada, *Breves apuntes de mesología criminal*

TABLE 5.9

INMATES AT THE LIMA PENITENTIARY,
BY TYPE OF OFFENSE, 1862–90

	N	%
Homicides and similar		
Homicide	1018	
Multiple homicide	35	
Frustrated homicide	31	
Homicide and other	49	
Parricide	8	
Filicide	3	
Uxoricide	16	
Infanticide	3	
Fratricide	4	
Shooting	5	
Uxoricide and other	2	
Attempted uxoricide	1	
Subtotal	1175	74.4
Injuries and violence		
Injuries	30	
Injuries and other	4	
Arson	4	
Arson and other	2	
Assault	48	
Subtotal	88	5.6
Economic crimes		
Theft	134	
Theft and other	39	
Petty theft	21	
Cattle rustling	17	
Highway robbery	10	
Falsification	25	
Subtotal	246	15.6
Sexual crimes		
Estupro	20	
Rape	6	
Pederasty	4	
Sodomy	1	

TABLE 5.9 (continued)

	N	%
Castration	1	
Estupro and other	1	
Subtotal	33	2.1
Crimes against public order		
Subversion	13	
Military mutiny	14	
Insubordination	1	
Rebellion	6	
Escaped prisoners	3	
Subtotal	37	2.3
Other	1	
Total	1580	

Source: Jiménez, "La sociedad y el delito"

TABLE 5.10

INMATES AT THE PENAL ISLAND EL FRONTÓN, BY TYPE OF OFFENSE, 1922

	N	%
Theft	73	40.1
Homicide	62	34.1
No data	18	9.9
Burglary	8	4.4
Petty theft	6	3.3
Injuries	5	2.7
Rape	4	2.2
Rape of a minor	3	1.6
Pederasty	1	0.5
Abduction	1	0.5
Cattle rustling	1	0.5
Total	182	

Source: Memoria, El Frontón, 1922

TABLE 5.11

INMATES AT THE LIMA PENITENTIARY, BY REGIONAL ORIGIN
(PLACE OF SENTENCE), 1877–1925

	1877		1900		1910		1921		1925	
	N	%	N	%	N	%	N	%	N	%
Ancash	19	5.1					39	7.7	27	7.6
Arequipa	18	4.9	17	5.7	31	7.8	18	3.6	14	4.0
Ayacucho	12	3.2	7	2.4	30	7.5	35	6.9	15	4.2
Cajamarca	28	7.6	26	8.8	41	10.3	44	8.7	42	11.9
Cusco					43	10.8	54	10.7	26	7.3
Huaraz			7	2.4	18	4.5				
Iquitos					4	1.0	18	3.6	8	2.3
Junin	8	2.2							16	4.5
Lambayeque									28	7.9
La Libertad	61	16.4	51	17.2	49	12.3	46	9.1	21	5.9
Lima	198	53.4	131	44.1	118	29.6	113	22.4	65	18.4
Piura	4	1.1	31	10.4	35	8.8	76	15.1	43	12.2
Puno	8	2.2	27	9.1	30	7.5	62	12.3	49	13.8
Tacna	15	4.0								
Total	371		297		381		505		354	

Source: Memorias, Penitentiary of Lima

NOTES

INTRODUCTION

1 Quoted in León y León, "El problema sexual," 71. Emphasis added.

2 Chavarría, *José Carlos Mariátegui*; Klaren, "The Origins of Modern Peru"; Pike, *The Modern History of Peru*.

3 See Basadre, *Historia de la República del Perú*, vols. 8, 9; Burga and Flores Galindo, *Apogeo y Crisis*; Gilbert, *La Oligarquía Peruana*; Klaren, "The Origins of Modern Peru"; Miller, "The Coastal Elite"; Nugent, "Building the State, Making the Nation"; Mallon, *Peasant and Nation*.

4 *Gamonalismo* is the term used to describe a variety of local bossism existing in the Peruvian highlands, in which the *gamonal* exercised political, economic, and even judicial power on the basis of personal dependence, servile labor, paternalistic control, violence, and the manipulation of local cultural codes. For an overview of gamonalismo, see Burga and Flores Galindo, *Apogeo y Crisis*, 104–13. See also various essays in Poole, ed., *Unruly Order*; Manrique, *Yawar Mayu*; and Jacobsen, *Mirages of Transition*.

5 López, "El estado oligárquico en el Perú" and "Crisis, formas, y reformas del estado," both included in López, *El Dios mortal*.

6 According to a commission of the Peruvian senate in 1895, "The man who does not know how to read or write is not, nor can he be, a citizen in modern society." Quoted in Mallon, *Peasant and Nation*, 275.

7 Mallon, *Peasant and Nation*; Thurner, " '*Republicanos.*' "

8 Mallon, *Peasant and Nation*, 315.

9 Burga and Flores Galindo, *Apogeo y Crisis*; Klaren, "Origins of Modern Peru"; Pike, *The History of Modern Peru*.

10 Taylor, *Bandits and Politics in Peru*; Burga and Flores Galindo, *Apogeo y Crisis*, 140–44.

11 Mallon, *The Defense of Community*; Klaren, *Modernization, Dislocation and Aprismo*; Jacobsen, *Mirages of Transition*.

12 Burga and Flores Galindo, *Apogeo y Crisis*, 146.

13 See especially Herbold, "Developments in the Peruvian Administrative System." The Peruvian state may be depicted as "highly despotic, yet infrastructurally

weak," to borrow the terms used by the sociologist Miguel Angel Centeno in his rendering of the Latin American state (Centeno, *Blood and Debt*, 10).

14 Klaren, "The Origins of Modern Peru," 614.

15 For an overview of urban changes in Lima, see Barbagelata and Bromley, *Desarrollo urbano de Lima*. See also Ramón, *La muralla y los callejones*.

16 Blanchard, *The Origins of the Peruvian Labor Movement*, 8; Pareja, *Anarquismo y sindicalismo*, 31.

17 Pareja, *Anarquismo y sindicalismo*, 30; Parker, *The Idea of the Middle Class*.

18 The literature on this topic is enormous. See, among others, Tejada, *La cuestión del pan*; Pareja, *Anarquismo y sindicalismo*; Sulmont, *El movimiento obrero en el Perú*; Kapsoli, *Las luchas obreras en el Perú*; Blanchard, *The Origins of the Peruvian Labor Movement*; Sanborn, "Los obreros textiles de Lima."

19 For valuable studies about urban life, popular culture, and socialization in Lima, see Muñoz, *Diversiones públicas en Lima*; Del Aguila, *Callejones y mansiones*; Ramón, *La muralla y los callejones*; and various articles in Panfichi and Portocarrero, eds., *Mundos interiores*.

20 Flores Galindo, *La tradición autoritaria*.

21 See Stein, "Cultura popular"; on women and domestic servants, see Miller, "La mujer obrera en Lima"; on schools, see Encinas, *La educación de nuestros hijos*. According to Francisco García Calderón, schools were "little military headquarters" (quoted in Stein, "Cultura popular," 61). On authoritarianism in the family, see González Prada, *Bajo el oprobio*.

22 Stein, "Cultura popular," 62, 73.

23 Melossi and Pavarini, *The Prison and the Factory*; Ignatieff, *A Just Measure of Pain*.

24 Meranze, *Laboratories of Virtue*.

25 Spierenburg, *The Spectacle of Suffering*.

26 Zinoman, *The Colonial Bastille*; Arnold, "The Colonial Prison"; Redfield, *Space in the Tropics*.

27 Davis, "Masked Racism"; Wacquant, "From Slavery to Mass Incarceration."

28 Foucault, *Discipline and Punish*, 304. As Nancy Fraser has recently summarized, "viewed through his [Foucault's] eyes, social services became disciplinary apparatuses, humanist reforms became panoptical surveillance regimes, public health measures became deployments of biopower, and therapeutic practices became vehicles of subjection." Fraser, "From Discipline," 160.

29 James, *Imprisoned Intellectuals*; Buntman, *Robben Island*.

30 Gatrell, "Crime, Authority, and the Policeman-State."

31 Garland, *Punishment and Modern Society*, 193–203.

32 Melossi, "The Cultural Embeddedness," 407.

33 Garland, *Punishment and Modern Society*, 195.

34 I take the expression from Barrows, *Distorting Mirrors*.

35 On this, see especially Wiener, *Reconstructing the Criminal*.

36 Perrot, "Delinquency and the Penitentiary System," 217.

37 On the strength of democratic practices see especially Forment, *Democracy*

in Latin America; on authoritarian traditions, see Flores Galindo, *La tradición autoritaria*.

38 For a brief account of female imprisonment during this period, see Aguirre, "Mujeres delincuentes."

CHAPTER 1. EMERGENCE OF THE CRIMINAL QUESTION

1 Born in Ecuador, Gutierrez lived in Lima most of his professional life. He is considered by the historian Jorge Basadre to be one of the best lawyers of his time. See Basadre, *Historia de la República*, 4:263.
2 The criminal was almost always constructed as a male subject.
3 According to Felipe Barriga, an acerbic critic of nineteenth-century liberal policies, an army of twenty thousand freed slaves was going to invade Lima and generate such a "horrendous quake" (*espantoso sacudimiento*) that society would be left with no choice but to "exterminate" them. Quoted by Dávalos y Lissón, *La primera centuria*, 4:107.
4 Távara, *Abolición de la esclavitud*, 43.
5 Fuentes, *Estadística general de Lima*, 211.
6 For the conservative newspaper *El Heraldo*, granting full citizenship to former slaves was "an insult to common sense." Abolition, it added, produced "the absolute idleness and total unbridledness of all blacks." *El Heraldo de Lima*, June 5 and 6, 1855.
7 Oviedo, *Colección de leyes*, 4:371–73.
8 Ibid., 12:255–57.
9 We lack a systematic study of the death penalty in colonial Peru. For references to public executions, see Flores Galindo, *Aristocracia y plebe*.
10 Valladares Ayarza, "La pena de muerte."
11 See Aguirre, "The Lima Penitentiary," 48.
12 An article in the newspaper *El Telégrafo de Lima* advanced the opinion that "to condemn any convict to death by a majority of votes is a crime. . . . capital penalties are deliberate homicides." *El Telégrafo de Lima*, September 20, 1833.
13 Loza, *Inviolabilidad de la vida humana*, 24, 30. I thank Charles Walker for sharing with me a photocopy of this rare pamphlet.
14 According to Gálvez, "Society does not have the right to kill." Quoted in Basadre, *Historia de la República*, 3:333. See also Valladares Ayarza, "La pena de muerte," 129.
15 Fuentes, *Estadística General de Lima*, 114–15.
16 Quoted in Francisco Javier Mariátegui, "La pena de muerte: El Ministerio y la Corte Suprema," *La Gaceta Judicial* (hereafter LGJ), 1:108, September 30, 1861.
17 Silva Santisteban, *Breves reflexiones*.
18 On the artisans' riots, see Méndez, "Importaciones de lujo y clases populares," and Gootenberg, "Artisans and Merchants."
19 *El Comercio* (hereafter EC), February 15, 1859.

20 Quoted in Basadre, *Historia de la República*, 3:380.

21 Ibid.

22 Shortly afterward, the Penal Code of 1862 established the types of homicides that would be punished by the death penalty. See *Códigos penal y de enjuiciamiento*, 78–79.

23 González Vigil, *Opúsculo sobre la pena de muerte*. Bartolomé Herrera responded to González Vigil in *El opúsculo sobre la pena de muerte*.

24 Luis E. Albertini, "Consideraciones legales y filosóficas sobre la pena de muerte," *LGJ*, 1:1, May 15, 1861, emphasis added. See also *LGJ*, 1:4, May 22, 1861, and 1:5, May 23, 1861. For other interventions in this debate, see Mariátegui, "La pena de muerte: El ministerio y la Corte Suprema," *LGJ*, 1:108, September 30, 1861; José Simeón Tejeda, "La ley que restablece la pena de muerte," *LGJ*, 1:110, October 2, 1861. Years later, in 1874, the Peruvian congress debated and rejected again the abolition of the death penalty. See "Documentos referentes a la abolición de la pena de muerte proyectada por el congreso," *LGJ*, 2:89, October 20, 1874, and 2:90, October 21, 1874.

25 Monsalve, "Elecciones, violencia y dominación racial."

26 Ibid., 15.

27 On inflation and unemployment, see Gootenberg, "Carneros y Chuño," and Quiroz, *La deuda defraudada*.

28 For the differences and similarities between liberals and conservatives during the early Republican period, see Gootenberg, "Beleaguered Liberal," and Aljovín, *Caudillos y constituciones*.

29 "Mensaje que el Libertador Presidente de la República dirije a la legislatura de 1860," *El Peruano*, July 28, 1860.

30 Espinosa, *Diccionario para el pueblo*, 463.

31 On the growing attention to statistics on the part of Peruvian state makers, see Ragas, "Ciudadanía, cultura política y representación," 39–43. An important statistical compilation was Córdova y Urrutia, *Estadística histórica*.

32 Fuentes was probably the most prolific writer in nineteenth-century Lima and one of the most influential legal experts and journalists. There is no comprehensive biography of this exceptional character. See some references in Gootenberg, *Imagining Development*, 64–71, and Xammar, *"El Murciélago" en la literatura peruana*. On the diffusion and importance of statistics in the Peruvian political imaginary during the 1860s and 1870s, see Chiaramonti, "Buscando el ciudadano 'virtuoso.'"

33 Fuentes, *Estadística general de Lima*. A second edition, "notably corrected," was published in 1866 in Paris by Tip. de A. Lainé et J. Havard. In this work I cite from the first edition.

34 Fuentes, *Estadística general de Lima*, 111–12.

35 Ibid., 74.

36 Ibid., 610.

37 Ibid., 700.

38 Ibid., 595–96, 601, 606.

39   Ibid., 606, footnote.

40   Ibid., 114–15.

41   The list of subscribers to Fuentes's book reads like a directory of the *limeño* intelligentsia and included Gutierrez, Mariátegui, Gonzalez Vigil, Albertini, Silva Santisteban, and many more. See the list in the 1858 edition of the *Estadística general de Lima*.

42   In her valuable study on statistics and nationalism in Italy, Silvana Patriarca argues that "statistics not only performed a work of ideological and political legitimation, but also contributed to the creation, the 'production' as it were, of the Italian nation, that is, of the very entity that they were supposed to describe." Patriarca, *Numbers and Nationhood*, 4.

43   Cole, *Suspect Identities*, 14. Cole attributes to the French philosopher Adolphe Quetelet the idea that crime, like other social phenomena such as birth, death, and suicide, were determined by "statistical laws."

44   Gootenberg, *Imagining Development*, 71.

45   Walker, "Voces discordantes."

46   Wade, *Race and Ethnicity*, 31; Méndez, "Incas Sí, Indios No."

47   Gootenberg, "Population and Ethnicity."

48   Walker, "The Patriotic Society."

49   Méndez, "República sin indios," 21.

50   Quoted in Poole, *Vision, Race, and Modernity*, 148.

51   See, for example, the following statement: "The Indians of Peru will declare themselves free today, since they do not have to pay tribute, but, is this all that true freedom entails? No, one thousand times, no: . . . let's enlighten the people [el pueblo] so that it be happy. Without morality, knowledge, and work there will not be in Peru enlightened, respected, and beloved peoples, but only ignorant, repudiated, and mistreated peoples." Fuentes, *Aletazos del Murciélago*, 1:22–23.

52   Fuentes, *Lima: Apuntes históricos*, 78.

53   Among the members of this society were the physician José Casimiro Ulloa, the liberal educator Sebastián Lorente, the future director of the penitentiary Tomás Lama, the future leading figure of the Sociedad Geográfica de Lima, Luis Carranza, among others. See McEvoy, *Forjando la nación*, 99.

54   Ibid., 100.

55   Quoted in Jacobsen, "Civilization and Its Barbarism," 101.

56   Espinosa, *Diccionario para el pueblo*, 609–21; quotation from 616–17.

57   Francisco Laso, "Croquis sobre el caracter peruano," *La Revista de Lima* 2, 7 (October 1, 1860), reprinted in Laso, *Aguinaldo para las señoras*.

58   See the landowners' responses to a survey on Chinese labor published in Elías and Rodríguez, *Inmigración de Chinos*.

59   García Jordán, "Reflexiones sobre el Darwinismo social."

60   Quoted in Muñoz, *Diversiones públicas*, 163.

61   José Simeón Tejeda, "Un delito de homicidio," LGJ, 1:134, November 6, 1861; Ignacio Noboa, "Homenaje a nuestros jueces," LGJ, 1:135, November 7, 1861.

62   Lorente, "Raterías del indio," in *Pensamientos sobre el Perú*, 43.

63 Manuel Atanasio Fuentes, "Arraigo de chinos," *LGJ*, 1:61, March 24, 1874.

64 See, for instance, Casanova, *Ensayo sobre la industria algodonera*; Pardo, "Algo sobre el código penal."

65 "The plebe's orgies, always promoted by vagrants, are the source of immorality and corruption, where crimes are prepared, where infamous criminals trained the novices in their execution and from where malefactors depart in all directions to effect their gloomy plans." Memoria, Gobierno, 1860, 41–42 (for full citations of the *Memorias*, see the bibliography).

66 Fuentes, *Estadística general de Lima*, 164.

67 *El Trabajo*, 6, October 3, 1874.

68 Isaac Alzamora, "La vagancia," *LGJ*, January 26, 1874.

69 *El Nacional*, March 16, 1877. See also Manuel A. Fuentes, "Vagancia de menores," *LGJ*, February 20, 1874.

70 "Una caridad mal entendida," *El Nacional*, March 9, 1877.

71 For late eighteenth-century concerns, see Ignacio de Lequanda, "Discurso sobre el destino."

72 For enlistment of vagrants in the army, see "Circular a los Prefectos," Ministry of Government, September 16, 1829, in Quirós, *Colección de leyes*, 3:211. The *boleto* was made obligatory for slaves in 1825, but in 1839 the Reglamento de Policía extended the requirement to all members of the laboring classes. See "Reglamento interior de las haciendas de la costa" (1825), in Quirós, *Colección de leyes*, 2:167–69, and "Reglamento de policía de Lima," November 11, 1839, in Oviedo, *Colección de leyes*, 3:76–77, articles 233, 238.

73 Oviedo, *Colección de leyes*, 3:326.

74 *EC*, October 29, 1855.

75 Código Penal, art. 365, and others.

76 "Reglamento de moralidad pública y policía correccional," October 12, 1877, art. 23, in Concejo Provincial de Lima, *Reglamento de la guardia urbana*, 75.

77 Ramón, *La muralla y los callejones*, 73. The urban historian Juan Bromley refers to this period as one of "febrile activity and brilliant material progress, but, at the same time, of intense megalomaniac craziness and profound private and public immorality." Bromley, "El plano de Lima," in Concejo Provincial de Lima, *Monografías históricas*, 1:425.

78 See Ramón, *La muralla y los callejones*, for a detailed account of the history of the Lima walls.

79 Ibid., 88.

80 Méndez, "Penalidad y muerte."

81 Archivo Histórico de la Municipalidad de Lima (hereafter AHML), Subprefecturas, June 2, 1860.

82 Majluf, *Escultura y espacio público*, 24.

83 Quoted in ibid., 27.

84 Bonilla, "La crisis de 1872," in *Guano y burguesía*.

85 Bonilla, "El problema nacional y colonial del Perú en el contexto de la Guerra del

Pacífico," in *Guano y burguesía*. On the 1872 riots, see Giesecke, *Masas urbanas y rebelión*.

86 Fuentes, *Lima: Apuntes históricos*, v.

87 *El Diario Judicial* (hereafter *EDJ*), April 15, 1890.

88 *EC*, September 12, 1893. The author, Paul Groussac, was a French writer living in Argentina. See also "La insalubridad de Lima," *EC*, May 24, 1898.

89 Dr. Vidrieras, "La podre de Lima: La ciudad de los chinos," *EDJ*, 2:462, December 1, 1891. The second article in the series was "La podre de Lima: Las casas de obreros," *EDJ*, 2:466, December 5, 1891. Note that despite the title, this article is not about working-class housing, but about working-class bordellos.

90 *EC*, March 6, 1885; *EC*, October 10, 1892, "Callejón de Otaiza"; Rodríguez Pastor, "La calle del Capón."

91 "Lo que es hoy Lima y lo que será mañana," *EC*, June 3, 1898.

92 For further developments of this trend emphasizing the role of health in the disadvantagedness of the Peruvian population, see Parker, "Civilizing the City of Kings."

CHAPTER 2. THE SCIENCE OF THE CRIMINAL

1 *Criminology*, a term invented by Rafaelle Garofalo in 1885, is used here synonymously with *criminal anthropology*, the first name given to the new discipline. See Bierne, *Inventing Criminology*, 233–38.

2 Garland, "Of Crimes and Criminals."

3 Garland, "The Criminal and His Science."

4 Lombroso, *L'Uomo delinquente*. See also Gibson, *Born to Crime*.

5 The term *born criminal*, however, was invented by Enrico Ferri and was not used by Lombroso until about eight years after the original publication of *L'Uomo delinquente*. See Gibson, *Born to Crime*, 22.

6 See Stephen J. Gould, "The Ape in Some of Us: Criminal Anthropology," in *The Mismeasure of Man*, 122–45, and Daniel Pick, "Lombroso's Criminal Science," in *Faces of Degeneration*, 109–52.

7 Quoted in Gibson, *Born to Crime*, 20.

8 Quoted in Wright, *Between the Guillotine and Liberty*, 121.

9 Renneville, "La réception de Lombroso."

10 Salvatore, "Criminology, Prison Reform"; Buffington, *Criminal and Citizen*; Rodríguez, "Encoding the Criminal."

11 A fuller account of these debates is in Aguirre, "Crime, Race, and Morals."

12 Prado, *El método positivo*.

13 [Paulino Fuentes Castro], "Atractivos de las penas," *EDJ*, 4:827, June 22, 1893.

14 Rodríguez, "Estudios criminológicos."

15 Paulino Fuentes Castro, "Manuel Peña y Chacaliaza," *EDJ*, 2:500, February 18, 1892. On Chacaliaza, see also Portal, *Del pasado limeño*, 99–100. Sources refer to him as both Chacaliaza and Chacallaza. I will use the former throughout this book.

16   Paulino Fuentes Castro, "Pedro Laredo," *EDJ*, 3:537, May 2, 1892.

17   Prado, *El método positivo*, 133.

18   See L. Barros Méndez, "La nueva escuela penal italiana," *EDJ*, 1:208, December 4, 1890; "Discurso pronunciado por el catedrático de la Facultad de Medicina, Dr. Manuel C. Barrios en la ceremonia de apertura del año escolar de 1891," *LGJ*, 1:8, 9, March 31 and April 1, 1891; Andrés Meneses, "Antropología," *EDJ*, 3:625, August 22, 1892; Enrique Ego Aguirre, "Escuela antropológica," *El Derecho*, September 1898; Salomón, "El factor económico"; Prado Ugarteche, "El tipo criminal"; Cedano, "Estudios sobre la criminalidad"; Julio E. Portella, "Algunas observaciones sobre la escuela penal positiva," *EC*, November 11, 1905; Pedro José Rada, "El derecho penal moderno," *EC*, October 13, 1905; Zamora Torres, "El delito y sus causas."

19   "The existence of the inborn criminal causes repugnance to our reason; we found it impossible to believe that there exist persons condemned to be devoured by the world of crime." Jiménez, "La sociedad y el delito," 118.

20   Ibid., 189. "Crime is not the exclusive product of an individual; society also encourages and fertilizes it" (159).

21   Ibid., 195.

22   Ibid., 121.

23   Ibid., 158–63, 221.

24   "Unlimited latifundia exhaust Indigenous property, driving them away from free labor, throwing them into the hands of the gamonal, and locking them up in order to steal their land, their cattle, and their children." Encinas, "Causas de la criminalidad indígena."

25   "In a context of servitude, under a regimen of incessant oppression, their violent reactions are easily understandable. And because these conditions, instead of decreasing, are being accentuated, the figures of Indian delinquency tend to grow." Valdizán, "La delincuencia en el Perú," 147.

26   Villavicencio, *Algunos aspectos*, 65. See also Miró Quesada, *Breves apuntes*.

27   Encinas indeed conducted "anthropometric" research. After measuring 116 Indian inmates at the Lima penitentiary, he concluded emphatically that "the Indian is not a born criminal." Encinas, "Causas de la criminalidad indígena," 261.

28   Palma, *El porvenir de las razas*. For similar racist statements, see Clavero, *El tesoro del Perú*, and Arrús, *Las razas china e india*.

29   Palma, *El porvenir de las razas*, 16.

30   Ibid., 6–7.

31   Ibid., 35.

32   Ibid., 38.

33   Portocarrero, "El fundamento invisible."

34   Pike, *The Modern History*, 159. Pike mentions the sociologist Carlos Lisson as one of the first to write in "optimistic" terms about the "regeneration" of the Indian and to retreat from biological explanations of racial inferiority (ibid., 161).

35   I am referring here to quite influential works such as González Prada, *Nuestros indios*; Haya de la Torre, *Por la emancipación*; and Mariátegui, *Siete ensayos*.

36   The writer Francisco Graña confessed that "it has been necessary [to face] this

painful experience, this years-long disillusion, to understand that we should not rely on immigration, if we, by our own effort, do not make a previous preparatory work, an initial work that can make this land friendly for ourselves and for the rest. Only then will they come to bring us the contribution of their blood, their intelligence, and their culture." Graña, *La población del Perú*, 46.

37   Villavicencio, *Algunos aspectos*, 72–73.

38   The literature on *Indigenismo* is enormous and impossible to summarize here. A recent provocative contribution is De la Cadena, *Indigenous Mestizos*.

39   Cerna, "El problema carcelario."

40   See Poole, "Ciencia, peligrosidad y represión." Indigenista ideology was also appropriated by the Leguía administration in the 1920s. A Bureau of Indian Affairs was created in 1921, and a Patronato de la raza indígena in 1924 for defending the Indian. As Leguía himself stated, the Indian needed to be protected for this also meant "defending our economic life of which he [the Indian] is a driving force." Quoted in Hurtado Pozo, *La ley 'importada,'* 82.

41   Opinions favoring white immigration as a means of "regenerating" Peruvian population were very popular up to the 1900s. See Polar, "Aptitudes políticas de nuestra raza"; Barros, "Aptitud de nuestra raza para el trabajo"; Arona, *La inmigración en el Perú*. See also Boisset, *El problema racial en el Perú*. The alternative view, emphasizing education and moral reform as the path to regeneration, gained strength in the early decades of the twentieth century. See León García, *Las razas en Lima*; Graña, *La población del Perú*; Medina, *Causas del estacionarismo*; Pesce, *Indígenas e inmigrantes*.

42   Graña, "Factores sociales." In 1919, J. F. Landaeta argued that "the racial factor . . . has 99% of influence in the commission of criminal acts." Landaeta, *Legislación sobre delincuencia alcohólica*, vii.

43   Villavicencio, *Defensas criminales*, 63.

44   De la Cadena, *Indigenous Mestizos*, 2–3.

45   Many racist commentators were in fact *mestizos*, which presented an obvious drawback to their pretensions to make white racial purity the main or exclusive sign of superiority.

46   Parker, "Civilizing the City of Kings," 153–78.

47   On medical ideas about hygiene and their relationship with discourses about gender and the body, see the important study by Maria Emma Mannarelli, *Limpias y modernas*.

48   Miró Quesada, *Mesología*, 99–100.

49   Portella, "La higiene en las casas de vecindad," 40, 41.

50   Villavicencio, *Algunos aspectos*, 40.

51   "Una casa de vecindad en Lima: Los grandes focos de infección. 'Pescante grande' y 'Pescante chico,'" *EC*, March 13, 1908.

52   Cueto, *El regreso de las epidemias*, chapters 1 and 2.

53   Eyzaguirre, "La tuberculosis pulmonar," 151.

54   See, for example, José Casimiro Ulloa, "Cuestiones médico-legales: La embriaguez erijida en crimen y castigada con la pena capital," *LGJ*, 5:109, March 31, 1861.

55 Jiménez, "La sociedad y el delito," 274.

56 Ibid., 282, 284.

57 Congreso Ordinario de 1887, *Diario de los debates de la H. Cámara de Senadores* (Lima, 1887), 491.

58 *EC*, March 30, 1902. See also "Desarrollo del alcoholismo," *EC*, September 1, 1908; and "Alcoholismo: Cifras reveladoras," *EC*, September 26, 1916.

59 See the data offered by Ruperto Algorta, secretary of the society, as an appendix to Stoddard, *Manual científico*. Algorta, a Methodist missionary, was a key figure in the antialcoholic campaign, in particular among working-class subjects. See Fonseca, *Misioneros y civilizadores*, 231, 249.

60 In response to this last proposal Vicente H. Delgado replied that, if approved, two million people would go to jail, for Indians were always drunk when not at work (*EC*, April 25, 1903). It is revealing that the entry for "Alcoholismo" in Leguía y Martínez, *Diccionario de la legislación criminal*, simply says, "See *Indígena*" (48).

61 Graña offered criminal statistics to support that idea. In a period of six years (1895–1901), 24.3 percent of all individuals arrested in the *Intendencia* of Lima were under the influence of alcohol, while 46.5 percent were accused of crimes committed while inebriated. See also Castañeda y Alvarez, "El alcoholismo en Lima." According to the author, "degenerated" criminals began their "careers" in the tavern and completed them in the penitentiary or the mental asylum.

Smy62 *EC*, January 3, 1903.

63 Ley 2282, October 14, 1916, and accompanying decree, February 3, 1917 (Archivo Digital de la Legislación Peruana, hereafter ADLP). The ADLP is available online at www.leyes.congreso.gob.pe, and was also issued as a CD-ROM set (Lima: Congreso de la República, 2000).

64 Jiménez de Asúa, *Derecho penal*, 39–74.

65 For examples of opposition to the death penalty among Peruvian authors, see Calderón, "La defensa social"; Pineda Iglesias, "Se justifica la pena capital"; Varela y Orbegoso, *La criminología de Garofalo*; Quintanilla, *La pena de muerte*; Castillo, "Una institución que debe desaparecer."

66 Several Peruvian commentators embraced the notion of social defense. See León y León, "La libertad y la responsabilidad"; Memoria, Penitenciaría, 1915; Carlos Bambarén, "La función preventiva del estudio psicopatológico del criminal" (1919), reprinted in *La Crónica Médica* 53, no. 874 (1936): 155–59; Avendaño, "La reforma de la legislación penal," 251.

67 According to Foucault, the idea of dangerousness gave rise to both Italian criminal anthropology and the theory of social defense, as developed in Belgium. Foucault, "About the Concept."

68 In the United States, social defense was understood as the need to eliminate "the recidivistic class of criminals" by sending them to prison. Boies, *The Science of Penology*, 97–98.

69 Quoted in Altmann Smythe, *Reseña histórica*, 104.

70 Penal Code, art. 51.

71 Avendaño, "La reforma de la legislación penal," 252.

72 Solano, *El estado peligroso.*

73 Solano, *El indígena y la ley penal.*

74 According to Juan Luis Hague, for example, if somebody showing "psychiatric abnormalities" was accused of a minor crime, it was advisable to inquire into the reasons such an insignificant offense was committed, for focusing on the crime alone may be misleading as to the real dangerousness of the subject. Conversely, if a so-called normal person was accused of a crime, it was necessary to consider the strong possibility of a wrongful accusation. Hague, *La caracterización del delincuente*, 15.

75 Jiménez de Asúa, "Elmore y Chocano."

76 López-Rey Arrojo, *Introducción al estudio*, 36.

77 *Código Penal (Ley No. 4868)*, edited by Juan José Calle (Lima: Librería e Imprenta Gil, 1924), arts. 44, 45.

78 This represented a radical change in relation to the Penal Code of 1862, according to which "unawareness of the penal law does not exempt the criminal from [legal] responsibility," a doctrine compatible with the notion that all Peruvians were equal before the law. On this, see Hurtado Pozo, *La ley 'importada,'* 77–78.

79 "El Código Maúrtua y la Sociedad General de Prisiones de Paris," *Revista de Derecho y Ciencias Políticas* 2, no. 1 (1937): 83–84.

80 Poole, "Ciencia, peligrosidad y represión," 354. See also Hurtado Pozo, *La ley 'importada,'* 69.

81 Hurtado Pozo compares the precepts of the penal code with Spanish colonial attitudes regarding Indians. Quite revealingly, the jurist Juan Bautista de Lavalle suggested that countries with a majority of indigenous population, such as Peru, Bolivia, and Ecuador, should learn from the French experience in its colonies, "particularly with respect to the Indigenous peoples in those regions." See "El Código Maúrtua."

82 Cueto, *Excelencia científica*, 62–63.

83 José Casimiro Ulloa, "Código Penal. Cuestión Médico-Legal," LGJ, 5:107, February 28, 1861. See also Fuentes and De la Lama, *Diccionario de jurisprudencia*, 434–36.

84 Plácido Jiménez, for instance, referred to the need to "cauterize" and "sterilize" society from crime. Jiménez, "La sociedad y el delito," 108–9.

85 Quoted in Pozo, *La ley 'importada,'* 49.

86 The sentence was eventually commuted to fifteen years of isolation at the penitentiary. All the documents pertaining to this case were published in *Foro Peruano: Proceso criminal.*

87 Quoted in Fuentes Castro, *Criminología peruana*, 70.

88 Fuentes Castro, comp. *Anales Judiciales*, 6:7–12. See also the fascinating study of Alejandrino Montes, a domestic servant who murdered his patrons. Miró Quesada, "El caso del asesino Montes."

89 "The enormous majority of Peruvian jurists have not been totally seduced by the notion of the dangerous state [*estado peligroso*]." Altmann Smythe, *Reseña histórica*, 109.

90   Hermilio Valdizán, "Peritaje: Un imbécil criminal," *Revista de Psiquiatría y Disciplinas Conexas* 1, no. 3 (1918): 166–76.

91   Carlos Bambarén and Luis Vargas Prada, "Alcoholismo y delincuencia," *Boletín de Criminología* (hereafter BC) 1 (1927): 97–100; Carlos Bambarén and Luis Espejo, "Perversión psicosexual y delincuencia," BC 1 (1927): 270–73; Carlos Bambarén and Luis Vargas Prada, "Epilepsia y delincuencia," BC 1 (1927): 558–65; Carlos Bambarén and Luis Vargas Prada, "Observaciones de clínica criminológica," BC 3 (1930): 207–35; Víctor M. Villavicencio, "El caso de un delincuente pederasta," BC 3 (1930): 235–50; José Max Arnillas Arana, "Las constituciones psicopáticas en su relación con la delincuencia," BC 4 (1931): 22–45; Bambarén, *Casos de clínica criminológica.*

92   Among them were the future criminologists Julio Altmann Smythe, Susana Solano, Juan Luis Hague, and Carlos Herrera Martínez.

93   Balbín, "El matrimonio y la eugenesia," 22.

94   Stepan, *"The Hour of Eugenics,"* 16–17.

95   Peñaloza, *Prevención eugénica.*

96   Fosalba, "La herencia como principal factor."

97   Mendoza and Martínez, "Las ideas eugenésicas." In the 1930s, Carlos Enrique Paz Soldán founded the Institute of Social Medicine and in 1939 organized the First Peruvian Conference on Eugenics.

98   Stepan, *"The Hour of Eugenics,"* 178–82.

99   Iberico, *Elementos psicológicos.*

100 Cueto, *Excelencia científica,* 58. For a document that laments this deficiency, see the Memoria, Penitenciaría, 1908.

101 "Informe de Honorio Delgado en torno a la escuela penitenciaria de vigilantes," November 14, 1930, Archivo General de la Nación [hereafter AGN], Ministerio de Justicia [hereafter MJ], 3.20.3.1.11.2.

102 The initial idea for the *Boletín* came from the psychiatrist Honorio Delgado, who considered it "an indispensable organ to create criminological consciousness among the justices of the Republic." Delgado to the Inspector General of Prisons, March 28, 1926 (AGN, MJ, 3.20.3.1.7.1).

103 In France, for instance, the social question was constructed as resulting from irregular employment, alarming poverty, criminality, and disease. Horne, *A Social Laboratory,* 18.

104 Barreda, "La asistencia pública," 22–25.

105 Revoredo, "Deficiencias de nuestra legislación."

106 Gandolfo, *El problema de la vagancia.*

107 Bailey, "The Fabrication of Deviance," 222.

108 Ibid., 230, 254.

109 On the birth of the working classes in Lima and their forms of organization and culture, see especially Tejada, *La cuestión del pan*; Blanchard, *The Origins of the Peruvian Labor Movement*; and Stein, ed., *Lima Obrera.*

110 This category encompassed all those who lived in the margins of lawful society:

vagrants, habitual drunkards, beggars, rateros, pimps, gamblers, and so forth. Joaquín Capelo called them the parasites of the city. Capelo, *Sociología de Lima*, 2:141–47.

111 On this, see Tejada, *La cuestión del pan*, passim.

112 Parker, "Civilizing the City of Kings," 168.

113 Parker, "Los pobres de la clase media," 169.

114 Panfichi, "Urbanización temprana de Lima," 39.

115 See, for instance, the numerous episodes of working-class violence against brothels and other sites of so-called criminal activities that took place in 1912. Torrejón, "Lima, 1912."

116 Quoted in ibid., 329.

117 See Tejada, "Malambo." See chapter 5 below for more details about faites and rateros.

118 For the case of Argentina, see especially Salvatore, "Criminology, Prison Reform."

CHAPTER 3. THE MAKING OF A CRIMINAL CLASS

1 Merino Arana, *Historia policial*, 7.

2 See Cosamalón, *Indios detrás de la muralla*, 207–10, for information on *serenos* in eighteenth-century Lima.

3 "Reglamento Provisional de Serenos," September 10, 1834 (ADLP).

4 See, for example, Peralta, "El mito del ciudadano armado," which describes the attempts by Domingo Elías to build a liberal political movement on the basis of transforming the Guardia Nacional into a sort of civilian militia.

5 Zapata Cesti, *Historia de la policía*, 44.

6 Memoria, Gobierno, 1867, 56.

7 McEvoy, *Un proyecto nacional*, 109. Years later, the newspaper *El Nacional* defended the Guardia Nacional against accusations of "degrading and repugnant" recruitment practices and of serving the interests of the political party in power. For *El Nacional*, the guardia was made up of honest, hard-working men, capitalists and workers, who enjoyed the support of the citizens and who had their own profession, which they practiced when not in service. "Guardias Nacionales," Editorial, *El Nacional*, May 25, 1877.

8 Concejo Provincial de Lima, *Reglamento de la guardia urbana*.

9 Because of disagreements between the government and the landowners, however, the implementation of the latter was suspended indefinitely. Zapata Cesti, *Historia de la policía*, 56.

10 "Reglamento de Policía Correccional," art. 29, in *Reglamento de la guardia urbana*, 76.

11 *La Patria*, May 23, 1877; "Lo que es hoy la Guardia Nacional," Editorial, *La Patria*, May 24, 1877.

12 Middendorf, *Perú: Observaciones*, 1:267.

13 By October 1889, there were eight such rural commissaries with ten men assigned to each besides the commissary and one officer. "Servicio rural de los valles de la capital de Lima," October 15, 1889, Biblioteca Nacional, D11500.

14 "Documentos sobre las quejas de los comisarios por la falta de fuerza para el cumplimiento del servicio rural," February 18, 1889, Biblioteca Nacional, D11540.

15 See several examples in AGN, Prefectura de Lima, Serie 3.9, Legajo 3.1.

16 Memoria, Gobierno, 1886, 20–24, and Aranda, ed., *Leyes y resoluciones*, 93.

17 August 31, 1899 (ADLP).

18 Memoria, Subprefecto, 1892. See also Memoria, Prefectura, 1893.

19 AGN, Prefectura de Lima, Serie 3.9, Legajo 16.6, August 8, 1891; ibid., 16.5, July 22, 1891. The census counted a total population of 107,114 inhabitants for the city of Lima. Memoria, Prefecto, 1893,

20 AGN, Prefectura de Lima, Serie 3.9, Legajo 16.6, October 9, 1891. Avendaño resigned in 1895 for political reasons. See Vargas Prada, "El servicio de identificación," 1.

21 Memoria, Subprefecto, 1895. See also Valdizán, "La delincuencia en el Perú," 126. The Bertillon system was created in France by Alphonse de Bertillon in the late 1870s. Its success derived from the belief that "it is altogether unlikely that among many thousands subjects, two will be found who will approximately reveal figures of the same head diameters, the same foot, finger, etc." See Bertillon, *Instructions for Taking Descriptions*; the quote comes from the introduction written by Gallus Muller, warden of Illinois State Penitentiary, 6–7. The Bertillon system was used in Lima until April 1915. A total of 8,541 individuals were measured between 1892 and 1915. Lozada Benavente, "La policía judicial científica," 44–45.

22 Memoria, Subprefecto, 1895, 46. See AGN, Prefectura de Lima, Serie 3.9, Legajo 16.10, December 30, 1895, for the case of someone who requested that his anthropometric records be destroyed.

23 Zapata Cesti, *Historia de la policía*, 69.

24 AGN, Prefectura de Lima, Serie 3.9, Legajo 16.6, July 11, 1892.

25 Ibid., Legajo 3.3, May 4, 1894.

26 Ibid., Legajo 16.7, October 20, 1892.

27 Ibid., Legajo 3.3, September 5, 1891; March 5, 1891; February 15, 1892; Legajo 3.1, February 1, 1886.

28 Ibid., Legajo 16.10, July 16, 1894.

29 Ibid., Legajo 3.3, January 8, 1892.

30 Ibid., Legajo 16.10, August 2, 1895.

31 Ibid., May 7, 1895.

32 Ibid., July 8, 1894.

33 Ibid., October 8, 1895.

34 Ibid., February 12, 1895.

35 Ibid., June 10, 1895. For additional cases of police-army rivalries, see ibid., Legajo 16.30, May 9, 1916.

36 Zapata Cesti, *Historia de la policía*, 72.

37 AGN, Prefectura de Lima, Serie 3.9, Legajo 16.12, August 14, 1900.

38 Memoria, Gobierno, 1907, xxxi.

39 Memoria, Gobierno, 1905, xx.

40 AGN, Prefectura de Lima, Serie 3.9, Legajo 16.20, October 7, 1907.

41 Ibid., January 9, 1908; ibid., January 10, 1908; ibid., Legajo 16.25, October 20, 1911; AGN, Ministerio del Interior, Prefecturas, Paquete 140, 1911, December 23, 1911.

42 Revollé, *Exposición que sobre el estado*, 42.

43 AGN, Prefectura de Lima, Serie 3.9, Legajo 16.10, July 19, 1895.

44 AGN, Prefectura de Lima, Serie 3.9, Legajo 16.12, May 7, 1900.

45 See EC, June 9, 1912, for a detailed description of this system and the expectations it created as an auxiliary in the struggle against both crime and anarchism in Peru.

46 On this, see especially Rodríguez, "Encoding the Criminal," chap. 4; Cole, *Suspect Identities*, 127–34; and Ruggiero, "Fingerprinting."

47 Zapata Cesti, *Historia de la policía*, 195. See also "Informe que la Comisión encargada de examinar el estado administrativo y técnico de la penitenciaría de Lima, ha presentado al Ministerio de Justicia," in *Revista del Foro* 7 (1920), and 8 (1921) (hereafter referred to as "Calle Commission, Informe."), 378, and Memoria, Justicia, 1916.

48 AGN, Ministerio del Interior, Prefecturas, Legajo 173, 1915, May 10, 1915.

49 Lozada Benavente, "La policía judicial científica," 46.

50 Zapata Cesti, *Historia de la policía*, 86.

51 Memoria, Gobierno, 1913, 41.

52 *La Prensa*, February 22, 1913.

53 "Reglamento para el ingreso en las gendarmerías o guardias civiles de la República," in Memoria, Gobierno, 1916, 96–97.

54 Vargas Prada, "El servicio de identificación," 4–10.

55 Memoria, Gobierno, 1920, XXVII.

56 In 1896, a similar French military mission was brought to Perú to reorganize and professionalize the army. Basadre, *Historia de la República*, 7:416.

57 Ibid., 9:414.

58 The decree creating the police academy had been issued on August 7, 1919. Zapata Cesti, *Historia de la policía*, 94–96.

59 See details in Memoria, Gobierno, 1923.

60 Memoria, Gobierno, 1923, 185. The first director of the cuerpo was Rufino Martínez, who would earn a reputation as a torturer.

61 Memoria, Gobierno 1916, xvi. See also AGN, Ministerio del Interior, Prefecturas, Lima, Paquete 148, 1917, December 20, 1916.

62 Memoria, Gobierno, 1923, 390.

63 AGN, Prefectura de Lima, Serie 3.9, Legajo 2.24, June 7, 1919.

64 See Salazar et al., *Historia de la noticia*, 55.

65 Zapata Cesti, *Historia de la policía*, 89.

66 Ibid., 195–99.

67 Solís, *Once años*, 51–59.

68 EC, May 24, 1891.

69 AGN, Prefectura de Lima, Serie 3.9, Legajo 16.20, January 10, 1908.

70 "Memoria del Inspector de Cárceles," LGJ, 3:11, January 15, 1875.

71 AGN, RPJ, Causas Criminales, Legajo 626, "Criminal de oficio contra Ramon Gonzales, Lizarto Detam, Manuel Escurra, Manuel Molina, Teodoro Jimenez, y Tomás Aliaga por homicidio," September 22, 1896.

72 AGN, Prefecturas, Legajo 183, November 25, 1916. See also Carrera, *El gran Dr. Copaiba*, which transcribes popular verses about the *carretilla*.

73 "Crónica: Las comisarías de la policía," EC, April 22, 1898; see also a report by the commissary of the 3d quarter on the *calabozo*'s neglected condition. AGN, Prefectura de Lima, Serie 3.9, Legajo 3.3, November 11, 1892. See also "Esa no es policía," *El Tiempo*, June 17, 1905, for a creepy description of the *calabozos*.

74 Adjustments in the height of the bar meant that sometimes only the head was lying on the floor, at other times the head and the torso. See descriptions of this practice in Valdez, "La patología"; Esparza, "Contribución al estudio," 35; and Villavicencio, *La Reforma penitenciaria*, 89. The chief of the police station in the Ate district warned that placing the barra at a certain height would cause the prisoner's death because of cerebral damage. AGN, Prefecturas, Legajo 16.12, December 31, 1902.

75 AGN, RPJ, Causas Criminales, Legajo 601, "Causa criminal contra Isidoro Torres y Cruz Vargas por robo," January 29, 1895.

76 For a description, see Garrido Malaver, *El Frontón*, 105.

77 AGN, RPJ, Causas Criminales, Legajo 630, "Criminal de oficio contra Marcos Cobián por robo," November 17, 1896.

78 AGN, Prefectura de Lima, Serie 3.9, Legajo 16.25, August 19, 1912.

79 AGN, Prefectura de Lima, Serie 3.9, Legajo 16.30, January 25, 1916. Both instances of torture were confirmed by the authorities.

80 AGN, MJ, 3.20.3.1.12.5.1, August 28, 1930.

81 J. M. Jiménez, "De la flajelación y resistencia a los mandatos judiciales," EDJ, 1:43, May 12, 1890.

82 EC, August 26, 1890. The newspaper *El País* denounced, in February 1900, the flagellation of a "decent young lady" in a police jail in the rural district of Barranco, a denunciation that the commissary found "grave" and the prefecto "alarming" (AGN, Prefecturas, Serie 3.9, Legajo 16.12, February 21, 1900).

83 "Expediente sobre los sucesos promovidos a raíz de la denuncia formulada por el periódico 'La Opinión Nacional' de abusos cometidos por la policía de la ciudad de Lima," April 20, 1896, Biblioteca Nacional, D5754.

84 González Prada, *Horas de lucha*. See also "La policía," in his *Bajo el oprobio*, 33–35, 79.

85 Legislatura ordinario de 1915, *Diario de los debates de la H. Cámara de Diputados* (Lima: Tip. de la Prensa, 1915), 474.

86 AGN, Prefectura de Lima, Serie 3.9, Legajo 16.25, January 19, 1895.

87 EC, March 30, 1902.

88 González Prada, *Sobre el militarismo*, 35.

89 AGN, Prefectura de Lima, Serie 3.9, Legajo 16.30, January 23, 1916, emphasis added.

90 AGN, Archivo Intermedio, Expedientes criminales, "Criminal de oficio contra José Fernández (a) Chuzaso, por robo," February 8, 1915. Another attorney, in defending his client against a similar indictment based on the *parte policial*, said that if one believed every police statement, the result would be that the real judge was the police agent. AGN, RPJ, Causas Criminales, Legajo 637, "Criminal de oficio contra Amador Illescas y otros por robo," May 22, 1897.

91 AGN, Prefectura de Lima, Serie 3.9, Legajo 3.4, January 18, 1906.

92 EC, August 25, 1901.

CHAPTER 4. LIMA'S PENAL ARCHIPELAGO

1 The report, entitled "Estado actual de las cárceles y presidios en el Perú," was published in Paz Soldán, *Examen de las penitenciarías*, 89–104.

2 Paz Soldán, "Estado actual," 103; Fuentes, *Estadística general de Lima*, 205–8.

3 Fuentes, *Estadística general de Lima*, 213.

4 For a description of Casasmatas, see Concejo Provincial del Callao, *Memoria del Alcalde Wenceslao Venegas (1887)* (Lima: Imprenta de Gómez y Ledesma, 1888), 24. See also "La cárcel del Callao," LGJ, 4:60, September 15, 1875.

5 Aguirre, "Violencia, castigo y control social."

6 Aguirre, "Disciplina, castigo y control social."

7 Ignatieff, *A Just Measure of Pain*, 93–113.

8 Hirsch, *The Rise of the Penitentiary*.

9 Rothman, *The Discovery of the Asylum*, 81.

10 Paz Soldán, *Examen de las penitenciarías*, 121–34.

11 García Yrigoyen, "Sistemas penitenciarios," 6.

12 Paz Soldán, "La reforma del régimen penitenciario," 11. See also Memoria, Gobierno, 1862.

13 In his final report, Paz Soldán considered it "one of the best buildings in South America." For the German visitor E. W. Middendorf, the penitentiary was "the biggest, most solid, and best constructed edifice in the city." Middendorf, *Perú*, 1:296.

14 Flores Galindo, *La tradición autoritaria*, 42.

15 Hirsch, *Rise of the Penitentiary*, 14–15.

16 The *Reglamento* mandated that prisoners should be called only by the numbers of their cells. This practice, the subject of criticism by inmates and reformers, was legally abolished only in the 1920s.

17 Fuentes and de la Lama, *Diccionario*, 523.

18 "Reglamento interno de la penitenciaría de Lima," in Fuentes and de la Lama, *Diccionario*, 527–47, arts. 323–40.

19 Middendorf, *Perú*, 1:297.

20 See various unsuccessful proposals for inmate classification and separation in

Memoria, Penitenciaría, 1870; Memoria, Penitenciaría, 1877, ff. 405–23; Memoria, Penitenciaría, 1891; Memoria, Penitenciaría, 1910.

21 The penitentiary held a small number of female inmates until 1881. They occupied a section in one of the departments and were under the authority of a matron. They were moved to Guadalupe that year and, in 1891, to the female-only Santo Tomás prison.

22 Memoria, Penitenciaría, 1906.

23 AGN, MJ, 3.20.3.3.1.3.1, f. 569, December 29, 1866.

24 The junta had been created to oversee the operation of the penitentiary and implement any necessary changes. It was also granted the right to appoint prison personnel and to draft new bylaws for the penitentiary and other prisons. See *El Peruano*, February 16, 1870 (Decree of January 31, 1870). The report was published in *El Comercio* in August 1873.

25 AGN, MJ, 3.20.3.3.1.3.3, f. 403 (July 25, 1873), f. 408 (July 26, 1873), and ff. 421–22 (August 7, 1873).

26 AGN, MJ, 3.20.3.3.1.1.2, March 1, 1881.

27 AGN, MJ, 3.20.3.3.1.1.2, February 27, 1888, f. 120.

28 Memoria, Penitenciaría, 1890.

29 Pradier-Foderé, *Compendio del curso*, 323–24.

30 Fuentes and de la Lama, *Diccionario*, 509.

31 García Yrigoyen, "Sistemas penitenciarios," 20; Puga, "Sistemas penitenciarios," 20.

32 Velasco, "Sistemas penitenciarios," 5, 21.

33 "Reglamento de la Penitenciaría," in Memoria, Justicia, 1901.

34 Driver, "Discipline Without Frontiers?"

35 See especially Morris, *Maconochie's Gentlemen*.

36 For a summary of the philosophy behind the progressive system, see Waite, "From Penitentiary to Reformatory." According to Waite, the third stage was crucial: "It was designed to filter prisoners, to identify those who were reformed and could function in society on their own." Ibid., 95.

37 Quoted in ibid.

38 Quoted in Rothman, *Conscience and Convenience*, 32.

39 Pradier-Foderé, *Compendio del curso*, 324; Manuel Umeres, "Sistemas carcelarios," EDJ, 1:202, November 27, 1890; Gerardo Chávez, "Evoluciones del régimen penitenciario"; Leonidas Avendaño, "Ejecución de las penas en caso de enfermedad sobreviniente," *El Derecho* 10 (1904–05): 2. See also Oscar Miró Quesada, "La reforma de nuestros códigos penales y el Congreso Penitenciario de Washington," EC, July 28, 1915; Fermín Carrión Matos, "Algunos aspectos de la reforma penitenciaria en el Perú," BC 2, no. 3 (1929): 378–89.

40 Elías Lozada Benavente, "Algo sobre represión," *Revista Universitaria*, 13 (1920): 461–513. Although the international reputation of the Elmira Reformatory was enormous, recent revisionist scholarship has shown that it was not the model prison its authorities pretended and that brutality and coercion were still im-

portant components of the treatment of inmates. See Pisciotta, *Benevolent Repression.*

41 Calle Commission, "Informe."

42 Herbold, "Developments."

43 AGN, MJ, 3.20.3.1.1.1, Ministerio de Justicia, Dirección General de Prisiones, Resoluciones Supremas (1921–26).

44 See Penal Code, arts. 10–18.

45 Salvatore, "Positivist Criminology."

46 The decree, signed on February 13, 1929, was printed in BC 2, no. 1 (1929): 85–87. In his 1927 study of penitentiary reform, Víctor Modesto Villavicencio had complained that "in our prisons, the most absolute ignorance about the true personality of the criminal exists. It is impossible to have a precise notion of their dangerousness. We see them daily, but we can never penetrate [their character.]" Villavicencio, *La reforma penitenciaria*, 31.

47 Carlos Bambarén, "La función preventiva del estudio psicopatológico del criminal," (1919), reprinted in *La Crónica Médica* 53, no. 874 (1936): 155–59, quote from 158. Bambarén had spent five months in Buenos Aires in 1926 taking courses in criminology and legal medicine with Dr. Nerio Rojas, during which time he became quite familiar with the operation of the Argentine Instituto de Criminología.

48 AGN, MJ 3.20.3.3.1.3.42, Ministerio de Justicia, "Correspondencia Recibida," February 12, 1927.

49 AGN, MJ, 3.20.3.3.1.3.45, f. 613, October 14, 1930, and November 11, 1930; DGP, "Instrucciones para los médicos de prisiones en el momento de expedir el certificado sobre el 'estado peligroso.'" (typescript, n.d.).

50 DGP, "Instrucciones."

51 Bambarén, *Sobre organización y fines*, 1.

52 Seminario Helguero, *Notas para la reforma*; Bambarén, *Sobre organización y fines*, 1.

53 See the interview with Bernardino León y León in BC 2, no. 1 (1929): 1–6, and legislative pieces published in every issue of the *Boletín*. On January 14, 1929, a "Reglamento de Clasificación de Conducta de los Presos" was issued. Before the tribunal was created, evaluation of prisoners who qualified for parole was carried out by the Consejo Local de Patronato, or Patronage Society. AGN, MJ, 3.20.3.1.4.1.

54 AGN, MJ, 3.20.3.1.12.1.4, December 7, 1931.

55 *Código Penal*, art. 135, 115.

56 AGN, MJ, 3.20.3.1.12.1.4, December 7, 1931.

57 "Calificación correspondiente al 10 de julio de 1935."

58 See BC 1 (1927): 127–28.

59 See AGN, MJ, 3.20.3.3.1.3.42, f. 207 (June 8, 1927), and f. 225 (June 22, 1927).

60 It was mandated by the Resolution of June 4, 1927, and began to operate by late 1928. AGN, MJ, 3.20.3.1.7.0.

61 "La cárcel de Guadalupe," EC, June 2, 1901.

62 I have been unable to establish precise dates for either the closing or the reopening of Guadalupe. According to Carlos Aurelio León, who visited the prison in 1920 and reviewed its records, the first surviving document was dated 1856. See León, *Nuestras cárceles*, 9. However, neither Paz Soldán nor Fuentes included Guadalupe in their surveys of Lima's prisons in 1853 and 1858. Paz Soldán, *Examen de las penitenciarías*, and Fuentes, *Estadística general*.

63 "Reglamento de la cárcel de Guadalupe," July 3, 1879 (ADLP).

64 "Una visita a la cárcel de Lima," *EDJ*, June 21, 1890. Ricardo Heredia, president of the Patronage Society, was horrified to see that one hundred Guadalupe inmates "of all conditions" remained sequestered inside an isolation cell with no beds, ventilation, or even pavement for twelve hours a day. "Cárcel de Guadalupe," *LGJ*, 2, 2, 461, November 16, 1892.

65 *EDJ*, 3:536, April 30, 1892.

66 "Cárcel de Guadalupe," *LGJ*, 2, 2, 456, November 10, 1892.

67 See, for example, letters from the Mayor of Lima, César Canevaro, to the minister of justice in *EC*, June 26, 1889; and from the president of the Supreme Court to the minister of justice in *EDJ*, 2:431, October 26, 1891.

68 Additional descriptions of Guadalupe can be found in Alvarez, "Visitas de cárcel," *EC*, March 21, 1893; *El Nacional*, June 14, 1898; Memoria, Corte Superior de Lima, 1905, 1907; Abelardo Gamarra, "La cárcel de la capital!" in *Cien años de vida perdularia*, 193–95; "Dos horas en la cárcel de Guadalupe," *EC*, November 9, 1919; *Variedades* 19, no. 786 (March 24, 1923); León, *Nuestras cárceles*; Cerna, "El problema carcelario en el Perú"; Angela Ramos, "Visitando la cárcel de Guadalupe: Un antro de vergüenza y de dolor," *La Crónica*, November 8, 1927.

69 "Nueva cárcel," *EDJ*, 4:821, June 15, 1893.

70 Memoria, Justicia, 1905, 705.

71 Reynoso and Galup, "La arquitectura carcelaria," 52; *BC* 2, no. 1 (January-April 1929): 171. An entirely new prison was being built to replace Guadalupe, but it would take a few more years for it to be fully in operation. Adjacent to the 6th police station, it came to be known as El Sexto, and its first inmates were political prisoners. Víctor Modesto Villavicencio, "La cárcel nueva," *BC* 1, no. 4 (January 1928): 209. A dramatic portrait of this prison is in Arguedas, *El Sexto*.

72 AGN, MJ, 3.20.3.1.12.5.1, May 12, 1931. A study of the population of the CCV in 1935 showed that 52.5 percent of the prisoners were recidivists (10 percent of them with more than one prison sentence). Seminario Helguero, *Cárcel*, 31.

73 Fermín Carrión Matos, "Régimen penal y condiciones materiales de la cárcel departamental de varones de Lima," *BC* 4, no. 1 (1931): 150–54.

74 AGN, MJ, 3.20.3.1.12.5.1, September 9, 1930; "Informe presentado a la Inspección General de Prisiones por el Director de la Cárcel Central de Varones," April 12, 1933, AGN, MJ, 3.20.3.1.12.5.2; Seminario Helguero, *Cárcel*, passim; see also a description of the appalling prison conditions by two physicians of the Direccion General de Salubridad Pública, in AGN, MJ, 3.20.3.1.7.2 (September 15, 1932).

75 AGN, MJ, 3.20.3.1.7.2, October 24, 1931.

76 The exact date it opened remains unclear. According to the historian Jorge Basadre,

it was established during the second administration of President José Pardo (1916–19). Basadre, *Historia de la república*, 9:193. In 1919, Lorenzo Esparza referred to El Frontón as being "just opened." Esparza, "Contribución al estudio," 26.

77 Memoria, El Frontón, 1922, 7.

78 AGN, MJ, 3.20.3.1.12.2.3, July 14, 1930.

79 Memoria, El Frontón, 1922, 5.

80 Memoria, El Frontón, 1922, 15.

81 See, for example, "En la Colonia Penal de 'El Frontón,'" *El Tiempo*, February 16, 1919.

82 Ramos, *Una vida sin tregua*, 129, 130.

83 AGN, MJ, 3.20.3.1.7.2, September 15, 1932.

84 Mendoza, *En las prisiones peruanas*, 129.

85 The Aprista leader Luis Felipe de las Casas, who spent time as a prisoner at El Frontón in the 1940s, depicted it as an "enclave or independent territory" run by three authorities who were "the lords, kings, and absolute monarchs." De las Casas, *El Sectario*, 91.

86 Only in 1928 was the cemetery closed and autopsies made mandatory.

87 Villavicencio, *La reforma penitenciaria*, 89.

88 AGN, MJ, 3.20.2.1.6.0, June 16, 1924.

89 AGN, MJ, 3.20.3.1.12.1.6, January 5, 1937.

90 Garrido Malaver, *El Frontón*, 107–09.

91 Ibid., 111–12. These descriptions are confirmed by the testimonies of Armando Villanueva del Campo (personal interview) and Nicanor Mujica (written statement). See also Cossio del Pomar, *Víctor Raúl Haya de la Torre*, 94–96, and De las Casas, *El Sectario*, 98–101.

92 Villavicencio, *La reforma penitenciaria*, 89–90.

93 Ramos, *Una vida sin tregua*, 121.

94 León y León, "El reciente mensaje."

95 In 1915, the Calle Commission had recommended that the administration of the penitentiary be given to a religious institution, but that proposal died. The commission quoted Tocqueville as saying that "no human power is comparable with religion for effecting the reform of the criminal." Calle Commission, "Informe," 226.

96 The documents about these negotiations are found in AGN, MJ, 3.20.3.1.7.1.

CHAPTER 5. *FAITES, RATEROS*, DISGRACED GENTLEMEN

1 Decree of March 5, 1868 (AGN, MJ, 3.20.3.3.1.4.1, ff. 240–41). For critics of this practice, who called it "a complete perturbation of our penal system," see Alvarez, "Visitas de cárcel" (quote from 129); Memoria, Penitenciaría, 1902; "Penitenciados," *El Derecho* 5 (May 1894): 18; AGN, MJ, 3.20.3.3.1.7.2, f. 106, October 25, 1904.

2 AGN, MJ, 3.20.3.3.1.1.2, September 13, 1904, and 3.20.3.3.1.1.2, November 3, 1917; AGN, MJ, 3.20.3.3.1.4.61, August 14, 1920.

3 The report was never published, but the data it contained were used by criminologists such as Oscar Miró Quesada and Víctor M. Villavicencio.

4 Between 1881 and 1885, the average number of new inmates was 266.8 per year, significantly lower than the average 671.5 new inmates per year between 1870 and 1880.

5 "Memoria del Inspector de Cárceles," *LGJ*, 3:7, January 10, 1875.

6 "Cárcel de Guadalupe," *EC*, November 9, 1919.

7 See, for instance, "Relación de rematados y penitenciados existentes en la Cárcel Central de Guadalupe (Lima)," July 3, 1925, in AGN, MJ, 3.20.3.1.12.4.1.

8 AGN, MJ, 3.20.3.1.12.2.3, December 26, 1929.

9 Memoria, El Frontón, 1922.

10 Fuentes, *Estadística de la penitenciaría*.

11 We still need studies of this process of the expansion and consolidation of a national judicial system. For references about the expansion of the state and the retreat of local *gamonales*, see Taylor, *Bandits and Politics*, and Burga and Flores Galindo, *Apogeo y crisis*.

12 See "Resúmen estadístico de la existencia de condenados a penas privativas de la libertad, en los establecimientos penales de la República, en 31 de diciembre de 1930," in *BC* 4, no. 1 (1931).

13 Alegre y Pacheco, *Los delincuentes tatuados*, 39–88.

14 Memoria, Penitenciaría, 1909.

15 Alegre y Pacheco, *Los delincuentes tatuados*, 46.

16 Ibid., 53.

17 Ibid., 80.

18 See chapters 2 and 8 for further details.

19 See above, chapter 2, for further details.

20 Fuentes Castro, *Criminología peruana*; "Crónica: Horrible crimen," *EC*, August 17, 1893.

21 Miró Quesada, "El caso del asesino Montes."

22 AGN, Archivo Intermedio, Expedientes Criminales, "Criminal de oficio contra Pablo Bambarén por homicidio," March 7, 1911.

23 AGN, RPJ, Causas Criminales, Leg. 627, "Causa criminal contra Melchor Bustamante por homicidio," October 7, 1896.

24 AGN, Archivo Intermedio, Expedientes criminales, "Criminal de oficio contra Ambrosio Flores por homicidio," June 3, 1914.

25 AGN, Archivo Intermedio, Expedientes criminales, "Criminal de oficio contra el asiático Acam por homicidio," October 9, 1900.

26 AGN, RPJ, Causas Criminales, Leg. 290, "Criminal de oficio contra Pedro Reyes por el homicidio de Manuel Cárdenas en la hacienda de Punchauca," September 23, 1869.

27 AGN, RPJ, Causas Criminales, Leg. 290, "Criminal de oficio contra Pedro Pablo García por homicidio de Cipriano Tenorio," September 23, 1869.

28 AGN, Archivo Intermedio, Expedientes criminales, "Criminal de oficio contra Pablo Alemán por homicidio," October 26, 1901.

29 Archivo del Congreso, Expedientes de indulto, Legajo 8, Cuaderno 1, document 12, "Expediente. Ricardo Carmona sobre indulto," August 7, 1909.

30 Ibid., document 15, "Expediente de Aurelio Cueto sobre indulto," August 23, 1909.

31 Ibid., document 25, "Expediente de Saturnino Fuentes sobre indulto," October 14, 1909.

32 "Rateros," *LGJ* 2, 2, 433, October 13, 1892. See also "Crónica: Los rateros," *EC*, May 28, 1886.

33 A deceptive story commonly used by thieves in Lima to take advantage of naive victims.

34 Angela Ramos, "Una ojeada a las cárceles: La congestión de presos en la cárcel central," *La Crónica*, October 10, 1929. Reprinted in Ramos, *Una vida sin tregua*, 225–26.

35 Gálvez, *Una Lima que se va*, 88.

36 AGN, RPJ, Causas Criminales, Legajo 640, "Causa criminal contra Rómulo Calonge (a) Marcolfa por robo," July 14, 1897.

37 AGN, RPJ, Causas Criminales, Legajo 660, "Criminal de oficio contra Aurelio Pinto por robo," December 3, 1898.

38 AGN, RPJ, Causas Criminales, Legajo 662, "Causa criminal contra Julián La Rosa por robo," January 25, 1899.

39 AGN, Archivo Intermedio, Expedientes criminales, "Criminal de oficio contra Andrés Farfán por robo," August 6, 1902.

40 AGN, Archivo Intermedio, Expedientes criminales, "Criminal de oficio contra Pedro Aguirre Villar (a) 'Chivatito' por robo," March 12, 1915.

41 "Cárcel de Guadalupe," *EC*, November 9, 1919.

42 Gálvez, *Una Lima que se va*, 53.

43 José Diez Canseco, "Kilómetro 83," in *Estampas mulatas*, 108. Chivato and Tintoreros were names of streets; Descalzos is the name of a promenade in the Rímac district, near the Malambo area; Tajamar was an area near the river that had the reputation of being infested with criminals; Abajo el Puente (literally, "below the bridge") is a popular denomination for the Rímac district.

44 Quoted in Tejada, *La cuestión del pan*, 143.

45 Luis Alberto Sánchez, for instance, the most prestigious literary critic of twentieth-century Peru and a member of the Aprista party, referred to a *soplón* who was being assaulted by a furious crowd as a "tragic black man, bold, very brave, who neither cried nor begged to the crowd. He was, no doubt, a relentless criminal, but he also was a noble and brave type. I have never seen a man more courageous than him!!" Sánchez, *Valdelomar o la "Belle Epoque*," 92.

46 The name Malambo was taken from certain "antifever" trees planted by Spanish colonists to combat mosquitos. For this and other details of the history of Malambo, see Marquina Ríos, "Cincuenta casas de vecindad."

47 Tejada, "Malambo."

48 For a fascinating study of contemporary faites, see Pérez Guadalupe, *Faites y atorrantes*.

49 "Duelo de caballeros," EC, May 3, 1915; Alegría, "Duelo de Caballeros." The story was written in 1953 and originally published in 1961.

50 "Carita en prisión," EC, August 6, 1915.

51 See, for example, "La muerte de Tirifilo," by José Torres de Vidaurre, in *Delitos, crímenes, y costumbres*, 48–49, and "Muerte de Tirifilo," *El cancionero de Lima*, no. 99 (n.d.).

52 EC, May 3, 1915.

53 Alegría, "Duelo de caballeros," 284–85.

54 EC, May 3, 1915.

55 Alegría, "Duelo de caballeros," 292.

56 José Carlos Mariátegui, "Cómo mató Wilmann a 'Tirifilo.' Conversando con el victimario en el Hospital Dos de Mayo," *La Prensa*, May 6, 1915.

57 Carita would have a long criminal career. He spent fifteen years in prison between 1924 and 1939, which he served at El Frontón and the penitentiary. He was quite visible in sporting and cultural events (he wrote a song for Angela Ramos, for instance) and in seeking parole through his political contacts. AGN, MJ, 3.20.3.1.12.4.1, August 8 and 14, 1925; 3.20.3.3.1.4.72, January 5, 1929; 3.20.3.3.1.5.22, "Calificación correspondiente al 10 de Julio de 1935"; 3.20.3.1.12.1.6, July 5, 1936; 3.20.3.1.7.4, December 18, 1936; Ramos, *Una vida sin tregua*, 160, 168–69.

58 Alegría, *Duelo de caballeros*, 292.

59 Ley 4891, ADLP, also reprinted as an appendix of the Penal Code of 1924. The Vagrancy Law was finally annulled in 1986.

60 Ramos, *Una vida sin tregua*, 117.

61 Memoria, Guardia Civil, 1928, 147.

62 Ramos, *Una vida sin tregua*, 112.

63 Ibid., 96–103. A Leguiísta congressman ratified the veracity of this denunciation. Ibid., 113–16.

64 Planas, *La república autocrática*, 32; Ramos, *Una vida sin tregua*, 41.

65 Law no. 4113, May 11, 1920. According to Basadre, it "only affected the Indian." Basadre, *Historia de la República*, 9:391. The Conscripción Vial was called the "republican mita"—in reference to the form of coercive labor used in colonial Peru. See also Davies, *Indian Integration in Peru*, 82–86.

66 Memoria, Prefecto, 1925, 19.

67 Pedro Barrantes Castro, "Primeros efectos de la ley de vagancia," BC 1 (1927–28): 159.

68 According to the *Memoria* of General Martínez, during the year 1927, 516 suspects were evaluated, of whom 230 were convicted, 284 were released, and 2 were sent to the mental asylum. Memoria, Guardia Civil, 144.

69 Barrantes Castro, "Primeros efectos," 162–64.

70 Ramos, *Una vida sin tregua*, 94.

71 Ibid.

72 AGN, MJ, 3.20.3.1.12.2.1, July 15, 1926.

73 For valuable efforts at illuminating the participation of subaltern groups in political battles during this period, see Mallon, *Peasant and Nation*; Thurner, *From*

Two Republics; and Jacobsen and Diez Hurtado, "Montoneras, la comuna de Chalaco."

74 See, for instance, the coverage of political prisoners during the first Leguía administration (1908–12). Numerous reports, photographs, and interviews were published in Lima's newspapers and magazines, especially *Variedades*.

75 See especially Blanchard, *The Origins of the Peruvian Labor Movement*, passim.

76 Among them Juan Durand, Luis Pardo y Barreda, Alejandro Revoredo, Luis Fernán Cisneros, Javier Prado, Víctor Andrés Belaúnde, and others. Basadre, *Historia de la República*, 9:257, 258, 269.

77 For sordid details on Leguía's repressive methods, see, among others, Solís, *Once años*, 51–59, who puts the number of victims of Leguía's repression in the thousands.

78 Basadre, *Historia de la República*, 9:261.

79 Solís, *Once años*, 54.

80 Basadre, *Historia de la República*, 10:46.

81 Cossio del Pomar, *Víctor Raúl*, 97–99. After a hunger strike, Haya was sent into exile to Mexico. He returned to Peru in 1931, after the fall of Leguía.

82 Basadre, *Historia de la República*, 9:300.

83 Del Prado, *En los años cumbres*, 85–86.

84 Melgar and Seoane spent ten years in prison before being indulted. Juan Seoane, brother of the prominent Aprista leader Manuel Seoane, wrote his novel-testimony *Hombres y rejas* while in prison. It is a gripping account of prison life in the panóptico.

85 See Castro Fernandini, *Breve estudio*.

86 March 21, 1859 (ADLP).

87 The Penal Code of 1924 later mandated that political prisoners occupy special facilities segregated from other criminals and perform obligatory work (art. 18).

88 Valdez, "La patología de los delincuentes," 6.

89 *Variedades* 4, no. 104 (February 26, 1910): 251–57.

90 Seoane, *Hombres y rejas*, 136.

91 Ibid., 22–23.

92 Juan Seoane, for instance, was addressed as doctor by both common criminals and the director of the penitentiary. Seoane, *Hombres y rejas*, 209. The Chilean René Mendoza, who was accused of spying and spent time at El Frontón, admitted that, in spite of his nationality, he was treated well by both authorities and soldiers on the island. He was actually addressed as Señor. Mendoza, *En las prisiones peruanas*.

93 In 1900, for example, a political prisoner at Guadalupe, Belisario Barriga, was allowed to have alcohol in his room, to write and publish articles while in prison, send private correspondence, and even contact the people he wanted to. AGN, Ministerio del Interior, Prefecturas, Paquete 68, 1900.

94 José de la Riva Aguero, a distinguished member of an aristocratic family and a prestigious historian and politician, was sent to the Intendencia after he published an article in 1911 defending those involved in the May 1909 conspiracy.

After a successful mobilization of students and a collective petition for his freedom, the government yielded and not only freed him, but also declared amnesty for all other political prisoners. Before they were released, a massive banquet was organized for Riva Agüero, which was reportedly attended by eight hundred guests. Once it concluded, a large crowd marched to the penitentiary to salute the soon-to-be-released political prisoners and asked the director to allow them to enter the prison and offer their greetings to the political inmates. The director acceded. More than one hundred persons entered and, for about an hour, held a political rally inside the panóptico. Planas, *El 900: Balance y recuperación*, 126–28; see also Planas, *La república autocrática*, 135.

95   *Variedades* 4, no. 14 (June 6, 1908): 458, "En la penitenciaría."

96   Ibid., 459.

97   See, for example, *Variedades* 4, no. 23 (August 8, 1908): 738, and 4, no. 24 (August 15, 1908): 773.

98   AGN, Prefectura de Lima, Serie 3.9, Legajo 16.44, April 22, 1927.

99   After several months, thanks to the intercession of individuals and institutions, Basadre was taken from the island back to the Intendencia, where he spent a night. The next day he was taken to see the minister of government, who greeted him courteously and then released him.

100   AGN, MJ, 3.20.3.1.11.2, "Informe del Dr. Dn. Carlos Alberto Izaguirre, Diputado 3°. del Instituto, acerca de la situación de los presos político-sociales," June 12, 1934.

101   De las Casas, *El Sectario*, 33–41.

102   Seoane, *Hombres y rejas*, 259.

103   Partido Aprista Peruano, *El proceso Haya de la Torre*, 106.

104   Ibid., 107.

105   AGN, MJ, 3.20.3.1.12.1.6, January 5, 1937.

CHAPTER 6. THE CUSTOMARY ORDER

1   Pisciotta, *Benevolent Repression*, 36.

2   See, for example, O'Brien, *The Promise of Punishment*; Zedner, *Women, Crime, and Custody*; Moczydlowski, *The Hidden Life*; Dikotter, *Crime, Punishment, and the Prison*.

3   Altmann Smythe, *El problema sexual*, 48.

4   On *meritorios* among Lima's employee population, see Parker, *The Idea of the Middle Class*, 48.

5   To avoid that situation the director of the penitentiary suggested they be put on the regular payroll. AGN, MJ, 3.20.3.3.1.7.1, ff. 340–41, October 1, 1901. Many years later, in 1932, the director of the penitentiary demanded that meritorio positions be eliminated because they "loosen discipline." AGN, MJ, 3.20.3.1.12.1.4, January 2, 1932.

6   AGN, MJ, 3.20.3.3.1.4.3, f. 329, August 17, 1870.

7   AGN, MJ, 3.20.3.3.1.4.2, Memoria, Penitenciaría, 1876, January 1, 1877, ff. 405–23.

8   AGN, MJ, 3.20.3.3.1.4.61, May 17, 1920.

9   For various examples, see AGN, MJ, 3.20.3.3.1.3.42, f. 7, January 22, 1927, and f. 64, February 18, 1927; AGN, MJ, 3.20.3.3.1.3.45, f. 677, October 30, 1930.

10 AGN, MJ, 3.20.3.1.12.1.2, June 15, 1929.

11 AGN, MJ, 3.20.3.1.12.1.1, September 1, 1925. For further details about the traffic in coca, see a report written in April 1936 by a workshop manager (AGN, 3.20.3.1.12.1.6, April 8, 1936).

12 See AGN, MJ, 3.20.3.1.12.1.1, December 5, 1925. The DGP sent a memo to the director of the penitentiary prohibiting the introduction and consumption of alcohol and chicha by both inmates and employees.

13 AGN, MJ, 3.20.3.3.1.4.19, April 18, 1892.

14 EC, November 5, 1877.

15 AHML, Cárceles, August 31, 1881.

16 For some examples, see AGN, MJ, 3.20.3.1.12.1.2, December 28, 1929; AGN, MJ, 3.20.3.1.12.1.1, October 22, 1925. Guadalupe inmates paid some employees as much as six hundred soles for helping them secure their conditional freedom (AHML, Cárceles, June 13, 1885).

17 See, for example, AGN, MJ, 3.20.3.1.12.1.1, October 9, 1926.

18 See, for instance, AGN, MJ, 3.20.3.3.1.4.1, October 1, 1872.

19 See, for example, AGN, MJ, 3.20.3.1.12.1.4, June 14, 1933.

20 AGN, MJ, 3.20.3.3.11.2, October 5, 1892.

21 AGN, MJ, 3.20.3.1.12.1.1, December 10, 1925.

22 AGN, MJ, 3.20.3.1.12.1.3, September 13, 1929.

23 See especially AGN, MJ, 3.20.3.1.12.1.2, June 2, 1928; and August 15, 1929.

24 There are numerous reports on this. In November 1883, the warden of Guadalupe was caught sending home twenty rations of food from the prison supply, instead of the five he was allowed (AHML, Cárceles, November 24, 1883). Cooks at Guadalupe sold food rations to both political and common criminals (AHML, Cárceles, June 13, 1885). The bookkeeper of the penitentiary formed with one prisoner a sort of partnership for trading coca, cigarettes, and even groceries they took from the prison supplies (AGN, MJ, 3.20.3.3.1.4.2, October 17, 1874).

25 In January 1928, for example, the director of the penitentiary, in complicity with the workshop supervisor, was accused of using prisoners to manufacture furniture he used in his own house or gave as presents to his friends (AGN, MJ, 3.20.3.3.1.3.43, f. 9, January 24, 1928).

26 In 1930, the former inspector general of the penitentiary was accused of abusing the inmates by forcing them to pay for their clothes and other supplies. In addition, he fed them poorly and was involved in coca trade inside the prison. He charged a fee to the administrator of the prison canteen for allowing him to sell coca. The inspector also had chicken farms inside the penitentiary (AGN, MJ, 3.20.3.1.12.1.3, September 4, 1930). Indeed, the inspector did not deny selling clothes to the inmates but tried to pass off his actions as favors. He declared that "there are very few employees or prisoners who have not come to me to ask some favors" (AGN, MJ, 3.20.3.1.12.1.2, January 3, 1929).

27 The director of the penitentiary in 1929, for instance, implemented food service inside the prison for himself and his friends from outside the prison (AGN, MJ, 3.20.3.1.12.1.2, June 17, 1929).

28 For a description of this, see "Cárcel de Guadalupe," EC, November 9, 1919. A similar description was made of El Canchón, the central patio of the CCV, by Seminario Helguero in *Cárcel*, 10, 71.

29 Calle Commission, "Informe," 382.

30 AGN, MJ, 3.20.3.3.1.4.11, ff. 108–09, November 1886. See AGN, MJ, 3.20.3.3.1.4.16, September 1880, ff. 651–60, for similar complaints about unrecorded infractions and inmate-employee connivance. See the Memorias of the penitentiary for 1897 and 1905 for additional descriptions of decadence, corruption, and employee-inmate partnerships.

31 AGN, MJ, 3.20.2.1.7.0, March 24, 1921.

32 While the accusation might lead one to think these cases were monitored and eventually sanctioned, that only happened when those situations threatened other interests. On this occasion, the accusation was made after the employee insulted the vice-warden (AGN, MJ, 3.20.3.1.12.4.1, June 6, 1922).

33 AGN, Ministerio del Interior, Prefecturas, Legajo 28, February 11, 1892.

34 EC, February 20, 1893.

35 See, for example, Clemmer, *The Prison Community*.

36 AGN, MJ, 3.20.3.3.1.4.2, f. 638, December 12, 1877.

37 "Reglamento de la penitenciaría de Lima," in Memoria, Justicia, 1901, art. 27.

38 Seoane, *Hombres y rejas*, 116.

39 Enrique Galdas, inmate, to the minister of justice (June 5, 1937, AGN, MJ, 3.20.3.1.12.1.6). The inmate who wrote this complaint stated that the *caporal* had threatened anybody who dared to denounce him with transferal to El Frontón.

40 AGN, MJ, 3.20.3.1.12.1.1, January 5, 1926.

41 AHML, Cárceles, June 13, 1885.

42 Seminario Helguero, *Cárcel*, 66–67.

43 "Miguel de Orueta: El prestamista asesinado," EC, September 11, 1910. Orueta's fortune was estimated at well over a million soles.

44 AGN, Prefecturas, Serie 3.9, Legajo 16.12, September 22, 1911.

45 *Cacique* was the name given to indigenous tribal rulers in the Caribbean and, later, elsewhere in Latin America. After the European conquest they became critical intermediaries between colonial authorities and indigenous communities. The name was used later and is used even today to refer to political bosses, especially in Mexico.

46 He was later transferred to the penitentiary, where he was spotted in 1919 by a reporter from *El Comercio* and was described as a "tall, smiling, and charming *moreno*." EC, November 30, 1919.

47 AGN, MJ, 3.20.3.3.1.4.11, f. 630, June 24, 1880. Following this denunciation the warder was suspended in his job.

48 Seoane, *Hombres y rejas*, 89–90.

49 Paz Soldán, "Reglamento de la penitenciaría de Lima," in Fuentes and de la Lama,

Diccionario de legislación, passim. The rain shower, or "baño de lluvia," was the uninterrupted exposing of the prisoner to a heavy shower, causing him or her serious breathing difficulties. It is revealing that in his report on U.S. prisons Paz Soldán expressed his horror toward such treatment, considering it a penalty that was even more horrendous than the shooting of a criminal. Later, he adopted it for the Lima penitentiary as a way of softening prison penalties. Paz Soldán, *Exámen de las penitenciarías*, 47. The Reglamento of 1901 contained similar rewards and penalties but added the barra as a legal form of punishment.

50 Memoria, Penitenciaría, 1877. Some inmates, it was reported, actually began to smoke only because they wanted to benefit from the bonus.

51 AGN, MJ 3.20.3.3.1.3.1, f. 309, October 1, 1864.

52 AGN, MJ, 3.20.3.3.1.4.2, March 12, 1886.

53 AGN, Penitenciaría, Legajo 242, March 7, 1867.

54 The physician César Valdez referred to the case of a prisoner who spent two years in solitary, receiving his food through the metal bar on a piece of paper. Valdez considered the overall system of penalties in the penitentiary as "cruel and inhumane." Valdez, "La patología."

55 "Relación de las faltas cometidas por los presos y los castigos impuestos durante el año que comprende el segundo semestre de 1906 y primero de 1907," in Memoria, Justicia, 1907. A warning about the accuracy of these statistics: it seems fair to assume, as any student of prison regimes would, that numerous, if not most, transgressions were neither recorded nor punished, usually because of some sort of inmate-guard complicity.

56 Quoted in Valdez, "La patología," 36.

57 AGN, MJ, 3.20.3.3.1.5.19, "Moralidad de los presos. Año 1918." See also Esparza, "Contribución al estudio," 35.

58 "Reglamento de la penitenciaría de Lima," 549. Additional workshops were set up later, including a shop for manufacturing buttons and equipment for the army, which opened in 1881, and a bakery and couch-making shop (*carrocería*) that were operating by 1883. Some time later, a printing and binding shop was added.

59 The contract with a Mr. Muratori to run all the existing workshops and any others to be created later was signed on February 15, 1865. He was given a profit of 4 percent of the sales, with the promise of a later increase to 6 percent. AGN, MJ, 3.20.3.3.1.3.2.

60 AGN, MJ, 3.20.3.3.1.3.2, January 15, 1867.

61 AGN, MJ, 3.20.3.3.1.4.1, April 17, 1868. See also Lama, *Refutación del informe*, 18.

62 This was to happen only if the prisoner's work was estimated to be worth more than ten soles, the calculated maintenance cost for each inmate.

63 AGN, MJ, 3.20.3.3.1.4.1, June 30, 1870. Later, he insisted that prison work must be "proportional to the strength and abilities of the prisoner," and that it should captivate "his will and his self-esteem," in order to serve the rehabilitative purpose; otherwise, if work is imposed by force without consideration of his intelligence and inclinations, it will only dishearten and exasperate him. Lama, *Refutación*, 22.

64 Ibid., 19.

65 Ibid., 11.

66 The amount of money the prisoners were entitled to had to be given to the director of the penitentiary for the purchasing of books, desk supplies, and other "licit goods." See AGN, MJ, 3.20.3.3.1.3.3, August 7, 1873. See also De la Lama, *Constitución del Perú*, 419, 430–31.

67 These transfers, obviously, did not take into account the overall disciplinary needs of the prison or the prisoner's individual rehabilitative process. In January 1877, for example, it was requested that forty-six handicapped convicts be transferred from the penitentiary to Guadalupe in exchange for a similar number of skilled prisoners.

68 AGN, MJ 3.20.3.3.1.4.2, January 17, 1877. More examples in AGN, MJ, 3.20.3.3.1.3.3, November 21, 1881.

69 AGN, MJ, 3.20.3.3.1.3.3, December 31, 1880; AGN, MJ, 3.20.3.3.1.3.7, April 22, 1884; AGN, MJ, 3.20.3.3.1.4.11, November 1886.

70 AGN, MJ, 3.20.3.3.1.4.11, November 30, 1878.

71 AGN, MJ, 3.20.3.3.1.3.6, June 6, 1881.

72 AGN, MJ, 3.20.3.3.1.3.3, December 18, 1883. Angel Cavassa, for instance, signed a contract to run the bakery. He offered to reward each prisoner "according to his performance." He had to pay the state thirty cents per prisoner, but all the bread made at the prison went to the contractor. Ibid., May 30, 1884.

73 Memoria, Penitenciaría, 1891.

74 *EC*, July 31, 1889.

75 "El panóptico," *LGJ* 2, 2, 436 (October 17, 1892).

76 *EDJ*, 4:961, December 4, 1893. See also *EC*, May 5, 1894, "Penitenciado," and Chavez, "Evoluciones," 84–85, 101–02.

77 Memoria, Penitenciaría, 1896.

78 "Visitando el panóptico," *EC*, November 30, 1919.

79 Memoria, Penitenciaría, 1890 and 1892.

80 AGN, MJ, 3.3.1.7.1, November 21, 1898. Responding to criticisms of the cost to the state of the system of direct administration, the director stated in April 1900 that what was much more important was "the supreme interest of the severe discipline of the panóptico," which had loosened under the contract system. AGN, MJ, 3.20.3.3.1.7.1, April 1900.

81 Memoria, Penitenciaría, 1900.

82 See Calle Commission, "Informe," 158.

83 Memoria, Penitenciaría, 1903, 203; Memoria, Justicia, 1903.

84 AGN, MJ, 3.3.1.7.2, October 25, 1904 (Memoria 1903); "Talleres del panóptico," in Memoria, Justicia, 1903.

85 "Informe de P. Doly sobre el estado y las reformas del orden económico y administrativo de la penitenciaría," in Memoria, Justicia, 1909. Still in 1907, according to the director, 350 out of 411 prisoners did work at the workshops. Memoria, Penitenciaría, 1907.

86 Memoria, Penitenciaría, 1912.

87 Calle Commision, "Informe," 161.

88 Memoria, Justicia, 1915.

89 They were the Comité de Solidaridad Obrera (Committee for working-class solidarity) and the Sociedad de Mosaístas del Perú (Association of Peruvian mosaic makers).

90 AGN, MJ, 3.20.3.1.12.1.1, August 23, 1921, and AGN, MJ, 3.20.2.9.12.0, Resolution of November 21, 1921. A precedent existed since October 21, 1911, when the government ordered that notebooks, books, and other stationery supplies for the Ministry of Justice be manufactured at the penitentiary. Quoted in Calle Commission, "Informe," 220.

91 Very rarely was prison work brought up in the debates about labor in Lima. One of the few times it was, Carlos B. Cisneros, the author of a socioeconomic study of Lima, stated in 1911 that the penitentiary had been inappropriately converted into a "vast industrial workshop," which was detrimental to "free and honest artisans." He suggested that prisoners' labor should be used only in public works. Cisneros, *Provincia de Lima*, 227.

92 Resolution of March 28, 1925, in AGN, MJ, 3.20.3.1.12.1.3; Penal Code, art. 79.

93 On the expanding state bureaucracy, see especially Herbold, "Developments," and Parker, *The Idea of the Middle Class*.

94 Memoria, Penitenciaría, 1926. The director insisted that the penitentiary should produce only for the state and that the state must place orders only with the prison workshops.

95 "Ayer la Junta del Patronato visitó la penitenciaría. Hay que llevar a cabo fundamentales reformas," *EC*, January 19, 1926.

96 AGN, MJ, 3.20.3.3.1.6.1.

97 AGN, MJ, 3.20.3.3.1.6.1, October 1, 1927.

98 AGN, MJ, 3.20.3.3.1.1.2, February 5, 1922, f. 456.

99 AGN, MJ, 3.20.3.1.12.1.2, June 5, 1929, and August 7, 1929.

100 AGN, MJ, 3.20.3.1.12.1.2, March 15, 1929.

101 AGN, MJ, 3.20.3.1.7.1, August 5, 1930, and October 15, 1930.

102 AGN, MJ, 3.20.3.1.12.1.4.

103 The phrase is taken from Hobsbawm, "Peasants and Politics."

CHAPTER 7. SUBCULTURES AND LIVING CONDITIONS

1 See, for example, O'Brien, *The Promise of Punishment*, especially chap. 3.

2 Sabo et al., "Gender and the Politics of Punishment." The term "hegemonic masculinities" is borrowed from Connell, *Masculinities*.

3 For classical studies of tattooing, see Lombroso, "The Savage Origin of Tattooing," and Lacassagne, *Les tatouages*.

4 Alegre y Pacheco, *Los delincuentes tatuados*, 25.

5 O'Brien, *The Promise of Punishment*, 81.

6 Valdizán, "El tatuaje."

7 Ibid., 109.

8   One inmate not included in this report wore the image of an Inca, for whom, he confessed, he had great admiration "because of their great accomplishments." See Altmann, *El problema sexual*, 43.

9   Alegre y Pacheco, *Los delincuentes tatuados*, passim. I thank Walter Huamaní for helping me locate a copy of this rare volume.

10 Ibid., 37.

11 A few of them underlined its importance for the study of criminal populations but were not too much attracted to empirical research. See, for example, Rada, *Apuntes sobre el estudio*, 145. For the glossaries of criminal argot, see "Cárcel de Guadalupe," EC, November 9, 1919, and Seminario Helguero, *Cárcel*, 75–84.

12 "Cárcel de Guadalupe," EC, November 9, 1919.

13 Rada, *Apuntes sobre el estudio*, 145.

14 Seminario Helguero, *Cárcel*.

15 For an overview of the history of coca consumption in Andean Peru, see Gagliano, *Coca Prohibition*.

16 Esparza, "Contribución al estudio," 38–43.

17 "Visitando el panóptico," EC, November 30, 1919.

18 Valdez, "La patología," 16–18.

19 Both *Reglamentos* of the penitentiary (1863 and 1901) gave permission to inmates to consume coca in solitude as a reward for good behavior.

20 Altmann, *El problema sexual*.

21 Valdez, "La patología," 41.

22 It is implied that the lesser impact of homosexuality at the penitentiary was related to the fact that inmates occupied individual cells, thus reducing considerably the possibilities for intimate contact.

23 Seminario Helguero, *Los presos*, 47.

24 Piccato, "Interpretations of Sexuality," 262.

25 The term *active* was used to refer to the "masculine" partner, the one who was conceived as doing the penetration, while the term *passive* referred to the "feminine" one, that is, the one who was sexually penetrated. Needless to say, this categorization was imposed by observers upon a reality that was much more complex. At the same time, though, this supposed division of roles within homosexual relations seems to have shaped at least in part the relations between partners, as we will see below.

26 Valdez, "La patología," 42–48.

27 Seminario Helguera, *Cárcel*, 72–73.

28 Altmann, *El problema sexual*, 38.

29 "C.G.C.," interviewed by Altmann. See *El problema sexual*, 42.

30 Seminario Helguero, *Cárcel*, 70.

31 Ibid., 73.

32 AGN, MJ, 3.20.3.1.12.1.4, April 26, 1932.

33 AGN, MJ, 3.20.3.1.12.1.4, October 3, 1931.

34 AGN, MJ, 3.20.2.1.7.0, April 18, 1925.

35 AGN, Archivo Intermedio, Expedientes criminales, Legajo 5, "Criminal de oficio contra Juan Marín por lesiones," February 17, 1913.

36 AGN, Archivo Intermedio, Expedientes Criminales, "Contra Manuel Chumpitaz por lesiones," December 18, 1911.

37 Seminario Helguera, *Cárcel*, 72.

38 León, *Nuestras cárceles*, 11.

39 O'Brien, *The Promise of Punishment*, 107.

40 Altmann, *El problema sexual*, 48.

41 AGN, MJ, 3.20.3.3.1.3.45, May 30, 1930.

42 This is suspicious, though. AGN, MJ, 3.20.3.3.1.1.2, August 1, 1907.

43 *EC*, August 4, 1894.

44 AGN, MJ, 3.20.3.1.12.4.1, November 21, 1924.

45 AGN, MJ, 3.20.3.3.1.4.61, September 18, 1920.

46 AGN, MJ, 3.20.3.1.12.1.2, February 9, 1929.

47 AGN, RPJ, Causas Criminales, Legajo 659, "Seguido de oficio contra Rafael Sosa por homicidio y otros delitos," November 16, 1878.

48 Inmates had easy access to knives and all sorts of hardware that they used as weapons to fight or impose their authority. They usually stole or fabricated them in the workshops. See, for example, AGN, MJ, 3.20.3.3.1.3.2, February 8, 1868; MJ, 3.20.3.3.1.4.73, June 17, 1930.

49 Scott, *Domination and the Arts of Resistance*, 26.

50 "Cárcel de Guadalupe," *EC*, November 9, 1919.

51 Seminario Helguero, *Cárcel*, 19.

52 In Mexico, for instance, the penitentiary regime included, among many classificatory criteria, the prisoners' race. See Piccato, "Mexico City Criminals."

53 According to Seminario Helguero, indigenous inmates at the CCV were "quiet, they live a reserved life, and do not have relationships with other inmates." Seminario Helguero, *Cárcel*, 21.

54 AGN, MJ, 3.20.3.1.12.1.6, June 5, 1937.

55 Esparza, "Contribución," 38.

56 Tawantinsuyo is the Quechua name for the Inca Empire.

57 AGN, MJ, 3.20.3.1.12.1.2, April 18, 1929.

58 Miguel Montenegro, "Informe relativo al estado sanitario de la penitenciaría," in AGN, MJ, 3.20.3.3.1.3.1, f. 548, December 1, 1866; and "Informe sobre el estado sanitario de la penitenciaría," AGN, MJ, 3.20.3.3.1.3.2, March 31, 1867.

59 Eyzaguirre, "La tuberculosis pulmonar." See also Portella, "La higiene."

60 Valdez, "La patología"; Esparza, "Contribución al estudio."

61 According to the director of the penitentiary in 1869, tuberculosis was not caused by harmful weather but by the lack of fresh air, physical exercise, hygiene, and "especially by the moral despair" (*abatimiento moral*) of the prisoners (AGN, MJ, 3.20.3.3.1.4.1, p. 28; AGN, MJ, 3.20.3.3.1.3.1, f. 294).

62 "Movimiento habido en el hospital de la penitenciaría de junio de 1905 a mayo de 1906 inclusive," in Memoria, Justicia, 1906.

63 Seminario Helguero, *Cárcel*, 9.

64   Memoria, Penitenciaría, 1911.

65   Valdez, "La patología," 62–72. Valdez's monograph is a detailed, sometimes gory depiction of health conditions inside the Lima penitentiary.

66   "Memoria que presenta el médico de la penitenciaría al Sr. director del establecimiento," AGN, MJ, 3.20.3.3.1.4.1, July 17, 1868, f. 271.

67   Seminario Helguero, Cárcel, 11.

68   Valdez, "La patología," 53. See also Esparza, "Contribución," 26.

69   See MJ 3.20.3.3.1.4.1, May 12, 1870, for details on the prisoners' diet and the administrators' self-serving statements about its nutritious character. A visitor to the penitentiary in 1919 reported that he found the food not only good but also tasty. The day of his visit the prisoners were going to get beans with "big chunks of meat." See "Visita al panóptico," EC, November 30, 1919.

70   See, for example, AGN, MJ, 3.20.3.3.1.3.6, f. 223, May 23, 1881.

71   AGN, MJ, 3.20.3.3.1.3.3, f. 237, March 8, 1872.

72   AGN, MJ, 3.20.3.3.1.4.1, f. 361, May 31, 1870.

73   AGN, MJ, 3.20.3.1.12.1.3, January 20, 1930.

74   EC, August 7 and August 22, 1889.

75   AHML, Cárceles, October 30, 1883.

76   AHML, Cárceles, November 11, 1883.

77   AHML, Cárceles, August 12, 1885.

78   AGN, MJ, 3.20.3.1.12.5.1, October 1, 1931.

79   The notion of "less eligibility" was developed by the German sociologists Georg Rusche and Otto Kirchheimer in their Punishment and Social Structure.

80   See, for instance, Zedner, Women, Crime, and Custody, 170–71 ("The local prison as refuge").

81   The living conditions for Chinese coolies in nineteenth-century Peru are discussed in Rodríguez Pastor, Hijos del celeste imperio.

82   Velasco, "Sistemas penitenciarios," 36.

83   "Atractivos de las penas," EDJ, 4:827, June 22, 1893.

84   "Carcel de Guadalupe," EC, November 9, 1919.

85   Ibid.

86   Seminario Helguero, Los presos, 18.

87   See, for instance, AGN, MJ, 3.20.3.3.1.4.61, July 13, 1920.

88   AGN, MJ, 3.20.3.3.1.3.42, f. 91, March 15, 1927.

89   Memoria, Penitenciaría, 1921.

90   AGN, MJ, 3.20.3.3.1.3.42, July 18, 1927; AGN, MJ, 3.20.3.1.12.1.2, February 25, 1929.

91   See Ramos, Una vida sin tregua, for abundant information about these events.

92   Altmann Smythe, El problema sexual, 49.

93   AGN, MJ, 3.20.3.1.12.1.1, January 3, 1926.

CHAPTER 8. BEYOND THE CUSTOMARY ORDER

1   AGN, MJ, 3.20.3. .3.1.3.1, September 15, 1862, and 3.20.3.3.1.4.1, September 28, 1862.

2   AGN, MJ, 3.20.3.3.1.3.1, February 17, 1863.

3   AGN, MJ, 3.20.3.3.1.4.1, July 2, 1867, November 22, 1868, and August 8, 1870.

4   AGN, MJ, 3.20.3.3.1.3.6, February, 18, 1880.

5   See AGN, RPJ, Causas Criminales, Legajo 352, 1877, "De oficio contra Manuel Peña Chacaliaza por fuga y José Estevan Guzman por ocultación," August 13, 1877.

6   Paulino Fuentes Castro, "Manuel Peña y Chacaliaza," EDJ, 2:500, February 12, 1892.

7   AGN, MJ, 3.20.3.1.4.2, September 21, 1876.

8   Variedades 6:97 (January 8, 1910): 42.

9   AGN, Ministerio del Interior, Prefecturas, Legajo 132, February 21, 1910. See also "La evasión de los presos políticos," EC, February 27, 1910; "La evasión de los presos políticos," Variedades 6:104 (February 26, 1910): 254–57. For Variedades, "political prisoners have not escaped from justice; what they have escaped from is vengeance." Ibid., 253.

10   AGN, MJ, 3.20.3.3.1.1.2, March 28, 1912, and November 26, 1915.

11   AGN, MJ, 3.20.3.1.12.5.2.

12   Letter from "Prisoners friends of order," EC, February 20, 1893.

13   AGN, Prefecturas, 3.9, Legajo 3.1, August 27, 1884.

14   AHML, Cárceles, October 14, 1884.

15   AGN, Prefectura de Lima, Series 3.9, Legajo 16.5, January 28, 1890. See also EC, January 28, 1890.

16   EC, February 27, 1892.

17   See, for various such cases, AGN, Ministerio del Interior, Prefecturas, Paquete 34, February 16, 1893; AGN, MJ, 3.20.3.1.1.2.41, October 4, 1924, February 21, 1927, and April 24, 1927.

18   AGN, MJ, 3.20.2.1.7.0, February 23, 1925.

19   He was recaptured a few months later in Lima after he stole some hens. AGN, Prefecturas, Serie 3.9, Legajo 16.45, August 6, 1927.

20   AGN, MJ, 3.20.3.1.12.2.3, May 27, 1930.

21   Garrido Malaver, El Frontón, 93.

22   AGN, MJ, 3.20.3.3.1.4.1, October 31 and November 2, 1864.

23   AGN, Penitenciaría, Legajo 242, March 7, 1867.

24   AGN, MJ, 3.20.3.3.1.4.1, December 7, 1867.

25   AGN, MJ, 3.20.3.3.1.4.1, December 24, 1867.

26   AGN, MJ, 3.20.33141, Memoria, Penitenciaría, 1868.

27   AGN, MJ, 3.20.3.3.1.3.2, February 8, 1868.

28   AGN, Penitenciaría, Legajo 242, September 6, 1866. In July 1867, after two prisoners escaped, a thorough inspection of the penitentiary cells made clear that prisoners were in possession of arms (AGN, MJ, 3.20.3.3.1.1.2, July 8, 1867).

29   AHML, Cárceles, July 12, 1887.

30   "Los presos de la cárcel de Guadalupe se amotinan. Atacaron al Alcaide y los empleados. Arzola jefe de los rebeldes. Varios heridos." EC, July 29, 1915, and August 2, 1915.

31   AGN, MJ, 3.20.2.1.7.0, March 24, 1921.

32   Amey in November 1869 (AGN, MJ, 3.20.3.3.1.4.1, November 4, 1869); José María

Así in April 1872 (AGN, MJ, 3.20.33141, April 22, 1872); and José Aley in October 1924 (AGN, MJ, 3.20.3.1.1.2.41, October 30, 1924). José had killed a guard and was sent to the calabozo, where he reportedly committed suicide.

33 AGN, MJ, 3.20.3.3.1.4.1, December 1, 1862.

34 Ruiz Zevallos, *Psiquiatras y locos*, 95.

35 AGN, MJ, 3.20.3.3.1.1.2, July 9, 1874.

36 AGN, MJ, 3.20.3.3.1.1.2, July 18, 1905.

37 AGN, MJ, 3.20.3.3.1.3.44, May 24, 1929.

38 AGN, Ministerio del Interior, Prefecturas, Legajo 103, August 24, 1905.

39 AGN, MJ, 3.20.3.3.1.4.2, February 20, 1875.

40 AGN, Prefecturas, 3.9, Legajo 16.12, February 19, 1900. Two days later, another suspect, Julio Sanchez, was arrested, for whom no details were offered. Ibid., February 21, 1900.

41 AGN, MJ, 3.20, 3.3.1.4.1, ff. 422–23, February 1, 1871.

42 Ruiz Zevallos, *Psiquiatras y locos*, 41–85.

43 See, for example, AGN, MJ, 3.20.3.3.1.4.1, f. 321, October 13, 1869; AGN, MJ, 3.20.3.3.1.3.3, June 13, 1870; "Informe presentado por el Inspector Principal Sr. Enrique Andía," in Memoria, Penitenciaría, 1927.

44 AGN, Archivo Intermedio, Expedientes criminales, "De oficio contra Leonardo Gomez por lesiones," March 11, 1904.

45 The proposal did not succeed. EDJ, 2:290, May 4, 1891.

46 This is not the same as denying that there were, in Lima's prisons, cases of individuals with symptoms of mental imparity who in fact needed to be treated at special institutions.

47 AGN, MJ, 3.20.3.3.1.3.2, April 28, 1867.

48 AHML, Cárceles, February 8, 1872.

49 AGN, MJ, 3.20.3.3.1.4.1, April 21, 1868. This was not an isolated case. In almost every other riot, reports referred to groups of inmates who, instead of joining the band of the rebels, sided with the authorities and helped put down the uprising.

50 "Cárcel de Guadalupe," EC, November 9, 1919.

51 AGN, MJ, 3.20.3.3.1.4.1, November 11, 1868.

52 José Félix Castro, "Las Cárceles y el panóptico," EC, March 21, 1893.

53 AGN, MJ, 3.20.3.1.12.1.3, n/d. [1932].

54 AGN, MJ, 3.20.3.1.1.2.51, March 28, 1931.

55 AGN, MJ, 3.20.3.1.12.1.1, March 27, 1925.

56 AHML, Cárceles, October 14, 1884.

57 This section draws from my article "Disputed Views of Incarceration in Lima."

58 I do not mean to suggest that collective letters were completely unknown in the late 1920s. Indeed, I have found a few such letters written several decades before. One notable example is a letter sent to the National Congress in September 1870 by dozens of penitentiary inmates requesting reductions in their sentences (National Congress, Historical Archive, Legajo 6, September 19, 1870). In 1892, prisoners from both the Lima penitentiary and the Guadalupe jail sent collective letters to the Congress also requesting a reduction in their sentences on the

occasion of the Fourth Centennial of Columbus's "Discovery" of America (National Congress, Historical Archive, Legajo 9, Memoriales, Doc. 327, September 30, 1892, and Doc. 328, September 28, 1892). I suggest, though, that in the late 1920s collective forms of representation became more common and revealed newly acquired political and doctrinal notions absent in previous periods.

59 For more details about these interventions, see Aguirre, "Disputed Views of Incarceration."

60 Common inmates, for instance, smuggled Aprista propaganda between the penitentiary and the ccv through the sewage system. In November 1932, the director of the ccv reported that Aprista inmates were receiving communications from their leader, Haya de la Torre, who was detained at the contiguous penitentiary (AGN, MJ, 3.20.3.1.12.5.1). The volume *Cartas de Haya de la Torre* contains a sample of letters written by Haya de la Torre and smuggled into the penitentiary and other prisons.

61 Personal written communication. See also Seoane, *Hombres y rejas*, 118.

62 Seoane, *Hombres y rejas*, 22.

63 AGN, MJ, 3.20.3.1.12.5.1.

64 AGN, MJ, 3.20.3.1.12.1.5, June 30, 1934. The director asks for the transfer of two or three Aprista leaders to El Frontón to prevent further contamination.

65 AGN, MJ, 3.20.3.1.11.1, November 12, 1930.

66 De las Casas, *El Sectario*, 95–97.

67 AGN, MJ, 3.20.3.1.12.1.5, October 28, 1935, and November 5, 1935.

68 Seoane called the penitentiary "this hell, where one always has to pretend [*fingir*]." Seoane, *Hombres y rejas*, 116.

69 Mariátegui, *Correspondencia*, 1:289–90, 293–94.

70 Mariátegui, *Correspondencia*, 2:681.

71 *El proceso Haya de la Torre*, 67.

72 AGN, Ministerio del Interior, Prefecturas, Legajo 16.45, August 25, 1927.

73 AGN, MJ, 3.20.3.1.12.2.3, April 8, 1930.

74 They based their request on a decree that mandated that political prisoners had to be placed in a special section of the prison. AGN, MJ, 3.20.3.1.12.1.5, February 20, 1934.

75 AGN, MJ, 3.20.3.1.12.1.5, September 30, 1935.

76 AGN, MJ, 3.20.3.1.7.2, December 23, 1933. Still, the petitioners resorted to clientelistic rhetoric: they praised Benavides for his policies of "concord and reconciliation."

77 AGN, MJ, 3.20.3.1.12.1.6, May 20, 1936.

78 AGN, MJ, 3.20.3.1.12.1.1, December 30, 1924.

79 AGN, MJ, 3.20.3.1.11.1., April 26, 1926.

80 AGN, MJ, 3.20.3.1.12.51, July 26, 1930. A similar tone runs through a letter written by Guadalupe inmates to Angela Ramos, in which they thank her for all the activities she was organizing in favor of prisoners. Ramos, *Una vida sin tregua*, 139–40.

81 AGN, MJ, 3.20.3.1.12.12, April 11, 1930.

82   AGN, MJ, 3.20.3.3.13.45, f. 10, n.d.

83   My review of prisoners' letters reveals that, in many instances, they seem to have been written not by the inmates themselves, but by other individuals. Who the writers were is difficult to establish: they could have been outside relatives, educated fellow inmates, lawyers or legal practitioners (*tinterillos*), or even prison employees paid by the inmates.

84   Chevalier, "Official Indigenismo."

85   AGN, MJ, 3.20.3.1.12.1.1, February 25, 1925.

86   AGN, MJ, 3.20.3.1.12.1.1, March 30, 1927.

87   Scott, *Domination and the Arts of Resistance*, 4.

88   See Stein, *Lima obrera*; Burga and Flores Galindo, *Apogeo y crisis*; Parker, *The Idea of the Middle Class*.

89   *La Crónica*, February 19, 1928, reproduced in Ramos, *Una vida sin tregua*, 175.

90   AGN, MJ, 3.20.3.1.12.1.2, June 12, 1929.

91   Ibid., May 2, 1930.

92   AGN, MJ, 3.20.3.1.1.2.51, August 28, 1930.

93   AGN, MJ, 3.20.3.1.12.1.3, November 3, 1930.

94   AGN, MJ, 3.20.3.1.1.2.51, September 20, 1930. See also EC, December 9, 1931, for another letter with a similar content. Prisoners at the CCV asked President Sánchez Cerro to pay a visit to the prison so they could inform him personally of their "pathetic situation."

95   Ramos, *Una vida sin tregua*, 133.

96   AGN, MJ, 3.20.3.1.1.2.51, April 10, 1929.

97   AGN, MJ, 3.20.3.1.1.2.51, May 22, 1930.

98   See, for example, "Carta de un preso de Guadalupe," EC, August 12, 1915.

99   AGN, MJ, 3.20.3.1.12.2.3, September 12, 1929.

100   AGN, MJ, 3.10.3.1.1.2.51, November 4, 1930.

101   AGN, MJ, 3.20.3.1.2.1, July 9, 1929.

102   AGN, MJ, 3.20.3.1.1.2.51, May 25, 1931.

103   AGN, MJ, 3.20.3.1.1.2.51, January 1932.

104   AGN, MJ, 3.20.3.1.12.1.1, January 3, 1926, emphasis added.

105   AGN, MJ, 3.20.3.1.12.2.2, August 15, 1928, emphasis added.

106   AGN, MJ, 3.20.3.1.1.2.51, December 9, 1931, emphasis added.

107   Villavicencio, who has been mentioned repeatedly throughout this book, was one of the most conspicuous penologists of this period. He wrote extensively on a variety of issues regarding penal regimes and served in various posts in the administration of prisons. See, among his numerous publications, *La reforma penitenciaria en el Perú*. I have also found evidence that Villavicencio was particularly harsh on prisoners, giving them generally low scores during the evaluations of the Tribunal de Conducta, which may explain the animosity the inmates felt for him. See on this AGN, MJ, 3.20.3.3.1.5.22.

108   AGN, MJ, 3.20.3.1.12.1.4, December 10, 1931.

CONCLUSION

1   The drawings were first published by the historian Pablo Macera in *Cielo Abierto* (Lima), 5:15 (1981).

2   McConville, *English Local Prisons*; Oshinsky, *"Worse than Slavery"*; Carrefiello, *The Tombs of the Living*.

3   Herbold, "Developments," 70–71.

4   Villavicencio, *La reforma penitenciaria*, 25.

5   Cueto, *Excelencia científica*, 58. See also Memoria, Penitenciaría, 1908.

BIBLIOGRAPHY

Most archival sources are given in the notes. What follows is the list of citations for the *Memorias* used throughout the book and the bibliographical references, including primary and secondary printed materials.

MEMORIAS FROM THE MINISTER OF JUSTICE

1872: *Memoria que debió presentar el Ministro de Estado en el despacho de Justicia, Culto, Instrucción y Beneficiencia D. Melchor T. García al Congreso Nacional de 1872* (Lima: Imprenta de la Sociedad, 1872).

1890: *Memoria que presenta el Ministro de Justicia, Culto, Instrucción y Beneficencia al Congreso Ordinario de 1890* (Lima: Imprenta de Torres Aguirre, 1890).

1891: *Memoria que presenta el Ministro de Justicia, Culto, Instrucción y Beneficencia al Congreso Ordinario de 1891* (Lima: Imprenta de El Diario, 1891).

1892: *Memoria presentada por el Ministro de Justicia, Culto, Instrucción y Beneficencia al Congreso Ordinario de 1892* (Lima: Imprenta Torres Aguirre, 1892).

1894: *Memoria presentada por el Ministro de Justicia, Culto, Instrucción y Beneficencia al Congreso Ordinario de 1894* (Lima: Imprenta El Rímac, 1894).

1896: *Memoria presentada por el Ministro de Justicia, Culto e Instrucción al Congreso Ordinario de 1896* (Lima: Imprenta Torres Aguirre, 1896).

1897: *Memoria presentada por el Ministro de Justicia, Culto e Instrucción al Congreso Ordinario de 1897* (Lima: Imprenta La Industria, 1897).

1900: *Memoria que presenta el Ministro de Justicia, Culto e Instrucción al Congreso Ordinario de 1900* (Lima: Imprenta Torres Aguirre, 1900).

1901: *Memoria que presenta el Ministro de Justicia, Instrucción y Culto al Congreso Ordinario de 1901* (Lima: Imprenta del Estado, 1901).

1902: *Memoria que presenta el Ministro de Justicia, Culto e Instrucción al Congreso Ordinario de 1902* (Lima: Imprenta Torres Aguirre, 1902).

1903: *Memoria que presenta el Ministro de Justicia, Culto e Instrucción al Congreso Ordinario de 1903* (Lima: Imprenta Torres Aguirre, 1903).

1904: *Memoria que presenta el Ministro de Justicia, Culto e Instrucción al Congreso Ordinario de 1904* (Lima: Imprenta Torres Aguirre, 1904).

1905: *Memoria presentada por el Ministro de Justicia, Instrucción y Culto, Dr. D. Jorge Polar al Congreso Ordinario de 1905* (Lima: Imprenta Torres Aguirre, 1905).

1906: *Memoria presentada por el Ministro de Justicia, Instrucción y Culto Dr. D. Jorge Polar al Congreso Ordinario de 1906* (Lima: Imprenta Torres Aguirre, 1906).

1907: *Memoria presentada por el Ministro de Justicia, Instrucción y Culto Dr. Carlos A. Washburn, al Congreso Ordinario de 1907* (Lima: Imprenta Torres Aguirre, 1907).

1908: *Memoria presentada por el Ministro de Justicia, Instrucción y Culto Dr. D. Carlos A. Washburn al Congreso Ordinario de 1908*, vol. 1, Justicia (Lima: Imprenta Torres Aguirre, 1908).

1909: *Memoria presentada por el Ministro de Justicia, Instrucción y Culto Dr. D. Carlos A. Washburn al Congreso ordinario de 1909* (Lima: La Oficina Nacional, 1910).

1910: *Memoria presentada por el Ministro de Justicia, Instrucción y Culto Sr. Dr. D. Antonio Flores al congreso ordinario de 1910*, vol. 1, Justicia (Lima: Tipografía La Revista, 1910).

1915: *Memoria presentada por el Ministro de Justicia, Instrucción, Culto y Beneficencia Dr. Don Plácido Jiménez al Congreso ordinario de 1915* (Lima: Imprenta del Estado, 1915).

1916: *Memoria que el Ministro de Justicia, Instrucción, Culto y Beneficencia Dr. D. Wenceslao Valera presenta al Congreso Ordinario de 1916*, 2 vols. (Lima: Empresa Tipográfica Lártiga, 1916).

1918: *Memoria que el Ministro de Justicia, Instrucción, Culto y Beneficencia presenta al Congreso Ordinario de 1918* (Lima: Oficina Tipográfica La Opinión Nacional, 1918).

1921: *Memoria que el Ministro de Justicia, Culto, Instrucción y Beneficencia Dr. D. Oscar C. Barrón presenta al Congreso Ordinario de 1921* (Lima: Imprenta Torres Aguirre, 1921).

1927: *Memoria que el Ministro de Justicia, Culto, Instrucción y Beneficencia, Dr. Pedro Olivera presenta al Congreso Ordinario de 1927* (Lima: Casa Editora La Opinión Nacional, 1928).

1929: *Memoria que el Ministro de Justicia, Culto, Instrucción y Beneficencia Dr. J. Matías León presenta al Congreso Ordinario de 1929* (Lima: Imprenta Larrabure & Ramirez, 1929).

MEMORIAS FROM THE DIRECTOR OF THE LIMA PENITENTIARY

1868: "Memoria que presenta el director de la penitenciaría al Ministro del Ramo," July 21, 1868 (AGN, MJ, 3.20.3.3.1.4.1, ff. 246–58).

1876: "Memoria del director de la penitenciaría de Lima," (AGN, MJ, 3.20.3.3.1.4.2, ff. 405–23).

1890: "Memoria presentada por el Presidente de la Junta Inspectora del Panóptico, Dr. D. Augusto S. Albarracin al Ministerio de Justicia, Culto, Instrucción y Beneficencia," in Memoria, Justicia, 1890.

1891: "Memoria que presenta el Señor Coronel D. José Rosendo Samanez, Director de la Penitenciaría," in Memoria, Justicia, 1891.

1892: "Memoria que presenta el Coronel Don José R. Samanez, Director de la Penitenciaría," in Memoria, Justicia, 1892.

1896: "Memoria que presenta el Señor Dr. Dn. Juan José Calle, Director de la Penitenciaría," in Memoria, Justicia, 1896.

1897: "Memoria que presenta el Director de la Penitenciaría Sr. Manuel Panizo y Zárate," in Memoria, Justicia, 1897.

1900: "Memoria que presenta el director del Panóptico de Lima, D. Manuel Panizo y Zárate al Sr. Ministro de Justicia, Culto e Instrucción," in Memoria, Justicia, 1900.

1901: "Memoria del director de la penitenciaría de Lima" (AGN, MJ, 3.20.3.3.1.7.1, ff. 303–08, May 31, 1901).

1903: "Memoria del Director del Panóptico, don Manuel Panizo y Zárate," in Memoria, Justicia, 1903.

1905: "Memoria que el director de la Penitenciaría de Lima presenta al señor Ministro de Justicia," in Memoria, Justicia, 1905.

1906: "Memoria que el Director del Panóptico eleva al Ministerio de Justicia," in Memoria, Justicia, 1906.

1907: "Memoria presentada por el Director del Panóptico de Lima, Coronel D. Pedro Portillo, al Ministerio de Justicia, Instrucción y Culto," in Memoria, Justicia, 1907.

1908: "Memoria presentada por el Director del Panóptico de Lima Coronel Pedro Portillo, al Ministerio de Justicia, Instrucción y Culto en el año de 1908," in Memoria, Justicia, 1908.

1909: "Memoria del director de la penitenciaría," in Memoria, Justicia, 1909.

1916: "Memoria que el Director de la Penitenciaría, señor Don Ramón Irigoyen, presenta al señor Ministro de Justicia," in Memoria, Justicia, 1916.

1921: "Memoria presentada por el Director de la Penitenciaría de Lima, Señor Hermilio Higueras, al Ministerio de Justicia, Instrucción y Culto," in Memoria, Justicia, 1921.

1925: *Memoria presentada por el director de la Penitenciaría de Lima, Sr. Hermilio Higueras al Ministerio de Justicia, Instrucción, Culto y Beneficencia* (Lima: Talleres Tipográficos de la Penitenciaría, 1925).

1926: *Memoria presentada por el director de la Penitenciaría Central de Lima Sr. Jesús A. Larco al Ministerio de Justicia, Instrucción y Culto* (Lima: Talleres Gráficos de la Penitenciaría, [1927]).

1927: "Memoria del director de la penitenciaría," in Memoria, Justicia, 1927.

MEMORIAS FROM OTHER AUTHORITIES

"Memoria leída por el Pdte de la Ilustrísima Corte Superior de Lima, el día de la apertura del nuevo año judicial," in Memoria, Justicia, 1896.

"Memoria leída por el Presidente de la Ilustrísima Corte Superior de Lima en la ceremonia de apertura del año judicial de 1897," in Memoria, Justicia, 1897.

"Memoria del Director de la Escuela Correccional de Varones de Lima, 1902–1903," in Memoria, Justicia, 1903.

"Memoria del Director de la escuela correccional de varones," in Memoria, Justicia, 1904.

"Memoria de la Escuela Correccional de Varones," in Memoria, Justicia, 1905.

"Memoria de la Superiora de la Escuela Correccional de Mujeres," in Memoria, Justicia, 1905.

"Memoria del Presidente de la Corte Superior de Lima en la apertura del año judicial de 1918," in Memoria, Justicia, 1918.

Colonia Penal El Frontón. Memoria presentada por el Director, Sr. Manuel Hermilio Higueras al Ministerio de Justicia, Instrucción y Culto, 1922 (Lima: Litografía e Imprenta T. Scheuch, 1923).

Memoria del Director General de la Guardia Civil y Policía General, Pedro P. Martínez correspondiente al año 1927 y primer semestre de 1928 (Lima: Talleres Gráficos de La Revista, 1928).

Memoria que el Ministro de Gobierno y Policía presenta al congreso ordinario de 1916 (Lima: Imprenta del Estado, 1916).

REFERENCES

Aguirre, Carlos. "Violencia, castigo y control social: Esclavos y panaderías en Lima, siglo XIX." *Pasado y Presente* 1, 1 (1988): 27–37.

———. "Disciplina, castigo y control social: Conductas sociales y mecanismos punitivos, Lima, 1821–1868," Licenciatura thesis, Universidad Nacional Federico Villarreal, Lima, 1990.

———. "Patrones, esclavos, y sirvientes domésticos en Lima, 1800–1860." In Pilar Gonzalbo and Cecilia Rabell, eds., *Familia y Vida Privada en la Historia de Iberoamérica*, 401–22. Mexico City: El Colegio de México, 1996.

———. "The Lima Penitentiary and the Modernization of Criminal Justice in Nineteenth-Century Peru." In Salvatore and Aguirre, eds., *The Birth of the Penitentiary in Latin America*, 44–77.

———. "Crime, Race, and Morals: The Development of Criminology in Peru (1890–1930)." *Crime, History and Societies* 2, 2 (1998): 73–90.

———. "Disputed Views of Incarceration in Lima, 1890–1930: The Prisoners' Agenda for Prison Reform." In Ricardo Salvatore, Carlos Aguirre, and Gilbert Joseph, eds., *Crime and Punishment in Latin America: Law and Society since Colonial Times*, 342–68. Durham: Duke University Press, 2001.

———. "Mujeres delincuentes, prácticas penales, y servidumbre doméstica en Lima, 1862–1930." In Scarlett O'Phelan et al., comps., *Familia y vida cotidiana en América Latina, Siglos XVIII–XX*. Lima: IFEA/Instituto Riva Agüero/Pontificia Universidad Católica, 2003.

Alegre y Pacheco, Marino C. *Los delincuentes tatuados de la penitenciaría nacional.* Lima: Tipografía y Encuadernación de la Penitenciaría, 1917.

Alegría, Ciro. "Duelo de caballeros." In *Relatos*, 279–92. Madrid: Alianza Editorial, 1983.

Aljovín, Cristóbal. *Caudillos y constituciones: Peru: 1821–1845*. Lima: Fondo de Cultura Económica/Instituto Riva Aguero, 2000.

Altmann Smythe, Julio. *El problema sexual en los establecimientos penales*. Lima: Sanmarti y Cia, 1931.

———. "Eugenesia y criminalidad." *Higiene Social* 1, 1 (1933).

———. "La esterilización en la lucha contra el delito." *Revista de Ciencias Jurídicas y Sociales* 1 (1934).

———. *Reseña histórica de la evolución del derecho penal, con conclusiones sobre la futura política criminal del Perú*. Lima: Sanmarti y Cía, 1944.

Anales. *Anales de las Religiosas de Nuestra Señora de la Caridad del Buen Pastor de Angers en Lima, 1871 a 1900*. Lima: Imprenta de El Lucero, 1903.

Arnold, David. "The Colonial Prison: Power, Knowledge and Penology in Nineteenth-Century India." *Subaltern Studies*, 8 (1994): 148–87.

Arona, Juan de (Pedro Paz Soldán y Unanue). *La inmigración en el Perú*. Lima: Imprenta Universo, 1891.

Arrús, Oscar. *Las razas china e india en el Perú: Disertación leída en la biblioteca científico-literaria del Callao*. Callao: Imprenta del Callao, 1906.

Avendaño, Leonidas. "La reforma de la legislación penal." *La Crónica Médica* 41 (1924).

Bailey, Victor. "The Fabrication of Deviance: 'Dangerous Classes' and 'Criminal Classes' in Victorian England." In John Rule and Robert Malcolmson, eds., *Protest and Survival: Essays for E. P. Thompson*, 221–56. New York: New Press, 1993.

Balbín, Eduardo Ismael. "El matrimonio y la eugenesia." Bachelor thesis, University of San Marcos, Medical School, 1929.

Bambarén, Carlos. *Sobre organización y fines del Instituto de Criminología*. Lima: Imprenta Enrique Lulli, 1945.

Barbagelata, José, and Juan Bromley. *Desarrollo urbano de Lima: Apuntes históricos*. Lima: Imprenta Lumen, 1945.

Barreda, Felipe. "La asistencia pública y el pauperismo." Bachelor thesis, University of San Marcos, Political and Administrative Sciences, n.d. [c. 1905–08].

Barros, Oscar César. "Aptitud de nuestra raza para el trabajo." Ph.D. diss., University of San Marcos, Political and Administrative Sciences, 1899.

Barrows, Susanna. *Distorting Mirrors: Visions of the Crowd in Late Nineteenth-Century France*. New Haven: Yale University Press, 1981.

Basadre, Jorge. *Historia de la República del Perú*, 7th ed., 11 vols. Lima: Editorial Universitaria, 1983.

———. *La multitud, la ciudad y el campo en la historia del Perú*. Lima: Imprenta A. J. Rivas Berrio, 1929.

Bertillon, Alphonse de. *Instructions for Taking Descriptions for the Identification of Criminals and Others by the Means of Anthropometric Indications*. Chicago: American Bertillon Prison Bureau, 1889.

Bierne, Piers. *Inventing Criminology: Essays on the Rise of 'Homo Criminalis.'* Albany: SUNY Press, 1993.

Blanchard, Peter. *The Origins of the Peruvian Labor Movement, 1883–1919.* Pittsburgh: University of Pittsburgh Press, 1982.

Boies, Henry M. *The Science of Penology: The Defense of Society Against Crime.* New York: G. P. Putnam's Sons, 1901.

Boisset, Felipe M. *El problema racial en el Perú (o el peligro de la raza amarilla).* Lima: Empresa Tipográfica Unión, 1919.

Bonilla, Heraclio. "Peru and Bolivia from Independence to the War of the Pacific." In Leslie Bethell, ed., *Cambridge History of Latin America* 3:539–82. New York: Cambridge University Press, 1985.

——. *Guano y Burguesía en el Perú,* 3d. ed. Quito: FLACSO, 1994.

Buffington, Robert. *Criminal and Citizen in Modern Mexico.* Lincoln: University of Nebraska Press, 2000.

Buntman, Fran Lisa. *Robben Island and Prisoner Resistance to Apartheid.* New York: Cambridge University Press, 2003.

Burga, Manuel, and Alberto Flores Galindo. *Apogeo y crisis de la república aristocrática.* Lima: Editora Rikchay Perú, 1979.

Calderón, Julián. "La defensa social, justifica la pena de muerte?" Bachelor thesis, University of San Marcos, Law School, 1899.

——. *Realidad del tipo criminal.* Lima: Imprenta Comercial de H. La Rosa, 1904.

Calle, Juan José, ed. *Código Penal (Ley No. 4868).* Lima: Librería e Imprenta Gil, 1924.

Calle, Juan José, et al. "Informe que la Comisión encargada de examinar el estado administrativo y técnico de la penitenciaría de Lima, ha presentado al Ministerio de Justicia." *Revista del Foro* 2 (1920), 8 (1921).

Capelo, Joaquín. *Sociología de Lima.* 4 vols. Lima: Imprenta Masías, 1895–1902.

Carrefiello, Susan B. *The Tombs of the Living: Prisons and Prison Reform in Liberal Italy.* New York: P. Lang, 1998.

Carrera, Eudocio. *El gran Dr. Copaiba: Protomédico de la Lima jaranera.* Lima: Sanmarti y Cia., 1943.

Casanova, Juan Norberto. *Ensayo sobre la industria algodonera en el Perú.* Lima: Imprenta de José Masías, 1849.

Castañeda y Alvarez, A. "El alcoholismo en Lima bajo el punto de vista médico-social." Bachelor thesis, University of San Marcos, Medical School, 1897.

Castillo, Luciano. "Una institución que debe desaparecer definitivamente de los sistemas penales actuales: la pena de muerte." Bachelor thesis, University of San Marcos, Law School, 1927.

Castro Fernandini, Alberto. *Breve estudio sobre el delito de rebelión en el Perú y de sus sistemas penales.* Lima: Imprenta del Centro Editorial, 1916.

Cedano, Carlos A. "Estudios sobre la criminalidad." Bachelor thesis, University of San Marcos, Law School, 1901.

Centeno, Miguel Angel. *Blood and Debt: War and the Nation-State in Latin America.* University Park: Pennsylvania State University Press, 2002.

Cerna, José M. "El problema carcelario en el Perú." Bachelor thesis, University of San Marcos, Law School, 1923.

Chavarría, Jesús. *José Carlos Mariátegui and the Rise of Modern Peru, 1890–1930.* Albuquerque: University of New Mexico Press, 1979.

Chávez, Gerardo. "Evoluciones del régimen penitenciario." *Anales de la Universidad Mayor de San Marcos de Lima,* 25 (1898): 75–106.

Chevalier, Francois. "Official Indigenismo in Peru." In Magnus Morner, ed., *Race and Class in Latin America,* 184–96. New York: Columbia University Press, 1977.

Chiaramonti, Gabriella. "Buscando el ciudadano 'virtuoso': El censo peruano de 1876 en el proyecto político de Manuel Pardo." In Marcello Carmagnani, comp., *Constitucionalismo y orden liberal: América Latina, 1850–1920,* 9–50. Turin: Otto Editore, 2000.

Cisneros, Carlos B. *Provincia de Lima (Monografía del Departamento de Lima).* Lima: Carlos Fabbri, 1911.

Clavero, José. *El tesoro del Perú.* Lima: Imprenta Torres Aguirre, 1896.

Clemmer, Donald. *The Prison Community.* Boston: Christopher Publishing House, 1940.

Códigos penal y de enjuiciamiento en materia criminal. Lima: Imprenta del Estado, 1880.

Cole, Simon. *Suspect Identities: A History of Fingerprinting and Criminal Identification.* Cambridge: Harvard University Press, 2001.

Concejo Provincial de Lima. *Reglamento de la guardia urbana y demás disposiciones relativas a gobierno local.* Lima, Imprenta del Comercio, 1879.

———. *Monografías históricas sobre la ciudad de Lima.* Lima: Librería e Imprenta Gil, 1935.

Connell, R. W. *Masculinities.* Berkeley: University of California Press, 1995.

Contreras, Carlos, and Marcos Cueto. *Historia del Perú contemporáneo.* Lima: Red para el desarrollo de las Ciencias Sociales en el Perú, 1999.

Copello, Juan, and Luis Petriconi. *Estudio sobre la independencia económica del Perú.* Lima: Imprenta El Nacional, 1876.

Córdova y Urrutia, José María. *Estadística histórica, geográfica, industrial y comercial de los pueblos que componen las provincias del departamento de Lima.* Lima: Imprenta de Instrucción Primaria, 1839.

Cosamalón, Jesús. *Indios detrás de la muralla.* Lima: Pontificia Universidad Católica del Perú, 1999.

Cossio del Pomar, Felipe. *Víctor Raúl Haya de la Torre: El Indoamericano.* Lima: Editorial Nuevo Día, 1946.

Cueto, Marcos. *Excelencia científica en la periferia: Actividades científicas e investigación biomédica en el Perú, 1890–1950.* Lima: Grade/Concytec, 1989.

———. *El regreso de las epidemias: Salud y sociedad en el Perú del siglo XIX.* Lima: Instituto de Estudios Peruanos, 1997.

Davalos y Lisson, Pedro. *La primera centuria.* Lima: Librería e Imprenta Gil, 1919–26.

Davies, Thomas. *Indian Integration in Peru: A Half Century of Experience, 1900–1948.* Lincoln: University of Nebraska Press, 1974.

Davis, Angela. "Masked Racism: Reflections on the Prison Industrial Complex." *Color Lines*, 1, 2 (1998): 11–13.

De la Cadena, Marisol. *Indigenous Mestizos: The Politics of Race and Culture in Cuzco, Peru, 1919–1991.* Durham: Duke University Press, 2000.

De las Casas, Alfonso. *La delincuencia infantil ante el concepto de la medicina legal.* Lima: Imprenta del Centro Editorial, 1913.

De las Casas, Luis Felipe. *El Sectario.* Lima: Ital Perú, 1981.

Del Aguila, Alicia. *Callejones y mansiones: Espacios de opinion pública y redes sociales y políticas en la Lima del 900.* Lima: Pontificia Universidad Católica del Perú, 1997.

Del Prado, Jorge. *En los años cumbres de Mariátegui.* Lima: Ediciones Unidad, 1983.

Delfín, M. J. "Asilos para bebedores." Bachelor thesis, University of San Marcos, Medical School, 1909.

Delitos, crímenes, y costumbres a través del cuento y de la narración peruanos. Supplement of the *Revista Policial del Perú* 25 (Lima, 1957).

Diez Canseco, José. "El Kilómetro 83" [1930]. In *Estampas mulatas*, 103–55. Lima: Editorial Universo, 1973.

Driver, Felix. "Discipline without Frontiers? Representations of the Mettray Reformatory Colony in Britain, 1840–1880." *Journal of Historical Sociology* 3, 3 (September 1990).

Encinas, José Antonio. "Causas de la criminalidad indígena en el Perú: Ensayo de Psicología criminal." *Revista Universitaria* XIV, I (1919): 192–268.

——. *La educación de nuestros hijos.* Santiago: Editorial Ercilla, 1938.

Esparza, Lorenzo. "Contribución al estudio de la tuberculosis en el presidio." Bachelor's thesis, University of San Marcos, Medical School, Lima, 1919.

Espejo Palma, Ernesto. *Necesidad de crear en el Perú el patronato de ex-carcelados como medio de evitar en los delincuentes la reincidencia en el delito.* Lima: Empresa Tipográfica Unión, 1918.

Espinosa, Juan. *Diccionario para el pueblo: Republicano, democrático, moral, político y filosófico.* Lima: Imprenta del Pueblo, 1855.

Eyzaguirre, Rómulo. "La tuberculosis pulmonar en Lima: Tratamiento higiénico-sanitario." *Anales de la Universidad Mayor de San Marcos de Lima* 25 (1898): 149–256.

Flores Galindo, Alberto. *Aristocracia y plebe: Lima, 1760–1830.* Lima: Mosca Azul Editores, 1984.

——. "República sin ciudadanos." In *Buscando un Inca: Identidad y utopía en los Andes*, 4th. ed. Lima: Editorial Horizonte, 1994.

——. *La tradición autoritaria: Violencia y democracia en el Perú.* Lima: Aprodeh/SUR, 1999.

Forment, Carlos. *Democracy in Latin America, 1760–1900.* Volume 1: *Civic Selfhood and Public Life in Mexico and Peru.* Chicago: University of Chicago Press, 2003.

Foro Peruano. *Proceso criminal seguido contra Lorenzo Machiavello por los delitos de triple homicidio y homicidio frustrado.* Lima: Imprenta del Estado, 1888.

Fosalba, Rafael. "La herencia como principal factor etiológico de la anormalidad mental y de ciertas degeneraciones y formas de criminalidad y su prevención eugénica, mediante la esterilización genital por la vasectomía de Sharp, de los legalmente declarados como incapaces." Bachelor thesis, University of San Marcos, Medical School, 1928.

Foucault, Michel. "About the Concept of the 'Dangerous Individual' in Nineteenth-Century Legal Psychiatry." In James D. Faubion, ed., *Power*, 176–200. Volume 3 of *Essential Works of Foucault, 1954–1984*. New York: New Press, 2000.

——. *Discipline and Punish: The Birth of the Prison*, trans. by Alan Sheridan. New York: Vintage Books, 1979.

Fraser, Nancy. "From Discipline to Flexibilization? Rereading Foucault in the Shadow of Civilization." *Constellations*, 10, 2 (2003): 160–71.

Fuentes, Manuel Atanasio. *Estadística general de Lima*. Lima: Tipografía Nacional de M. N. Corpancho, 1858.

——. *Aletazos del Murciélago, I*, 2d ed. Paris: Imprenta de AD. Laine y J. Havard, 1866.

——. *Lima: Apuntes históricos, descriptivos, estadísticos y de costumbres*. Paris: Librería de Firmin Didot hermanos, hijos y Co., 1867.

——. *Estadística de la penitenciaría, cárcel y lugares de detención de la provincia de Lima en 1877*. Lima: Imprenta del Estado, 1878.

Fuentes, Manuel Atanasio, and M. A. de la Lama. *Diccionario de jurisprudencia y de legislación peruana: Parte criminal*. Lima: Imprenta del Estado, 1877.

Fuentes Castro, Paulino. *Criminología peruana: Rojas y Cañas condenado a muerte*. Lima: Imprenta del Estado, 1894.

Gagliano, Joseph. *Coca Prohibition in Peru: The Historical Debates*. Tucson: University of Arizona Press, 1994.

Gálvez, José. *Una Lima que se va*. 1921; repr. Lima: Editorial PTCM, 1947.

Gamarra, Abelardo. "¡La cárcel de la capital!" In *Cien años de vida perdularia*, 193–95. Lima: Tip. Abancay, 1921.

Gandolfo, José Benjamín. *El problema de la vagancia en el Perú*. Lima: Librería Escolar e Imprenta de E. Moreno, 1900.

García Jordán, Pilar. "Reflexiones sobre el Darwinismo social: Inmigración y colonización, mitos de los grupos modernizadores peruanos (1821–1919)." *Boletín del Instituto Francés de Estudios Andinos* 21, 2 (1992): 961–75.

García Yrigoyen, Alberto. "Sistemas penitenciarios." Bachelor thesis, University of San Marcos, Law School, 1887.

Garland, David. "The Criminal and His Science: A Critical Account of the Formation of Criminology at the End of the Nineteenth Century." *British Journal of Criminology* 25, 2 (1985): 109–37.

——. *Punishment and Modern Society: A Study in Social Theory*. Chicago: University of Chicago Press, 1990.

——. "Of Crimes and Criminals: The Development of Criminology in Britain." In Mike Maguire et. al., eds., *Oxford Handbook of Criminology*, 17–68. Oxford: Clarendon Press, 1994.

Garrido Malaver, Julio. *El Frontón*. Lima: Editorial Universo, 1977.

Gastón, Alfredo. *Compilación de las vistas fiscales que en materia judicial y administrativa se han expedido en el Perú, desde el año 1840 hasta 1871 por los Doctores D.*

José Gregorio Paz Soldán y D. Manuel Toribio Ureta. Lima: Imprenta del Estado, 1873.

Gatrell, V. A. C. "Crime, Authority, and the Policeman-State." In *Cambridge Social History of Britain, 1750–1950*, vol. 3, 243–310. Cambridge: Cambridge University Press, 1990.

Gibson, Mary. *Born to Crime: Cesare Lombroso and the Origins of Biological Criminology.* Westport, Conn.: Praeger, 2002.

Giesecke, Margarita. *Masas urbanas y rebelión en la historia: Golpe de estado, Lima 1872.* Lima: CEDHIP, 1978.

Gilbert, Dennis. *La oligarquía peruana: Historia de tres familias.* Lima: Editorial Horizonte, 1982.

González Prada, Manuel. "Nuestros indios." 1904; repr. Caracas: Universidad Central de Venezuela, 1983.

——. *Horas de lucha*, 2d ed. Callao: Tipografía Luz, 1924.

——. *Bajo el oprobio.* Paris: Tipografía de Louis Bellenad et fils, 1933.

González Vigil, Francisco de Paula. *Opúsculo sobre la pena de muerte.* Lima: Tipografía Nacional, 1862.

Gootenberg, Paul. "Artisans and Merchants: The Making of an Open Economy, Lima, 1830–1860." M.A. thesis, Oxford, St. Anthony's School, 1981.

——. "Beleaguered Liberals: The Failed First Generation of Free Traders in Peru." In Joseph Love and Nils Jacobsen, eds., *Guiding the Invisible Hand: Economic Liberalism and the State in Latin American History*, 63–97. New York: Praeger, 1988.

——. *Between Silver and Guano: Commercial Policy and the State in Postindependence Peru.* Princeton: Princeton University Press, 1989.

——. "Carneros y Chuño: Price Levels in Nineteenth-Century Peru." *Hispanic American Historical Review* 70, 1 (1990): 1–56.

——. *Imagining Development: Economic Ideas in Peru's "Fictitious Prosperity" of Guano, 1848–1880.* Berkeley: University of California Press, 1993.

Gould, Stephen J. *The Mismeasure of Man.* New York: W. W. Norton, 1981.

Graña, Francisco. *La población del Perú a través de su historia.* Lima: Tipografia del Centro Editorial, 1916.

Graña, Ladislao. "Factores sociales de la delincuencia en el Perú." Bachelor thesis, University of San Marcos, Law School, 1899.

Hague, Juan Luis. *La caracterización del delincuente: Estudio técnico-jurídico.* Lima: n.p., 1932.

Haya de la Torre, Víctor Raúl. *Por la emancipación de América Latina.* Buenos Aires: Gleizer, 1927.

——. *Cartas de Haya de la Torre a los prisioneros apristas.* Lima: Editorial Nuevo Día, 1946.

Herbold, Carl. "Developments in the Peruvian Administrative System, 1919–1939: Modern and Traditional Qualities of Government under Authoritarian Regimes." Ph.D. diss., Yale University, 1973.

Herrera, Bartolomé. *El opúsculo sobre la pena de muerte por Francisco de Paula González Vigil es incontestable.* Lima: Imprenta de José Masías, 1862.

Hirsch, Adam. *The Rise of the Penitentiary: Prisons and Punishment in Early America*. New Haven: Yale University Press, 1992.

Hobsbawm, Eric. "Peasants and Politics." *Journal of Peasant Studies* 1, 1 (1973): 3–22.

Horne, Janet R. *A Social Laboratory for Modern France: The Musée Social and the Rise of the Welfare State*. Durham: Duke University Press, 2002.

Hurtado Pozo, José. *La ley 'importada': Recepción del derecho penal en el Perú*. Lima: CEDYS, 1979.

Iberico, Mariano. *Elementos psicológicos del delito*. Lima: Sanmartí y Cía, 1918.

Ignatieff, Michael. *A Just Measure of Pain: The Penitentiary in the Industrial Revolution, 1750–1850*. New York: Penguin Books, 1978.

Jacobsen, Nils. *Mirages of Transition: The Peruvian Altiplano, 1780–1930*. Berkeley: University of California Press, 1993.

——. "Civilization and Its Barbarism: The Inevitability of Juan Bustamante's Failure." In Judith Ewell and William Beezley, eds., *The Human Tradition in Latin America: The Nineteenth Century*, 82–102. Wilmington, Del.: Scholarly Resources, 1989.

Jacobsen, Nils, and Alejandro Diez Hurtado. "Montoneras, la comuna de Chalaco y la revolución de Piérola: La sierra piurana entre el clientelismo y la sociedad civil, 1868–1895." In Antonio Escobar O. and Romana Falcón, eds., *Los ejes de la disputa: Movimientos sociales y actores colectivos en América Latina, siglo XIX*, 57–132. Madrid/Frankfurt: AHILA/Iberoamericana, 2002.

James, Joy, ed. *Imprisoned Intellectuals. America's Political Prisoners Write on Life, Liberation, and Rebellion*. Lanham, Md.: Rowman and Littlefield Publishers, 2003.

Jiménez, Plácido. "La sociedad y el delito." Ph.D. diss., University of San Marcos. *Anales de la Universidad Mayor de San Marcos de Lima* 25 (1898): 107–354.

Jiménez de Asúa, Luis. *Derecho penal en la república del Perú*. Valladolid: Universidad de Valladolid, 1926.

——. "Elmore y Chocano: El crimen de Lima." In *Política. Figuras. Paisajes*. Madrid: Historia Nueva, 1927, 173–83.

Kapsoli, Wilfredo. *Las luchas obreras en el Perú, 1900–1919*. Lima: Editorial Delva, 1976.

Klaiber, Jeffrey. "Los cholos y los rotos: Actitudes raciales durante la Guerra del Pacífico." *Histórica* 2, 1 (1978): 27–37.

Klaren, Peter. *Modernization, Dislocation and Aprismo: Origins of the Peruvian Aprista Party, 1870–1932*. Austin: University of Texas Press, 1973.

——. "The Origins of Modern Peru, 1880–1930." In Leslie Bethell, ed., *Cambridge History of Latin America*, vol. 5., 587–640. New York: Cambridge University Press, 1986.

——. *Peru: Society and Nationhood in the Andes*. New York: Oxford University Press, 2000.

Lacassagne, Alexandre. *Les tatouages, étude anthropologique et médico-légale*. Paris: Baillière, 1881.

Lama, Tomás. *Refutación del informe de la comisión inspectora de la Penitenciaría publicado en agosto de 1873*. Lima: Imprenta de El Nacional, 1874.

Laso, Francisco. *Aguinaldo para las señoras del Perú y otros ensayos, 1854–1869*. Edited by Natalia Majluf. Lima: IFEA/Museo de Arte de Lima, 2003.

Leguía y Martínez, Germán. *Diccionario de la legislacíon criminal del Perú*. Lima: Librería e Imprenta Gil, 1931.

León, Carlos Aurelio. *Nuestras cárceles*. Lima: Librería e Imprenta Gil, 1920.

León García, Enrique. *Las razas en Lima: Estudio demográfico*. Lima: Sanmarti y Cia, 1909.

León y León, Bernardino. "La libertad y la responsabilidad en el derecho penal contemporáneo." Bachelor thesis, University of San Marcos, Law School, 1907.

——. "El problema sexual en las prisiones." *Revista del Foro* 21 (1934).

Lequanda, Ignacio de. "Discurso sobre el destino que debe darse a la gente vaga que tiene Lima." *Mercurio Peruano* 10 (1794): 103–8, 111–17, 119–25, 127–32.

Lisson, Carlos. *Breves apuntes sobre la sociología del Perú en 1886*. Lima: Imprenta Gil, 1887.

Lombroso, Cesare. *L'Uomo delinquente: Studiato in rapporto alla antropologia, alla medicina legale ed alle discipline carcerarie*. Milan, 1876.

——. "The Savage Origins of Tattooing." *Popular Science Monthly* (April 1896): 793–803.

López, Sinesio. *El Dios mortal: Estado, sociedad y política en el Perú del siglo XX*. Lima: Instituto Democracia y Socialismo, 1991.

López-Rey Arrojo, Manuel. *Introducción al estudio de la criminología*. Buenos Aires: Librería y Editorial El Ateneo, 1945.

Lorente, Sebastián. *Pensamientos sobre el Perú*. 1855; repr. Lima: Universidad Nacional Mayor de San Marcos, 1967.

Loza, José Manuel. *Inviolabilidad de la vida humana, o discurso sobre la pena de muerte*. Lima: Imprenta de Félix Moreno, 1851.

Majluf, Natalia. *Escultura y espacio público: Lima, 1850–1879*. Lima: IEP, 1994.

Mallon, Florencia. *The Defense of Community in Peru's Central Highlands*. Princeton: Princeton University Press, 1983.

——. *Peasant and Nation: The Making of Post-Colonial Mexico and Peru*. Berkeley: University of California Press, 1995.

Mannarelli, Maria Emma. *Limpias y modernas: Género, higiene y cultura en la Lima del novecientos*. Lima: Ediciones Flora Tristán, 1999.

Manrique, Nelson. *Yawar Mayu: Sociedades Terratenientes serranas, 1879–1910*. Lima: IFEA/Desco, 1988.

Mariátegui, José Carlos. "Cómo mató Wilmann a 'Tirifilo.' Conversando con el victimario en el Hospital Dos de Mayo." *La Prensa*, May 6, 1915.

——. *Siete ensayos de interpretación de la realidad peruana*. Lima: Biblioteca Amauta, 1928.

——. *Correspondencia (1915–1930)*. Lima: Biblioteca Amauta, 1984.

Marquina Ríos, Hugo. "Cincuenta casas de vecindad en la Avenida Francisco Pizarro." In Carlos Enrique Paz Soldan, ed., *Lima y sus suburbios*, 76–91. Lima: Universidad Nacional de San Marcos, 1957.

McConville, Sean. *English Local Prisons, 1860–1900: Next Only to Death*. New York: Routledge, 1995.

McEvoy, Carmen. *Un proyecto nacional en el siglo XIX: Manuel Pardo y su visión del*

Perú. Lima: Pontificia Universidad Católica del Perú, 1994.

——. *Forjando la nación: Ensayos de historia republicana*. Lima: Universidad Católica/University of the South, 1999.

Medina, Pío Máximo. *El tipo criminal*. Lima: Imprenta de San Pedro, 1907.

——. *Causas del estacionarismo de la raza indígena y el remedio eficaz para su regeneración*. Lima: Imprenta La Industria, 1906.

Melossi, Dario. "The Cultural Embeddedness of Social Control: Reflections on the Comparison of Italian and North-American Cultures Concerning Punishment." *Theoretical Criminology* 5, 4 (2001): 403–24.

Melossi, Dario, and Massimo Pavarini. *The Prison and the Factory. Origins of the Penitentiary System*. Translated by Glynis Cousin. Totowa, N.J.: Barnes and Noble Books, 1981.

Méndez, Cecilia. "Importaciones de lujo y clases populares: Un motín limeño." *Cielo Abierto*, 29 (1984): 11–14.

——. "Penalidad y muerte en el Perú." *Márgenes* 1 (1987): 182–91.

——. "República sin indios: La comunidad imaginada del Perú." In Henrique Urbano, ed., *Tradición y modernidad en los Andes*, 15–41. Cusco: Centro Bartolomé de las Casas, 1992.

——. "Incas Sí, Indios No: Notes on Peruvian Creole Nationalism and Its Contemporary Crisis." *Journal of Latin American Studies* 28, 1 (1996): 197–225.

Mendoza, René. *En las prisiones peruanas*. Santiago de Chile: Imprenta y Encuadernación Moderna, 1921.

Mendoza, Walter, and Oscar Martínez. "Las ideas eugenésicas en la creación del Instituto de Medicina Social." *Anales de la Facultad de Medicina* (Lima) 60, 1 (1999): 55–60.

Meranze, Michael. *Laboratories of Virtue: Punishment, Revolution, and Authority in Philadelphia, 1760–1835*. Chapel Hill: University of North Carolina Press, 1996.

Middendorf, E. W. *Perú: Observaciones y estudios del país y sus habitantes durante una permanencia de 25 años*. Lima: Universidad Nacional Mayor de San Marcos, 1973.

Miller, Laura. "La mujer obrera en Lima, 1900–1930." In Miller et. al., *Lima obrera, 1900–1930*, vol. 2, 11–152. Lima: Ediciones El Virrey, 1987.

Miró Quesada, Oscar. *Breves apuntes de mesología criminal peruana*. Lima: n.p., 1922.

——. "El caso del asesino Montes: Ensayo de criminología aplicada." *Revista Universitaria*, 2d trimester (1916): 165–299.

Moczydlowski, Pawel. *The Hidden Life of Polish Prisons*. Bloomington: Indiana University Press, 1992.

Monsalve, Martín. "Elecciones, violencia y dominación racial en Lima a mediados del siglo XIX: Las elecciones de 1850 y 1855." Paper presented at the Peruvian History Workshop, Oxford, March 2002.

Morris, Norval. *Maconochie's Gentlemen: The Story of Norfolk Island and the Roots of Modern Prison Reform*. Oxford: Oxford University Press, 2001.

Muccielli, Laurent, ed. *Histoire de la criminologie française*. Paris: Editions L'Harmattan, 1994.

Muñoz, Fanni. *Diversiones públicas en Lima, 1890–1920: La experiencia de la moderni-dad*. Lima: Red para el desarrollo de las Ciencias Sociales en el Perú, 2001.

Nugent, David. "Building the State, Making the Nation: The Bases and Limits of State Centralization in 'Modern' Peru." *American Anthropologist* 96, 2 (1994): 333–69.

O'Brien, Patricia. *The Promise of Punishment: Prisons in Nineteenth-Century France*. Princeton: Princeton University Press, 1982.

Oliart, Patricia. "Poniendo a cada quien en su lugar: estereotipos raciales y sexuales en la Lima del siglo XIX." In Panfichi and Portocarrero, eds., *Mundos interiores*, 261–88.

Oshinsky, David M. *"Worse than Slavery": Parchman Farm and the Ordeal of Jim Crow Justice*. New York: Free Press, 1996.

Oviedo, Juan. *Colección de leyes, decretos y órdenes publicadas en el Perú desde el año 1821 hasta el 31 de diciembre de 1859*. Lima: F. Bailly, 1861–72.

Palma, Clemente. *El porvenir de las razas en el Perú*. Lima: Imprenta Torres Aguirre, 1897.

Panfichi, Aldo. "Urbanización temprana de Lima, 1535–1900." In Panfichi and Porto-carrero, eds., *Mundos interiores*, 15–42.

Panfichi, Aldo, and Felipe Portocarrero, eds. *Mundos interiores: Lima 1850–1950*. Lima: Universidad del Pacífico, 1995.

Pardo, Manuel. "Algo sobre el código penal: Vagancia." *La revista de Lima* 4 (1861): 103–10.

Pareja, Piedad. *Anarquismo y sindicalismo en el Perú*. Lima: Ediciones Rikchay Peru, 1978.

Parker, David. "Los pobres de la clase media: Estilo de vida, consumo e identidad en una ciudad tradicional." In Panfichi and Portocarrero, eds., *Mundos interiores*, 161–86.

——. "Civilizing the City of Kings: Hygiene and Housing in Lima, Peru." In Ronn Pineo and James A. Baer, eds., *Cities of Hope: People, Protests, and Progress in Urbanizing Latin America, 1870–1930*, 153–78. Boulder: Westview Press, 1998.

——. *The Idea of the Middle Class: White-Collar Workers and Peruvian Society, 1900–1950*. University Park: Pennsylvania State University Press, 1998.

Partido, Aprista Peruano. *El proceso Haya de la Torre: Documentos para la historia del ajusticiamiento de un pueblo*. Guayaquil: Imprenta La Reforma, 1933.

Patriarca, Silvana. *Numbers and Nationhood: Writing Statistics in Nineteenth-Century Italy*. New York: Cambridge University Press, 1996.

Paz Soldán, Carlos Enrique. "La reforma del régimen penitenciario en el Perú y el lib-ertador Ramón Castilla." In Paz Soldán, *Medio siglo de magisterio hipocrático*. Lima: Biblioteca de Cultura Sanitaria, 1964.

Paz Soldán, Mariano Felipe. *Examen de las penitenciarías de los Estados Unidos*. New York: Imprenta de S. W. Benedict, 1853.

——. "Reglamento para la penitenciaría de Lima." In Fuentes and de Lama, *Dic-cionario de jurisprudencia*, 525–47.

Peñaloza, Augusto. *Prevención eugénica de la criminalidad en el Perú*. Lima: Imprenta La Voce d'Italia, 1916.

Peralta, Víctor. "El mito del ciudadano armado: La 'semana magna' y las elecciones de 1844 en Lima." In Hilda Sábato, ed., *Ciudadanía política y formación de las naciones: Perspectivas históricas de América Latina*, 231–52. Mexico: El Colegio de Mexico/Fondo de Cultura Económica, 1999.

Pérez Guadalupe, José Luis. *Faites y atorrantes: Una etnografía del penal de Lurigancho*. Lima: Centro de Investigaciones Teológicas, 1994.

Perrot, Michelle. "Delinquency and the Penitentiary System in Nineteenth-Century France." In Robert Forster and Orest Ranum, eds., *Deviants and the Abandoned in French Society: Selections from the Annales, Economies, Societies, Civilisations*, 213–45. Baltimore: Johns Hopkins University Press, 1978.

Pesce, Luis. *Indígenas e inmigrantes en el Perú*. Lima: Imprenta de la Opinión Nacional, 1906.

Piccato, Pablo. "Mexico City Criminals: Between Social Engineering and Popular Culture." Paper presented at CLAH Conference, Atlanta, January 1996.

———. "Interpretations of Sexuality in Mexico City's Prisons: A Critical Version of Roumagnac." In Robert McKee Irwin, Edward J. McCaughan, and Michelle Rocío Nasser, eds., *The Famous 41: Sexuality and Social Control in Mexico City, 1901*, 251–66. New York: Palgrave, 2003.

Pick, Daniel. *Faces of Degeneration: A European Disorder, c. 1848–c. 1918*. New York: Cambridge University Press, 1989.

Pike, Fredrick. *The Modern History of Peru*. New York: Praeger, 1967.

Pineda Iglesias, Gonzalo. "Se justifica la pena capital en el nuevo campo del positivismo?" *Anales de la Universidad Mayor de San Marcos de Lima* 26 (1899): 65–86.

Pisciotta, Alexander. *Benevolent Repression: Social Control and the American Reformatory-Prison Movement*. New York: New York University Press, 1994.

Planas, Pedro. *La república autocrática*. Lima: Fundación Friedrich Ebert, 1994.

———. *El 900: Balance y recuperación. I. Aproximaciones al 900*. Lima: Citdec, 1994.

Polar, Jorge. "Aptitudes políticas de nuestra raza." *Anales de la Universidad Mayor de San Marcos de Lima* 27 (1900).

Poole, Deborah. "Ciencia, peligrosidad y represión en la criminología indigenista peruana." In Carlos Aguirre and Charles Walker, eds., *Bandoleros, abigeos y montoneros: Criminalidad y violencia en el Perú, siglos XVIII–XX*, 335–67. Lima: Instituto de Apoyo Agrario, 1990.

———. *Vision, Race, and Modernity: A Visual Economy of the Andean Image World*. Princeton: Princeton University Press, 1997.

Poole, Deborah, ed. *Unruly Order: Violence, Power, and Cultural Identity in the High Provinces of Southern Peru*. Boulder: Westview Press, 1994.

Portal, Ismael. *Del pasado limeño*. Lima: Librería e Imprenta Gil, 1932.

Portella, Juan Antonio. "La higiene en las casas de vecindad: Necesidad de construir casas higiénicas para obreros." Bachelor thesis, University of San Marcos, Medical School, 1903.

Portocarrero, Gonzalo. "El fundamento invisible: Función y lugar de las ideas racistas en la República Aristocrática." In Panfichi and Portocarrero, eds., *Mundos interiores*, 219–60.

———. *Racismo y mestizaje*. Lima: SUR, 1994.

Pradier-Foderé, Paul. *Compendio del Curso de Derecho Administrativo profesado en la Facultad de Ciencias Políticas y Administrativas de Lima por el Sr. Pradier-Foderé, fundador y decano de la Facultad*, 2d ed. Translated by Manuel A. Fuentes. Lima: Imprenta del Estado, 1878.

Prado, Javier. *El método positivo en el derecho penal*. Lima: Benito Gil Editor, 1890.

Prado Ugarteche, Mariano I. "El tipo criminal." *El Ateneo* 1 and 2 (1899–1900).

Puga, Nicolás. "Sistemas penitenciarios." Bachelor thesis, University of San Marcos, Political and Administrative Sciences, 1899.

Quintanilla, Aparicio. *La pena de muerte es injusta y debe abolirse de nuestra legislación*. Lima: Imprenta Comercial de Horacio La Rosa, 1906.

Quirós, Alfonso. *La deuda defraudada: Consolidación de 1850 y dominio económico en el Perú*. Lima: INC, 1987.

Quirós, Mariano Santos de. *Colección de leyes, decretos y órdenes publicadas en el Perú desde su independencia en el año de 1821 hasta el 31 de diciembre de 1830*. Lima: Imprenta de José Masías, 1831.

Rada, Pedro José. *Apuntes sobre el estudio del derecho en el Perú*. Arequipa: Imprenta de la Bolsa, 1894.

Ragas, José. "Ciudadanía, cultura política y representación en el Perú: La campaña electoral de 1850." Licenciatura thesis, Pontificia Universidad Católica del Perú, 2003.

Ramón, Gabriel. *La muralla y los callejones: Intervención urbana y proyecto político en Lima durante la segunda mitad del siglo XIX*. Lima: Sidea/PromPerú, 1999.

Ramos, Angela. *Una vida sin tregua*, vol. 1. Lima: Concytec, 1990.

Ramos, Carlos M. "El delito, es o no hereditario?" Bachelor thesis, University of San Marcos, Law School, 1900.

Redfield, Peter. *Space in the Tropics: From Convicts to Rockets in French Guiana*. Berkeley: University of California Press, 2000.

Revollé, Lizardo. *Exposición que sobre el estado y necesidades de la policía presenta a la Subprefectura e Intendencia el Comisario del Cuartel 2º. de esta capital*. Lima: Imprenta de El Lucero, 1908.

Revoredo, Alejandro. "Deficiencias de nuestra legislación penal." Bachelor thesis, University of San Marcos, Law School, 1919.

Rodríguez, Abraham. "Estudios criminológicos. Primera parte: Los caracteres del hombre criminal." Bachelor thesis, University of San Marcos, Medical School, 1899.

———. *Reflexiones antropológicas relativas al hombre universal, al americano, y al peruano*. Lima: Imprenta de El Nacional, 1897.

Rodríguez, Julia. "Encoding the Criminal: Criminology and the Science of 'Social Defense' in Modernizing Argentina (1880–1921)." Ph.D. diss., Columbia University, 1999.

Rodríguez Pastor, Humberto. *Hijos del celeste imperio en el Perú, 1850–1900*. Lima: Instituto de Apoyo Agrario, 1989.

———. "La calle del Capón, el Callejón Otayza, y el barrio chino." In Panfichi and Portocarrero, eds., *Mundos interiores*, 397–430.

Rothman, David. *The Discovery of the Asylum: Social Order and Disorder in the New Republic.* Boston: Little, Brown, 1971.

———. *Conscience and Convenience: The Asylum and Its Alternatives in Progressive America.* Boston: Little, Brown, 1980.

Ruggiero, Kristin. "Fingerprinting and the Argentine Plan for Universal Identification in the Late Nineteenth and Early Twentieth Centuries." In Jane Caplan and John Torpey, eds., *Documenting Individual Identity: The Development of State Practices in the Modern World*, 184–96. Princeton: Princeton University Press, 2001.

Ruiz Zevallos, Augusto. *Psiquiatras y locos: Entre la modernización contra los andes y el nuevo proyecto de modernidad, Peru: 1850–1930.* Lima: Instituto Pasado y Presente, 1995.

———. *La multitud, las subsistencias y el trabajo: Lima, 1890–1920.* Lima: Pontificia Universidad Católica del Perú, 2001.

Rusche, Georg, and Otto Kirchheimer. *Punishment and Social Structure.* New York: Columbia University Press, 1939.

Sabo, Don, et al. "Gender and the Politics of Punishment." In Sabo et al., eds., *Prison Masculinities*, 3–18. Philadelphia: Temple University Press, 2001.

Salazar, Jorge, et al. *Historia de la noticia: Un siglo de homicidios a sangre y tinta*, vol. 1. Lima: Universidad de San Martín de Porres, 1996.

Salomón, Alberto. "El factor económico como base de los fenómenos sociales: Proyecciones sociales del delito." Bachelor thesis, University of San Marcos, Law School, 1899.

Salvatore, Ricardo. "Criminology, Prison Reform, and the Buenos Aires Working Class." *Journal of Interdisciplinary History* 23, 2 (1992): 279–99.

———. "Positivist Criminology and State Formation in Modern Argentina, 1890–1940." In Peter Becker and Richard F. Wetzell, eds., *Criminals and Their Scientists: The History of Criminology in International Perspective.* New York: Cambridge University Press, forthcoming.

Salvatore, Ricardo, and Carlos Aguirre, eds. *The Birth of the Penitentiary in Latin America.* Austin: University of Texas Press, 1996.

Sanborn, Cynthia. "Los obreros textiles de Lima: Redes sociales y organización laboral, 1900–1930." In Panfichi and Portocarreo, eds., *Mundos interiores*, 187–218.

Sánchez, Luis Alberto. *Valdelomar o la "Belle Epoque,"* 3d ed. Lima: Inpropesa, 1987.

Scott, James C. *Domination and the Arts of Resistance: Hidden Transcripts.* New Haven: Yale University Press, 1990.

Seminario Helguero, Gabriel. *Cárcel.* Lima: Editorial Rímac, 1935.

———. *Los presos.* Lima: Editorial Lumen, 1937.

———. *Notas para la reforma del régimen de prisiones en el Perú.* Lima: Talleres Gráficos de la Penitenciaría, 1945.

Silva Santisteban, José. *Breves reflexiones sobre los sucesos ocurridos en Lima y el Callao con motivo de la importación de artefactos.* Lima: José Sánchez, 1859.

Solano, Susana. *El estado peligroso: Algunas de sus formas clínicas no delictivas.* Lima: Universidad de San Marcos de Lima, 1937.

——. *El indígena y la ley penal,* 2d ed. Lima: Librería e Imprenta Miranda, 1950.

Solf y Muro, Alfredo. "Penalidad de la reincidencia." *Anales de la Universidad Mayor de San Marcos de Lima* 25 (1898): 51–74.

Solís, Abelardo. *Once años.* Lima: Talleres Gráficos Sanmartí y Cia, 1934.

Spierenburg, Pieter. *The Spectacle of Suffering: Executions and the Evolution of Repression, from a Pre-Industrial Metropolis to the European Experience.* New York: Cambridge University Press, 1984.

Stein, Steve. "Cultura popular y política popular en los comienzos del siglo XX en Lima." In Stein, ed., *Lima obrera,* 53–83.

——. *Populism in Peru: The Emergence of the Masses and the Politics of Social Control.* Madison: University of Wisconsin Press, 1980.

Stein, Steve, ed. *Lima obrera, 1900–1930,* vol. 1. Lima: Ediciones El Virrey, 1986.

Stepan, Nancy. *"The Hour of Eugenics": Race, Gender, and Nation in Latin America.* Ithaca: Cornell University Press, 1991.

Stoddard, O. F. *Manual científico de temperancia.* Lima: Imprenta Americana, 1923.

Sulmont, Denis. *El movimiento obrero en el Perú.* Lima: Tarea, 1975.

Távara, Santiago. *Abolición de la esclavitud en el Perú.* Lima: Imprenta de J.M. Monterola, 1855.

Taylor, Lewis. *Bandits and Politics in Peru: Landlord and Peasant Violence in Hualgayoc, 1900–1930.* Cambridge: Center of Latin American Studies, c. 1986.

Tejada, Luis. *La cuestión del pan: El anarcosindicalismo en el Perú.* Lima: INC, 1987.

——. "Malambo." In Panfichi and Portocarrero, eds., *Mundos interiores,* 145–60.

Thurner, Mark. "'*Republicanos*' and '*La comunidad de Peruanos*': Unimagined Political Communities in PostColonial Andean Peru." *Journal of Latin American Studies* 27 (1995): 291–318.

Torrejón, Luis. "Lima, 1912: El caso de un motín popular urbano." In Panfichi and Portocarrero, eds., *Mundos interiores,* 315–42.

Valdez, César. "La patología de los delincuentes en el panóptico de Lima." Bachelor thesis, University of San Marcos, Medical School, 1914.

Valdizán, Hermilio. "La delincuencia en el Perú: Ensayo de criminología nacional." *La Crónica Médica* 22 (1910).

——. "El tatuaje entre nuestros criminales." *La crónica médica* 22 (1910): 95–96, 108–12.

Valladares Ayarza, Carlos. "La pena de muerte." Thesis, University of San Marcos, Law School, 1946.

Varela y Orbegoso, Luis J. *La criminología de Garofalo.* Lima: Librería Escolar e Imprenta de E. Romero, 1900.

Velasco, Alcibiades. "Sistemas penitenciarios." Bachelor thesis, University of San Marcos, Law School, 1890.

Villavicencio, Víctor M. *La reforma penitenciaria en el Perú.* Lima: Imprenta A. J. Rivas Berrio, 1927.

——. *Algunos aspectos de nuestra sociología criminal.* Lima: n.p., 1930.

——. *Defensas criminales y otros ensayos*. Lima: Librería y Editorial Peruana, 1933.

Wacquant, Loïc. "From Slavery to Mass Incarceration: Rethinking the 'Race Question' in the U.S." *New Left Review*, 13 (2002): 41–60.

Wade, Peter. *Race and Ethnicity in Latin America*. London: Pluto Press, 1997.

Waite, Robert G. "From Penitentiary to Reformatory: Alexander Maconochie, Walter Crofton, Zebulon Brockway, and the Road to Prison Reform—New South Wales, Ireland, and Elmira, New York, 1840–70." *Criminal Justice History* 11 (1991): 85–106.

Walker, Charles. "Voces discordantes: Discursos alternativos sobre el indio a fines de la colonia." In Walker, ed., *Entre la retórica y la insurgencia: Las ideas y los movimientos sociales en los Andes, siglo XVIII*, 89–112. Cusco: Centro Las Casas, 1996.

——. "The Patriotic Society: Discussions and Omissions about Indians in the Peruvian War of Independence." *The Americas* 55, 2 (October 1998): 275–98.

Wiener, Martin J. *Reconstructing the Criminal: Culture, Law, and Policy in England, 1830–1914*. New York: Cambridge University Press, 1990.

Wright, Gordon. *Between the Guillotine and Liberty: Two Centuries of the Crime Problem in France*. New York: Oxford University Press, 1983.

Xammar, Luis Fabio. *"El Murciélago" en la literatura peruana*. Lima: Librería e Imprenta Gil, 1945.

Zamora Torres, Víctor. "El delito y sus causas." Bachelor thesis, University of San Marcos, Law School, 1916.

Zedner, Lucia. *Women, Crime, and Custody in Victorian England*. Oxford: Clarendon Press, 1991.

Zinoman, Peter. *The Colonial Bastille: A History of Imprisonment in Vietnam, 1862–1940*. Berkeley: University of California Press, 2001.

INDEX

Note: Page numbers in italics indicate illustrations. Those with a t. or n. indicate a table or end note.

Boletín de Criminología, 59
Boleto (certificate of employment), 35, 242n.72
Bonilla, Heraclio, 37
Borja, César, 33
Bossism (gamonalismo), 4, 48, 107, 130, 132, 237n.4
Boy's Reformatory of Surco, 108
Brigada de Asuntos Sociales, 75
Brigada de Investigación y Vigilancia, 74
Brockway, Zebulon, 96
Bromley, Juan, 242n.77
Bustamante, Juan, 32

Cáceres, Andrés, 68, 70
Cacique, 151, 264n.45
Caivano, Tomás, 113
Calabozos (dungeons), 138, 144
Calle, Juan José, 96, 97; 1915 commission of, 149, 161
Callejones: criminality in, 51, 116, 117; Policia de Seguridad and, 67. *See also* Neighborhoods
Cambiaos, 171
Canasteros, 148
Candamo, Manuel, 52
Canevaro, César, 256n.67
Canta province, 112
Canteras (quarries), *105*
Capitalism, 6
Capital punishment, 18, 20, 22–24
Caporales: Cárcel de Guadalupe and, 151; collaboration of, 149–51, 173, 176, 197, 264n.39; customary order in prisons and, 149–51, 264n.39; guards and, 102; in penitentiary, 150, 264n.39
Cárcel Central de Varones (ccv): employment of inmates by, 197; escapes from, 187–88, 197; homosexuality and, 170, 171, 172; living conditions in, 104, 180, 181, 183; political prisoners in, 112, 132, 133; population of, 112
Cárcel de Guadalupe. *See* Guadalupe jail
Cárcel de policía, 87

Carceletas jail, 21, 28, 87
Carreras de vaqueta, 107
Casamatas jail, 87, 112, 132
Casas de vecindad, 51, 179
Castilla, Ramón, 21, 25–26, 66
Castro Pozo, Hildebrando, 137
Cellular regime, 89, 95, 218
Chacaliaza, 44, *45*, 115, 116
Chinese (coolies): arbitrary arrests of, 77; biological inferiority of, 47; criminality of, 33–34, 37–38; hygiene of, 38; imprisonment of, 88; living conditions of, 182–83; morality issues and, 34, 37–38; race and racism and, 32–33; stereotypes of, 37; suicide among, 191, 271n.32
Chocano, José Santos, 54
Citizenship: of Indians, 30–31, 32; literacy, 5, 237n.6; in Peru, 4–5; of slaves, 21; social class and, 3
Civility, European model of, 37, 38
Civil rights, 4–5
Civil war (1894–95), 70
Classes. *See* Lower class; Social class; Working class
Clientelism, 206–7
Coca trade in prisons, 146–47, 168–69
Cole, Simon, 28
Collaboration: of caporales, 149–51, 173, 176, 197, 264n.39; of guards, 194–96; of inmates, 194–96, 199–202, 206, 220–21, 273n.60; with political prisoners, 199–202, 206, 220–21, 273n.60; of soplones, 124, 126, 194, 259n.45
Colonialism, 48, 247n.81
Colored races, 30. *See also names of specific peoples*
Comercio, El: on abuses in workshops, 158; on alcoholism, 52; on arrests and releases, 79, 82; on casas de vecindad, 51; condemns torture, 78; on criminal slang, 167; on Duelo de caballeros, 126–27; on faites, 126–27; on jaranas, 146; letter by inmate in, 208; on passes, 35; on prisoner evaluation, 76

221; racial identity of, 125; violence and, 175

Ferri, Enrico, 42

Fingerprinting (dactyloscopy), 73, 74, 101

Flores Galindo, Alberto, 9, 91

Fosalba, Rafael, 58

Foucault, Michel, 10, 246n.67

Frontón, El, penal colony. *See* El Frontón penal colony

Fuentes, Manuel Atanasio: 56–57, 95, 102; on abolition of slavery, 21; on Cárcel de Guadalupe, 256n.62; on Chinese (coolies), 34; on crime, 26–28, 31, 241n.51; on education of Indians, 31, 241n.51; *Estadística general de Lima*, 26–28; on Lima's society, 37; on race and racism, 31; on vagrancy and vagrants, 34

Fuentes Castro, Paulino, 37, 43, 44

Gaceta Judicial, La, 103, 120

Galton, Francis, 58

Gálvez, José, 120–21, 124

Gamarra, Agustín, 66

Gamonales, 4, 48, 107, 130, 132, 237n.4

García Calderón, Francisco, 52

Garland, David, 11, 41

Garofalo, Rafaelle, 42, 54, 243n.1

Garrido Malaver, Julio, 107, 188–89

Gatrell, V. A. C., 11

Gendarmería, 67

Godínez, Julio Alberto, 213

González Prada, Manuel, 48, 79

González Vigil, Francisco de Paula, 24

Gootenberg, Paul, 29

Graña, Francisco, 52, 112, 244n.36, 246n.61

Guadalupe jail, 101–2; age groups of inmates at, 233t5.8; Arzola at, 151, 190, 264n.46; caciques at, 151, 264n.45; caporals at, 151; corruption in administration of, 263n.24; criminal slang at, 167; customary order in, 144, 149, 151, 264n.45; disciplinary regimes at, 103–

4, 112, 149; enjuiciados at, 111; escapes from, 186, 188, 193, 197; heterogeneity of inmates at, 112; homosexuality at, 170, 173; jaranas at, 146; mental condition of inmates at, 192–93; nutrition at, 181; occupations of inmates at, 231t5.6; operating dates of, 256n.62; political prisoners at, 133, 135, 136; population size of, 112–13, 227t5.1, 258n.4; presos tranquilos at, 196; racial identities of inmates at, 229t5.4; rateros at, 123; recruitment of inmates at, 195; regional origins of inmates at, 114; release of inmates from, 112–13; rematados at, 111; replacement of, 104, 256n.71; riots at, 190–91; socialization in, 123; subculture of, 123; tattooing at, 166–67; torture and violence at, 107, 174–75; workshops at, 221

Guano, 36, 37, 94

Guardia Civil de Lima, 67, 68–69

Guardia Nacional, 66–67, 68

Guardia Republicana, 74

Guardia Urbana, 67

Guards: accommodation strategies and, 144, 145; alcaides (prison wardens), 102; alcoholism and, 146, 215, *216*, 263n.12; caporals and, 102; collaboration amongst, 194–96; corruption of, 148, 263nn.24, 25, 26, 264nn.27, 28; loyalties of, 152, 264n.47, 265n.55; military service of, 93–94. *See also* Prison administration

Guerrero, Julio, 43

Gutiérrez, Gabriel, 17, 18, 19, 239n.1

Hague, Juan Luis, 247n.74

Haya de la Torre, Víctor Raúl, 48, 134, 202

Health issues: crime and, 56–57, 99; dangerousness of, 54–55; diseases, 51, 99, 107, 179, 180, 269n.61; epidemics, 51; hygiene, 38, 46, 50–51, 99; living conditions and, 50–51, 179–80, 269n.61; nutrition, 180–81, 270n.69; penalties and

106; suicides of, 191, 271n.32; tattooing and, 99, 115, 164, 165–67, 268n.8; wages for, 106; women, 79, 87, 252n.82; workshops and, 156, 221, 265n.63. *See also* Customary prison order; Letters of inmates; Penitentiary inmates; Political prisoners; Prison populations; Subcultures in prisons; *names of specific prisons*

Inspección General de Prisiones, 97–98. *See also* Dirección General de Prisiones

Instituto de Criminología (Argentina), 99

Instituto de Criminología (Lima), 99–100, 101, 255n.53

Intendencia de Policía, 76, 129, 137, 138, 261n.94, 262n.99

Irish system, 96

Izaguirre, Carlos Alberto, 138

Jaranas, 8, 116, 146, 213, *214*

Jargon, criminal, 164, 165, 167–68, 268n.11

Jiménez, Plácido, 44–45, 51–52, 97

Jiménez de Asúa, Luis, 2, 54–55, 99

Junta Administradora, 160

Junta Calificadora, 129

Junta Económica, 159

Junta Inspectora, reports on, 94, 254n.24

Labor force: boleto and, 35, 242n.72; child labor, 34; competition of segments of, 161, 162, 267nn.89, 91; crime and criminality of, 34, 61; discipline of, 34; public works projects and, 130–31; slavery and, 21; strikes and, 63; surveillance of, 75; vagrancy and vagrants and, 129

Lacassagne, Alexandre, 42–43, 45

Lama, Tomás, 156, 265n.63

Landowners, and slavery, 21–22

Laso, Francisco, 32

Lavalle, Juan Bautista de, 247n.81

Leguía, Augusto B.: administration of, 5–6, 7, 74–76, 137; Basadre on, 137; on

Cárcel de Guadalupe, 104; political prisoners and, 133, 134; public works program of, 129; reform initiatives of, 74–76, 97–98, 108; Road Conscription law and, 130; vagrancy law and, 128–29

Leguía y Martínez, Germán, 74, 97, 133, 134

León, Carlos Aurelio, 256n.62

León y León, Bernardino, 2

Letters of inmates: 198, 201–9, 273n.80, 274n.83; accusatory tone of, 208; of Aprista party members, 202–3; clientelism in, 206–7; collaboration with political prisoners and, 199–202, 206, 273n.60; collective approaches in, 198, 199, 209; effects of, 207–8; of Indians, 204–5; to newspapers, 201, 208–9; pardons and, 203, 204; petitions and, 203; political loyalties in, 205–6; prison reform rhetoric in, 209–12; resigned tone of, 203–4, 205; rights of political prisoners and, 201–9, 273n.74

Ley de Represión, 135

Libro de Conducta, 101

Lima: census of, 69; Chilean occupation of, 37, 68, 190; class-based neighborhoods in, 7; cosmopolitanism of, 7; criminal behavior in, 27; demographics of, 6; industrial factories in, 7; map of, *8*; modernization and, 6, 35–36, 108, 242n.77; morality issues in, 37–39; Peruvian society and, 9, 216–18, 221; police of, 68–69; riots in, 23, 36, 37; urban plebeians of, 7–8; urban reform in, 6–7; War of the Pacific and, 37; working class of, 7. *See also* Penitentiary; *names of specific prisons*

Lima penitentiary inmates. *See* Penitentiary inmates

Lisson, Carlos, 244n.34

Literacy, 5, 115, 237n.6

Living conditions: in Cárcel de Guadalupe, 103, 256n.64; at CCV, 104; of Chinese (coolies), 182–83; crimes and

Panizo y Zárate, Manuel, 93–94

Panóptico. *See* Penitentiary

Panopticon (prison model), 88

Parada, La, 107

Pardo, Manuel, 36–37, 67

Pardons (indulto), 100, 127, 203, 204

Parker, David, 50, 62

Parole, 98, 100, 176, 255n.53

Patria, La, 68

Patria Nueva, 5

Patriarca, Silvana, 241n.42

Patrimonialism, 6

Patronage Society, 158

Pauperism, 60–61, 62, 128, 182–83

Paz Soldán, Enrique Carlos, 57, 58

Paz Soldán, Mariano Felipe, 86–87, 88, 89, 180, 256n.62

Peasants, indigenous, 5. *See also* Indians

Peña Chacaliaza, Manuel, 44, *45*, 115, 116

Penal Code (1862): author of, 56; inmates' earnings under, 156, 157, 265n.62, 266n.66; knowledge of, by criminals, 247n.78; theft, 123; vagrancy and vagrants under, 35

Penal Code (1924): cash incentives for inmates under, 161; death penalty under, 53, 99; judicial guidelines of, 54; penalties under, 54, 98; positivist criminology and, 53

Penal codes, 53–54, 55, 98, 246nn.67, 68

Peñaloza, Augusto, 58

Penal regimes. *See names of specific regimes*

Penal theory. *See* Criminology; Positivist criminology

Penalties: at agricultural penitentiary, 98; dangerousness of, 53–55, 98, 99, 246n.67, 247n.74; health issues and, 54–55; individuation of, 53, 54–55, 99, 247n.74; internamiento and, 98, 188; judicial guidelines for, 54; pardons and, 100, 127, 203, 204; parole and, 98, 100, 176, 255n.53; penitenciaría and, 98; at penitentiary, 153; pentágono and,

154; prisión and, 98; probation and, 98; Reglamento (1901) and, 152, 153; solitary confinement, 154, 265nn.54, 55. *See also* Death penalty; Disciplinary regimes; Punishments

Penitenciados, 111–12, 114, 149, 157, 196

Penitentiary: agricultural workers as inmates of, 118; Auburn (N.Y.) model of, 88–89; caporals in, 150, 264n.39; CCV and, 104; construction of, 1–2, *90*, 91–92, *92*; control of inmates at, 92; corruption in administration of, 263nn.25, 26, 264n.27; customary order at, 144, 153; disciplinary regimes at, 3, 88, 89; escapes from, 116, 186–87, 271n.28; funding for, 94–95; guards at, 93; health conditions at, 179, 269n.61; homosexuality at, 170, 172, 268n.22; Indians at, 89; Junta Administradora and, 160; Junta Económica and, 159; Junta Inspectora reports on, 94, 95, 254n.24; living conditions at, 183; nutrition at, 180–81, 270n.69; Pampa de los Criollos and, 177; Pampa del Tawantinsuyo and, 177; penalties at, 153; political prisoners at, 133, 134; political rally at, 137; productive work at, 88–89, 91; prototypes of, 88; religious instruction, 89; as research facility, 99; riots at, 189–90, 200; schedule of activities at, 92; sentences served at, 92–93; size of population at, 112; tattooing at, 167; torture and violence at, 144, 191–92; workshops at, 155–56, 157, 211, 265nn.58, 59, 63

Penitentiary inmates: age groups of, 232t5.7; classification of, 93; occupations of, 230t5.5; offenses of, 234t5.9; race and racism and, 228t5.2, 229tt5.3, 5.4, 269n.52; regional origins of, 114, 236t5.11; sentencing of, 114

Penology, 2

Perrot, Michelle, 12

Peru: birth of, 4; citizenship of, 4–5; eco-

Peru (*cont.*)

nomic issues of, 4, 5, 6, 36; oligarchic state of, 4; society of, 9, 216–18, 221

Philadelphia penitentiary regime, 89, 95, 218

Piccato, Pablo, 170

Piérola, Nicolás de, 4, 70, 71

Pike, Fredrick, 244n.34

Plantation-like regimes, 106, 144

Police force: alcoholism and, 70; arbitrary arrests and, 77; brutality, 77–78; caudillista struggles and, 66; corruption in, 70–71; disciplinary regimes and, 70–71; faites and, 124; history of, in Lima, 66–67, 68–69; intraforce tensions and, 71; legislation and, 68; merit-based promotions in, 71; oncenio and, 74–76; organization of, 67–69; police academy and, 71, 72, 74; political units and, 75; professionalization of, 71, 74; punishments and, 219; recruitment of, 68, 249n.7; relations with society, 71; reorganization of, 74–76; in rural areas, 68, 70–72, 75; serenos and, 66; soldiers in, 72; statistics of arrests made by, 70; surveillance by, 72–73; urban plebeians and, 7; use Bertillon system of criminal identification, 69, 73, 250n.21; War of the Pacific and, 112

Policía de Seguridad, 67

Political prisoners: Aprista inmates as, 202–3; in Casamatas jail, 132; in ccv, 112, 132, 133; collaboration with inmates and, 199–202, 206, 220–21, 273n.60; at Cárcel de Guadalupe, 133, 135, 136; at El Frontón, 132, 133, 135, 202–3; at El Sexto prison, 132, 133, 134, 138, 256n.71; influences of, 186; institutions for, 112; Intendencia de Policia and, 137, 261n.94, 262n.99; Leguía y Martinez on, 133, 134; mistreatment of, 137–39; as noncriminals, 136; oncenio and, 137; at penitentiary, 133, 134; pop-

ulation diversity of, 111, 135, 136, 138, 139; racial stereotypes of, 136; rights of, 201–9, 273n.74; at San Lorenzo Island, 132, 133, 134; social class of, 132–33; special treatment of, 136–37, 261nn.92, 93, 94; subaltern groups and, 133

Politics: Aprista inmates and, 202–3; Aprista party, 107, 134, 136, 257n.85, 259n.45; blacks and, 25; criminality and, 43; lower class and, 25. *See also* Political prisoners

Poole, Deborah, 55

Poor people, 60–61, 62, 128, 182–83

Popular culture, 26, 28–29, 63

Portella, Juan Antonio, 51

Porvenir de las razas en el Perú, El (Palma), 47

Positivist criminology, 39–42; biological determinism, 42–44; criticism of, 42–43, 44; Indians and, 44; interventionism and, 59–60; Leguía regime penal reform and, 97; Penal Code (1924) and, 53; race and racism, 42; research on, 59

Pradier-Foderé, Paul, 95

Prado, Javier, 43, 44, 57

Prado, Mariano I., 67–68

Prensa, La, 201, 209

Presos tranquilos (quiet inmates), 195–96

Prison administration: corporals and, 150; corruption in, 263nn.25, 26, 264n.27; employment of inmates and, 196–97; faites and, 125–26; homosexuality and, 172–73; oversight an overseers, 113; recruitment of inmates and, 145, 146, 194; religious orders for, 108–9; violence against guards and, 191–92. *See also* Disciplinary regimes; Guards

Prisoners. *See* Inmates; Political prisoners; Prison populations

Prison populations: enjuiciados and, 111; heterogeneity of, 110–12, 135, 136, 138, 139, 213–14, *215*, 221; loyalties within, 165; race and racism and, 21; resistance

Riva Agüero, José de la, 261n.94
Road Conscription law, 130
Rodrigues, Nina, 43
Rodríguez Dulanto, Abraham, 43–44, 97
Rojas, Nerio, 255n.47
Rojas y Cañas, Enrique, 57, 115, 116
Roumagnac, Carlos, 43
Ruiz Zevallos, Augusto, 191, 192
Rural areas: jails in, 88; police forces in,
    68, 71–72, 75

Samanez, Rosendo, 94–95
Sánchez Cerro, Luis M., 134
San Lorenzo Island, 132, 133, 134
Scott, James, 175, 206
Sección de Identificación y Estadística
    (SIE), 69
Sección de Vigilancia, 75
Selective eugenics (Galton), 58
Seminario Helguero, Gabriel, 170, 171,
    172, 180, 183
Sentencing criminals, 119
Seoane, Juan: arrest of, 134; on caporales,
    150; on coca consumption in prisons,
    169; on living conditions, 136; on polit-
    ical activism of inmates, 200; on
    prison administration loyalties, 152;
    special treatment of, 261n.92
Sepultura, La, 107
Serranos, 176, 177, 221. See also Indians
Sex and sexuality issues, 99, 164, 169–73,
    184, 268nn.22, 25
El Sexto prison, 132, 133, 134, 138, 256n.71
Silva Santisteban, José, 23, 102
Slavery, 18, 20, 21, 22, 239n.3
Slaves, imprisonment of, 88
Social class: bossism and, 4, 48, 107, 130,
    132, 237n.4; civil disobedience and,
    132–33; civil rights and, 4–5; condi-
    tions of imprisonment and, 79–80, 81–
    82; criminality and, 19–20; cultural
    traditions of, 36; death penalty and, 33;
    decency as value of, 62–63; elites, 49–
    50, 245n.45; exclusionary practices

and, 4–5; housing and, 8; hygiene and,
    38, 50–51; jaranas, 8, 116, 146, 164, 213,
    214; labor discipline and, 34; modern-
    ization and, 7; morality issues and, 29;
    in neighborhoods, 7; pauperism and,
    60; police units and, 67; political par-
    ticipation by, 25; political power and,
    132–33; of political prisoners, 132–33;
    slavery and, 21; vagrancy and vagrants
    and, 34, 37, 51, 60–61, 242n.65. See also
    Lower class; Working class
Social hygiene, 50–51
Social medicine, 58
Social question, the, 60, 61, 248n.103
Sociedad Amigos del Indio, 32, 241n.53
Sociología criminal peruana (Villavicen-
    cio), 46
Solano, Susana, 54
Soldiers. See Military service
Solís, Abelardo, 75, 133
Soplones , 124, 126, 194, 259n.45
Spencer, Herbert, 42
Sports in prisons, 183–84
State patronage, of workshops, 155–56,
    160, 161–63, 265n.59, 266n.80,
    267nn.90, 94
Statistics and statistical data: an-
    thropometrics, 69, 73, 98, 250n.21; on
    arrests, 70, 223t3.1, 224t3.2, 225t3.3; be-
    havior assessments, 100–101; Cartilla
    criminológica and, 99; on crime, 26–
    28, 52, 69, 241n.43; estado peligroso,
    99; fingerprinting, 73; prison demo-
    graphics, 112–13, 258n.4; role of,
    241n.42
Stein, Steve, 9–10
Stepan, Nancy, 58
Sterilization of criminals, 58
Strikes, 63, 106
Subcultures in prisons, 164–74, 219; coca
    consumption and, 168–69; criminal
    slang and, 164, 165, 167–68, 268n.11;
    homosexuality and, 169–73, 268nn.22,
    25; jaranas and, 164; sexual behavior

and, 164; tattooing and, 99, 115, 164, 165–67, 268n.8

Surveillance, 70, 72–76

Tarde, Gabriel, 42–43, 44, 45
Tarjetazo, 6
Tattooing, 99, 115, 164, 165–67, 268n.8
Távara, Santiago, 21
Tejada, Luis, 125
Tejerina, Nicanor, 24
Tequile Island, 134
Tiempo, El, 208
Tinterillos, 148, 274n.83
Tirado, Gonzalo, 51
Torture, 77, 78–79, 87, 107, 144, 252nn.74, 82
Trabajo, El, 34
Tribunal de Conducta, 100, 255n.53
Tribunal de la Acordada, 22
Tuberculosis, 51, 179, 180, 269n.61
Tupac Amaru rebellion, 30

Ulloa, José Casimiro, 56
University of San Marcos: Law School, 99; Medical School, 57
Urban poor, 62, 128, 182–83

Vagrancy and vagrants: criminality and, 34–35, 37, 51, 60–61, 242n.65; defined, 128–29; El Frontón penal colony and, 106, 129, 130–31; forced labor and public works and, 129; imprisonment for, 112; law of Leguía and, 128–29; legislation on, 128; military service and, 35, 242n.72; occupations and, 130–31; Penal Code (1862) and, 35; penal colony and, 130; sentences for, 129; social class and, 34, 37, 51, 60–61, 242n.65
Valdez, César, 169, 170, 180, 181
Valdizán, Hermilio, 46, 57, 112, 166
Vales de cuartas partes, 156
Vargas Prada, Luis, 73, 74
Variedades, 137
"Vidrieras, Dr.", 103

Villanueva del Campo, Armando, 257n.91
Villavicencio, Víctor Modesto: on dangerousness, 255n.46; on illegal prison activities, 148; on Indians, 46, 48; on letters for inmates, 211; on penal theory, 219; *Sociología criminal peruana*, 46; on sociological explanations for criminal behavior, 58
Violence: abuse, 176; death of inmates from, 175; faites and, 175; in Cárcel de Guadalupe, 174–75; against guards, 191–92; hierarchies of, 177–79; homicide in prisons, 174; jaranas and, 164; lower class and, 117–18; in penitentiary, 191–92; power structures and, 175–76; riots, 193; social and cultural climates of, 175–79; weapons and, 174, 175, 200, 269n.48, 271n.28
Visita de cárcel (prison inspection), 199
Viterbo Arias, José, 56
Voting rights, 5
Vucetich system, 73

War of the Pacific: dislocates police forces, 68; effects of, 4, 37, 94; penitentiary workshops and, 157; prison population fluctuations and, 112, 258n.4
Willman, Emilio "Carita," 115, 116, 126–28, 260n.57
Wines, Enoch, 96
Women inmates, 79, 87, 252n.82
Work habits, 88
Working class: criminals from, 61; in penitentiary, 116; political mobilization of, 7; registration of domestic servants and, 70; surveillance of, 73–74, 75; urban plebeians, 8; values of, 62–63. *See also* Lower class; Social class
Working poor, 60–61
Workshops, 155–63, 221; abuses in, 157, 158, 159; in Cárcel de Guadalupe, 221; cash incentives of, 157, 160, 161–62, 163; civilian labor vs. labor in, 161, 162, 267nn.89, 91; contract system of, 155–

Index | 309

Carlos Aguirre is associate professor of history at the University of Oregon. He is the author of *Agentes de su propia libertad: los esclavos de lima y la desintegración de la esclavitud, 1821–1854* (1993). He has edited, with Ricardo D. Salvatore and Gilbert M. Joseph, *Crime and Punishment in Latin America: Law and Society since Late Colonial Times* (Duke, 2001); with Ricardo D. Salvatore, *The Birth of the Penitentiary in Latin America: Essays on Criminology, Prison Reform, and Social Control, 1830–1940* (1996); and with Charles Walker, *Bandoleros, Abigeos, y Montoneros: Criminalidad y Violencia en el Peru, Siglos XVIII–XX* (1990).

Library of Congress Cataloging-in-Publication Data

Aguirre, Carlos.

The criminals of Lima and their worlds : the prison experience,

1850–1935 / Carlos Aguirre.

p. cm.

Includes bibliographical references and index.

ISBN 0-8223-3457-7 (cloth : alk. paper)

ISBN 0-8223-3469-0 (pbk. : alk. paper)

1. Prisons—Peru—Lima—History—19th century.

2. Prisons—Peru—Lima—History—20th century. 3. Criminals—

Peru—Lima—History—19th century. 4. Criminals—Peru—

Lima—History—20th century. I. Title.

HV9625.L5A48 2005   365'.6'09852509034—dc22

2004019864